OXFORD ISLAMIC LEGAL STUDIES

*Series Editors:*
*Anver M. Emon, Clark Lombardi, and Lynn Welchman*

# THE ANTHROPOLOGY OF ISLAMIC LAW

OXFORD ISLAMIC LEGAL STUDIES

*Series Editors:*
*Anver M. Emon, Clark Lombardi, and Lynn Welchman*

Satisfying the growing interest in Islam and Islamic law, the *Oxford Islamic Legal Studies* series speaks to both specialists and those interested in the study of a legal tradition that shapes lives and societies across the globe. Islamic law operates at several levels. It shapes private decision making, binds communities, and it is also imposed by states as domestic positive law. The series features innovative and interdisciplinary studies that explore Islamic law as it operates at each of these levels. The series also sheds new light on the history and jurisprudence of Islamic law and provides for a richer understanding of the state of Islamic law in the contemporary Muslim world, including parts of the world where Muslims are minorities.

ALSO AVAILABLE IN THE SERIES:

*The Legal Thought of Jalāl al-Dīn al-Suyūṭī*
Authority and Legacy
Rebecca Hernandez

*Coercion and Responsibility in Islam*
A Study in Ethics and Law
Mairaj U. Syed

*Islamic Legal Revival*
Reception of European Law and Transformations in Islamic Legal Thought in Egypt, 1875–1952
Leonard Wood

*Shari'a and Muslim Minorities*
The Wasati and Salafi Approaches to Fiqh al-aqalliyyat al-Muslima
Uriya Shavit

*Domestic Violence and the Islamic Tradition*
Ayesha S. Chaudhry

*Shari'a and Social Engineering*
The Implementation of Islamic Law in Contemporary Aceh, Indonesia
R. Michael Feener

*Religious Pluralism and Islamic Law*
Dhimmis and Others in the Empire Law
Anver M. Emon

*Narratives of Islamic Legal Theory*
Rumee Ahmed

# The Anthropology of Islamic Law

## *Education, Ethics, and Legal Interpretation at Egypt's Al-Azhar*

ARIA NAKISSA

OXFORD
UNIVERSITY PRESS

**OXFORD**
UNIVERSITY PRESS

Oxford University Press is a department of the University of Oxford. It furthers the University's objective of excellence in research, scholarship, and education by publishing worldwide. Oxford is a registered trademark of Oxford University Press in the UK and certain other countries.

Published in the United States of America by Oxford University Press
198 Madison Avenue, New York, NY 10016, United States of America.



---

Library of Congress Cataloging-in-Publication Data

Names: Nakissa, Aria, author.
Title: The anthropology of Islamic law : education, ethics, and legal interpretation at Egypt's al-Azhar / Aria Nakissa.
Description: New York : Oxford University Press, 2019. | Based on author's thesis in cultural anthropology (doctoral—Harvard University, 2012) issued under title: Islamic law and legal education in modern Egypt. | Includes bibliographical references and index.
Identifiers: LCCN 2018048553 | ISBN 9780190932886 ((hardback) : alk. paper)
Subjects: LCSH: Jami ʿat al-Azhar. | Islamic law—Study and teaching. | Islamic law—Egypt.
Classification: LCC KBP43.E32 J36 2019 | DDC 297.1/40181—dc23
LC record available at https://lccn.loc.gov/2018048553

---

1 3 5 7 9 8 6 4 2

Printed by Sheridan Books, Inc., United States of America

# *Series Editors' Preface*

The Oxford Islamic Legal Studies Series is pleased to include Aria Nakissa's *The Anthropology of Islamic Law* among its lauded list of monographs. Nakissa's monograph is an important study that blends two distinct disciplinary approaches to the study of Islam. Historically, the study of Islam and Islamic law (especially in North America) has been framed by the poles of philology on the one hand, and anthropology on the other. The former informs the curriculum of long-standing area studies programs, whereas the latter has increasingly informed the curriculum, training, and production of knowledge in religious studies departments. The two disciplinary vantage points present distinct orientations and starting points in the study of Islam and Islamic law.

Nakissa's study is an attempt to bring the two approaches together. Through a close study of Islamic law as taught in the seminary classroom, Nakissa not only illuminates a specific environment of teaching, training, and knowledge transmission, but also interrogates the disciplinary formation of Islamic legal studies as a subfield of study and research. He blends a rich and deliberate ethnographic account of seminary training in al-Azhar, a major Sunni institution of learning, with close readings of the texts taught in those classrooms. His ethnographic account integrates the texts from which al-Azhar's instructors teach. By locating his ethnography in the classroom, Nakissa brings together ethnography with text-based analysis to perform a composite study that, by this very characteristic, makes his study an important contribution to advanced research on Islamic legal studies.

Anver M. Emon<br>Clark B. Lombardi<br>Lynn Welchman

# *Contents*

# *Acknowledgments*

Like any human work, I know that this book is not free from error. I ask the reader to forgive my ignorance. Whatever insights this text contains have only been possible through the help and guidance of others. I would like to take this opportunity to thank them.

First, I would like to express my gratitude to the Islamic scholars of Egypt and Malaysia. I have learned so much from all of them. Special thanks are due to Shaykh Ḥabīb al-Raḥmān Mohtisham, Shaykh Yāsir Fahmī, Professor Muḥammad al-Ṭāhir al-Mīsāwī, Professor Ibrāhīm Zayn, Shaykh Salāḥ Ḥasan Manṣūr, and Professor Muḥammad al-Dusūqī.

Second, I wish to thank all those who have given generously of their time and expertise to help me improve the manuscript at various stages of its development. These include Baber Johansen, Talal Asad, Arzoo Osanloo, Asad Ahmed, Morgan Liu, Malika Zeghal, David Powers, Flagg Miller, Carl Sharif El-Tobgui, Daniel Reza Jou, Payam Mohseni, Jonathan Brown, Aron Zysow, Hussein Agrama, Nada Moumtaz, Charles Hirschkind, and Andrew Shryock. Although my views are not always in agreement with these scholars, I owe a deep intellectual debt to all of them.

Special thanks are due to Steven Caton, Brinkley Messick, John Bowen, and Hayrettin Yücesoy. In addition to offering insightful comments and criticisms, they have been patient and encouraging mentors.

Special thanks are also due to Wael Hallaq, who has not only provided valuable scholarly feedback, but has shown me exceptional kindness.

Special thanks are additionally due to Anver Emon and four anonymous readers from Oxford University Press. Their comments and suggestions have greatly improved the manuscript. Without Emon's patience as a series editor and guidance as a scholar, this book would not have been possible. I have also had the privilege of working with Jamie Berezin, who has been an exemplary editor distinguished by his professionalism and courteousness.

Third, I would like to acknowledge the generous financial support that I received from the Fulbright program and from Brandeis University's Crown Center for Middle East Studies. I would also like to thank al-Azhar University and Cairo University for permitting me to conduct research on their campuses.

Finally, I wish to thank my parents for giving me the unstinting love, encouragement, and support that only a mother and father can. It is to them that I dedicate this work.

# Introduction: Theoretical Orientation and Methodology

This book is concerned with cultural, legal, and religious traditions. It examines how knowledge of such traditions is transmitted through time. I focus specifically on the Islamic tradition, which is simultaneously a cultural, legal, and religious tradition. Many traditions contain rules, and hence transmitting a tradition frequently entails transmitting knowledge of its rules. The Islamic tradition centers on a corpus of rules known as "Islamic law" or "Sharīʿa." These rules are commonly referred to as "Sharīʿa rules" (*al-aḥkām al-sharʿiyya*). I provide an analysis of Sharīʿa rules and the system of religious education which transmits knowledge of these rules.

I situate my analysis in relation to the system of higher religious education found in modern Egypt. Here, I draw on over two years of ethnographic fieldwork among formally trained Muslim religious scholars. The majority of the fieldwork took place between October 2009 and October 2011. It continued uninterrupted through the January 25th revolution, which toppled Egyptian president Ḥusnī Mubārak in early 2011. During this two-year period, I attended classes at al-Azhar University's Faculty of Sharīʿa, Cairo University's Dār al-ʿUlūm, and the network of traditional study circles operating in and around the al-Azhar mosque. These sites are all located in the city of Cairo. Together these sites constitute the most important venue for the transmission of religious learning in the contemporary Muslim world.[1] I also passed a great deal of time with students and teachers outside of lessons. This enabled me to familiarize myself with their broader social and religious lives.

In terms of disciplinary orientation, this book is primarily meant as a contribution to the fields of anthropology and history. However, it also engages with relevant sociological scholarship. Some further clarification on these points will be helpful.

[1] There is a wide variety of evidence for such an assertion. I base it in part on conversations with Muslim religious scholars in various countries across the world. Generally speaking, these religious scholars express the opinion that Egypt is uniquely significant. Moreover, they constantly reference the ideas and writings of Egyptian religious figures. Cairo is, of course, a center of Sunni (rather than Shiʿī) Muslim learning, but the overwhelming majority of contemporary Muslims are Sunni.

The Anthropology of Islamic Law. Aria Nakissa.

In the early twentieth century, texts provided a convenient dividing line separating the disciplines of anthropology and history. The (stereotypical) historian sought to construct an account of past societies based on the written texts which they had left behind. By contrast, the (stereotypical) anthropologist sought to construct an account of contemporary non-Western societies based on ethnographic fieldwork. Such fieldwork involved long-term residence in a non-Western society for the purpose of directly observing its practices and directly conversing with its members. Hence, whereas the historian relied upon texts, the anthropologist collected data not found in texts. Indeed, at this time, anthropologists focused primarily on "primitive" nonliterate societies without writing or texts. But matters were to change. Hence, in the latter half of the twentieth century, anthropologists embraced texts as a source of data, thereby unsettling (though not eliminating) the disciplinary boundary separating anthropology and history. Nevertheless, anthropology's initial rejection of texts has left an enduring but problematic legacy.

One aspect of this legacy is anthropology's limited openness to textual analysis. In this respect, there remain significant differences between anthropological studies and historical studies, especially where Islam is concerned. Historians who study religious ideas or institutions in Muslim societies are often referred to as "Islamicists" (or "Orientalists"). Whereas anthropological studies of Islam typically incorporate a handful of religious texts, Islamicist studies often provide in-depth analyses of sizable religious literatures (e.g., *Tafsīr, Uṣūl al-Fiqh*, Sufism). Such analyses frequently draw on dozens (if not hundreds) of Arabic primary source texts. Methodologically, the present book is best seen as a hybrid of anthropology and Islamicist history, taking its inspiration from Brinkley Messick's seminal *Calligraphic State* (1993). Accordingly, the book combines ethnography with in-depth Islamicist-style analysis of Arabic religious texts. It will become clear that the present book is also deeply indebted to the writings of (anthropologist) Talal Asad and (Islamicist) Wael Hallaq, who have laid down key foundations for the future study of the Islamic legal tradition.

In advancing its arguments, the present book gives special attention to the sizable anthropological literature on Islamic law that has developed over the past four decades. This literature has sought to expand knowledge of Islamic law by providing ethnographic case studies of Sharīʿa courts and Islamic educational institutions in different parts of the world, including (but not limited to) Iran (Fischer 1980; Osanloo 2009), Morocco (Eickelman 1985; Rosen 1989), Yemen (Messick 1993), Mayotte (Lambek 1993), Kenya (Hirsch 1998), Malaysia (Peletz 2002), Indonesia (Bowen 2003), Egypt (Dupret 2007; Agrama 2012), Tanzania (Stiles 2009), Lebanon (Clarke 2012), Britain (Bowen 2016), and China (Erie 2016) (Also see Starrett 1998; Mir-Hosseini 1999; Asad 2003; Mahmood 2005; B. Silverstein 2011).

In addition to addressing key topics in the anthropology of Islam, the book also addresses key topics in legal anthropology. However, its methodological approach differs from that favored in many works of legal anthropology. Since the 1940s, legal anthropology has been associated with the study of "law in action" through the so-called "trouble case" method (see Llewellyn and Hoebel 1941). This approach involves empirical research on individual disputes and legal problems, investigating how law and other mechanisms of "social control" are used to resolve them (see e.g., Gluckman 1967; Bohannan 1968; Comaroff and Roberts 1981; Moore 1986; Merry 1990). With respect to Islamic law, such research has typically centered on Sharīʿa courts.[2]

Nevertheless, over the past three decades, the trouble case method has faced mounting criticism (see Conley and O'Barr 1993; von Benda-Beckmann 2009). For instance, it is not obvious that studying individual cases provides the best means of grasping the sociological dynamics of a larger legal system. Moreover, legal discourses exert influence over human political, cultural, and intellectual life in an enormous variety of ways, most of which have little to do with issues of individual dispute resolution (see Kahn 1999; Sarat and Simon 2003; Erlanger et al. 2005). With these facts in mind, an increasing number of legal anthropologists have moved away from the trouble case method. This shift is particularly noticeable in recent research on Western legal systems. Instead of limiting itself to dispute resolution, such research addresses topics like pedagogy in Western law schools (Mertz 2007), the style and structure of legal documents (Riles 2001), and the dissemination of transnational legal norms (Merry 2006). I believe that this is a welcome development. To be sure, the trouble case method has value in some circumstances. Still, there is little reason it should be regarded as the defining feature of legal anthropology or of legal anthropological research on Islamic law. Hence, although the present book examines some legal disputes, it does not revolve around the trouble case method. Rather, following Mertz (2007), the book concentrates its attention on institutions of legal education.

Although the present book offers an ethnographic study of legal/religious learning in the modern period, it has much to say about the premodern period as well. Accordingly, the book engages with Islamicist scholarship on premodern Islamic legal doctrine (e.g., Schacht 1967[1950]; Schacht 1965; Zysow 2013[1984]; Crone 1987; Calder 1993; Melchert 1997; Johansen 1998; Weiss 1998; Dutton 1999; Hallaq 2001; Yunis Ali 2000; Motzki 2002; Hallaq 2005; Lowry 2007; Vishanoff 2011; Gleave 2012; El Shamsy 2013; Sadeghi 2013; Ahmed 2016). The book likewise engages with Islamicist scholarship on premodern religious education (e.g., Makdisi 1981; Berkey 1992; Chamberlain 1994; Ephrat 2000).

While the present book focuses primarily on anthropological and historical scholarship, it also takes note of the smaller sociological literature on Islam and Muslim societies, giving special attention to studies informed by the ideas of Max Weber (Rodinson 1973; Turner 1974; Arjomand 1984; Stauth 1987; Salvatore 1997; Bamyeh 1999; Huff and Schluchter 1999; Abaza 2002; Zubaida 2003). By integrating relevant anthropological, historical, and sociological literatures, the book offers a comprehensive cross-disciplinary perspective absent from existing scholarship on Islam and Muslim societies. Such a perspective makes it possible

[2] Examples are given above.

to critically engage with theoretical currents which run across the boundaries of these disciplines.

## I. THEORETICAL ORIENTATION

In terms of theoretical orientation, the present book engages with two highly influential analytic frameworks; namely, hermeneutic theory and practice theory. "Hermeneutic theory" is a (loose) term that can be used to cover "hermeneutics," "historicism," "interpretive" social science, as well as elements of "action theory" and "phenomenological sociology." These intellectual currents are all interconnected, sharing a common genealogy going back to the early nineteenth century. Hermeneutic theory (broadly defined) encompasses contributions from a range of philosophers, jurists, historians, sociologists, and anthropologists. Leading figures include Friedrich Schleiermacher, Friedrich Karl von Savigny, Johann Gustav Droysen, Wilhelm Dilthey, Max Weber, Alfred Schutz, Talcott Parsons, R.G. Collingwood, Emilio Betti, Hans-Georg Gadamer, Paul Ricoeur, Clifford Geertz, Donald Davidson[3], Ronald Dworkin, and Quentin Skinner. Meanwhile, "practice theory" is a (loose) term that can be used to cover "historicist genealogy," particular strains of "poststructuralism," and forms of social analysis indebted to Aristotelian virtue ethics. Practice theory emerged in the 1970s and 1980s, subsequently assuming a dominant place in anthropological, sociological, and historical research. Leading proponents of practice theory (broadly defined) include Pierre Bourdieu, Michel Foucault, Anthony Giddens, Marshall Sahlins, Sherry Ortner, and Talal Asad.

Hermeneutic theory and practice theory are both concerned with the relationship between action and mind. However, they analyze this relationship in different ways. Hermeneutic theory emphasizes that actions reveal the mind. Hence, if a woman purchases vegetables, her action reveals that she has a desire for vegetables. Similarly, if she prays, her action reveals that she has a belief in God. In this sense, her actions are evidence of the content of her mind (i.e., her desires, beliefs, emotions, intentions, etc.). As we will see, hermeneutic theory suggests that human beings, by nature, seek to understand the minds of others. They acquire such understanding by intuitively and unconsciously inferring the content of others' minds from the evidence supplied by others' actions (which function as "signs"/"symbols"). This process deeply shapes social life, for it enables communication and the transmission of cultural knowledge.

Practice theory posits a different relationship between action and mind, emphasizing that repeated action (i.e., "practice") alters the mind. Hence, through the repeated action of eating vegetables, a woman may develop a desire for vegetables. Similarly, through the repeated action of prayer, she may develop a

[3] Even though Davidson is conventionally labeled an analytic philosopher, it is widely recognized that his work addresses key issues in hermeneutic theory. See Davidson 2001[1984]; 2001[1980]; Ramberg 2015.

belief in God. Likewise, through the repeated action of bike-riding she may develop knowledge of how to ride a bike (i.e., a skill, "practical knowledge"—and knowledge is conventionally located in the mind). Through these practices, the woman has acquired a desire, a belief, and a type of knowledge that she did not previously possess. Practice theory tends to speak of mind in terms of "subjectivity," or in terms of the "dispositions" of a "habitus." Here, dispositions/habitus denote mental content acquired through practice (although the concept of habitus blends notions of mind and body).

Practice theory pushes this line of analysis further by asserting that institutions of power prescribe particular forms of practice (i.e., "discipline") to alter minds in particular ways. Hence, a government health organization may prescribe the practice of eating vegetables to instill a desire for vegetables in the population. Similarly, a church may prescribe the practice of prayer to instill a belief in God in the population. By altering minds, powerful institutions thereby exert influence and control over behavior. Hence, by instilling a desire for vegetables, a health organization creates a population which is inclined to eat vegetables. Similarly, by instilling belief in the Christian God, a church creates a population inclined to obey teachings ascribed to that God (e.g., in the Bible). The notion that institutions ("structure") can alter people's minds, and thereby influence (though not strictly determine) their future behavior/actions ("agency") is central to practice theory—and this notion underlies practice theory's efforts to conceptualize the temporally extended dialectical relationship between structure and agency.

For practice theory, human social life revolves around powerful institutions and their efforts to alter minds (and influence/control behavior) by prescribing practices. I will refer to practices of this type as "power-laden practices." Building on the preceding perspective, leading proponents of practice theory (like Bourdieu and Foucault) have criticized hermeneutic theory for not paying attention to power-laden practices. Thus, for Bourdieu (1977:4, 21) hermeneutic notions (like Schutzian phenomenological sociology) are flawed in that they ignore the power of "objective" structures to generate "subjectivity" (i.e., mental content) through practice. Similarly, Foucault consciously distances himself from hermeneutic analysis (especially the idea that the analysis of a text should focus on determining the intentions/mental content of the text's author) (Foucault 1998[1969]). Rather, Foucault suggests that the analysis of texts (i.e., "discourse") and society should focus on power-laden practices (i.e., "discipline") (1972;1995[1977];1990[1985]). Consequently, the rise of practice theory in recent decades has coincided with the increasing marginalization of hermeneutic theory within many fields of social research, including anthropology and history.

For practice theory, an emphasis on power-laden practices goes hand in hand with an interest in the "body" or "embodiment" (see esp. Bourdieu 1977; Foucault 1995[1977]; 1990[1985]). Thus, most practices involve the human body (i.e., the movement of body parts). For instance, the practice of bike-riding involves pedaling *with the legs*. The practice of prayer involves *bowing one's head* and reciting sacred formulae *with one's tongue and lips*. For proponents of practice theory, hermeneutic theory's neglect of power-laden practices leads to a neglect of the body. By contrast, practice theory seeks to place the body at the center of social analysis. For practice theory, the body is an object to be manipulated, trained, and remade through practices prescribed by powerful institutions. By seizing control of the body, powerful institutions seize control of the mind.

In assessing these theoretical developments, the anthropological contributions of Geertz and Asad deserve special attention. In the late nineteenth and early twentieth centuries, Franz Boas and Alfred Kroeber worked to incorporate hermeneutic ideas into American anthropology (see Boas 1887; Stocking 1974; Bunzl 1996; Buckley 1996). However, between the 1960s and 1980s, Geertz emerged as the most influential anthropological proponent of hermeneutic ideas (i.e., "interpretive anthropology"; also see Agar 1980; Rabinow and Sullivan 1987; Clifford 1988:21–54; Lambek 1991; 2015). Geertz is especially well known for his writings on religion. Despite the existence of earlier colonial-era precedents (e.g., Edward Lane, Christiaan Snouck Hurgronje, Paul Marty), Geertz is widely credited with establishing the anthropology of Islam in the 1960s, publishing a number of ethnographic studies on Muslim religiosity in Indonesia and Morocco (1960; 1968; 1983). Between the 1970s and the 1990s, Geertz's work shaped much anthropological research on Muslim societies (see, e.g., Rabinow 1977; Crapanzano 1980; Dwyer 1982; Hefner 1985; Rosen 1989; Fischer and Abedi 1990; Lambek 1993; also see Bowen 1993). However, Geertz's writings have also attracted a great deal of criticism, and since the 1990s his ideas have fallen out of favor. Geertz's work has been attacked on a variety of grounds (see Shankman 1984; Clifford and Marcus 1986; M. Schneider 1987). Yet, the most common criticism of Geertz has been that he ignores issues of power (Roseberry 1982; Ortner 1999).

Asad is Geertz's foremost critic. Influenced by Foucault, Asad is a major anthropological proponent of practice theory, and has led efforts to apply insights from practice theory to the study of religion (generally) and to the study of Islam (specifically). As we will see, Asad attacks Geertz for ignoring power-laden religious practices and the body in favor of a concern with religious signs/symbols. For Asad, the study of religion/Islam should center on power, practice, and the body.

Over the past two decades, Asad's ideas have come to dominate the anthropology of Islam, most evidently in research on the Middle East (Mahmood 2005; Hirschkind 2006; Hamdy 2009; Mittermaier 2011; Silverstein 2011; Agrama 2012). Moreover, Asad's ideas have found a receptive audience outside of anthropology, greatly impacting interdisciplinary scholarship on Islam, especially among Islamicist historians (see, e.g., Zaman 2002; Salvatore 2009; Anjum 2012; Hallaq 2013; Katz 2013; Ahmed 2016; Farquhar 2017). Much of this interdisciplinary scholarship specifically centers on the "body" or "embodiment" (Kugle 2007; Bashir 2011; Ware 2014). The shift from Geertz to Asad within the anthropology of Islam reflects a broader shift in anthropology (and related fields) from hermeneutic theory to practice theory.

In the past, when insights from practice theory were less familiar, it made sense to give them heavy (or even exclusive) emphasis. And indeed, scholarship inspired by practice theory has greatly advanced our understanding of cultural, legal, and religious traditions. This is particularly true of recent practice theoretical work by Asad, Mahmood, and Hallaq, which has greatly advanced our understanding of the Islamic tradition. Nevertheless, at present, there is good reason to reject a narrow focus on ideas drawn from practice theory. For such an approach risks simply rehashing lines of analysis that have already been explored in depth.

In this book, I argue against the current trend toward marginalizing hermeneutic theory in favor of practice theory. This is because cultural, legal, and religious traditions (like Islam) have important dimensions which can only be addressed through hermeneutic theory, and which have typically been overlooked by proponents of practice theory. However, I not interested in championing hermeneutic theory at the expense of practice theory. Rather, I am interested in thinking about how these two frameworks can be brought together in a coherent and fruitful manner. More specifically, I am interested in thinking about how these two frameworks can be brought together in a manner which facilitates the analysis of traditions—especially traditions (like Islam) which contain rules.

In the next chapter, I further explain both hermeneutic theory and practice theory, showing how they can be brought together in a manner relevant to the Islamic tradition. However, at present, I would like to give the reader a preliminary understanding of how these two frameworks relate to my fieldwork.

## II. HERMENEUTIC THEORY, PRACTICE THEORY, AND ETHNOGRAPHY

Throughout the book, I cite (somewhat reworked) excerpts from my fieldnotes in appropriate places. These excerpts appear in italics. The following excerpt gives the reader some sense of the environment in which my research was conducted:

> *The area surrounding Cairo's famous al-Azhar mosque is crowded with tightly packed medieval buildings. The narrow corridors that wind haphazardly between them are crammed full of small shops and kiosks selling all variety of goods. A large number of shops deal in low-cost printed versions of medieval religious texts. Other businesses traffic in pickled vegetables, pungent meats, live chickens, perfumes, women's garments, and household wares. The alleyways are filled with people haggling over prices and transporting merchandise using wagons and carts. Others sit on wooden chairs, sipping tea out of small glass cups, talking with customers and friends. Nestled in the midst of these bustling goings-on are innumerable mosques. No matter where one stands there is always a mosque within a five-minute walk. In some places, different mosques are immediately adjacent to one another. Certain mosques are large and impressive, but most are lesser in size. Some are no larger or more conspicuous than the modest shops that surround them.*

*The al-Farūq mosque is of middling proportions. It is a tall single-story rectangular structure. Constructed of smoothened yellowish-brown stone blocks, from the outside the mosque looks little different from its other ancient counterparts. Patrolled by mangy cats, the poorly paved back alley leading up to the mosque is strewn with refuse and buzzing with flies. Nothing about the area suggests anything special. But the location of the mosque and its modest exterior are deceiving. Entering the mosque reveals an uncommonly sumptuous interior. The floor is blanketed with a dozen large Oriental carpets of various patterns, mingling hues of blue, red, and white. A matrix of dull gray marble columns is interspersed through the middle of the building. Suspended above its center is an ornate bronze chandelier studded with tiny turquoise lamps. The walls of the mosque are decorated with alternating rectangular blocks of burgundy and white marble.*

*Every Tuesday, at the time of the afternoon prayer (ʿAsr), the mosque is visited by Shaykh ʿAbdullah. Shaykh ʿAbdullah is a professor at al-Azhar University. He is one of the most respected authorities on Islamic law in Egypt. While the* shaykh *does some teaching within the university itself, he also gives periodic lessons open to the public at a number of select local venues. One of them is the al-Farūq mosque. Around 70 years old, Shaykh ʿAbdullah has a long grayish-white beard. He wears a special garb reserved for male graduates of al-Azhar. The garb has two primary components. First, there is a loose outer garment with widely flared sleeves. Known as a "*jubba,*"[4] it resembles a long coat. Some* jubbas *have pinstripes. Others are plain. Their colors are always understated and solemn. Varying shades of gray, blue, and brown are typical. The garb also includes a particular kind of headwear. Known as an "Azhari turban,"[5] it consists of a cap of red felt with a white cloth wound around its sides. The uppermost portion of the cap peeks out from above the area covered by the white cloth. It is pinched at the top, with a small blue or black tassel attached. The turban represents an Azhari scholar's religious authority, and he will often take it off when he wishes to ceremoniously disclaim the attendant privileges.*

*The lesson begins as soon as Shaykh ʿAbdullah takes his place. He seats himself upon a squat wide-bottomed wooden chair fitted with a striped green cushion. The back of the chair is positioned against one of the mosque's walls. A small table has been placed before it. The students who are present sit on the floor in front of the* shaykh. *Facing him, they are arrayed in a circular pattern. The* shaykh's *chair is positioned on the edge of the circle. The area immediately before the* shaykh *is empty. In Arabic, this arrangement is known as a "*ḥalaqa*"[6] or "study-circle."*

*There are about 20 students in attendance. They range in age from the mid-20s to the mid-30s. All but one of them is male (the lone female in attendance sits off to the side, separate from the study-circle). Three-quarters of those present have beards and about half wear a type of robe-like garment known as a "*jallābiyya.*" Some wear traditional caps as well. The remainder of the students dress in Western clothing. Even though many of them are formally enrolled at al-Azhar University, none of them wear the special garb sported by Shaykh*

[4] Also known as a "*kākūla.*"
[5] "*Al-ʿimāma al-azhariyya.*"
[6] Also known as a "*ḥalqa.*"

*ʿAbdullah. However, many are recognizable as up-and-coming religious authorities themselves. Some lead their own study-circles in other places.*

*Shaykh ʿAbdullah delivers his lesson by reading from a centuries-old legal text. As he proceeds through the work in a soft, calm voice he intermittently stops to comment upon its contents. Sometimes he even makes a humorous remark and laughs. The students follow along in their own printed copies of the text. After a time, an older heavy-set woman of rural origins comes in. She is carrying a large iron tray. On top of the tray are steaming glasses of intensely sweetened green tea. Everyone in attendance takes a glass, and the* shaykh *continues his commentary on the text. The lesson concludes after about an hour and a half. The* shaykh *takes general questions for about 15 minutes and then proceeds to rise from his seat. When he rises, so do the students. They file forward to kiss the top of his hand, as a sign of their respect and affection.*

*The* shaykh *slowly walks toward the exit, with all of the students thronging around him. They follow the* shaykh *outside the mosque as he makes his way through narrow corridors and back alleys. After a few minutes walking he finally emerges from the inner regions of the bazaar on to a major road. There is an old sedan waiting to meet him, with the driver sitting inside. The students give the* shaykh *their final goodbyes and help him into the front passenger seat. Two students open up the rear door of the car and take seats behind the* shaykh. *They will continue on with him, although it is unclear where they are headed. As the car rattles off, the week's session draws to an end.*

Shaykh ʿAbdullah's students attend his lessons to acquire knowledge of Sharīʿa rules. How is this process to be understood? Islamic legal texts certainly play a role. As noted previously, the *shaykh* reads these texts to his students while offering clarificatory comments. But, as we will see, there is an additional nontextual dimension to Shaykh ʿAbdullah's pedagogy. Hence, it is expected that the *shaykh* will set an authoritative example for his students by living in accordance with Sharīʿa rules. The *shaykh* practices these rules when he eats, worships, travels, and interacts with others. Meanwhile, students observe and imitate the *shaykh*. More specifically, they practice Sharīʿa rules based on the model provided by the *shaykh*. They thereby acquire knowledge of Sharīʿa rules.

For instance, before the lesson begins, Shaykh ʿAbdullah prays the afternoon prayer with his students. When the *shaykh* stands in prayer, he faces in the direction of Mecca. From this, students infer that there exists a Sharīʿa rule which requires Muslims to face Mecca when praying. Moreover, the *shaykh* drinks green tea when it is brought to him. From this, students infer that Sharīʿa rules permit the drinking of green tea. Finally, when women appear, the *shaykh* looks away from them. From this, students infer that there exists a Sharīʿa rule which requires males to look away from females. The students then imitate the *shaykh*'s actions, facing Mecca when praying, permitting themselves to drink green tea, and looking away from females. When students fail to properly practice Sharīʿa rules, the *shaykh* uses his power and authority to correct them.

This form of learning can be analyzed using practice theory. Recall that through the practice of bike-riding a person may develop knowledge of how to ride a bike (i.e., a skill). Here we could say that through the practice of Sharīʿa rules, the *shaykh*'s students develop knowledge of how to (properly) practice Sharīʿa rules. Power also clearly enters into this process. After all, al-Azhar University is a powerful institution. Shaykh ʿAbdullah is part of this institution and shares in its power. As a representative of al-Azhar, he prescribes the practice of Sharīʿa rules, and he uses his power to correct students who deviate from these rules. We can push this practice-theoretical line of analysis still further. Hence, through the power-laden practice of Sharīʿa rules, Shaykh ʿAbdullah's students not only acquire knowledge of how to practice Sharīʿa rules (i.e., a skill). They also acquire other mental content. For instance, through the practice of prayer (i.e., through practice of Sharīʿa rules on prayer), students develop belief in God.

In this way, we see how practice theory can be used as a theoretical framework for analyzing ethnographic data (e.g., Shaykh ʿAbdullah's lessons). Yet, while I find such a framework helpful, it also has limitations. These limitations work to obscure the nature of Sharīʿa rules and Sharīʿa knowledge.

As we will see, for Muslim scholars, knowledge of Sharīʿa rules is knowledge of God's mind (i.e., mental content). More specifically, knowledge of Sharīʿa rules is knowledge of God's will/intentions, desires, and beliefs.

Thus, Sharīʿa rules embody God's "will" or "intentions. Meanwhile, God's will/intentions are based on His desires and beliefs. For instance, there is a Sharīʿa rule which requires that Muslim men refrain from looking at women who are not their wives or relatives. This is known as "lowering the gaze" (i.e., *ghaḍḍ al-baṣar*) (See Qurʾan [24:30]). In the view of Muslim scholars, it is God's "will" or "intention" that Muslim men lower their gaze. Moreover, God's will/intention is based upon God's desires and beliefs. Thus, God desires to prevent extramarital sex. Moreover, God believes (i.e., "knows") that if a man looks upon a woman he may be tempted to pursue extramarital sex with her. Hence, it is possible to say the following: God desires to prevent extramarital sex, and He believes (i.e., knows) that if men look at women, they will be tempted to pursue extramarital sex. Therefore, it is God's will/intention that men lower their gaze. Hence, the Sharīʿa rule embodies God's will/intention, which is based upon God's desires and beliefs. Accordingly, knowledge of the Sharīʿa rule is knowledge of God's will/intention, as well as the desires and beliefs upon which it is based.

The preceding points have implications for how we analyze Shaykh ʿAbdullah's lessons. Practice theory suggests that the *shaykh*'s students acquire knowledge of Sharīʿa rules by observing and imitating the *shaykh* (i.e., by modeling their practice on his example). But although this line of analysis is valid, it also obscures an important fact. In reality, the *shaykh*'s students are not simply acquiring knowledge of "Sharīʿa rules." At a deeper level, they are also acquiring knowledge of God's mind. More specifically, they are acquiring knowledge of God's will/intentions, beliefs, and desires.

For example, when women appear, Shaykh ʿAbdullah lowers his gaze. What do students infer from this? At one level, they infer that there exists a *Sharīʿa rule* which requires that men lower their gaze. But at a deeper level, students infer that it is *God's will/intention* that men lower their gaze. Moreover, it can be argued that students make additional inferences about God's mental content. Hence, they may also infer that God *desires* to prevent extramarital sex, and that God *believes* (i.e., knows) that if men look at women they will be tempted to pursue extramarital sex. This gives rise to an interesting but perplexing phenomenon. The students observe Shaykh ʿAbdullah's actions, and from these actions they infer God's mental content (i.e., His intentions, beliefs, desires).

This basic phenomenon is hardly limited to Islamic learning. Consider a Russian general and his soldiers. If we see the soldiers marching toward the French capital Paris we might infer that the general *intends* to attack Paris. We might further infer that the general *desires* to force France to surrender, and that the general *believes* France will surrender if Paris is attacked. Thus, just as we infer God's mental content from Shaykh ʿAbdullah's actions, we infer the general's mental content from his soldiers' actions. Similarly, we might infer the mental content of a factory owner from the actions of his/her workers, and we might infer the mental content of an architectural planner from the actions of his/her builders.

I will argue that the preceding phenomenon plays an important role in many (or perhaps all) cultural, legal, and religious traditions. I will also argue that the phenomenon can only be understood through hermeneutic theory. This is because hermeneutic theory provides a way of grasping how actions (e.g., Shaykh ʿAbdullah's actions) reveal minds (e.g., God's mind).

Insights from hermeneutic theory are not only helpful in analyzing the non-textual dimension of Islamic legal education (e.g., how students learn from Shaykh ʿAbdullah's actions). These insights are also helpful in analyzing the textual dimension of such education. Hence, we will see that the texts used in Islamic legal education do not simply lay out a list of explicit verbal rules (e.g., "Face Mecca in Prayer," "Lower the Gaze"). On the contrary, these texts report the actions of pious Muslim authorities like the Prophet Muḥammad, ʿUmar, and Abū Ḥanīfa (e.g., in Hadith reports and *āthār*). For instance, it might be reported that the Prophet or Abū Ḥanīfa lowered his gaze in the presence of women. From the actions of these authorities the reader makes inferences about the mind of God (e.g., it is God's will/intention that men lower their gaze, God desires to prevent extramarital sex). Consequently, there is a parallel between (1) inferences made from the observed actions of figures like Shaykh ʿAbdullah, and (2) inferences made from the textually reported actions of figures like the Prophet Muḥammad and Abū Ḥanīfa. I suggest that this parallel is of fundamental importance in the analysis of Islamic learning and legal doctrine. Although the parallel is overlooked by practice theory, I will argue that it can be understood using hermeneutic theory. Once again, this is because hermeneutic theory provides a way of grasping how actions reveal minds whether these actions are directly observed or reported in texts.

The foregoing points indicate the need for a new perspective on Islamic legal doctrine and religious learning. According to such a perspective, knowledge of Sharīʿa rules consists in knowledge of God's mental content. Knowledge of God's mental content is inferred from actions, whether these actions are directly observed or reported in texts. This process is analogous to the process whereby we infer knowledge of a general's mental content from the actions of his soldiers.

It can be said that practice theory, taken alone, does not suffice for analyzing how knowledge of Sharīʿa rules is transmitted in Shaykh ʿAbdullah's lessons. Recourse to hermeneutic theory is also necessary. Hence, it becomes necessary to integrate practice theory and hermeneutic theory. I would suggest that in achieving such integration, we help bridge the gap between anthropological and Islamicist approaches to Islamic law. After all, contemporary anthropological approaches are indebted to practice theory. Meanwhile, Islamicist approaches are frequently concerned with the sorts of issues addressed by hermeneutic theory (e.g., "How do Muslim jurists determine the will/intentions of God?," "How do Muslim jurists analyze Hadith reports and other texts reporting the actions of religious authorities?"). Consequently, in integrating hermeneutic theory and practice theory, conceptual resources are provided for scholars who wish to work between anthropological and Islamicist approaches. I would count myself among this group of scholars.

## III. METHODOLOGICAL REMARKS

Before closing out this introductory chapter, I would like to briefly touch on a few methodological issues. The first concerns whether it is valid to make broad generalizations about the (Sunni) Islamic tradition. One view is that generalizations of this type are fundamentally problematic. Proponents of this view emphasize (correctly) that there exists substantial temporal and geographic variation in Muslim religiosity. For instance, it is common to distinguish between different periods in Islamic legal history (e.g., a formative period from the seventh to tenth centuries, a classical period from the tenth to twelfth centuries, a postclassical period from the twelfth to nineteenth centuries).[7] It is likewise common to distinguish between the types of religiosity found in different regions of the Muslim world (i.e., the Middle East and North Africa, Sub-Saharan East and West Africa, Central Asia, South Asia, and Southeast Asia).[8] In light of the preceding facts, some scholars have asserted that it is inappropriate to speak of a coherent Islamic tradition (see, e.g., El-Zein 1977; Gilsenan 1982; Al-Azmeh 1993). Such scholars dismiss general claims about an Islamic tradition as insufficiently nuanced, "essentialist," and ignorant of Islam's enormous historical diversity (i.e., there are "Islams" rather than an "Islam"). It is also asserted that general claims about an Islamic tradition are problematic because they are, by nature, prescriptive rather than merely descriptive. According to this line of

[7] For works addressing legal change and periodization in Islamic legal history see Johansen 1988; Hallaq 2001; Burak 2015.

[8] For works that discuss regional differences in Islamic religiosity see Laffan 2011; Ware 2014; Ahmed 2016.

reasoning, general claims are frequently based on politically dominant/elite/orthodox forms of Islam, and imply that other forms of Islam are inauthentic or illegitimate. Scholars committed to the preceding perspective hold that good academic work concerns itself with local and historically specific forms of Islam. The most respectable and scholarly of claims are those which are most modest and extensively qualified.

I do not deny the value of studies which focus on local and historically specific forms of Islam. However, I do not believe that this style of scholarship is the only legitimate one. Scholars like Talal Asad (1986) and Shahab Ahmed (2016:113–404) have challenged the view that it is inappropriate to speak of a coherent Islamic tradition. While Asad and Ahmed acknowledge substantial temporal and geographic variation in the Islamic tradition, they hold that this tradition exhibits a type of coherence because its different currents share a general orientation; namely, they all take the Qurʾan and (perhaps) the Hadith reports as fundamental (though not necessarily exclusive) sources of religious knowledge (see Asad 1986:14; Ahmed: 345–356). Although this is a radical oversimplification of Asad and Ahmed's views, it captures a key insight found in their work.

Building on the preceding insight, I would posit that, *broadly speaking*, different currents of the Islamic tradition take (either explicitly or implicitly) the Qurʾan, the Prophet Muḥammad, and past religious scholars as fundamental sources of religious knowledge. This fact does not preclude substantial variation in forms of Islamic religiosity. Nevertheless, it engenders certain widely shared transhistorical and transregional patterns in Islamic education and legal thought. I am concerned with patterns of this kind, and in describing them I will make a number of general claims about the Islamic tradition. I qualify these claims to some extent, and I recognize that some scholars would prefer to see them qualified still further. Nevertheless, I do not believe that maximal qualification is necessarily a virtue. Maximal qualification is useful when delineating local and historically specific forms of Islam, but it can also obscure broader patterns which are also worthy of attention.

I realize that generalizing about broader patterns will invite criticism from scholars who are methodologically committed to the view that wide generalizations are inherently problematic, and that the sole aim of proper Islamicist scholarship is to precisely delineate local and historically specific forms of Islam. However, to my mind, scholarship on Islam can give attention both to broader patterns as well as local and historically specific forms. In fact, the present book attempts to do exactly this. In other words, it attempts to discern broad patterns within the Islamic tradition, while also examining a local and historically specific form of Islam in modern Egyptian religious education.

I am inclined to say that this book makes credible generalizations about the Sunni Islamic tradition. However, it could be asserted, more cautiously, that the book makes credible generalizations about a dominant current of religiosity within the Sunni Islamic tradition. Ultimately, I want to leave it to the reader to evaluate my arguments and then decide how to best understand the book.

I regard scholarly debate and disagreement over the proper scope of a work as legitimate and productive.

My general claims about the Islamic tradition are meant to be read as descriptive rather than prescriptive. Hence, this book does not seek to privilege one form of Islam as legitimate and authentic, or to dismiss others as illegitimate and inauthentic. While there may be value in discussions of legitimacy and authenticity, such discussions fall outside the scope of the present work.

A second methodological issue pertains to the division between the "premodern" and "modern" periods. I use the term "modernity" to designate an ensemble of technologies and modes of institutional organization originating in post-medieval Europe. In the nineteenth century, this ensemble was increasingly disseminated outside of Europe, reaching Egypt and other Muslim lands. To understand modernity's impact on Egyptian religious education, it is necessary to consider the character of Islamic learning in the premodern period.

In subsequent chapters, I use the expression "traditional Islamic learning" as a shorthand way of referring to religious education in Arab Muslim lands (particularly Egypt) from the eleventh century until the coming of modernity. I will cite the writings of various Muslim authors who lived during this span, using their texts to elucidate specific educational practices that were challenged by modern Egyptian educational reforms. Yet the validity of such an approach may be questioned.

Past Islamicist historical scholarship was accustomed to portraying the premodern period as entirely static. This view was forcefully attacked in Edward Said's *Orientalism* (1978). As a result, much recent scholarship both emphasizes the dynamism of premodern Muslim societies and is acutely sensitive to the dangers posed by overbroad historical generalizations. Thus, many anthropologists feel the need to stress that the Islamic tradition is in a constant state of change, and that to believe otherwise is mistaken. Here is where I stand on these matters. Every era is similar to those before and after it in some ways, and different from them in others. To assert (in the abstract) that traditions change is no more true than to assert (in the abstract) that they stay the same. Decontextualized assertions of either type have little methodological value. Rather, claims regarding change or continuity only have value when related to specific issues.

The appropriate periodization for one's study will depend on the type of issues addressed. For some investigations (e.g., archaeology) it may be appropriate to lump many millennia together. In others, going beyond a century (or decade) may be ill-advised. My contention is that modernity inaugurated radically new educational practices. In comparison to these modern practices, the premodern practices constituent of what I have termed "traditional Islamic learning" can be looked at as broadly similar, at least with respect to the issues with which I am concerned (for a similar perspective, see Ware 2014). I suggest that many traditional Islamic learning practices can still be witnessed in Cairo. In analyzing these practices, I cite relevant premodern texts, along with relevant modern Egyptian texts and ethnographic data. When used with adequate caution, this approach can be fruitful.

Another important reason to pay attention to premodern texts is that contemporary religious scholars constantly reference them. Hence, many of the key texts currently used in Islamic education originate in the medieval period. As a result, texts authored in the medieval period are still "contemporary" texts, in the sense that they are still being taught and read today. Thus, in providing an account of contemporary Islamic education, there is no way to avoid extensive references to "medieval" texts. Throughout the following chapters, virtually all of the medieval texts I cite are in widespread use today.

Consider that contemporary religious scholars see themselves as faithful representatives of an ancient tradition extending back to the Prophet. They relate many aspects of their lives, both scholarly and personal, to this ancient tradition. When scholars invoke the past, they do so with reference to ancient texts (Qur'an, Hadith reports, etc.). Oftentimes they memorize the exact wording of these texts. Alternatively, they may closely paraphrase them or deploy formulaic expressions drawn from them. These habits are ingrained by religious education itself, instilling within scholars thoroughly "textualized" patterns of discourse. This, of course, does not mean that contemporary scholars merely reproduce ancient views. After all, they decide what to cite, when to cite it, and what other citations to combine it with—choices that deeply inflect the communicated content. At any rate, when dealing with contemporary religious scholars, simple dichotomies like "past versus present" and "written versus oral" become problematic. Such scholars strive to keep a past tradition alive in the present, while constantly referencing and paraphrasing written texts in their speech. It is this situation that has led me to weave together ethnographic data (on living scholars) with (ancient) Islamic texts.

An additional methodological issue pertains to gender. In the premodern period, those who participated in Islamic learning were overwhelmingly male. As we will see, at present, al-Azhar and the Dār al-ʿUlūm educate both sexes. Nevertheless, they remain predominantly male institutions, especially at the highest levels. Furthermore, owing to Islamic norms of gender segregation, male researchers (like myself) are limited in their ability to interact with females at these institutions. Consequently, my fieldwork focused primarily (though not exclusively) on male religious scholars.

I will conclude by saying a couple of words about my own identity, and how it shaped my research. Although I think that exercises of this type are always selective, they can still be beneficial. My father comes from a largely secular (but not anti-religious) Shiʿite Iranian Muslim family, and my mother comes from a largely secular (but not anti-religious) white Catholic American family. I was not brought up within any particular religious tradition. At the same time, I have always been dissatisfied with hegemonic secular liberal descriptions of human experience (i.e., the notion of Homo economicus). More specifically, I have never subscribed to the notion that human existence consists in the egoistic attempt to maximize individual happiness by consuming as many goods and services as possible. By extension, I have never believed that an ideal society is simply one in which a capitalist economy produces an ever-increasing range of goods and services through constant advances in science and technology.

The notion that human experience centers on happiness maximization through material consumption has, of course, been challenged in many works of classical social theory, as well as more recent research in psychology, biology, and cognitive anthropology. In keeping with such research,[9] I strongly suspect that the human mind/brain is in some sense "naturally" inclined to search for purpose in the cosmos, and to process experience through particular forms of "mythical" thinking (although I do not equate "myth" with "falsehood"). I also suspect that the human mind/brain is in some sense "naturally" inclined toward physically enacted ritual, affection for kin, and concern with "identity" (i.e., concern with one's people/in-group, its history, and traditions). I recognize that such a perspective is controversial, I will not seek to argue for it in this book, and the book's findings are in no way dependent upon accepting it. Nevertheless, at both a personal and academic level, I think matters of myth, ritual, kin, and identity are profoundly important. Put differently, I do not think they can simply be dismissed as ignorance and barbarism which lack relevance in a modern age dominated by empirical science, atomized individualism, and consumer capitalism. I genuinely respect Islamic religious scholars for taking matters of myth, ritual, kin, and identity seriously, and this respect doubtlessly shaped my research.

## IV. THE OVERALL STRUCTURE OF THE BOOK

The remainder of this book is divided into 10 chapters. The 10 chapters are distributed among four sections.

The first section is titled "Theory, Ethnography, History." It contains chapters 1 and 2. In chapter 1, I explain how hermeneutic theory and practice theory can be brought together in the analysis of cultural, legal, and religious traditions, giving special attention to the Islamic tradition. Throughout the remainder of the book I draw on hermeneutic theory and practice theory to analyze central aspects of Islamic learning and legal doctrine. In chapter 2, I offer an ethnographic and historical account of higher religious learning in modern Egypt.

The second section is titled "Traditional Islamic Learning and Legal Doctrine." It contains chapters 3, 4, 5, and 6. In chapter 3, I take up the key concepts of Sharīʿa, Sunna, and ethics (*akhlāq*), clarifying their place in Islamic learning and legal doctrine. In chapter 4, I examine the traditional Islamic pedagogy of companionship (*ṣuḥba*). In chapter 5, I examine the place of the *sanad* in the traditional Islamic learning. In chapter 6, I consider how written texts are used in traditional Islamic learning.

[9] Some relevant research on this topic includes the work of cognitive anthropologists like Dan Sperber, Stewart Guthrie, Scott Atran, Pascal Boyer, and Emma Cohen. Related work has also been done by evolutionary anthropologists like Richard Sosis, William Irons, and Robin Dunbar.

The third section is titled "A New Perspective on Islamic Legal Doctrine." It contains a sizable chapter 7. In chapter 7, I examine the overall structure of Islamic legal thought, and explain how it relates to the pedagogical practices characteristic of Islamic learning. Here I develop hermeneutic ideas using insights from "planning theory," an influential approach in recent philosophical and legal scholarship. This allows for a new perspective on an entire range of Islamic legal concepts including: *maṣlaḥa, taʿabbud, Maqāṣid al-Sharīʿa, qiyās, istiṣlāḥ, istiḥsān, ijmāʿ, ijtihād, taqlīd*, and *madhhab*. I link my analysis to ideas and practices found at al-Azhar University, al-Azhar mosque, and the Dār al-ʿUlūm.

The fourth section is titled "Modern Reform." It contains chapters 8, 9, and 10. In chapter 8, I examine how modern reform efforts have sought to transform Islamic learning by reordering time and space. In chapter 9, I examine how reform efforts have introduced new practices of reading texts. In chapter 10, I examine how reform efforts have given rise to two modern currents of Islamic legal thought: namely, Salafism and Wasaṭism.

# Section I

# Theory, Ethnography, History

present tense
odd

intellectual
genealogy

# 1

# Hermeneutic Theory and Practice Theory in the Study of Cultural, Legal, and Religious Traditions

In this chapter, I explain how hermeneutic theory and practice theory can be brought together in the analysis of cultural, legal, and religious traditions. I begin by introducing some basic hermeneutic ideas, situating them in relationship to the work of Geertz and Asad. Next, I consider how these hermeneutic ideas can be developed in new directions and applied to the Islamic tradition. I then use these ideas to critique certain key aspects of practice theory's approach to rules. I conclude by offering some suggestions on how ideas from hermeneutic theory and practice theory can be integrated.

In this chapter, I utilize a list of terms associated with hermeneutic theory and practice theory. I pay special attention to terms that have near (or exact) Arabic equivalents, and which are important in the Islamic tradition. These terms include "mind" (*qalb*), "action" (*fiʿl* or *ʿamal*), "mental attribute" (*ṣifa al-qalb* or *waṣf al-qalb*), and "disposition" (*malaka* or *khuluq*). In subsequent chapters, I will make use of these terms to explicate Islamic learning and legal doctrine.

## I. SIGNS AND HERMENEUTIC THEORY

As noted previously, hermeneutic theory encompasses a diverse but interconnected range of intellectual currents. I will focus on one specific current which has deeply influenced social theory. This largely German current is rooted in the early nineteenth century ideas of Hegel and Schleiermacher. In the later nineteenth century, this current is developed into an expansive program for social and historical research by Dilthey (1988[1883]; 1972[1900]; 2002[1910]) and Droysen (1893) (i.e., the notion of *Geisteswissenshaften*). At the beginning of the twentieth century, Weber (1978[1922]) draws on this current to produce a systematic sociology (i.e., "interpretive sociology"). Weber's ideas are then reworked in the early and mid-twentieth century by Parsons (1949[1937]; 1964[1951]) and Schutz (1967[1932]; Schutz and Luckmann 1973). In the 1960s, Schutz's ideas are further extended by Berger and Luckmann (1991[1966]). Moreover, in the latter portion of the twentieth century, Davidson builds on and refines concepts

The Anthropology of Islamic Law. Aria Nakissa.

which are central to this general current (esp. "action" and "interpretation"; see Davidson 2001[1980]; 2001[1984]). During the same period, the jurist Betti (1990; 2017) seeks to revive older lines of analysis associated with this current.

Geertz's work can only be appreciated when situated with respect to the preceding current. Nevertheless, this current is habitually overlooked in contemporary anthropological and historical work which identifies itself as hermeneutic/interpretive in character. Such work tends to focus on ideas from Gadamer ([1960]2006) and Ricoeur (1981)—two hermeneutic theorists who also influenced Geertz (see, e.g., Agar 1980; Rabinow and Sullivan 1987; Lambek 1991; 2015). But the ideas of Gadamer and Ricoeur often diverge significantly from the current of hermeneutic theory developed by Droysen, Dilthey, Weber, Parsons, Schutz, Berger, Davidson, and Betti.

Hermeneutic theory is concerned with knowledge of other minds. According to conventional views, an individual's mind contains his/her beliefs, desires, emotions, intentions, etc.[1] Hence, beliefs, desires, emotions, and intentions may all be referred to as "mental attributes," for they are all "located" in the mind. It would be possible to mention a wide range of additional mental attributes. Nevertheless, given their special importance in social theory, I focus on (1) beliefs, (2) desires, (3) emotions, and (4) intentions.

An individual's mind can be distinguished from his/her body. The body is a corporeal entity which walks (with its legs), eats (with its mouth), talks (with its tongue), and so on. A major difference between the mind and body is that the mind cannot be seen. Thus, it is impossible for me to directly look into the mind of another person and see the mental attributes it contains (i.e., I cannot see another person's particular beliefs, desires, emotions, etc.). But if another person's mental attributes are hidden in this way, how can one acquire knowledge of them? Hermeneutic theory seeks to address this question (Dilthey 1972[1900]:231–232).

In doing so, hermeneutic theory draws attention to the concept of "action." An individual's actions include behaviors like walking, eating, studying, driving, and so forth. Hermeneutic theory also treats intentional refusal to perform an action as a type of action. Hence, intentionally abstaining from alcohol is an action. Similarly, avoiding extramarital sex is an action. Finally, for hermeneutic theory, making a verbal statement is considered an action. (Dilthey 2002[1910]:79–209; Weber 1978[1922]:3–26).

Hermeneutic theory holds that it is (often) possible to infer an individual's mental attributes from his/her actions. For instance, if a man performs the action of purchasing chocolate ice cream, one may infer from this action that he has a desire to eat chocolate ice cream. Similarly, if he performs the action of putting on a raincoat, one may infer that he has a belief that it will rain. If he picks up a tennis racket, one may infer that he has an intention to play tennis. Just as individuals may perform actions, groups of individuals may also perform

[1] For a critique of this general (Cartesian) perspective see Ryle 2002[1949].

actions (e.g., cooperative actions, customs, communal rituals). For instance, a group of individuals might together hunt a buffalo. From their action, it may be inferred that they desire to eat buffalo meat.

Because verbal statements are simply one type of action, they can be analyzed in the same way. Hence, if a woman states: "Shut the door," one can infer from her statement that she has a belief that the door is open. If she states: "I am going to the ice cream shop," one can infer that she has a desire to eat ice cream. (See Dilthey 1972[1900]; 2002[1910]; Weber 1978[1922]:3–26; Schutz 1967[1932]).

Hermeneutic theory expands upon the preceding ideas in a manner relevant to cultural and historical analysis. Hence, hermeneutic theory notes that actions can either be directly observed or reported by others. Just as one may infer mental attributes from directly observed actions, one may also infer mental attributes from actions that are reported by others. For instance, if I directly observe John go to the ice cream shop, I may infer that he desires to eat ice cream. Similarly, if someone reports to me that John went to the ice cream shop, I may infer that he desires to eat ice cream.

For hermeneutic theory, actions (including statements) reported in texts are essential linkages to the minds of individuals from the past (see Droysen 1893; Dilthey 2002[1910]; Schutz 1967[1932]; Gadamer [1960]2006). Such individuals might be ordinary people (e.g., my great-grandfather). Or they might be major historical personalities (e.g., Alexander the Great, Prophet Muḥammad, William Shakespeare). In most cases, what I know about a figure from the past will be based on what has been reported about that figure's actions (including statements). From a historical figure's reported actions, I come to know that historical figure's mind (i.e., I infer his/her various mental attributes).

Building on Hegel, hermeneutic theory also notes that, through their actions, human beings shape their material world and their social world. Human beings shape their material world through actions whereby they produce different material structures and artifacts (e.g., bridges, churches, rice fields, sculptures, paintings, swords, pottery, cars). Human beings shape their social world by implementing specific rules, decrees, and plans through their actions (e.g., military decrees, building plans, rules of law, rituals, ceremonies, and customs) (Droysen 1893:18; Dilthey 2002[1910]:106–107, 175–178; 1972[1900]:231; Schutz and Luckmann 1973:16–17). Such often involves obedience on the part of a group. Hence, to implement a rule, decree, or plan in a given society, people within the society must obey the rule, decree, or plan by acting in accordance with it. I will refer to this as "obedient action." Obedient action differs from ordinary action in that ordinary action may not involve acting in accordance with a rule, decree, or plan. For instance, a person may kick the television, but this is not an obedient action, as there is no rule, decree, or plan which prescribes kicking the television.

For hermeneutic theory, one may infer mental attributes from material structures/artifacts and obedient actions. Hence, when people build a church, it may be inferred that they believe Jesus is God. If they produce soccer balls, it may be inferred that they desire to play soccer. If they act in accordance with legal rules which forbid theft (i.e., obedient action), it may be inferred that they desire to protect property rights. If they perform prescribed rituals of mourning when parents die (i.e., obedient action), it may be inferred that they experience emotions of sadness when their parents die (see Dilthey 1972[1900]:232; 2002[1910]:101–102, 168-170; Droysen 1893:11–19).

Thus, for hermeneutic theory, mental attributes can be inferred from actions, statements, material structures/artifacts, and obedient actions. Hermeneutic theorists refer to these things as "expressions," "externalizations," or "objectifications" of mind (i.e., mental attributes) (see Dilthey 2002[1910]:101–109,168–174; Droysen 1893:12; Schutz and Luckmann 1973:16–17; Berger and Luckmann 1991[1966]). These things are also frequently referred to as "signs" of mental attributes (Dilthey 1972[1900]:231–232; also see Schutz and Luckmann 1973:17, 63, 75). Thus, when a woman purchases chocolate ice cream it is a *sign* she desires to eat chocolate ice cream. When a man states: "Shut the door," it is a sign that he believes the door is open. When a group of people plants a rice field, it is a sign that they desire and intend to eat rice. In the context of hermeneutic theory, inferring mental attributes from signs is referred to as "interpretation," which leads to "interpretive understanding" (*Verstehen*) (Dilthey 1972[1900]:231–232; Weber 1978[1922]:3–26; Schutz and Luckmann 1973:16). Hence, one *interprets* the woman's action of purchasing chocolate ice cream cone as a sign that she desires to eat chocolate ice cream (i.e., one infers the woman's desire for chocolate ice cream from her action of purchasing chocolate ice cream).

Hermeneutic theory draws on the preceding insights to offer a distinctive perspective on human social life. For hermeneutic theory, human beings, by their very nature, are intensely concerned with understanding others. Humans are concerned with understanding the other individuals they live and interact with. They are likewise concerned with understanding the other individuals they hear about and read about in texts (including individuals from the past) (see Schutz 1967[1932]; 1962; Schutz and Luckmann 1973; Betti 1990:160). The process of understanding others involves acquiring knowledge of their minds. For hermeneutic theory, ordinary people intuitively and unconsciously infer such knowledge from the signs they encounter in society (e.g., actions, statements, structures, artifacts). Thus, if an ordinary woman sees a man smash a television, she will infer that he has an emotion of anger. If she sees an irrigation system in a village, she will infer that the villagers desire to water their crops. The woman makes these inferences in an intuitive and unconscious manner, thereby accumulating an intuitive and unconscious "stock of knowledge" concerning the minds of others (see Schutz 1962; Schutz and Luckmann 1973). For hermeneutic theory, human social life centers largely on inferring the mental attributes of others from signs (i.e., interpreting signs)—a process which enables communication and the transmission of cultural knowledge (see Schutz 1967[1932]; Schutz and Luckmann 1973:esp.16–17, 270–271; Parsons and Shils 1951:159–189). Addressing this issue, Betti (1990:160) remarks:

> Nothing is of greater importance to man than living in mutual understanding with his fellow-men. Nothing appeals as much to his understanding as the lost traces

> of man that come to light again and address him. Whenever we come into contact with meaning-full forms [i.e. signs] through which an other mind addresses us, we find our interpretative powers stirring to get to know the meaning contained within these forms. From fleeting speech to fixed documents and mute remainders, from writing to *chiffres* and to artistic symbol, from articulated language to figurative or musical representation, from explanation to active behavior, from facial expression to ways of bearing and types of character—in short, whenever something from the mind of an Other approaches us there is a call on our ability to understand. . . .

The notion that human social life centers largely on interpreting signs can be developed in a number of different directions. This is because the concept of the "sign" has been theorized in myriad ways (e.g., by Saussure, Peirce, Wittgenstein, Bakhtin). However, I wish to focus on the concept of the sign in hermeneutic theory, giving special attention to the work of Geertz.

## II. GEERTZ, SIGNS, AND THE ANTHROPOLOGICAL ANALYSIS OF RELIGION

Geertz was trained at Harvard by Parsons in the 1950s. Accordingly, his work reflects the influence of Parsons, as well as related thinkers such as Dilthey, Weber, and Schutz. Geertz's work also reflects the broader interest in signs (or "symbols") characteristic of anthropological scholarship between the 1960s and the 1980s; that is, the "symbolic" anthropology associated with figures like Victor Turner (1967), David Schneider (1968), and Mary Douglas (2002[1962]; 2003[1970]). Geertz's analysis of signs is partially indebted to hermeneutic theory (e.g., Dilthey, Weber, Parsons), but it draws on other intellectual currents as well (e.g., Ryle, Wittgenstein, Susanne Langer). In his writings, Geertz sometimes refers to "signs" (1973:14). More often he refers to "symbols." Yet, for Geertz, symbols are signs. Geertz is not entirely consistent in how he defines signs/symbols. However, to keep matters simple, it can be said that for Geertz a sign (or "symbol") is "anything that denotes, describes, represents, exemplifies, labels, indicates, evokes, depicts, expresses— *anything that somehow or other signifies* [emphasis mine]" (1980:135; also see 1973:14, 91–92). Turner (1967:19) offers a similarly broad definition of signs/symbols. In adopting such a position, Geertz (and Turner) acknowledge that there are many different types of signs. Hence, there are signs that function through conventional association (which enables "label[ing]" and "denot[ing]"). For example, the English word "apple" is a sign/label for apples because it is conventionally associated with apples. There are also signs that function through resemblance (which enables "depict[ion]" and "exemplifi[cation]). For instance, a painting of a king is a sign/depiction of the king because it resembles the king (i.e., a Peircean "icon"; see Silverstein 1976:27; Daniel 1984:31–32; Kohn 2013:8). Geertz recognizes there are also signs which function as evidence "indicat[ing]" the presence of something else (i.e., a Peircean "index"; see Silverstein 1976:27; Daniel 1984:31–32; Kohn 2013:8). Hence, smoke is a sign of fire because it is evidence indicating the presence of fire. Similarly, Geertz tells us that "dark clouds are the symbolic precursors of on-coming rain" (1973:91; i.e., dark clouds are evidence indicating the future presence of rain). Signs of this sort function as evidence because the presence of the sign is statistically correlated with what it indicates (i.e., the presence of smoke is statistically correlated with the presence of fire, so the presence of smoke is evidence indicating the presence of fire).

Geertz often invokes forms of hermeneutic analysis which treat actions, statements, and material structures/artifacts as signs of mental attributes (i.e., the "verstehen approach," 1973:3–30). Yet, Geertz does not limit himself to these forms of analysis. Rather, Geertz tends to analyze different types of signs together in a fairly loose and imprecise manner. The loose form of analysis employed by Geertz (simply) highlights the fact that, in a given culture, a particular set of signs is somehow "linked" (through signification) to a particular set of beliefs or ideas (i.e., "meanings") (see esp. 1960; 1980). In other words, this particular set of cultural signs somehow "denotes, describes, represents, exemplifies, labels, indicates, evokes, depicts, [or] expresses" a particular set of cultural beliefs or ideas. Rather than explain exactly how a given sign is linked to a given idea or belief, Geertz simply remarks that each sign is linked, in various ways, to many ideas and beliefs. For Geertz, signs are "richly polysemic (that is, have multiple senses), their significance spreading out profusely in an embarrassment of directions" (1980:105; also see Turner 1967:27–30).

Echoing Parsons (see Parsons and Shils 1951:159–189), Geertz suggests that any culture or any religion can be treated as a system of "signs" (or "symbols") (1973:14, 89–94). These signs include things as various as "carvings, flowers, dances, melodies, gestures, chants, ornaments, temples, postures, and masks" (1980:103). For Geertz, signs cause people to adopt beliefs, especially religious beliefs. Hence, when people encounter a set of (religious) signs, they will be inclined to accept the (religious) beliefs with which these signs are linked (1980:104; 1973:87–125). Signs are most effective in fostering religious belief when people are repeatedly exposed to them, and when the signs are embedded in awe-inspiring, emotionally evocative, and aesthetically beautiful cultural events or products (i.e., "pomp and ornament," 1980:105, 100, 121, 18). Such a stance seems to imply that religious signs/symbols operate akin to political propaganda or commercial advertisements. Geertz also argues that when people in a given society are exposed to signs/symbols, they will be inclined to accept the religious beliefs conveyed by these signs/symbols, if the beliefs serve to justify their particular "way of life" (see 1973:89–90).

Thus, Geertz develops hermeneutic ideas in a distinctive way. First, he claims that any cultural or religious tradition can be treated as a system of signs. Second, he promotes a loose and imprecise approach to the analysis of signs—one which is partially indebted to hermeneutic theory. Third, he asserts that, under the right conditions, signs cause people to adopt religious beliefs. These ideas define Geertz's distinctive approach to anthropology (i.e., "interpretive anthropology").

## III. BREAKING FROM GEERTZ'S ANALYSIS OF SIGNS IN CULTURE AND RELIGION

Different hermeneutic theorists develop different approaches to signs in social analysis. Geertz develops one approach, but there are others. Indeed, I think that hermeneutic theorists like Droysen, Weber, Schutz, Parsons, and Davidson develop a more productive approach. Their work suggests that, in social analysis, signs are often best understood in terms of "mental causation" and its effects.

### A. Mental Causation

Discussions of "mental causation" go back to Aristotle, but are refined by hermeneutic thinkers like Weber and Davidson (also see Heil and Mele 1993; Audi 2006). Weber recognizes that causal explanation takes different forms depending upon whether we are dealing with matter or with mind (also see Dilthey 1988[1883]; Collingwood 1993). Thus, we causally explain the behavior of material objects without reference to mental attributes. Take the movement of a rock. Thus, the rock might be caused to move by being struck (e.g., by a falling tree). The rock might also be caused to move (i.e., fall) by gravity. Notice that causal explanation of this type makes no reference to mental attributes. However, a human being differs from a material object (like a rock) in that s/he has a mind. This means that it is possible to causally explain human behavior (i.e., action) with reference to mental attributes. For instance, a woman was caused to purchase ice cream by a *desire* for ice cream. A man was caused to smash the television by his *emotion* of anger. Weber does not deny that, in theory, human action can also be causally explained without reference to mental attributes. For instance, one might say that a woman was caused to purchase ice cream by a biochemical reaction in her brain. Here there is no reference to mental attributes (like belief, desire, etc.). Yet, for Weber (an antipositivist), social analysis centers on causal explanation, which does reference mental attributes (see Weber 1975:125–129). Collingwood endorses the same position (1993:214–215).

Thus, for Weber, *mental attributes (like belief, desire, emotion, intention) cause actions*. In other words, *actions are effects of mental attributes* (see Weber 1975:125–129; 1978[1922]:12; Huff 1984. Also see Schluchter 1999:68; Beiser 2011:539–544). For instance, a belief that the door is open causes a man to state: "Shut the door." An intention to play basketball causes a man to put on his basketball shoes. Like Weber, Parsons, Collingwood, and Davidson affirm that mental attributes cause actions (Parsons and Shils 1951:161 ft.1; Collingwood 1993:214–215; Davidson 2001[1980]:3-19). Notably, however, this key idea drops out of the work of Geertz, and anthropological work inspired by Geertz.

## B. Mental Causation, Rational Action, and Instrumental Rationality

At any rate, the notion of mental causation has a further level of complexity. Scholarship on action recognizes that action is of (at least) two types: (1) rational action, and (2) non-rational action. Let us focus on rational action. One way to describe a rational action is as follows: an individual performs a rational action when s/he performs an action which s/he believes will help realize his/her desires.

The preceding idea can be traced back to Aristotle. Aristotle draws attention to a particular case. In this case a single desire and a single belief combine together to cause an action. For instance, John may desire to lose weight. He may also believe that bike-riding will result in weight loss. John's desire and belief combine together to cause him to perform the action of riding a bike.

For Aristotle, when we describe how an individual's belief and desire combine to cause an action, we describe his/her reasoning (i.e., the "practical syllogism" see Davidson 2001[1980]:3–42; Audi 2006:10–28). Thus, in the previous example, John reasons as follows: "I desire to lose weight. It is my belief that bike-riding results in weight loss. Therefore, I should perform the action of riding a bike." In this way, John's belief and desire form the basis of his reasoning and cause him to perform the action of riding a bike. Where reasoning leads to action it is typically referred to as "practical reasoning." Thus, for Aristotle, beliefs and desires form the basis of (practical) reasoning and cause action.[2]

Within hermeneutic theory, the topic of (practical) reasoning is taken up by Weber and then Davidson. Like Aristotle, Weber and Davidson hold the view that beliefs and desires combine to cause action. However, Weber and Davidson offer an analysis of (practical) reasoning which is more sophisticated than that of Aristotle.

Weber's discussion of (practical) reasoning focuses on the concept of "instrumentally rational action" (1978[1922]:24–26). Weber's concept of instrumentally rational action has exercised a strong influence over twentieth century social theory (see Lukacs 1971[1923]; Schutz 1967[1932]; Parsons 1949[1937]; Horkheimer 2004[1947]; Habermas 1984). This concept is partially inspired by Utilitarian and neoclassical economic models of human action (e.g., Homo economicus). However, it is also critical of these models, rejecting some of their basic premises. For instance, Weber rejects the assumption that all human action is self-interested and caused by a desire to acquire material goods. (For classic anthropological critiques of such models see Malinowski 1984[1922]; Mauss 2000[1950]; Sahlins 1976. Also see Chibnik 2011).

[2] This idea continues to enjoy widespread support even though it was attacked in the middle of the twentieth century on the dubious grounds that "reasons" cannot simultaneously be "causes." Ryle (2002[1949]) and Anscombe (2000[1957]) criticize the view the reasons are causes, but Davidson (2001[1980]) and Audi (2006) convincingly rebut these criticisms.

Weber's concept of instrumentally rational action can be explained as follows. Similar to Aristotle, Weber holds that desires and beliefs are causes of action.[3] Nevertheless, Weber turns away from the Aristotelian idea that a single desire and a single belief combine to cause an action. Rather, for Weber, an individual is caused to perform an action by his/her various beliefs and desires (see Weber 1946[1915]:280; 1978[1922]:24–26; Also see Habermas 1984:87–88). This means that the individual acts to pursue the strongest of his/her various desires in light of his/her various beliefs about the world.

Weber's point is articulated with greater clarity and refinement by prominent philosopher of action Donald Davidson (2001[1980]; 2001[1984]). Davidson explains that when analyzing action, it is necessary to adopt a holistic approach. Such an approach takes all of an individual's beliefs and desires into account. This is necessary because an individual's beliefs and desires can always offset one another. Recall the example of John the bike-rider. A simple Aristotelian analysis would hold that John is caused to ride the bike by his desire to lose weight and his belief that bike-riding will result in weight loss. But such an analysis tacitly presumes that John does not have any offsetting beliefs and desires. First, consider the case of offsetting desires. For instance, imagine that John desires to rest in bed more than he desires to lose weight. In this situation John would not ride the bike. More specifically, in this situation, John's desire to lose weight would not cause him to perform the action of bike-riding because it is offset by a stronger desire to rest in bed. There can also be offsetting beliefs. For instance, imagine that even though John believes that bike-riding will result in weight loss, he also believes it will result in a fatal heart attack. In this situation, he would also not perform the action of bike-riding. More specifically, in this situation his belief that bike-riding results in weight loss would not cause him to ride the bike because it is offset by a belief that bike-riding will result in a heart attack.

Davidson (2001[1980]) also points out that intention and action are closely related. This is because an intention is usually an intention to perform an action. Hence, I might intend to eat a hamburger or to visit China. In both cases I intend to perform a particular action (namely, the action of eating a hamburger and the action of visiting China). Furthermore, an individual's intentions have a causal relationship to his or her actions. Thus, once I form an intention to perform an action, the intention generally causes me to perform the action (unless I am prevented from doing so or unless I make a mistake). Hence, if I form an intention to eat a hamburger, the intention then causes me to perform the action of eating a hamburger. In other words, I eat the hamburger because I intended to do so.

For Davidson, it is possible to speak of an individual's beliefs and desires causing his/her actions. Yet, this is a *derivative* phenomenon. In Davidson's view, the totality of an individual's beliefs and desires first cause the individual to form intentions. These intentions then cause the individual to perform corresponding

[3] Weber refers to beliefs as "ideas" or "expectations." Meanwhile, he refers to desires as "interests" or "ends."

actions. Here we may return to the case of John the bike-rider. On Davidson's view, John's desire to lose weight and his belief that bike-riding results in weight loss cause him to form an intention to ride a bike. This intention then causes John to perform the action of riding a bike.

In explaining his views on intention, Davidson once again emphasizes the importance of a holistic approach. After all, an individual's intentions are caused by his/her beliefs and desires, but these beliefs and desires can offset one another. Hence, it is necessary to take all of an individual's beliefs and desires into account. For instance, imagine that John desires to rest in bed more than he desires to lose weight. In this situation, John would not *form an intention* to ride the bike. Similarly, imagine that even though John believes that bike-riding will result in weight loss, he also believes it will result in a fatal heart attack. In this situation, John would not *form an intention* to ride the bike. Consequently, one must take all of John's desires and beliefs into account to determine which intentions he will form.

The preceding points can be summarized as follows. The totality of an individual's beliefs and desires cause him/her to form intentions. More specifically, an individual forms an intention to perform a particular action based on the strongest of his/her desires and in light of all his/her beliefs about the world. This intention then causes the person to perform the corresponding action. Since an individual's actions follow directly from his/her intentions, it can also be said that the person acts based on the strongest of his/her desires and in light of his/her beliefs about the world. I will use the term "instrumental rationality" to refer to the notion that an individual forms intentions (and/or performs actions) based on the strongest of all his/her desires and in light of all his/her beliefs about the world.

As noted previously, human actions can be divided into two (simplistic) categories: (1) rational actions, and (2), non-rational actions. To put things in simplistic terms, where an action is rational it can be described in terms of instrumental rationality[4] (i.e., an individual is caused to form intentions and perform actions based on the totality of his/her beliefs and desires). Yet, where an action is non-rational such a description is not valid. Hermeneutic theorists like Weber recognize that not all human actions are rational. For instance, Weber (1978[1922]:24–26) recognizes that actions can be caused by emotions (i.e., "affectual action") or even habits (i.e., "traditional action").

Indeed, Weber points out that human actions typically do not fit into simple categories. Hence, an action can be partially rational and partially non-rational. For instance, a woman might be caused to perform a particular action partially based on the totality of her beliefs and desires (i.e., instrumentally rational action), but also partially based on her emotions and habits. Nevertheless, for both Weber and Davidson, human actions are largely (though not completely) rational. Hence, in analyzing actions, one should start with the presumption that

[4] This simplification omits Weber's notion of "value rational action."

they are rational (see Weber 1978[1922]:6–7, 18–19; Parsons 1949[1937]:640–649; Habermas 1984:6; also see Beiser 2011:548–550). Yet, one may abandon this presumption in the face of contrary evidence.

All of this leaves us with a more complex model of mental causation. The model focuses on rational action (i.e., instrumentally rational action), while recognizing that action is not purely rational. Insofar as action is rational (i.e., instrumentally rational), it can be described as follows. An individual's beliefs and desires combine to cause the individual to form intentions, and these intentions then cause the individual to perform actions. Notice that, according to this model, the individual's beliefs, desires, and intentions all cause his/her actions (i.e., this is "mental causation"). Hence, an individual's actions are effects of his/her beliefs, desires, and intentions. In other words, *actions are effects of mental attributes.*

## C. Mental Causation and Chains of Effects

Hermeneutic theorists like Weber hold that actions are effects of mental attributes. However, not all effects of mental attributes are actions. Thus, Droysen (1893:12) points out that "man's mind has touched, formed, [and] stamped" the material and social world. Such a view suggests that things like material structures and artifacts are also effects of mental attributes. Parsons and Schutz espouse a similar stance (See Parsons and Shils 1951:161 ft.1; Schutz and Luckmann 1973:16–17, 272). This stance can be understood as follows. Consider that a cause can produce a "chain of effects." Here, the cause produces an effect. This effect then causes a second effect. The second effect then causes a third effect, and so on. For example, my emotion of anger can cause me to shoot a gun, and my action of shooting the gun can cause someone's death. In this case, there is a cause (anger), which produces an effect (the action of shooting a gun). This effect (the action), then causes a further effect (someone's death). Similarly, I may have a desire to eat corn, and a belief that corn plants will grow if I plant corn kernels in the earth. My belief and my desire then cause me to perform the action of planting corn kernels in the earth. My action of planting the corn kernels has the effect of changing the earth into a cornfield. Hence, the cornfield is an effect of my action of planting, which is an effect of my desire to eat corn and my belief that corn plants will grow if I plant corn kernels in the earth. In this way, my "mind" has "formed [and] stamped" the earth by making it into a cornfield.

Synthesizing the insights of Droysen, Weber, Schutz, Parsons, and Davidson, I would suggest the following. Actions (including statements), material structures/artifacts, and the like can be viewed as the effects of mental attributes. Moreover, these effects can be conceptualized as "signs." Such signs function as evidence indicating the presence of something else (i.e., a Peircean index). Hence, just as smoke is a sign of fire because it indicates the presence of fire, the action of purchasing ice cream is a sign of a desire for ice cream because it indicates the presence of a desire for ice cream. Moreover, when one sees a cornfield in a village, the cornfield is a sign that the villagers desire to eat corn and believe that corn plants will grow if kernels are planted in the earth.

As a general principle, wherever a mental attribute causes a chain of effects, all of these effects are evidence indicating the presence of the mental attribute. In other words, *all of these effects are signs of the mental attribute which caused them.* In such a situation, one infers the presence of a mental attribute from an effect, by tracing back from the effect to the mental attribute which caused it. For instance, suppose we see a woman purchasing ice cream. We infer that she desires ice cream by tracing back her action of purchasing ice cream to a desire for ice cream (which we presume caused her action). In this case, we have traced an effect (i.e., the action of buying ice cream) directly back to a mental attribute (i.e., a desire for ice cream). Nevertheless, in other cases we may need to trace back through a longer chain of effects. Hence, when we encounter a cornfield, we see it as an effect of the action of planting corn kernels, and we see the action of planting kernels as an effect of a desire to eat corn and a belief that corn plants will grow if kernels are planted in the earth. In this way, from a cornfield we infer a desire to eat corn by tracing back through a chain of effects. Schutz alludes to something like the preceding method of inference: "It is a basic fact that acts . . . change [the world] . . . Some acts . . . leave behind traces . . . We can formally describe all such traces as the results [i.e., effects] of acts . . . [From the results/effects of an act] one can infer back to a determinate action and from this to certain subjective [i.e., mental] processes" (Schutz and Luckmann 1973:272).

All of this leads to a particular perspective on social analysis. According to such a perspective, the minds (i.e., mental attributes) of individuals cause countless chains of effects. These chains of effects radiate outward across space and through time to generate social and material worlds. Ordinary people within a given society (e.g., Egyptian society) confront a particular social and material world, consisting in effects. These effects include actions and statements (which may be recorded in texts), as well as material structures and artifacts. As we will see, these effects also include obedient actions through which particular rules, plans, and decrees are implemented. To put things in hermeneutic terms, all these effects are "expressions," "externalizations," or "objectifications" of mind (i.e., mental attributes). Cultural, religious, and legal traditions consist (at least partly) in effects of this type, and such traditions are an element of the human social and material world. People naturally seek to understand their world (and its traditions). This typically involves tracing back the effects (which constitute the world and its traditions) to mental attributes. *These people thereby treat the effects as signs of mental attributes.* Since traditions consist (at least partly) in effects, they also consist (at least partly) in signs. Schutz puts forth an analytic framework of this type when he discusses the intuitive stance that ordinary people have toward the world (i.e., the "natural attitude"): "In the natural attitude I [as an ordinary person] am already cognizant of the historicity of the social and cultural world. The questionableness of the social and cultural world is of a historical character. Its objectivations [i.e., objectifications] are traceable back to human doings, which can be explicated as regards their meaning. By means of the latter, I 'understand' the purpose of the tool, I grasp what a sign stands for . . . " (Schutz and Luckmann 1973:17).

In a sense, Geertz (and other symbolic anthropologists) are correct to suggest that any cultural or religious tradition can be seen (at least in part) as a system of signs. However, I wish to break from Geertz by insisting that it is (often) useful to conceptualize signs as effects of mental attributes. Here I adopt a hermeneutic approach closer to that of Schutz. As we will see, such a hermeneutic approach is particularly helpful in analyzing Sharīʿa rules and Islamic religious education. Yet, before we explore this approach, it is necessary to consider the criticisms of Geertz set forth by Asad.

## IV. ASAD'S CRITIQUE OF GEERTZ, AND ITS IMPLICATIONS FOR THE ANTHROPOLOGY OF RELIGION/ISLAM

Asad develops a perspective very different from Geertz's. In particular, Asad criticizes Geertz's assertion that signs/symbols generate religious belief, noting that a person can view signs/symbols without acquiring religious belief. For instance, a Hindu or an atheist might frequently encounter Christian signs/symbols (e.g., crucifixes, churches), but not acquire Christian religious beliefs (e.g., belief in the divinity of Jesus). For Asad, religious belief is not acquired through viewing signs/symbols, but through power-laden practices. Asad emphasizes that such practices engage the body. In Asad's view, the anthropology of religion should investigate how (bodily) practices prescribed by powerful religious institutions generate/instill belief and other mental attributes. Asad rejects Geertz's notion of religion as a system of signs/symbols because it is not attentive to power-laden (bodily) practices (see Asad 1993:27–54).

Extending this perspective, Asad holds that the anthropology of Islam should investigate how institutions like Muslim governments, Muslim families, Sufi orders, and religious schools use their power to prescribe (bodily) practices which generate/instill belief and other mental attributes (1986). For instance, these institutions require Muslims to pray, and through the practice of prayer Muslims acquire belief in God. These institutions also prescribe practices (i.e., ethical discipline) to instill other mental attributes (i.e., dispositions) valued in Islam (e.g., a desire to give to the poor, emotional feelings like fear of God and shame at exposing one's private parts). This particular analytic framework underlies Asad's influential concept of Islam as a "discursive tradition" (1986; 2003). As noted earlier, Asad's views have won wide acceptance, while Geertz's work (and hermeneutic theory) have been marginalized within the anthropology of religion/Islam.

I am sympathetic to Asad's criticisms of Geertz. Hence, like Asad, I see no need to endorse Geertz's assertion that signs/symbols generate religious belief. But while this assertion is central to Geertz's work, it is not central to the broader body of hermeneutic theory. Therefore, one can reject Geertz's assertion while affirming the general usefulness of hermeneutic ideas. The most important of these ideas is that actions (including statements), structures/artifacts, and obedient actions can be analyzed as signs of mental attributes. This type of analysis is neglected by Asad and other proponents of practice theory. Accordingly, it has no place in Asad's concept of Islam as a discursive tradition.

Hermeneutic ideas are essential for exploring aspects of religious, cultural, and legal traditions which cannot be reduced to power and practice. Thus, if the Islamic tradition incorporates power and practice, it also incorporates signs. Building on Geertz, I suggest that it is useful to treat the Islamic tradition as, in part, a system of "signs" (i.e., symbols). Indeed, this basic idea has been considered in a number of influential Islamicist works (see Waardenburg 2007; Ahmed 2016). However, I break from existing scholarship by conceptualizing signs as effects of mental attributes. Hence, I propose to treat the Islamic tradition as (in part), a system of signs *conceptualized as effects of mental attributes*. I would add that these signs should specifically be conceptualized as effects of *God's mental attributes*, for, as we will see, in the view of Muslims, Islamic knowledge is (largely) knowledge of God's mental attributes. Furthermore, unlike Geertz, I do not wish to assert that signs (i.e., symbols) generate religious belief. Rather, I would like to consider how signs operate to transmit a complex body of Islamic knowledge (including knowledge of Sharīᶜa rules), especially in contexts of higher religious learning.

In considering how signs operate to transmit Islamic knowledge, I also break from Weber, whose ideas have deeply shaped the interdisciplinary study of Islam and Muslim societies. On the whole, Weber's work is oriented by particular concern. He wishes to identify the distinctive religious and economic factors responsible for the rise of modern Western societies. Here he adopts a comparative approach, contrasting the history of Western societies with the history of different non-Western societies. In this context, Weber puts forth a variety of claims about Islamic law and Muslim societies. Hence, Weber claims that Muslim societies are governed through "patrimonialism"/"sultanism" (see 1978[1922]:231–232). He claims that Islamic legal systems exemplify "Qadi justice" (see 1978[1922]:818–822, 976–980). He claims that Muslim populations lack the rationalized and disciplined work patterns characteristic of Protestantism (see Rodinson 1973; Turner 1974; Huff and Schluchter 1999).

Weber's various claims about Islamic law and Muslim societies have generated a sizable literature within anthropology, sociology, and (Islamicist) history, especially since the 1970s (see e.g., Rodinson 1973; Turner 1974; Arjomand 1984; Rosen 1989; Gerber 1994; Johansen 1998; Crone 1999; Peletz 2002; Powers 2002). This literature has sought to explicate, defend, refute, qualify, or extend Weber's claims. Nevertheless, such Weber-related scholarship is guided by a set of concerns very different from my own. This is because such scholarship does not examine how signs (conceptualized as effects of mental attributes) operate to transmit Islamic knowledge (including knowledge of Sharīᶜa rules). However, I am interested in this issue. And I will now turn to it.

## V. KNOWLEDGE OF SHARĪʿA RULES AS KNOWLEDGE OF MENTAL ATTRIBUTES

Knowledge is of many different types. One specific type of knowledge is knowledge of others' minds (i.e., others' mental attributes). Knowledge of others' minds is especially important where rules are concerned. This is because, in many (but not all) cultural, legal, and religious traditions, rules are equated with the "will" or "intentions" of one or more authority figures. Hence, rules might be equated with the will or intentions of a lawgiving king. Likewise, rules might be equated with the will or intentions of a parliament, or "the people," or "the ancestors" (see Savigny 1831:33; Dilthey 1989[1883]:77–148; 216; 2002[1910]:106–107; Tönnies 2001[1887]:32–34; Schutz and Luckmann 1973:16; Ekins 2012, esp.127–142; Poscher 2015). In such contexts, the concepts of "will" and "intention" are largely interchangeable. Hence, I shall refer to "will/intention." Notably, will/intention is a mental attribute. Accordingly, in these contexts, knowledge of rules is knowledge of another's mental attributes (e.g., the mental attributes of the king, the parliament, or the ancestors). Since hermeneutic theory is concerned with grasping another's mental attributes it has great relevance to the analysis of rules. In explicating these points, I draw on influential recent work in "planning theory," which has sought to extend the ideas of Davidson (Bratman 1987; 2014; Shapiro 2002; 2011; Holton 2009; Ekins 2012; Vargas and Yaffe 2014). I offer a fuller introduction to planning theory later on.

Where rules are equated with intentions, such intentions can be conceptualized as being based on beliefs and desires, in accordance with the notion of instrumental rationality. Thus, imagine a king who wishes to lay down rules for his subjects (see Ekins 2012:127–142). The king forms rules by forming intentions. In other words, the king's rules are his intentions. As we will see, according to planning theory, such intentions take a particular form. Hence, the king intends that his subjects act in a particular way. For instance, the king might form an intention that his subjects refrain from dumping toxic waste in the ocean. The intention is equivalent to a rule mandating that subjects refrain from dumping toxic waste in the ocean. The king might then communicate this intention/rule to his subjects by making the statement "It is prohibited to dump toxic waste in the ocean."

In accordance with the notion of instrumental rationality, the king forms his intention/rule based on the strongest of all his desires and in light of all his beliefs about the world. For instance, suppose the king *desires* to protect the animals and the plants which live in the ocean. Moreover, he *believes* that toxic waste will kill these animals and plants. Based on his beliefs and desires, the king forms an intention that his subjects refrain from dumping toxic waste in the ocean. This is the king's "will." It is his rule.

Notably, proponents of planning theory hold that this line of analysis can also be extended to groups (Shapiro 2011; Ekins 2012; Bratman 2014). Moreover, such a perspective has long been affirmed by hermeneutic thinkers (see Savigny 1831;

Dilthey 1989[1883]:77–148; 216; 2002[1910]; Habermas 1984; 1996; Poscher 2015). Thus, a group of individuals may share a set of desires, beliefs, and intentions. Take the American people as a group. The American people may share a desire to protect the animals and plants which live in the ocean. They may also believe that toxic waste will kill these animals and plants. Based on these beliefs and desires, the American people form an intention that all citizens refrain from dumping toxic waste in the ocean. This is the will of the American people, which becomes (through the legislative process) an American legal rule. Of course, this is a simplistic idealization. Yet it is one which is central to political discourse in liberal polities (like the United States) (see Habermas 1984; 1996).

Moreover, just as this line of analysis can be extended to groups living in the present, it can also be extended to groups from the past. Hence, it can be argued that the past group laid down a set of rules. These rules embody their shared intentions (i.e., will), and are based upon their shared desires and beliefs. An example is the U.S. Constitution, which is widely held to embody the shared will of the American people at the time the United States was established (in the late eighteenth century). In some circumstances, this line of analysis can also be applied to informal rules found in nonliterate societies (e.g., rules of customary law, cultural norms) (see Savigny 1831; Dilthey 2002[1910]). These rules are part of a cultural tradition. It can be argued that such rules were laid down in the distant past by anonymous ancestors. Accordingly, these rules embody the shared intentions (i.e., will) of the ancestors, which are based upon the shared beliefs and desires of the ancestors.

I suggest that knowledge of Sharīʿa rules is best conceptualized as knowledge of another's mental attributes; namely, knowledge of God's mental attributes. This is because Muslims view God as a divine lawgiver, and equate Sharīʿa rules with the "will" or "intentions" of God. As noted previously, the concepts of "will" and "intention" are largely interchangeable, and in the Arabic language both are denoted by terms such as "*qaṣd*" and "*irāda*." The Arabic language also contains a variety of related terms which denote "a thing which is intended (or willed)" (e.g., *maqṣūd/maqṣad, murād*). Such terms are important because Muslim jurists continually invoke them when discussing the will/intentions of God (see, e.g., al-Ghazālī 2000:179; al-Shāṭibī 2004:219; al-Shāfiʿī n.d.:91–92). For instance, it is God's will/intention that Muslims pray five time a day, refrain from drinking alcohol, and punish theft with amputation of the hand. Because God wills/intends these things, they are considered Sharīʿa rules (*al-aḥkām al-sharʿiyya*). Therefore, it is a Sharīʿa rule that Muslims pray five times a day. Likewise, it is a Sharīʿa rule that theft be punished with amputation of the hand. As we will see, in the view of Muslim jurists, God has communicated His will/intentions to human beings (in part) through divine scripture.

The fact that Muslim religious scholars equate Sharīʿa rules with God's intentions has important implications. Thus, it implies that Sharīʿa rules are based on the desires and beliefs of God. This idea finds strong support in Arabic Islamic religious discourse. Hence, Muslim scholars hold that God is a beneficent being (*al-Raḥmān*). Accordingly, He desires to secure benefits for human beings (see

Hallaq 1997; al-Raysūnī 2006; Emon 2010; Opwis 2010). Such benefits are referred to by the Arabic term "*maṣlaḥa.*" For instance, it is a benefit for human beings if their lives are protected (*ḥifẓ al-nafs*). It is likewise a benefit for human beings if their property rights are protected (*ḥifẓ al-māl*). God desires to secure such benefits. God's desire to secure benefits for human beings causes Him to lay down rules which aid in securing these benefits. Hence, because God desires to protect human life, He has laid down a rule which punishes murder by execution (*qiṣāṣ*) or payment of blood money (*diya*) (though with the possibility of forgiveness by the victim's heirs) (al-Ghazālī 2000:174; al-Shāṭibī 2004:222; also see Peters 2005:38–53; Hallaq 2009:320–322). This rule is God's will. In other words, God has formed an intention that Muslims punish murder by execution or payment of blood money. Similarly, because God desires to protect property rights, He has laid down a rule which punishes theft with amputation of the hand (though only when very restrictive conditions are met) (al-Ghazālī 2000:174; al-Shāṭibī 2004:222; also see Peters 2005:55–57; Hallaq 2009:316–318).

Thus, it can be said that God has a desire (*gharaḍ*)[5] to secure benefits (*jalb al-maṣlaḥa*) for human beings, and that He lays down His rules (*aḥkām*) for this purpose. As we will see, this perspective undergirds the famous medieval theory of Islamic law referred to as *Maqāṣid al- Sharīʿa* (i.e., the Intended Aims of the Sharīʿa).

Muslim religious scholars also attribute an extensive body of beliefs to God. However, here a clarificatory comment is necessary. Some beliefs are true, while others are false. True beliefs are generally referred to as knowledge.[6] So knowledge is a kind of belief (i.e., true belief). Now, Muslim scholars, never speak of God as possessing beliefs (*muʿtaqadāt*). Rather they speak of God as possessing knowledge (*ʿilm*). This is because scholars hold that God is an omniscient being who only possesses true beliefs.

Muslim jurists tacitly assume that every Sharīʿa rule is based on God's (true) beliefs (i.e., knowledge) about the world. Take the Sharīʿa rule which mandates amputation for theft as a means of protecting property rights. This rule only makes sense based on a belief that amputating the hands of thieves deters theft. Were it the case that this punishment had no deterrent effect, then it would not help protect property rights. Hence, it may be said that God has laid down amputation as a penalty for theft based on his "knowledge" (i.e., true belief) that amputating hands deters theft.

In Islamic legal discourse, direct references to God's knowledge are often replaced by references to *facts* about the world. Thus, a Muslim jurist might state that God has laid down amputation as a penalty for theft based on the *fact* that amputating hands deters theft. There is a particular reason that references to facts can substitute for references to God's knowledge. Because God is an omniscient being, He has knowledge about every fact in the world. Hence, to say

[5] I recognize that *gharaḍ* can also be translated "intention" or "aim."

[6] Although some assert that a belief must be both true and justified to be called "knowledge."

that it is a fact that amputating hands deters theft implies that God knows (i.e., believes) that amputating hands deters theft.

To sum up, Muslim scholars equate Sharīʿa rules with God's will/intentions. Muslim legal discourse presumes that God's will/intentions are based on His desires and beliefs. Consequently, *knowledge of Sharīʿa rules is knowledge of God's will/intentions, and the desires and beliefs on which they are based.* Put differently, *knowledge of Sharīʿa rules is knowledge of God's mental attributes*, for intentions, desires, and beliefs are mental attributes.

## VI. HERMENEUTIC ANALYSIS AND THE TRANSMISSION OF KNOWLEDGE OF SHARĪʿA RULES

As noted previously, mental attributes cause chains of effects. One may trace back from the effects to the mental attributes which caused them. In this sense, the effects are signs of the mental attributes which caused them.

As we will see, Muslim scholars hold that God's mental attributes have caused chains of effects. Muslim scholars seek to acquire knowledge of God's mental attributes by tracing the effects back to God's mental attributes. In this sense, the effects are signs of God's mental attributes.

Such signs/effects of God's mental attributes take countless forms. However, I will briefly address four of the most important: (1) the Qurʾan, (2) the reported obedient actions of the Prophet Muḥammad (Sunna), (3) the reported obedient actions of religious scholars from the past, and (4) the observed obedient actions of present-day religious scholars. These four types of signs can be seen as a system of signs from which Muslims acquire knowledge of God's mental attributes (i.e., knowledge of Sharīʿa rules). Let us examine each type of sign.

### A. The Qurʾan

According to the Islamic tradition, God has guided human beings throughout history by sending them a line of prophets, including Abraham, Moses, and Jesus. God has conveyed his teachings to each of these prophets through divine revelation (*waḥī, tanzīl*). The last of these prophets was Muḥammad, whose life spanned from 570 to 632 C.E.. Muḥammad was a merchant from the Arabian town of Mecca. He was called to his prophetic mission at age 40, and over the next two decades God gradually revealed to him a large number of teachings. Prophet Muḥammad proclaimed these teachings, thereby establishing the religion of Islam.

The foundation of the Islamic religion is the Qurʾan, a 600-page Arabic text believed to be the literal word of God. The Qurʾan is essentially a collection of statements made by God to the Prophet over the course of the latter's mission. These statements cover a variety of matters. Some statements lay down Sharīʿa rules, while others explain theological doctrine, offer political advice, or recount stories of past prophets.

As noted earlier, for hermeneutic theory, verbal statements are simply one type of action. Statements (like other actions) are effects caused by mental attributes. One may trace a statement back to the mental attributes which caused it. In other words, one may infer, from a statement, the mental attributes which caused it. For instance, in the Qurʾan, God states: "Amputate the hand of the thief."[7] From this statement it can be inferred that it is God's will/intention that Muslims amputate the hands of thieves. Moreover, it can further be inferred that God desires to protect property rights and that He believes (i.e., knows) that amputation will deter theft. After all, God's intentions are based on His desires and beliefs.

Nevertheless, as we will see, interpreting the Qurʾan is more complex than the preceding example suggests. This is because, for Muslim jurists, God's intentions may diverge significantly from the literal meaning (*ẓāhir*) of His statements in the Qurʾan. Hence, read literally, the statement "Amputate the hand of the thief" indicates that all thieves should have their hands amputated. Yet, Muslim jurists infer that, in actuality, God only intends that Muslims amputate the hands of adult sane thieves, sparing thieves who are children or insane. God also intends to spare thieves who steal out of severe hunger and thieves who steal something trifling in value (see Peters 2005:20–24, 55–57; Hallaq 2009:316–318; Biltājī 2006:214–223). Thus, inferring God's intentions is not a simple or straightforward process, even when explicit statements from God are available.

Arabic Islamic discourses refer to God's statements in the Qurʾan as "signs" (*āyāt*) and "evidence" (*dalīl*). It is believed that one can infer both Sharīʿa rules and God's intentions from Qurʾanic statements. This is natural, given that Sharīʿa rules are equated with God's intentions. According to formal Islamic legal theory (*Uṣūl al-Fiqh*) the Qurʾan is the first source (*aṣl*) of knowledge about Sharīʿa rules (*Fiqh*).

## B. The Reported Obedient Actions of the Prophet Muḥammad (Sunna)

For Muslims, the Qurʾan is not the only source of divine guidance. Thus, as a general principle, it is believed that all of the Prophet's actions (including statements) are based on teachings received from God. Moreover, many of these teachings are not found in the Qurʾan. For instance, the Qurʾan does not prohibit eating from gold and silver vessels. However, the Prophet has proclaimed such a prohibition (Ibn Ḥajar 2008:56). In the view of the Islamic tradition, the Prophet's prohibition is equated with a prohibition from God. Because the Prophet's actions (including statements) are held to be divinely inspired, they are treated as a second form of revelation alongside the Qurʾan.

[7] Qurʾan [5:38].

Muslim scholars use the Arabic word "Sunna" to refer to the totality of the Prophet's actions (including statements). Dating back to early Islamic times, efforts have been made to collect and record reports on the Prophet's actions (including statements). A report of this type is known as a "Hadith." For instance, there is a Hadith report which records that the Prophet destroyed/removed the idols found in the city of Mecca (see al-Bukhārī 2002:1172). Similarly, there is a Hadith report which records that the Prophet stated: "Verily God loves kindness in all things." (al-Bukhārī 2002:1510). Muslim scholars have collected together many thousands of Hadith reports. These reports are contained in a number of large multivolume works (e.g., *al-Muwaṭṭaʾ*, *Ṣaḥīḥ al-Bukhārī*, *Ṣaḥīḥ Muslim*).

According to formal (Sunni) Islamic legal theory (*Uṣūl al-Fiqh*), the Sunna is the second key source (*aṣl*) of knowledge about Sharīʿa rules (*Fiqh*) after the Qurʾan. Hence, Muslim jurists seek to derive knowledge of God's mental attributes (i.e., His intentions/Sharīʿa rules) from the Prophet's actions (i.e., Sunna) as described in Hadith reports. Just as the Qurʾan is a type of "evidence" (*dalīl*) about God's mental attributes, the Prophet's actions are likewise a type of "evidence" (*dalīl*) about God's mental attributes.

How are we to understand the idea that the Prophet's actions are a type of evidence from which God's mental attributes may be inferred? Here I wish to turn back to the notion of "obedient actions." Recall that an obedient action is an action whereby a person obeys a rule, plan, or decree by acting in accordance with it. As noted earlier, obedient actions may be viewed as effects of mental attributes (i.e., "expressions" or "externalizations" of mind). However, in order to fully appreciate this point, it is necessary to consider obedience in relationship to communication. Here I draw on the highly influential (but not universally accepted) "intentionalist" model of communication developed by (some) hermeneutic theorists and analytic philosophers (see Schleiermacher [1838]1998, Grice 1957; 1969; 1989; Austin 1962; Searle 1969; 1983; Ekins 2012:180–217).[8] The intentionalist model presumes that communication involves communicating intentions through actions (including statements).

Obedience generally requires communication. Hence, before a person can obey a rule, decree, or plan (by acting on it), that rule, decree, or plan must be communicated to him/her. Consider a king who forms a rule/intention that his subjects refrain from dumping toxic waste in the ocean. The king's subjects cannot obey his rule/intention before he communicates it to them. In order for the king to communicate it to them, he must perform an action (i.e., an act of communication). This action may consist in a statement. Therefore, the king may state: "O my subjects, do not dump toxic waste in the ocean." The action might also be nonverbal. Hence, the king may simply beat anyone who dumps toxic waste in the ocean. People who see the king habitually beating waste-dumpers realize that he has prohibited waste-dumping. Once the king has communicated his rule/intention, it will (ideally) causally determine the actions of his subjects.

[8] For critical discussions of the intentionalist model see Gadamer [1960]2006; Ricoeur 1971; Rosaldo 1982; Duranti 2015.

Hence, once the subjects know of the king's rule/intention, it will cause them to refrain from dumping toxic waste in the ocean. Consequently, the subjects' action of refraining from waste-dumping is an *effect* of the king's rule/intention.

We may situate the king's communication within a causal chain which ends with the actions of his subjects. Hence, the king first forms his intention/rule that subjects refrain from dumping toxic waste. The king's intention then causes him to perform an act of communication. For instance, the king's intention that his subjects refrain from waste-dumping causes him to state: "O my subjects, do not dump toxic waste in the ocean." The king's act of communication (i.e., statement) (ideally) causes his subjects to act in accordance with this intention/rule. Hence, if the subjects now refrain from dumping waste, their action is an effect of the king's intention/rule. Notice that what we have here is mental causation, which generates a chain of effects. The chain begins in the king's mind (with his intention) and ends in his subjects' obedient actions.

Plans raise similar issues (and later on we will see that rules can be conceptualized as plans). For instance, take a Russian general who formulates a military plan. The general's plan consists of his intentions (e.g., he intends that his soldiers bomb Paris). The general's intentions cause him to perform the act of communicating his intentions to his soldiers. For instance, his intention that his soldiers bomb Paris causes him to state "Listen soldiers, I order you to bomb Paris." Ideally, the general's soldiers are obedient, and then act in accordance with his plan/intentions. This means that the actions of the soldiers are effects of the general's plan/intentions.

If the soldiers' obedient actions are effects of the general's plan/intentions then they are also signs of the general's plan/intentions. Or, to put things more broadly, the soldiers' obedient actions are signs (and effects) of the general's mental attributes. If the soldiers' obedient actions are signs of the general's mental attributes, we can infer the general's mental attributes from the soldiers' obedient actions. For instance, if we see the soldiers loading bombs into planes, we might infer from the soldiers' *actions* that the general *intends* to bomb enemy cities with planes. We may further infer that the general *desires* to force the enemy to surrender and that he *believes* the enemy will surrender if its cities are bombed. Similarly, if we see the planes bombing military bases, but sparing schools and homes, we may infer that the general intends to refrain from killing civilians. We may further infer that he desires to reduce loss of life and that he believes it is possible to force the enemy to surrender without killing its civilians. Here we see how the general's mental attributes can be inferred from the obedient actions of his soldiers. The material structures and artifacts produced by the soldiers are likewise effects/signs of the general's mental attributes. Hence, if we see that the soldiers have constructed a prison facility equipped with tools for torture, we may infer it is the general's intention to torture enemy soldiers. We may further infer that the general desires to extract information from the enemy soldiers, and that he believes torture is an effective method for procuring such information.

There are many other situations which are analogous to the situation described previously (e.g., a factory owner and his/her obedient workers, an architectural planner and his/her obedient builders). Yet, for our purposes, the most relevant analogous situation is a lawgiving king and his obedient subjects. As mentioned earlier, such a king might formulate rules, which consist of his intentions. The king then communicates his rules/intentions to his subjects. Ideally, his subjects are obedient, and they then act in accordance with his rules/intentions. The obedient actions of the subjects are effects/signs of the king's mental attributes. I suggest that this line of analysis is important for how we conceptualize knowledge of Sharīʿa rules. In the Islamic tradition, God is spoken of as a lawgiving "king" (*al-Mālik*). Meanwhile, all pious Muslims are expected to live as obedient "slaves" (i.e., subjects) of God (*ʿibād*). *Such implies that the actions of all pious Muslims are effects/signs of God's mental attributes. Similarly, the material structures and artifacts produced by Muslims are likewise effects/signs of God's mental attributes.*

This line of thinking helps us appreciate why Muslim jurists consider the Prophet's actions (i.e., Sunna) to be evidence of God's mental attributes. In the Islamic tradition, it is assumed that God communicated His rules/intentions to the Prophet through divine revelation. The Prophet then obediently acted in accordance with these rules/intentions. For instance, there is a Hadith report which recounts that the Prophet broke the idols found at Mecca's central shrine (the Kaʿba) (see al-Bukhārī 2002:1172). From the Prophet's action of idol-breaking we might infer that God's desires to prevent idol-worship in Mecca, that God believes (i.e., knows) that the presence of idols encourages idol worship, and that it is therefore God's intention/will that Muslims forever keep all Mecca free of idols. In other words, it is a Sharīʿa rule that Muslims forever keep all Mecca free of idols. Similarly, the Prophet has stated that Muslims should not spit in mosque (Ibn Ḥajar 2008:130). From the Prophet's statement (which is an action), we may infer that God intends that Muslims refrain from spreading any sort of filth in the mosque (e.g., spit, urine, feces, trash).

Notice that here we are tracing back to God's mental attributes from the reported actions of the Prophet. Thus, we begin with the Prophet's reported action of breaking the idols. We assume that the Prophet's action is an effect of God communicating His will/intention to the Prophet (i.e., His will/intention that Muslims keep Mecca free of idols). Notably, when God communicated His will/intention to the Prophet, this was an action on the part of God (i.e., an act of communication). We assume that God was caused to perform this action of communicating His intention by His intention. In other words, God's intention that Muslims keep Mecca free of idols caused God to communicate to the Prophet that His intention is that Muslims keep Mecca free of idols. Moreover, we assume that God's intention is based on His desire to prevent idol-worship in Mecca and His belief that the presence of idols encourages idol-worship. In this manner, we have traced back from the Prophet's reported action to God's mental attributes. In other words, we have an instance of mental causation which generates a chain of effects. God's beliefs, desires, and intentions are at the beginning of this chain, and the Prophet's actions are at the end of this chain. The Prophet's actions are signs (or evidence) of God's mental attributes because we can trace back from these actions to God's mental attributes.

## C. The Reported Obedient Actions of Past Religious Scholars

Just as God's mental attributes can be inferred from the obedient actions of the Prophet, they can also be inferred from the obedient actions of other pious Muslims—in particular, religious scholars. Common Arabic terms for religious scholar include "*shaykh*" and "*ʿālim*." The preceding notion is important for understanding the structure of Islamic religious education. According to traditional Muslim views, all religious knowledge is passed down through history via an unbroken chain of religious scholars (*sanad, isnād, silsila*). Here the idea is that God communicated knowledge of his rules/intentions to the Prophet (via divine revelation). The Prophet, as "God's Messenger" (*Rasūl Allah*) then communicated knowledge of God's rules/intentions to the earliest Muslims, the most knowledgeable of whom became the first generation of Muslim scholars. This first generation of Muslims scholars (*Ṣaḥāba*) then communicated knowledge of God's rules/intentions to their students, who became the second generation of religious scholars (*Tābiʿūn*). It is held that this process of knowledge transmission has continued on until the present. On such a view, scholars today have received knowledge of God's rules/intentions through an unbroken chain extending back to the Prophet.

Based on their knowledge of God's rules/intentions, Muslim scholars address a wide variety of legal issues that are not explicitly addressed in the Qurʾan or in the Hadith reports. For instance, the Qurʾan and Hadith reports do not address the permissibility of smoking tobacco, and they are (arguably) ambiguous on the permissibility of endowments (*awqāf*) (see Powers 1989:564). Similarly, the Qurʾan and the Hadith reports do not spell out, in detail, all the rules of inheritance law. Yet, Muslim scholars take up these matters.

Reports on the actions (including statements) of Muslim scholars are regarded as an important source of religious guidance. Consequently, dating back to early times, efforts have been made to collect these reports. Although there exist reports on scholars from every era, reports on the first (three or so) generations (*Salaf*) are especially prized. The Arabic word "*āthār*" is used to denote reports on early Muslim scholars.

Reports on the actions (including statements) of Muslim scholars have been collected in a large number of places. For instance, the earliest collections of Hadith reports also contain large numbers of reports on the early generations (e.g., *Muṣannaf ʿAbd al-Razzāq, Muṣannaf Ibn Abī Shayba, al-Muwaṭṭaʾ*). Thus, Mālik's *Muwaṭṭaʾ* contains 527 Hadith reports on the Prophet, 613 reports on the first generation of Muslim scholars, and 285 reports on the second generation of Muslim scholars (Brown 2009:25). However, collections of this type are only one place where reports on religious scholars can be found. In fact, an enormous proportion of premodern Islamic writing is devoted to biographies/hagiographies of religious scholars (e.g., *manāqib, ṭabaqāt, siyar, tarājim, tārīkh, ʿilm al-rijāl*). Such writing incorporates countless reports on Muslim scholars. Moreover, many Islamic legal works are, in large part, collections of reports on the actions (including statements) of Muslim scholars (e.g., Ibn Qudāma's *al-Mughnī*, al-Nawawī's *al-Majmūʿ*, Ibn ʿĀbidīn's *Radd al-Muḥtār*). These reports are arranged in terms of their relevance to different legal topics (e.g., prayer, marriage, commercial contracts, criminal punishment). For instance, it may be reported that a particular scholar (e.g., ʿUmar, ʿAlī, Abū Ḥanīfa) prayed with his hands clasped, or punished people for drinking date wine, or awarded custody of small children to mothers rather than fathers. This line of analysis can also be applied to books and treatises written by past religious scholars (e.g., al-Shāfiʿī's *Risāla*, al-Ghazālī's *Iḥyāʾ ʿUlūm al-Dīn*). After all, a book or treatise written by a scholar reports his statements (for it records his statements).

In the Islamic tradition, it is expected that religious scholars obey God by acting in accordance with His rules/intentions. Since religious scholars act in accordance with God's rules/intentions, their actions are effects of God's rules/intentions (e.g., God intends that Muslims pray five times a day, and as an effect, religious scholars pray five times a day). Given this situation, God's mental attributes can be inferred from the obedient actions (including statements) of religious scholars. Hence, if a religious scholar refuses to smoke tobacco, we might infer that it is God's will/intention that Muslims refrain from smoking tobacco. It may further be inferred that God desires to protect human health and that God believes/knows that tobacco is harmful to human health. Consider a more concrete example involving the Day of ʿĀshūrāʾ (the tenth day of the Islamic month of Muḥarram). At one time, the Prophet obliged Muslims to fast on this day. However, there was some doubt about whether the Prophet had canceled this obligation before he died. It is reported that Ibn Masʿūd (a scholar from the first generation) was seen eating during the Day of ʿĀshūrāʾ following the Prophet's death. From Ibn Masʿūd's action of eating, it may be inferred that it is no longer God's intention that Muslims refrain from eating on the Day of ʿĀshūrāʾ (see Muslim 1426h:503).[9] Using a similar line of analysis, Muslim jurists established the permissibility of endowments (*awqāf*) by noting that the first generation of Muslims had established endowments (i.e., it may be inferred from the action of the first generation in establishing endowments that it is not God's intention that Muslims refrain from establishing endowments) (see Powers 1989:564).

As we will see, students at al-Azhar and the Dār al-ʿUlūm devote extensive time to studying texts reporting the actions (including statements) of past religious scholars (especially the *Salaf*). Such texts are studied alongside the Qurʾanic text and textual Hadith reports. All of these texts are studied together, because knowledge of God's mental attributes (and hence knowledge of Sharīʿa rules) can be inferred from them. It is only by grasping this point that it is possible

[9] Or, to be more precise, Muslims are no longer obligated to fast on the Day of ʿĀshūrāʾ, though it is still praiseworthy for them to do so.

to appreciate the type of textual curriculum characteristic of higher Islamic learning.

### D. The Observed Obedient Actions of Present-Day Religious Scholars

Although Islamic learning has an important textual component, it also has an important non-textual component. Thus, a central element in traditional Islamic learning is a pedagogy known as "companionship" (*ṣuḥba, mulāzama*). As we will see, this pedagogy is still practiced by particular groups of Egyptian religious scholars today. In companionship, a student and a religious scholar (i.e., *shaykh*) enter into a long-term personal relationship. The scholar adopts the student into his household as a type of personal servant (i.e., *khidma*), and they spend their time eating together, worshipping together, and traveling together. The student is expected to continuously observe (*mushāhada*) and imitate (*iqtidāʾ*) the religious scholar. Meanwhile, the scholar takes on the role of a fatherly teacher, and is expected to continuously monitor and correct (*taʾdīb*) the student's behavior (i.e., *tarbiya*). The pedagogy of companionship operates on the assumption the student may derive knowledge of God's mental attributes (i.e., Sharīʿa rules) by continuously observing the obedient actions of the teacher. Hence, companionship, as a pedagogy, is grounded in the notion that the obedient actions of religious scholars are signs of God's mental attributes.

## VII. THE HOLISTIC CHARACTER OF HERMENEUTIC CULTURAL ANALYSIS

In the preceding sections, I have argued that in the Islamic tradition, signs/effects of God's mental attributes take a variety of forms, including: (1) the Qurʾan, (2) the reported obedient actions of the Prophet Muhammad (Sunna), (3) the reported obedient actions of past religious scholars, and (4) the observed obedient actions of present-day religious scholars. These can all be seen as chains of effects radiating out from God's mind and down through history. Accordingly, traditional Islamic learning emphasizes that religious knowledge flows through a "chain" (i.e., *isnād*) which extends back through history, to the Prophet, and from the Prophet ultimately to God (i.e., to the mind of God).

For hermeneutic theory, knowledge of an individual's mind consists in an overall picture of the mind. Such a picture is an understanding of that individual's various beliefs, desires, and intentions. Moreover, it is necessary that this overall picture be (relatively) coherent. Coherence presumes that an individual's desires, beliefs and intentions are not independent separate entities. Rather, the mind is an integrated structure, and an individual's desires, beliefs, and intentions are interrelated elements in this structure.

## A. Interrelations among Desires, Beliefs, and Intentions

Desires, beliefs, and intentions are interrelated in at least three ways. First, as a general principle, an individual does not have contradictory beliefs (even if perfect coherence is elusive). Thus, if an individual believes that Mecca is located in Saudi Arabia, s/he cannot simultaneously believe that Mecca is located in France. Second, as a general principle, an individual does not have contradictory intentions (even if perfect coherence is elusive). Thus, if I intend to go the library at 7:00 p.m., I cannot simultaneously intend to eat dinner at home at 7:00 p.m. Similarly, if a king intends that his subjects marry, he cannot simultaneously intend that his subjects refrain from marriage. Third, as a general principle, an individual's intentions are based on his/her desires and beliefs in accordance with the concept of instrumental rationality.

Thus, beliefs, desires, and intentions are interrelated (in at least three ways). If these mental attributes are interrelated, then positing that an individual has a particular desire (or belief or intention), implies things about the individual's other desires, beliefs, and intentions (See Davidson 2001[1984]). For instance, positing that an individual has a particular belief, implies that s/he does not have other beliefs which contradict it. Similarly, positing that an individual has a particular intention, implies that s/he does not have other intentions which contradict it. Moreover, in accordance with the concept of instrumental rationality, whenever we posit that an individual has a particular belief or desire, such implies that s/he has the sort of intentions which can be based on this belief or desire. Hence, suppose we posit that God desires to protect property rights. Protecting property rights might be accomplished by punishing thieves in some way (e.g., by fining them, lashing them, amputating their hands, etc.). Consequently, the fact that God desires to protect property rights implies that God may intend that Muslims punish thieves in some way. Similarly, suppose we posit that God believes that the presence of idols encourages idol-worship. God's belief that idols encourage idol-worship implies that God may intend that Muslims destroy such idols. The concept of instrumental rationality has an additional consequence. In accordance with this concept, whenever we posit that an individual has a particular intention, such implies that s/he has the sort of beliefs and desires which could serve as a basis for the intention. For instance, if we posit that God intends that Muslims amputate the hands of thieves, such implies that He desires to protect property rights and believes that amputation will deter theft. After all such a desire and a belief could serve as the basis of the intention.

## B. A Coherent Overall Picture of the Mind

Each sign/effect of an individual's mind, taken alone, provides some evidence of his/her beliefs, desires, and intentions. Yet, what one sign suggests about mental attributes might be contradicted or qualified by what other signs suggest. Hence, all the signs must be considered together and synthesized into a coherent overall picture of an individual's mind. Accordingly, in an Islamic context, all the signs of God's mental attributes must be considered together and synthesized into a coherent overall picture of God's mind. In such a coherent overall picture, God's beliefs, desires, and intentions fit together as interrelated elements.

One way to think about this is the following. We begin by looking at all the signs/effects of God's mental attributes. We then ask: "Which set of mental attributes (i.e., beliefs, desires, and intentions) would God need to have in order to cause these signs/effects?" For instance, which set of beliefs, desires, and intentions would God need to have in order to cause Him to utter the statements found in the Qurʾan? Which set of beliefs, desires, and intentions would God need to have in order to cause the Prophet and later scholars to perform the obedient actions which have been reported (or directly witnessed) from them? As we will see, Muslim religious scholars address this process (i.e., *istiqrāʾ*) in legal theoretic discussions of God's intended aims (*Maqāṣid al-Sharīʿa*).

In reality, the process at issue is not a rare or unfamiliar one. Rather human beings habitually engage in this process, albeit in an intuitive and largely unconscious manner (a distinct but related point is made by Schutz 1967[1932]:139–214; Schutz and Luckmann 1973:15–18, 59–98). Hence, recall the earlier example of the general and his soldiers. By observing the various obedient actions of the soldiers we intuitively and unconsciously acquire a coherent overall picture of the general's mind (i.e., his various, beliefs, desires, and intentions). The more we observe the soldiers, the richer and more detailed this picture becomes. In building this picture, we are asking ourselves which set of beliefs, desires, and intentions would the general need to have in order to cause the soldiers to perform these obedient actions. The same approach applies if we add in additional signs of the general's mental attributes, such as the general's statements. Here we derive a coherent overall picture of the general's mind by looking both at his various statements and at the various obedient actions of his soldiers. In doing so, we ask ourselves which set of mental attributes would the general need to have in order to cause him to utter these statements and in order to cause the soldiers to perform the obedient actions. In the same way, we might acquire a coherent overall picture of a king's mind by examining his statements and the obedient actions of his subjects.

Hermeneutic thinkers have long recognized that a process of this type exists, treating it under the heading of the "hermeneutic circle." The hermeneutic circle has been theorized in different ways by different scholars (e.g., Schleiermacher 1998[1838]; Dilthey 1972[1900]; Gadamer ([1960]2006). However, a common theme is that we interpret individual signs to gain a coherent overall (i.e., holistic) understanding (i.e., the movement from the "parts" to the "whole") (see Dilthey 1972[1900]:243–244; Geertz 1983:69; Davidson 2001[1984]).

This process is also relevant to groups (see Savigny 1831; Dilthey 1989[1883]:77–148; 216; 2002[1910]). Thus, just as an individual may have a particular set of beliefs, desires, and intentions, a group may share a particular set of beliefs, desires, and intentions. In such circumstances, it is possible to derive a coherent overall picture of the "group mind" (i.e., *Volksgeist*, "corporate mind," see Bunzl1996; Collingwood 1993:219). Here the notion of "group mind" simply refers to mental attributes which are shared (for the most part) among a group of individuals.[10] As such, "group mind" is similar to some definitions of "culture." For instance, we may assume that the group lays down particular rules, which embody its shared intentions (i.e., will). Members of the group obey the group by acting in accordance with its rules/intentions. In this way, the obedient actions of group members are effects/signs of the group's rules/intentions. This is analogous to how the obedient actions of a king's subjects are effects/signs of the king's rules/intentions. Just as we derive an overall picture of the king's mind by examining the obedient actions of his subjects, we derive an overall picture of a group's mind by examining the obedient actions of its members. Thus, suppose we see the group members refraining from dumping toxic waste in the ocean. Such is an obedient action on the part of group members. From this we infer that the group desires to protect sea animals, believes toxic waste is harmful to sea animals, and has formed an intention that group members refrain from dumping toxic waste in the oceans. By examining more of the group members' obedient actions, we acquire a richer and more detailed picture of the group's mind. Of course, the group's mind does not only reveal itself in obedient actions. Rather, it reveals itself in every action, statement, material structure, and artifact wherein the shared mental attributes of the group are manifested. These are all signs of the group mind. By considering all the signs together, we synthesize a coherent overall picture of the group mind.

## VIII. RELATIVISM IN HERMENEUTIC CULTURAL ANALYSIS

The process of synthesizing a coherent overall picture of a mind is best approached in relativistic terms. Thus, suppose that a particular group of people synthesizes a coherent overall picture of a given individual's mind (e.g., a general, a king, a factory owner). In one sense, this picture is based on the individual's actions (including statements) and the effects of these actions. However, strictly speaking, the picture is actually based on what the group *subjectively believes* to be the individual's actions and what the group *subjectively believes* to be the effects of these actions. Thus, a particular group's picture of the general's mind will not necessarily be based on the general's actual statements. Rather it will be based on what the group believes to be the general's statements. Similarly, the group's picture of the general's mind will not necessarily be based on the actions actually performed by his soldiers. Rather, it will be based on what the group subjectively believes about the actions performed by his soldiers. The same applies to the Islamic tradition. Muslims' picture of God's mind is based upon

[10] "Group mind" does not refer to a mystical entity which exists independently from the individuals.

what they subjectively believe to be God's actions (including statements) and what they subjectively believe to be the effects of God's actions. Thus, Muslims subjectively believe that God uttered the statements recorded in the Qur'an. Moreover, they subjectively believe that the actions of the Prophet and later Muslim scholars are effects of God's mental attributes. If one is interested (as I am) in how Muslims build an overall picture of God's mind, it does not matter whether these subjective beliefs are true. All that matters is that Muslims treat them as true.

As a broader methodological point, such a relativistic approach is helpful when analyzing cultural, religious, and legal traditions. These traditions do not exist in a vacuum. Rather they exist for particular social groups. Particular social groups engage with a tradition via their subjective beliefs about the nature and history of that tradition. For instance, suppose there is a nonliterate group. The cultural tradition of the group includes rules. The group obeys these rules. Moreover, the group believes that the rules have been handed down from the ancient ancestors. Accordingly, the rules are identified with the intentions of the ancient ancestors. Hence, in the view of the group, knowledge of the rules is knowledge of the shared intentions of the ancient ancestors, and knowledge of the shared beliefs and desires on which these intentions are based. Now, suppose John is a member of the group. John subjectively believes that other group members act in accordance with the intentions/rules of the ancient ancestors. Consequently, in John's view, the obedient actions of the group members are signs/effects of the ancient ancestors' shared mental attributes. Thus, John will build a coherent overall picture of the ancient ancestors' mind by examining the obedient actions of other group members. As a matter of fact, John's subjective beliefs may be incorrect. For instance, the rules of the group may not actually derive from a set of ancient ancestors with shared beliefs, desires, and intentions. Yet, if we are interested in how John builds an overall picture of the ancient ancestors' mind, it does not matter whether or not his subjective beliefs are true.

Anthropological proponents of practice theory typically reject the hermeneutic notion that cultural, legal, and religious traditions can be conceptualized as coherent wholes. Instead, they assert that every tradition is, by nature, "contradictory" and "contested." On this view (inspired by Marxist ideology critique), different groups put forth different interpretations of the tradition, which advance their different political interests. Each group then uses its power to champion its favored interpretation. This leads to a power struggle, wherein the strongest group usually gets its favored interpretation accepted as authoritative (see Bourdieu 1977; Merry 2003; Ortner 2006). Legal anthropologists have often endorsed similar views (see Moore 2000[1978]; Comaroff and Roberts 1981). I do not think that, in the abstract, it is helpful to assert that a given tradition is (or is not) a coherent whole. What is more important is that members of a given tradition (e.g., the Islamic tradition) typically *perceive* it as a coherent whole. As explained previously, perceptions of this type are generated through a specific hermeneutic/interpretive process whereby a coherent picture of a mind is derived from signs/effects. This process is socially important. Yet, it is habitually ignored by proponents of practice theory (as well as legal anthropologists). Even if there is some sense in which every tradition is contradictory and contested, attention must also be paid to the hermeneutic/interpretive process whereby members of a tradition come to perceive it as a coherent whole. Ignoring this process leads to simplistic accounts of how people engage with tradition. At their worst, such accounts reduce engagement with tradition to a power struggle. By contrast, hermeneutic theory recognizes that people engage with tradition in order to *understand* others (i.e., to understand their minds), *not merely to advance a set of political interests through power*. For example, Muslims engage with the Islamic tradition to understand the mind of God (i.e., God's will/intentions), not merely to advance a set of political interests through power. As recognized by Habermas, the hermeneutic/interpretive process (whereby people understand others) is distinctive. Accordingly, an analysis of this process cannot be reduced to "ideology critique" (i.e., the critical analysis of power and political interests), even if "ideology critique" is also worthwhile (see Habermas 1971).

## IX. HERMENEUTIC THEORY VERSUS PRACTICE THEORY ON THE ANALYSIS OF RULES

At the outset, I remarked that cultural, legal, and religious traditions (like Islam) have important dimensions that can only be addressed through hermeneutic theory. Proponents of practice theory have tended to overlook these dimensions. This has led proponents of practice theory to promote a perspective on rules and rule-learning which is incomplete and misleading. I will now critically examine practice theory's perspective on rules and rule-learning.

As noted previously, practice theory highlights the way in which power-laden practices instill mental attributes. Expanding upon this idea, practice theory offers a sweeping and influential critique of conventional perspectives on rules. This critique involves (at least) four key claims.

### A. First Claim: Rules and Control

First, practice theory claims that conventional perspectives exaggerate the role of rules in controlling human behavior. Such perspectives are not adequately attentive to the fact that powerful institutions often control behavior by prescribing practices which instill mental attributes. Hence, a government health organization may prescribe the practice of eating vegetables to instill a desire for vegetables in the population. This practice-instilled desire then influences the behavior of the population (i.e., it causes them to eat vegetables). In this way, the government health organization is able to control the population (i.e., make them eat vegetables). However, it does not do so by laying down a rule (i.e., a rule requiring them to eat vegetables). Rather, it does so by instilling a mental attribute through practice.

Practice theory develops another related line of analysis, which focuses on decision-making in complex and changing circumstances. The basic idea is this. Every individual faces complex and changing circumstances. The individual must decide how to act in response to these circumstances (which involves practical reasoning). An individual's decision about how to act in a particular set of circumstances will depend on his/her mental attributes—including those which have been instilled through practice (i.e., his/her dispositions/habitus). For instance, suppose a woman is offered ice cream. She will decide how to act in this set of circumstances based on her mental attributes. Hence, if she has a desire for ice cream she will decide to perform the action of eating the ice cream. However, if she has no desire for ice cream she will perform the action of refusing the ice cream. Similarly, if she has a belief that the ice cream is poisoned she will perform the action of refusing the ice cream.

If individuals decide how to act based on their mental attributes, then a powerful institution can "guide" decision-making (and subsequent action) by instilling particular mental attributes through prescribed practice (i.e., the institution can thereby shape an individual's practical reasoning). As we will see, Asad (2003) emphasizes that Islamic religious institutions do not merely guide Muslim action/behavior through rules. Rather, they also guide Muslim action/behavior by instilling various mental attributes (i.e., dispositions—including "character traits" like generosity, patience, and humility).

On the whole, I agree with practice theory that conventional perspectives exaggerate the role of rules in controlling (and guiding) human behavior. Likewise, I agree with practice theory that attention must be given to how mental attributes (i.e., dispositions) control (and guide) human behavior. Accordingly, I integrate these valuable insights into my analysis of Sharīʿa rules and religious education.

## B. Second Claim: Rules as Guides for Human Behavior

We now come to a second related claim made by practice theory. Practice theory argues that conventional perspectives exaggerate the basic capacity of rules to guide human behavior. This argument is informed by a particular idea; namely, that a rule can be equated with the literal meaning of a verbal statement (i.e., the "explicit" meaning of a statement). On such a view, knowledge of rules is a form of "discursive knowledge" (see esp. Bourdieu 1977:16–21; 1987:840, 849; Asad 2003:249). For example, in the Qurʾan, God makes the verbal statement: "Amputate the hand of the thief." For practice theory, God's rule can be equated with the literal meaning of His statement.

Practice theory asserts that human life is characterized by complex circumstances, and in these complex circumstances, rules do not provide adequate guidance (i.e., the literal meaning of statements does not provide adequate guidance). Thus, although the literal meaning of God's statement indicates that every thief must have his/her hand amputated, this rule may not apply in all circumstances. For instance, the rule may apply in standard circumstances, where the thief is adult and sane. Yet, it may not apply in more exceptional circumstances, where the thief is a child or insane. Hence, a judge who is faced with exceptional circumstances cannot simply apply the rule in accordance with its literal meaning. In other words, in exceptional circumstances, the rules cannot guide the judge's behavior. This basic line of argument is developed in Aristotle's *Nicomachean Ethics* (Ross 2009:99) and it resonates with the later work of Wittgenstein (2001[1953]). This line of argument is subsequently championed by practice theorists like Bourdieu, Asad, and (to an extent) Giddens (see Bourdieu 1977:16–21; 1987:840, 849; Asad 2003:249; also see Giddens 1979; 1984).[11]

Nevertheless, while the preceding line of argument captures an important insight, it is also misleading. Hence, it is correct that the literal meaning of verbal statements cannot adequately guide human behavior in complex circumstances. *Yet it is wrong to presume that every rule can be equated with the literal meaning of a verbal statement.* Rather, (in many cases) a rule should be equated with an intention based upon a set of beliefs and desires. Recall that in the Islamic tradition, rules are not equated with the literal meaning of verbal statements (i.e., *ẓāhir al-naṣṣ*). Rather, rules are equated with the intentions of God, which are based upon God's desires and beliefs. Accordingly, Muslim jurists hold that it is not God's intention that Muslims amputate the hands of thieves if they are children, if they are insane, or if they have stolen due to hunger (see Peters 2005:55–57; Hallaq 2009:316–318; Biltājī 2006:214–223). This is despite the fact that God states: "Amputate the hand of thief."

To understand the position of Muslim jurists, it should be emphasized that, in seeking knowledge of God's intentions, they do not limit themselves to the Qurʾan. Rather, they also give attention to Hadith reports and reports on the actions of past scholars. Thus, there is a Hadith report wherein the Prophet states: "The Pen is lifted from three [i.e., they are not held accountable for their deeds]: one who is asleep until he wakes up; a child until he reaches puberty; an insane person until he regains his reason." (Abū Dāwud 1998:v.5, 85). Moreover, there is a relevant report on the actions of the esteemed Muslim religious authority/scholar ʿUmar bin al-Khaṭṭāb (d.644). ʿUmar was a close companion of the Prophet, and assumed political leadership of the Muslim community two years after the Prophet's death. During the reign of ʿUmar there was a severe famine in which hunger forced people to steal for survival. ʿUmar responded by temporarily suspending the amputation punishment for theft (see Biltājī 2006:214–223).

In analyzing the issue of theft, Muslim jurists pay attention to God's statement (in the Qurʾan), the Prophet's statement (described in a Hadith report),

[11] Bourdieu equates rules with the "explicit" (i.e., literal meaning) of texts declaring rules. Meanwhile, Asad distinguishes between "knowledge of rules" and knowledge of the "application" of these rules. In this context, knowledge of the rules implies knowledge of the literal meaning of texts declaring these rules. Asad insists that knowledge of the rules does not entail knowledge of the application of the rules.

and ʿUmar's action (described in a report). For Muslim jurists, these are all signs of God's mental attributes, and these signs must be synthesized into a coherent overall picture of God's mind. This raises the following question: "Which set of beliefs, desires, and intentions would God need to have in order to cause Him to make the Qurʾanic statement, while also causing the Prophet [to] make the statement (described in the Hadith report), and causing ʿUmar to perform the action of suspending the amputation penalty during a time of famine?" Here we might posit the following picture of God's mind. God desires to protect property and believes that amputation deters theft. As a result, He forms an intention to punish thieves through amputation. This intention then causes Him to state: "Amputate the hand of the thief." God also desires to spare people lacking rational capacity (*ʿaql*) from punishment. Moreover, He believes/knows that children and the insane lack rational capacity. Hence, He forms an intention to exclude children and the insane from punishment. God then communicates this intention to the Prophet via divine revelation. This causes the Prophet to state: "The Pen is lifted from [a child and insane person]" (as described in the Hadith report). In other words, the Prophet's statement is an effect (and sign) of God's intention. We may continue the analysis a step further. As noted previously, God's mind is an integrated structure wherein His intentions do not contradict one another (i.e., *taʿāruḍ*). Hence, God cannot have an intention to punish all thieves by amputation (including thieves who are children or insane), for this would contradict his intention to exclude children and the insane from punishment. Thus, we must assume that when God stated "Amputate the hand of the thief," in actuality, His intention was only to punish adult sane thieves. This is true, even though the literal wording of His statement suggests a punishment which applies categorically to all thieves (including thieves who are children or insane). By qualifying God's intention in this way (*takhṣīṣ*), we remove the problem of contradictory intentions. For there is no contradiction between an intention to punish sane adult thieves with amputation and an intention to exclude children and the insane from punishment.

Finally, we come to the action of ʿUmar. We already know that God desires to protect property. However, it is also possible that He desires to protect human life. Moreover, there are certain circumstances in which these two desires cannot be realized simultaneously—like a severe famine. If the amputation penalty is applied during a severe famine, impoverished individuals may be dissuaded from taking the food they need to survive. Thus, in a famine, a choice needs to be made between protecting property and protecting life. We may posit that God desires to protect life (*nafs*) more than He desires to protect property (*māl*). Recall that the concept of instrumental rationality holds that individuals form intentions based on the strongest of their desires. Hence, in a famine situation, since God desires protecting life more than protecting property, He will form an intention to suspend the amputation penalty. Now, this knowledge of God's intentions, and the desires on which they are based, is knowledge of Sharīʿa rules. Such knowledge was presumably communicated by God to the Prophet via divine revelation. The Prophet then communicated this knowledge to ʿUmar.

Thus, ʿUmar knew that God intended to suspend the amputation penalty at a time of famine. This caused ʿUmar to suspend the amputation penalty at a time of famine. In other words, God formed an intention to suspend the amputation penalty, and ʿUmar's action is an effect (and hence a sign) of God's intention.

In this way, Muslim jurists begin with three signs of God's mental attributes (i.e., the Qurʾanic statement, the Hadith report, and the report on ʿUmar). They then synthesize these reports into a coherent overall picture of God's mind. This involves ascribing to God a particular set of intentions, and such intentions are Sharīʿa rules. As we will see, the existence of such a hermeneutic process is richly attested in Islamic legal texts and contemporary discussions at al-Azhar and the Dār al-ʿUlūm. Yet, this process is obscured by practice theory's identification of rules with the literal meaning of verbal statements. As we will also see, intentions are more complex than literal meanings, which gives intentions (and hence rules) a greater capacity to guide human behavior under complex and changing circumstances. This is why religious scholars at al-Azhar and the Dār al-ʿUlūm believe that Sharīʿa rules (dating from the seventh century) are capable of providing guidance to Muslims living in the twenty-first century.

To be clear, I think that practice theory is correct in suggesting that conventional perspectives overestimate the capacity of rules to guide behavior in complex circumstances. However, practice theory goes to the opposite extreme of underestimating the capacity of rules to guide behavior in such circumstances. It is to justify this dubious stance that practice theory incorrectly identifies rules with the literal meaning of statements.

Practice theory extends its critique of rules into a critique of texts. Hence, texts often report verbal statements declaring rules. For instance, the verbal statement "Amputate the hand of the thief" is reported in a text. The literal meaning of this text implies that every thief must have his/her hand amputated, but, as noted previously, there are complex circumstances where this penalty might not apply. Consequently, the text does not provide adequate guidance in such circumstances. In this way, practice theory uses the same line of argument to suggest that neither rules nor texts can guide human behavior in complex circumstances. Once again, this basic line of argument is directly traceable to Aristotle's *Nicomachean Ethics* (Ross 2009:99) and resonates with the later work of Wittgenstein (2001[1953]). The line of argument is then championed in the work of practice theorists like Bourdieu, Asad, and (to an extent) Giddens (see Bourdieu 1977:16-21; 1987:840, 849; Asad 2003:249; also see Giddens 1979; 1984).

Nevertheless, practice theory's approach to texts is problematic. First of all, practice theory tacitly assumes that all texts concerning rules simply record/report verbal statements declaring rules. Such texts ideally take the form of a "code" or "rulebook," which records/reports a series of verbal statements (e.g., "Do not kill," "Do not steal," "Do not worship idols") (see Bourdieu 1977:16–21; 1987:840, 849). This perspective suggests that the study of texts (concerning rules) revolves around the analysis of verbal statements. However, it would be more accurate to assert that the study of texts (concerning rules) revolves around the analysis of *effects of mental attributes*. This is because texts (concerning rules) do not simply report verbal statements. Rather they report the effects of mental attributes.

Here the Islamic tradition provides a helpful example. Muslim scholars seek knowledge of Islamic legal rules by consulting particular texts. It can be said that such texts concern rules. As we have seen, these texts include the Qurʾan, the Hadith reports, and reports on the actions of past scholars. All of these texts report the effects/signs of (God's) mental attributes. Hence, the text of the Qurʾan reports God's statements (which are effects of His mental attributes). Hadith reports are texts which report the actions of the Prophet (which are effects of God's mental attributes). Reports on past scholars are texts which report the actions of past scholars (which are effects of God's mental attributes). *When Muslim scholars study these texts they are not simply analyzing verbal statements. Rather, they are analyzing the effects of God's mental attributes.* Admittedly, the effects of God's mental attributes may be verbal statements (e.g., "Amputate the hand of the thief"). However, these effects need not be verbal statements. Consider the following two texts: The first is a Hadith report which says "The Prophet Muḥammad wore a silver ring." The second is a report which says "ʿUmar suspended the amputation penalty during a time of famine." When Muslim scholars study these texts they are interested in the (nonverbal) actions of the Prophet and ʿUmar, which are effects of God's mental attributes. It is misleading to suggest that the study of such texts revolves around the analysis of verbal statements (even though the actions of the Prophet and ʿUmar are described/reported through verbal statements). Moreover, notice that texts of this type do not report verbal statements declaring rules (e.g., "Amputate the hand of the thief"). Consequently, these texts do not fit the model of a "code" or "rulebook." Nevertheless, texts of this type are central to the Islamic legal tradition. Indeed, such texts are central to (almost) every cultural, religious, and legal tradition which involves precedent, for precedents are often reported nonverbal actions (and the actions of the Prophet and past Muslim scholars may be seen as similar to precedents). Yet, such texts are ignored by practice theory.

There is a second problem with practice theory's approach to texts. Practice theory suggests that a written verbal statement (i.e., text) does not communicate information beyond its literal meaning (i.e., its explicit wording). But this is mistaken. As emphasized by hermeneutic theory, one may infer a variety of mental attributes from a (written) verbal statement, even though these mental attributes are not part of the statement's literal meaning. Take the statement "Amputate the hand of the thief." Among other things, one may infer from this statement that God *desires* to protect property rights and *believes* that amputation will deter theft. Yet this information about God's beliefs and desires (i.e., His mental attributes) is not contained in the literal meaning (i.e., explicit wording) of the statement "Amputate the hand of the thief." Proponents of practice theory overlook the range of information which may be inferred from a text, because they wish to strengthen their claim that texts containing rules have a limited capacity to guide human behavior (see Bourdieu 1977:16–21; 1987:840, 849; Asad 2003:249).

## C. Third Claim: Transmitting Knowledge of Rules through Practice

Practice theory criticizes conventional perspectives on rules for failing to realize that knowledge of rules is largely acquired through practice. Again, this basic line of argument is directly traceable to Aristotle's *Nicomachean Ethics* and resonates with the later work of Wittgenstein (2001[1953];1965[1958]; McGinn 1984; Bloor 2006[1997]). In the *Nicomachean Ethics*, Aristotle draws attention to the importance of *repeated action* (i.e., practice). Hence, he refers to the "repetition of . . . acts" (Ross 2009:23). For Aristotle, through repeated action (i.e., practice) an individual may acquire knowledge of how to competently do something (i.e., do it in a competent/skillful fashion). Thus, through the repeated action (i.e., practice) of playing a musical instrument (e.g., a piano), an individual may acquire knowledge of how to competently play the musical instrument (Ross 2009:23). Notably, there is a difference between playing a musical instrument competently and incompetently. Playing the musical instrument incompetently involves deficiencies, mistakes, and errors. Consider another example. Through the practice of bike-riding, an individual may acquire knowledge of how to competently ride a bike. There is a difference between competently and incompetently riding a bike. One who cannot competently ride a bike falls off the bike, or wobbles while on the bike. If this can be called bike-riding at all, it is deficient and mistake-filled bike-riding (i.e., incompetent bike-riding).

Knowledge of how to competently do something is usually referred to as a "skill." Thus, if one knows how to competently play a piano, s/he has skill in piano-playing. Likewise, if one knows how to competently swim, s/he has skill in swimming. Hence, Aristotle's view is that a person may acquire a skill through repeated action (i.e., practice). Indeed, Aristotle goes a step further. For Aristotle, *many skills can only be acquired through repeated action* (i.e., *practice)*.

Consider the case of a man who wishes to acquire skill in piano-playing or bike-riding. It is possible to think of (at least) three ways in which he might seek to acquire this skill. First, he might seek to acquire it by reading a text. Such a text might offer instructions, expressed in verbal statements (e.g., "To ride a bike, first sit on the bike. Then put your feet on the pedals . . . etc.). Second, he might seek to acquire the skill by observing the actions of someone with the skill (e.g., by observing a skilled piano-player play the piano, by observing a skilled bike-rider ride a bike). Third, he might seek to acquire the skill by practicing himself (e.g., he himself practices piano-playing or bike-riding). For Aristotle, there are many skills which a person cannot acquire simply by reading texts or observing others. Rather, a person must acquire them through practice. To be clear, Aristotle's stance does not preclude multifaceted forms of learning, in which a skill is acquired through a combination of reading, observation, and practice. However, in the *Nicomachean Ethics*, Aristotle asserts that practice is often an essential element in learning a skill.

Aristotle and the later Wittgenstein (2001[1953];1965[1958]; McGinn 1984; Bloor 2006[1997]) extend the preceding line of analysis to rules, and their ideas are taken up by proponents of practice theory (see Bourdieu 1977; Asad 2003:249; also see Giddens 1979; 1984). Thus, Wittgenstein equates knowledge of a rule with knowledge of how to competently apply the rule (i.e., skill in applying the rule). Take knowledge of Arabic grammatical rules. One knows these rules if s/he knows how to competently apply them when speaking Arabic. When one competently applies the rules, s/he does not make grammatical errors. On the other hand, if one makes grammatical errors, s/he does not know Arabic grammar rules. Two relevant examples from the Islamic tradition are ritual prayer and criminal law. Thus, Islamic ritual prayer (*ṣalāh*) involves a set of rules. One knows the rules of ritual prayer if one knows how to competently apply them when praying. On the other hand, if one makes errors when praying, s/he does not know the rules. Likewise, a judge knows the rules of Islamic criminal law if he knows how to competently apply them when punishing criminals (e.g., he applies the amputation penalty to adult sane thieves but not to thieves who are children or insane). If the judge makes errors in punishing criminals (e.g., amputating the hand of an insane person), he does not know the rules.

Wittgenstein makes a number of further points about rules. For Wittgenstein, it is typically through practice than an individual acquires knowledge of a rule (i.e., knowledge of how to competently apply the rule or skill in applying the rule). Hence, an individual acquires knowledge of the rules of Arabic grammar through the practice of applying these rules when speaking Arabic. An individual acquires knowledge of the rules of ritual prayer through the practice of applying these rules when praying. An individual acquires knowledge of the rules of criminal law through the practice of applying these rules when punishing criminals.

The Aristotelian-Wittgensteinian notion of learning rules through practice tacitly implies the existence of knowledgeable authorities with the capacity to offer guidance and correction. Hence, suppose there is a person who wishes to practice applying a rule. In some cases, this person may experience confusion in how to apply the rule. In other cases, the person may unwittingly err in applying the rule. In these cases, there is need for guidance and correction by someone knowledgeable about the rule. For instance, if a student learning Arabic errs in applying the rules of Arabic grammar s/he may be corrected by a native speaker with greater knowledge of the language. If a Muslim judge errs in applying the rule of criminal punishment, he may be corrected by a more knowledgeable (and higher-ranking) judge. Therefore, guidance and correction by knowledgeable authorities make it possible to practice applying a rule. As we will see, such guidance and correction are a key element in the Islamic pedagogy of companionship, wherein a student learns through practice, but is subject to the guidance and correction of a teacher who monitors the student's practice.

Wittgenstein makes a further point about knowledge of rules. For Wittgenstein, when a rule is learned through practice, knowledge of that rule is often tacit and unconscious. Hence, a person may know how to competently apply a rule, but not be able to verbally articulate his/her knowledge of the rule. For example, suppose a woman has acquired knowledge of Arabic grammar rules and Islamic prayer rules through practice. Perhaps she has been speaking Arabic and praying since her childhood. Consequently, she may be able to competently apply these rules (by speaking Arabic and praying perfectly). Nevertheless, she may find it difficult or impossible to adequately explain these rules to others through words. Following Wittgenstein, proponents of practice theory frequently emphasize that knowledge of rules (acquired through practice) is largely tacit and unconscious (see Bourdieu 1977; Giddens 1979; 1984).

The preceding ideas from practice theory are valid and insightful. However, practice theory does not explicate how these ideas relate to hermeneutic theory. I suggest that *practice theory and hermeneutic theory can be brought together by considering the linkage between rules and intentions.* As noted earlier, in many traditions, rules can be equated with intentions (e.g., Sharīʿa rules can be equated with God's intentions). Meanwhile, practice theory argues that knowledge of rules can be acquired through practice. But *if rules are intentions, this implies that knowledge of intentions can be acquired through practice*. Moreover, *if knowledge of intentions is tied to knowledge of beliefs and desires, it may be argued that knowledge of a mind* (i.e., *a coherent overall picture of a mind) can be acquired through practice.* Such a line of analysis allows us to bring together practice theory's concern with practice and hermeneutic theory's concern with knowledge of other minds.

## X. ACQUIRING KNOWLEDGE OF ANOTHER MIND THROUGH PRACTICE

*I suggest that, in many cultural, religious, and legal traditions, knowledge of mind* (i.e., *mental attributes) can be acquired through practice of the tradition's rules.* More specifically, in an Islamic context, knowledge of God's mind can be acquired through practice of Sharīʿa rules. These claims can be explained as follows. According to practice theory, knowledge of rules is knowledge of how to competently apply the rules, and knowledge of how to competently apply the rules is acquired through the practice of applying the rules. Now, in traditions where rules are intentions (e.g., the Islamic tradition), "knowledge of how to competently apply rules" can be equated with "knowledge of how to act in accordance with intentions" (e.g., how to act in accordance with God's intentions). Moreover, "the practice of applying rules" can be equated with "the practice of acting in accordance with intentions." This being the case, we can say that in the Islamic tradition, a Muslim acquires knowledge of how to act in accordance with God's intentions (i.e., rules) through the practice of (obediently) acting in accordance with God's intentions (i.e., rules). For instance, a Muslim judge acquires knowledge of how to act in accordance with God's intentions/rules on criminal punishment through the practice of (obediently) acting in accordance with God's intentions/rules when punishing criminals (i.e., he does not impose the amputation penalty on child thieves). Similarly, a Muslim woman acquires knowledge of how to act in accordance with God's intentions/rules on ritual prayer through the practice of (obediently) acting in accordance with God's intentions/rules.

Hence, she begins her prayer by uttering "*Allahu Akbar*" or "God is great" (for it is God's intention that Muslims begin the prayer by uttering the words "*Allahu Akbar*"). Likewise, she wears a veil when praying and avoids prayer during menstruation (for it is God's intention that women veil their hair when praying, and avoid prayer during menstruation).

The preceding line of analysis can be pushed a step further. If one knows how to act in accordance with God's intentions, one must know what God's intentions are. Admittedly, this knowledge of God's intentions may be tacit and unconscious. Consequently, a person with this knowledge may be unable to verbally articulate it (at least with any precision). Yet, Wittgenstein (and practice theory) recognize that much knowledge is tacit and unconscious, and hence difficult (or impossible) to verbally articulate. With this in mind, it is possible to state the following. Through the practice of obediently acting in accordance with God's intentions/rules, a Muslim not only acquires knowledge of how to act in accordance with these intentions/rules. S/he also acquires knowledge of what God's intentions are, even if this knowledge is largely tacit and unconscious. And this knowledge of what God's intentions are constitutes knowledge of God's mind (i.e., mental attributes).

This line of analysis can be pushed yet further. Recall that a mind (including God's mind) is an integrated structure, wherein beliefs, desires, and intentions are interrelated. Hence, if one knows an individual's intentions, s/he may infer the individual's beliefs and desires. Suppose, for instance, that there is a Muslim judge. Through the practice of punishing criminals, he acquires knowledge that God intends to amputate the hands of sane adult thieves, but that God intends to spare thieves who are children or insane. Once the judge knows that these are God's intentions, he may infer God's beliefs and desires. As explicated previously, the concept of instrumental rationality indicates that, whenever an individual has a particular intention, such implies that s/he has the sort of beliefs and desires which could serve as a basis for the intention. Hence, if the judge knows that God intends to amputate the hands of adult thieves, the judge may infer that God desires to protect property rights and believes that amputation will deter theft. Similarly, if the judge knows that God intends to spare thieves who are children and insane from punishment, the judge may infer that God desires to spare people lacking rational capacity (*ʿaql*) from punishment. The judge may also infer that God believes that children and the insane lack rational capacity. As noted previously, inferences of this type are intuitive, and are typically made in a largely unconscious manner

To recapitulate: A Muslim may acquire knowledge of God's intentions through practice, and then infer God's beliefs and desires from these intentions. Hence, a Muslim also comes to know God's beliefs and desires through practice. In this way, a Muslim may synthesize a coherent overall picture of God's mind through practice. One may imagine a similar process in other traditions. Take a cultural tradition ascribed to the anonymous ancient ancestors. Those who practice the rules of this tradition may thereby acquire a coherent overall picture of the mind of the ancestors.

## XI. ACQUIRING KNOWLEDGE OF RULES THROUGH TEXTS, OBSERVATION, AND PRACTICE

In many cultural, legal, and religious traditions, knowledge of rules is learned through a combination of methods. Three of the most important methods are: (1) learning through texts, (2) learning through observation, and (3) learning through practice. Such methods operate together in an integrated fashion because they all contribute to a coherent overall picture of a mind (and, in many traditions, knowledge of rules is knowledge of a mind). These interrelated methods can be understood by bringing together ideas from hermeneutic theory and practice theory. I will explicate the preceding points with reference to the Islamic tradition.

Knowledge of Sharīʿa rules is knowledge of God's mind (i.e., mental attributes). More specifically, it is knowledge of God's intentions, as well as the beliefs and desires on which these intentions are based. Because God's mind is an integrated structure, what is needed is a coherent overall picture of God's mind. Such a picture can be acquired through a combination of (1) learning through texts, (2) learning through observation, and (3) learning through practice.

Let us begin by considering learning through texts and learning through observation. Hermeneutic ideas are helpful in analyzing these two methods of learning. In these two methods, it is necessary to focus on the effects/signs of (God's) mental attributes. As noted previously, in the Islamic tradition, the effects/signs of God's mental attributes take a variety of forms, including: (1) God's statements as reported in the Qurʾan, (2) the obedient actions of the Prophet as described in Hadith reports, (3) the obedient actions of past religious scholars as described in other reports, and (4) the obedient actions of present-day religious scholars, which are directly observed.

In the Islamic tradition, the *method of learning through texts* involves study of God's statements as reported in the Qurʾanic text, study of the obedient actions of the Prophet as described in textual Hadith reports, and study of the obedient actions of past scholars as described in other textual reports. Based on these various effects/signs of God's mental attributes, a Muslim student seeks to construct a coherent overall picture of God's mind.

In the Islamic tradition, the *method of learning through observation* involves observing the obedient actions of present-day religious scholars. As noted previously, such observation is a core element in the traditional pedagogy of companionship. Recall that in companionship, a student is adopted into the household of a scholar and observes his actions over an extended period. The observed obedient actions of the scholar are effects/signs of God's mental attributes. The student draws on these signs to construct a coherent overall picture of God's mind.

It is important to recognize that the methods of learning through texts and learning through observation do not operate separately and independently. Rather these methods are integrated together. Hence, a Muslim student utilizes both of these methods together in constructing a coherent overall picture of God's mind. In other words, the student synthesizes a coherent overall picture of God's mind based on (1) God's statements as reported in the Qurʿanic text, (2) the Prophet's obedient actions (as described in textual Hadith reports), (3) the obedient actions of past scholars (as described in textual reports), and (4) the obedient actions of the teacher (and other present-day scholars) which are directly observed. The student asks: "Which set of beliefs, desires, and intentions would God need to have to cause these various effects/signs?" This produces a coherent overall picture of God's mind—and knowledge of God's mind is knowledge of Sharīʿa rules.

We now come to the third method; namely, learning through practice. To analyze this method we must draw on ideas from practice theory as well as hermeneutic theory. As explained previously, through practice, a Muslim student may acquire knowledge of God's intentions, beliefs, and desires. In theory, the student might synthesize a coherent overall picture of God's mind on the basis of practice alone. Put differently, the student might synthesize a coherent overall picture of God's mind only using the method of learning through practice. But, in reality, students do not use this method alone. Rather, any student's knowledge of God's mind is also informed by what s/he has learned through texts and through observation. Put differently, students always combine the method of learning through practice with the methods of learning through texts and learning through observation. These methods together yield a coherent overall picture of God's mind.

For example, suppose that a student begins by using the methods of learning through texts and learning through observation (i.e., he studies texts and observes his teacher). Using these two methods, he constructs a coherent overall picture of God's mind, which includes a variety of intentions, desires, and beliefs. According to this picture (1) God desires to protect property rights, (2) God believes that amputation will deter theft, (3) it is God's intention to amputate the hands of adult male thieves, (4) it is God's desire to spare those without rational capacity from punishment, (5) God believes that children and the insane lack rational capacity, and (6) it is God's intention to spare thieves who are children and insane from punishment. The student will add to (and hence revise) this overall picture whenever he learns something new. And he may learn something new by the method of learning through practice. For example, he may learn through practice that it is God's intention to spare a thief the amputation penalty if s/he has only stolen something of trifling value (e.g., a towel, a stapler). This intention must then be added into the overall picture of God's mind (and the overall picture must be adjusted such that it maintains its coherence). In this way, the overall picture is revised, and this revised picture incorporates knowledge learned through practice, as well as knowledge learned through texts and observation.

Of course, learning through practice may engender more complex forms of revision. Hence, suppose that the student learns through practice that it is God's intention to spare a thief the amputation penalty if s/he has only stolen something of trifling value. The student then makes further inferences. Hence the student infers that God *desires* that criminal punishment be proportional, such that severe punishment (like amputation) is reserved for crimes which result in substantial harm. The student also infers that God *believes* that stealing something of trifling value does not result in substantial harm. After all, the preceding desire and the preceding belief could serve as the bases for God's intention to spare a thief the amputation penalty if s/he has only stolen something of trifling value. Consequently, the student has not only learned God's intention through practice, but also the desire and belief on which the intention is based. The student will add this intention, this desire, and this belief to his overall picture of God's mind.

In this manner, it is possible to gradually build up an increasingly detailed coherent overall picture of God's mind. This picture incorporates knowledge acquired by the three methods of learning through texts, learning through observation, and learning through practice. I will argue that all three of these methods structure Islamic learning at al-Azhar and the Dār al-ʿUlūm. Through these methods, students at al-Azhar and the Dār al-ʿUlūm acquire an increasingly detailed coherent overall picture of God's mind, which is simultaneously an increasingly detailed coherent overall picture of the system of Sharīʿa rules.

## XII. CONCLUSION

In the preceding pages, I have sketched out some preliminary ideas about how hermeneutic theory and practice theory can be brought together to facilitate the analysis of cultural, legal, and religious traditions (especially those which contain rules). My basic argument has been that in many traditions, knowledge of rules is knowledge of a mind/mental attributes (i.e., intentions, beliefs, and desires). Mental attributes cause chains of effects, and these effects are signs of the mental attributes which have caused them. It is possible to synthesize a coherent overall picture of a mind from its effects/signs (i.e., from the effects/signs caused by mental attributes). This mode of analysis is an intuitive one. Hence, we engage in this mode of analysis when we synthesize a coherent overall picture of a general's mind from the obedient actions of his soldiers (as these actions are effects/signs caused by the general's mental attributes). Here we "read"/"interpret" an army rather than a "text." Likewise, we engage in this mode of analysis when we synthesize a coherent overall picture of a king's mind (e.g., God's mind) from the obedient actions of his subjects (e.g., the Prophet and Islamic scholars). As explicated earlier, this mode of analysis is often tied to particular methods of learning (i.e., learning through texts, learning through observation, learning through practice). These methods enable a student to synthesize a coherent overall picture of a mind.

Admittedly, many of the ideas I have laid out require further explanation, qualification, and refinement. I will undertake these tasks in the following chapters. Moreover, I will apply the preceding ideas to offer a historical and ethnographic analysis of Islamic learning and legal doctrine, focusing on modern Egypt. It is to Islamic learning in Egypt that I now turn.

# 2

# Higher Religious Learning in Modern Egypt

In this chapter, I offer an ethnographic and historical account of higher religious learning in modern Egypt.

## I. PREMODERN EGYPTIAN RELIGIOUS EDUCATION

Egypt's reputation for religious knowledge extends back many centuries. Spared the Mongol invasions which decimated Baghdad and crippled Syria in the thirteenth century, Cairo became a haven for displaced religious authorities and established itself as the principle center of medieval Arab-Islamic scholarship.

During the Middle Ages Cairo was home to a number prominent educational institutions, including the al-Azhar mosque. However, the mosque would only acquire its unique standing over time. The Shiʿite Fatimid government constructed the al-Azhar mosque in the early 970s, shortly thereafter providing stipends and living quarters for scholars to teach there. By the twelfth century, the Fatimid regime had given way to Sunni rulers. Al-Azhar was converted into a Sunni institution and was made the beneficiary of new renovations and endowments. Still, it was not until the coming of Ottoman rule in the sixteenth century that al-Azhar was elevated above other Egyptian institutions of learning. In recognition of al-Azhar's unique status, the Ottomans created the post of Shaykh al-Azhar toward the end of the seventeenth century.[1] Filled by a leading scholar, the Shaykh al-Azhar was given authority over the mosque.

When Napoleon invaded Egypt in 1798, al-Azhar sat at the top of the nation's educational hierarchy. Its international reputation attracted scholars from across the globe. Indeed, at the close of the eighteenth century, al-Azhar was probably the most prominent Islamic educational establishment in the world, enjoying a status at least equal to that of the Süleymaniye in Istanbul, the Qarawiyyīn in Fez, and the Zaytūna in Tunis. On the other hand, the fame associated with these institutions should not lead to exaggerated notions about the scope of their operations. In the premodern period, the Muslim world knew nothing comparable in size and organization to a modern European university. Thus, even the most world-renowned venues were, by contemporary standards, extremely

[1] Dodge 1961:82.

small-scale. Around 1800, al-Azhar was a place in which 40 to 60 teachers served between 1,500 and 3,000 students.[2] Due to their small size, neither al-Azhar nor other centers of learning knew anything akin to the mass schooling techniques and forms of bureaucratic organization characteristic of modern education. At al-Azhar, there were no formal admission procedures. Students were not divided into fixed age grades. There were no departments or classrooms. Likewise, there was neither a standard curriculum nor periodic tests to evaluate student progress. Institutional certification in the form of a degree was absent.

Before coming to al-Azhar and other institutions of higher education, students prepared themselves by attending a type of school called a "*kuttāb*." Spread throughout the country, *kuttābs* taught children how to memorize the Qur'an. While learning the Qur'an, students also picked up basic reading skills. Some learned to write as well. *Kuttābs* could admit women, but their attendance in the premodern period seems to have been rare.[3] Graduates of the *kuttāb* were not necessarily destined to become religious scholars. On the contrary, it was ordinary for those who spent time at the *kuttāb* to pursue other professions, frequently taking up the trades of their fathers.[4]

There was no set age for entry into the *kuttāb*. Students often began between the ages of 5 and 10. The amount of time required for memorizing the entire Qur'an depended on a student's abilities, his level of motivation, and the age at which he had entered the *kuttāb*. This period could range from two to six years.[5] Given the early age at which *kuttāb* education was completed, graduates usually embarked on higher education in their early teens, perhaps even as early as eight or nine. During the eighteenth century, it was at these ages that students began their studies at al-Azhar.[6]

Education at al-Azhar was structured around informal study-circles, continuing a mode of learning whose basic format is traceable to the earliest Islamic times.[7] Every study-circle was presided over by a particular *shaykh*. The *shaykh* sat on a stool or a sheepskin, resting his back either against the wall or upon one of the mosque's many pillars.[8] Students were seated on the floor, arraying themselves in a circle before him. Study-circles ranged widely in size. They usually met a number of times every week in accordance with a loose schedule. However, their proceedings were not subject to any strict temporal regulations. There were no lesson plans dictating what needed to be covered or setting dates for its completion. A *shaykh* was free to cover the material at whatever pace he wished.

Study-circles were open to the public and anyone was free to attend. Students would pick and choose among the available lessons in accordance with their

[2] Gesink 2010:41. [3] Heyworth-Dunne 1939:14. [4] Heyworth-Dunne 1939:6–7.

[5] Scholars have given differing estimates regarding the length of this time period. See, e.g., Heyworth-Dunne 1939:2; Aroian 1983:7; Khafājī 1987, 1:128. Also see Eickelman 1978:493.

[6] Heyworth-Dunne 1939:36; Eccel 1984:126. [7] See Melchert 2004.

[8] See Heyworth-Dunne 1939:39.

interests. It was left to them to decide how long they wished to spend with any teacher.

During the eighteenth century, lessons at al-Azhar were only held about six months out of the year. There was a long three-month vacation extending through Ramadan, as well as three separate month-long vacations for various religious festivals.[9] There was no set timetable for the completion of one's studies. Heyworth-Dunne estimates that serious students could finish all the general books in 8 to 10 years, although he notes that some students left after only two or three. Students were permitted to carry on indefinitely,[10] and there was no assumption that once an individual had assumed teaching responsibilities he should cease his own studies. Those who aspired to enter the higher echelons of the scholarly class might spend their entire lives in study.[11]

A number of different subjects were taught in the study-circles. Among the most important were: (1) the art of properly reciting the Qur'an (*Tajwīd*), (2) Qur'anic exegesis (*Tafsīr*), (3) Hadith reports, (4) law (*Fiqh*), (5) legal theory (*Uṣūl al-Fiqh*), (6) theology (*Tawḥīd*), (7) Arabic-language syntax (*Naḥw*), (8) Arabic-language morphology (*Ṣarf*), (8) rhetoric (*Balāgha*), and (9) logic (*Manṭiq*).[12]

Throughout the eighteenth century, Egypt's only establishments of learning were religious. Elementary education was provided by *kuttābs*. Higher-level studies took place in various schools or mosques. As mentioned earlier, al-Azhar was the most prestigious venue. At neither the lower nor the higher levels was education subject to any type of central organization. Each institution operated more or less independently.

The vast majority of the general Egyptian population was nonliterate. Owing to their literacy and legal training, products of religious education were the backbone of the government administration that existed at the time. They supplied almost all of Egypt's clerks, scribes, and judges. They also served as teachers, administered the mosques, and oversaw the performance of religious rituals. Religious scholars varied from one another in terms of wealth and status. Yet, on the whole, they were comparatively well-off financially and occupied a place at the apex of society.[13]

## II. MODERNIZING EDUCATION

Throughout the modern period, Muslim societies have been confronted with the superior political, military, and economic might of European societies. From the seventeenth century onward, European societies steadily expanded their control over Muslim populations, routing indigenous armies while appropriating

[9] Heyworth-Dunne 1939:37. [10] Heyworth-Dunne 1939:37.

[11] See Lane 2005[1836]:214.

[12] For a more complete listing see Heyworth-Dunne 1939:41-42. For a discussion of subjects taught in medieval Islamic learning see chapter 2 in Makdisi 1981. Also see chapter 3 in Berkey 1992.

[13] See Crecelius 1972; Sayyid-Marsot 1972; Skovgaard-Petersen 1997:40.

indigenous land and resources. Struggling for survival, Muslim states attempted to eliminate this imbalance in power by replicating the socioeconomic infrastructure of the West—importing interrelated techniques of governance, organization, and production. Success in these areas required new forms of knowledge and expertise. Accordingly, educational reforms came to be perceived as a pressing necessity.

The Ottoman Empire was at the forefront of efforts to reform education along European lines. By the late eighteenth century, the Ottomans had opened up Western-style academies for military engineering. In the nineteenth century, the Ottomans established institutes for translation, medicine, military science, civil administration, and law.

The Napoleonic invasion (1798–1801) jolted Egypt on to the same course as the Ottomans. Although the French occupation was only temporary, it revealed the extent of European military superiority. The power vacuum left in the wake of Napoleon's departure was filled by Muḥammad ʿAlī, whose reign extended from 1805 to 1848. Although Egypt was technically a province of the Ottoman Empire, in practice Muḥammad ʿAlī ruled autonomously. His first priority was creating an army comparable to Napoleon's by importing Western technologies and by using Western administrative techniques to maximize the productive capacity of the national economy. Muḥammad ʿAlī sought to acquire the personnel needed to effectuate his project by creating an indigenous workforce trained in European forms of knowledge. This necessitated restructuring Egyptian education.

Rather than reform al-Azhar or other existing institutions, Muḥammad ʿAlī elected to establish a parallel European-style system. He proceeded to open new schools for advanced education in military training (1816), engineering (1820), veterinary science (1827), medicine (1827), civil administration (1829), and translation (1836).

After a brief lull, the effort to build a Western-style educational infrastructure was given new impetus by Muḥammad ʿAlī's grandson Khedive Ismāʿīl. Committed to remaking Egypt in the image of Europe, the 1860s and 1870s saw the beginnings of a national system of primary schools. These were meant to systematically extend basic education to the masses. They embodied a "modern" alternative to the type of learning found at religious institutions like al-Azhar.

In 1882 the British occupied the country, initiating a period of imperial rule. An indigenous monarchy remained in place, but ultimate authority resided with the British authorities. Independence from the British came in the 1950s. Since independence, Egypt has been ruled by a string of successive military dictatorships. Under Gamāl 'Abd al-Nāṣir, the Egyptian government was ideologically committed to pan-Arabism and socialism. Upon ʿAbd al- Nāṣir's death in 1970, Anwār Sādāt took power and shifted the nation into America's sphere of influence. In 1981, Sādāt was assassinated by Islamic militants. He was succeeded by Ḥusnī Mubārak.

Mubārak maintained Egypt's close ties to the United States, ruling until early 2011. Mass street protests broke out on January 25th and continued for three weeks before forcing him to step down. In the aftermath of these events, steps were taken toward a democratic transition. Islamists prevailed in the nation's first parliamentary and presidential elections. Nevertheless, at the behest of secular liberal forces and elements from the Mubārak regime, the military staged a coup in mid-2013. The military proceeded to carry out mass arrests and killings of opposition figures. These efforts primarily targeted Islamist protestors and political personalities, however they eventually extended to other groups as well, including secular liberal activists who believed that military repression had gone too far. In mid-2014, a pro forma presidential election officially established General ʿAbd al-Fattāḥ al-Sīsī as Egypt's new ruler.

Both the British imperial authorities and Egypt's post-independence military rulers have been committed to modernizing the country along Western lines. As we will see, this has involved a conscious program of propagating Western cultural practices. Within Egypt, European-style education has been championed as a key tool for introducing Western cultural practices to the broader populace. With this aim in mind, state authorities have pushed for the constant expansion of Egypt's educational system over the course of the twentieth century.

In 1908, Egypt's first modern university was established. Currently it is known as Cairo University.[14] Modeled on European lines, Cairo University was intended to be a resolutely secular institution.[15] In the 1940s the Egyptian state began rapidly expanding the number of European-style public universities. Alexandria University was founded in 1942, ʿAyn Shams in 1950, and Asyūṭ University in 1957. Seven more universities were founded in the 1970s, distributed among the nation's population centers. At the beginning of the twentieth century higher education had been restricted to the elite. The rapid expansion of the university system was intended to open it up to all social classes. In 1962, all university education was officially made free of charge.[16]

The preceding account provides a rough genealogy of Egypt's system of public education, from its beginnings in the wake of the Napoleonic invasion up until the present day. So what happened to the older indigenous tradition of religious learning alongside which the European-style system was built? To answer this question we must return to the first reforms initiated by Muḥammad ʿAlī in the early nineteenth century.

In the premodern period, all of Egypt's institutions of religious learning were funded by charitable endowments known as "*awqāf*" (sing. *waqf*). As an act of piety, rulers and wealthy individuals often dedicated agricultural lands and commercial property to support particular religious institutions. Once a property was dedicated to an institution, its revenue would support the institution in perpetuity. Religious scholars typically oversaw administration of the properties and their revenue. This revenue was used to provide stipends, food, lodging, and other necessities to students and teachers affiliated with the institution,

14 At the time of its founding it was known as "Egyptian University" and then later as "Fuad I University."

15 See Reid 1990:31.

16 Reid 1990:110.

allowing them to devote their time to religious learning rather than work. Remaining monies were used for non-academic staff and upkeep of the facilities. At al-Azhar, stipends for teachers and students were usually paid in periodic disbursements of bread. Some loaves were eaten while others were traded for supplies.[17]

At the time of Napoleon's invasion, the *awqāf* dedicated to al-Azhar were the most extensive and lucrative in Egypt.[18] The fact that al-Azhar and other institutions of religious learning possessed an independent source of funding helped insulate them (partially) from outside political pressures. Beginning with Muḥammad 'Alī, the government began to rapidly centralize the religious establishment and place it under state control. This was done by appropriating control of their *awqāf*. Smaller institutions ceased receiving funds and collapsed from neglect. Larger ones, like al-Azhar, would no longer have direct access to *awqāf* revenue. Instead they would receive money from the government. Once in control of funding, the state acquired the ability to condition financial support on acquiescence to various aspects of its modernization programs. However, pressure of this kind was not exerted immediately.

Nevertheless, the state still required some skills traditionally associated with religious learning, such as expertise in the Arabic language and in Islamic law. Because scholars within al-Azhar were resistant to efforts at modernizing religious education, the state proceeded to establish new parallel institutions. In 1892 the Dār al-ʿUlūm was founded to provide Arabic teachers capable of teaching language courses in the new national school system. In 1907 the School for Islamic Judges (*Madrasa al-Qaḍāʾ al-Sharʿī*) was established with the aim of supplying assorted personnel for the judiciary. They were necessary to administer those portions of the legal system which remained religious in nature (e.g., the law of personal status). Both institutions combined courses in traditional religious disciplines with new non-religious subjects. Students learned in classrooms using Western teaching methods. The School for Islamic Judges did not continue long before it was dissolved. On the other hand, the Dār al-ʿUlūm has been able to retain its importance up until the present day.

Beginning in the late nineteenth century the state began to force reforms inside of al-Azhar itself. In 1872, a fixed curriculum was installed and standardized examinations leading to institutional certification were brought into being. In 1930, specific religious faculties were established. They were housed in new buildings constructed alongside the mosque. At the same time, lessons were moved out of the mosque into these buildings. However, the biggest changes would only come after national independence in the 1950s. In an effort to push al-Azhar into the modern era, a series of sweeping reforms were introduced in 1961.[19] A full array of non-religious faculties were introduced alongside those dedicated to the Islamic disciplines. The Islamic studies curriculum itself was diluted to make more room for non-religious subjects, and the administration of

[17] Sayyid-Marsot 154–155. [18] Gesink 2010:10. [19] See Zeghal 1999.

al-Azhar was increasingly turned over to individuals with Western educational backgrounds.

The reform of education at the al-Azhar mosque was paralleled by movements demanding the reform of traditional Islamic legal doctrine. Traditional Islamic legal doctrine revolves around deference to past authority. In the premodern period, it was assumed that early Muslim scholars were more knowledgeable about scripture than later generations. Hence, later generations were obliged to defer to early scholars' interpretations of scripture. Such deference to past Muslim scholars is known as "*taqlīd.*" For reasons to be explained, (Sunni) Islam singled out four early scholars as particularly important: Abū Ḥanīfa (d.767), Mālik (d.795), al-Shāfiʿī (d.820), and Ibn Ḥanbal (d.855). Each of these scholars is given the title "Imam" (leader). Together they are known as the four Imams. Each Imam, through the interpretation of scripture, produced a set of opinions on Islamic law. The legal opinions of an Imam are known as his legal school (*madhhab*). Accordingly, (Sunni) Islam recognizes four legal schools established by the four Imams. The Ḥanafī school is based on the opinions of Imam Abū Ḥanīfa, the Mālikī school on the opinions of Imam Mālik, the Shāfiʿī school on the opinions of Imam al-Shāfiʿī, and the Ḥanbalī school on the opinions of Imam Ibn Ḥanbal. This is an extreme oversimplification, but it will suffice for the time being. Dating back to about the tenth century, Muslims have affiliated themselves with a particular legal school, deferring (via *taqlīd*) to the opinions of its founding Imam. Hence, adherents of the Shāfiʿī school defer to the opinions of al-Shāfiʿī.

For the most part, the doctrines of the four legal schools are consistent with a literalistic interpretation of the Qurʾan and the Hadith reports. Nevertheless, disparities are not uncommon. Generally speaking, proponents of the legal schools assume that when the Imams depart from a literal interpretation of scripture they have valid grounds for doing so. Later generations may not always know what these grounds are. However, they should still defer to the Imams. I will refer to this overall school-oriented juristic perspective as it exists in the modern period by the name "Traditionalism." Later on, I will offer a deeper and more detailed analysis of Traditionalism, drawing on hermeneutic theory and practice theory.

The emergence of significant opposition to Traditionalism within an Egyptian context is conventionally associated with three Muslim religious scholars: Jamāl al-Dīn al-Afghānī (1839–1897), his student Muḥammad ʿAbduh (1849–1905), and ʿAbduh's student Rashīd Riḍā (1865–1935). The story of these figures can be given briefly, if somewhat simplistically, as follows. Al-Afghānī was deeply concerned with the threat that European imperialism posed to the Muslim world. He came to believe that the Europeans derived their superior power from their liberal ideas. These ideas venerated both scientific progress and liberal forms of governance. In al-Afghānī's eyes, Muslims could only acquire enough power to defend themselves against Europe if they adopted the same liberal ideas. Consequently, al-Afghānī promoted the notion of a new reformed Islam that would incorporate liberal ideas and reconcile them with traditional religious doctrines. Al-Afghānī himself was not entirely certain how to achieve such a reconciliation, and as a result he developed a complex and ambivalent attitude toward both Islam and toward liberalism.

Though Persian by birth, and Shiʿite in upbringing, al-Afghānī traveled widely in the Sunni Muslim lands. To blend in, he disguised his origins, putting himself forth as a Sunni from Afghanistan. In 1872, al-Afghānī came into contact with a young Azhar student named Muḥammad ʿAbduh. Al-Afghānī took ʿAbduh into his inner circle and helped familiarize him with liberal ideas. Like al-Afghānī, ʿAbduh was a fervent opponent of European imperialism. Thus, he assumed a prominent role in the Egyptian nationalist ʿUrābī revolt (1879–1882), which sought to reduce British and French influence in the country. In 1882, the British put down the revolt and exiled ʿAbduh from Egypt. In 1884, ʿAbduh journeyed to France to join al-Afghānī in producing the journal "*al-ʿUrwā al-Wuthqā*" (*The Firmest Bond*). The journal promoted al-Afghānī's ideas and condemned European imperialist aggression against Muslims. Combined with al-Afghānī's tutelage, time spent in Europe convinced ʿAbduh of the need to harmonize Islam with liberal ideas concerning governance and scientific progress. As ʿAbduh's admiration for liberal Europe deepened, he became increasingly critical of non-liberal traditional learning at al-Azhar. ʿAbduh would later remark: "If I have a portion of sound knowledge . . . I have only acquired it after remaining for ten years sweeping out from my mind the filth stuck in it from al-Azhar. And even to this day it is not as clean as I wish."[20]

Despite its grand aspirations *al-ʿUrwā al-Wuthqā* had little impact on the real political situation of Muslims. As a result, ʿAbduh became disillusioned with al-Afghānī's brand of anti-imperialism, seeing it as futile. Instead ʿAbduh eventually came to believe that Muslims in Egypt would need to tolerate some period of European imperial rule, and could even derive benefits from it. Thus, British rule promised to bring valuable economic and technological development. Moreover, British influence might help Muslims integrate empowering liberal ideas into their religious tradition. In 1888, ʿAbduh returned to Egypt and struck out on the path of Islamic religious reform.

ʿAbduh describes his life as devoted to "liberating thought from the fetter of *taqlīd*."[21] For ʿAbduh, this entailed, among other things, leaving off deference to the four legal schools. Instead, he encouraged scholars to read scripture for themselves and produce their own interpretations. ʿAbduh himself produced innovative new interpretations which sought to reconcile liberal ideas with traditional religious doctrines.

Over the course of his life, ʿAbduh's general liberal-mindedness won him support from a number of prominent political figures. The most important was Lord Cromer, who was the top British imperial official in Egypt at the time. British imperial policy aimed at compelling non-Europeans to adopt Western liberal culture. Cromer embraced this policy, writing, "the new generation of Egyptians

[20] ʿAbduh 2006, 3:192.

[21] Quoted in Riḍā 2006, 1:(al-Qism al-Awwal) 11.

has to be persuaded or forced into imbibing the true spirit of Western civilization."[22] Cromer believed that ʿAbduh could be useful in achieving British aims.

Backing from high places gave ʿAbduh abundant opportunities to promote his ideas. In addition to being granted a forum in newspapers and journals, he was given a place on the state committee responsible for reforming education at al-Azhar. ʿAbduh's career culminated with his appointment as state Mufti (*Muftī al-Diyār al-Miṣriyya*), a position officially created in the late nineteenth century, and second only to the Shaykh al-Azhar in stature. ʿAbduh held the Muftiship from 1899 until his death in 1905. As Mufti, ʿAbduh encouraged Muslims in Algeria and Tunisia to submit to the French imperial regime which had occupied their land.[23] Not only did he believe that resistance would be futile, but he hoped that they could draw some benefits from French rule in the same way that Egyptians were drawing benefits from British rule.

In the end, ʿAbduh (like al-Afghānī) was a conflicted figure facing a difficult political situation. Grappling with this situation, at different times he both opposed and promoted imperial rule. ʿAbduh's willingness to cooperate with the European empires was actually relatively commonplace among Muslims in the late nineteenth and early twentieth centuries. Hence, generally favorable views on imperialism were expressed by leading religious scholars and intellectuals like Sayyid Aḥmad Khān (d.1898) and Sayyid Amīr ʿAlī (d.1928) in India, ʿUthmān bin Yaḥyā (d.1913) in Indonesia, al-Hajj Malik Sy (d.1922) and Amadou Bamba (d.1927) in Senegal, Sayyid Shaykh bin Aḥmad al-Hādī (d.1934) and Haji Abdul Majid bin Zainuddin (d.1943) in Malaysia, ʿAbd al-Ḥamīd bin Bādīs (d.1940) in Algeria, and Muḥammad al-Ḥajwī (d.1956) in Morocco. Most of these figures are revered by Muslims today, although their (now disfavored) views on imperialism have largely been forgotten.

The complexity of ʿAbduh's life is important to keep in mind, for among contemporary religious scholars memories of ʿAbduh are selective and highly politicized. Those opposed to ʿAbduh's ideas are inclined to depict him as a simple agent of European imperialism. Meanwhile, those favorable to ʿAbduh's ideas are inclined to depict him as a nationalist hero opposed to European imperialism.

During his lifetime, ʿAbduh's ambitious efforts to reform al-Azhar were largely derailed by unfavorable political conditions and Traditionalist opposition from within al-Azhar. However, ʿAbduh's proposals steadily gained ground after his death, being aided by pro-liberal government forces as well as the tireless journalistic efforts of Rashīd Riḍā.

Born in Ottoman Syria, Riḍā became acquainted with ʿAbduh's ideas through reading *al-ʿUrwa al-Wuthqā*. He migrated to Egypt to join ʿAbduh and in 1898 established the journal "*al-Manār*" (*The Lighthouse*), for which he served as editor until his death. Through *al-Manār*, Riḍā helped spread ʿAbduh's views across the Muslim world. Although Riḍā developed a more critical view on liberal European

[22] Baring 1916, 2:538.

[23] See Riḍā 2006, 1:(al-Qism al-Awwal) 871–874.

civilization than ʿAbduh, both of them were united in a categorical rejection of *taqlīd*.

As indicated previously, religious scholars within al-Azhar initially opposed ʿAbduh's reforms. Nevertheless, their resistance gradually softened over time owing to new social and economic challenges faced by religious scholars as a group. Throughout the nineteenth century the wealth and prestige possessed by this group steadily declined, being appropriated by the graduates of European-style schools. By the early twentieth century, religious scholars faced increasing poverty and an uncertain future. The government made it clear that if Azhari education was not restructured along European lines its students would no longer be considered for jobs within the schools, administrative offices, and judiciary. Fearful for their futures, a rising generation of religious scholars came to see some measure of reform as necessary and inevitable.

Thus, in the decades following ʿAbduh's death, the reform of al-Azhar was promoted by liberal and socialist Egyptian politicians, the British imperial authorities, and liberal-minded religious scholars within al-Azhar. These combined forces helped ensure that high administrative positions were conferred on those sympathetic to ʿAbduh's ideas. Two particularly important figures were the religious scholars Muṣṭafā al-Marāghī (1881–1945) and Maḥmūd Shaltūt (1893–1963).[24] A student of ʿAbduh and an ally of Riḍā, al-Marāghī was appointed to the post of Shaykh al-Azhar for two separate terms (1928–1929 and 1935–1945). Shaltūt supported al-Marāghī during this time, and would later himself serve as Shaykh al-Azhar (1958–1963). Both al-Marāghī and Shaltūt still had to confront Traditionalist opposition to reform. Corresponding with the British authorities, al-Marāghī reported that the opposition was so severe that he could not even install modern toilets, for Traditionalists would cite copious scriptural texts against this simple hygienic measure.[25] Nevertheless, under al-Marāghī and Shaltūt, decisive steps were taken to achieve ʿAbduh's vision of a reformed al-Azhar.

As reformers increasingly put ʿAbduh's ideas into effect, he came to acquire official acknowledgment as the father of modern-day al-Azhar. In the late 1940s ʿAbduh's canonical status was given permanent architectural form. An imposing "Hall of Muḥammad ʿAbduh" was erected on al-Azhar's grounds to be used for special conferences and speeches.[26]

ʿAbduh and Riḍā succeeded in largely undermining the authority of *taqlīd*, and with it, that of the four legal schools. In the place of Traditionalism arose two new approaches to Islamic legal interpretation: "Salafism" and "Wasaṭism." Later on, I will provide a detailed analysis of these approaches in light of hermeneutic theory and practice theory. However, for now, I simply offer a few preliminary remarks.

Salafism demands a direct return to the sacred texts (i.e., the Qurʾan and Hadith reports). Such is combined with an insistence that they be applied in a

[24] For works on these figures see Lemke 1980; Zebiri 1993; Costet-Tardieu 2005.

[25] Costet-Tardieu 2005:68.

[26] See al-Shinnāwī 1984, 2:820.

staunchly literalistic fashion. Salafis criticize Traditionalist doctrine for falling short in this respect. They do not accept the argument that the founders of the legal schools had legitimate reasons for departing from the letter of the Qurʾan and Hadith reports.

This brings us to "Wasaṭism." I use the word "Wasaṭism" to translate the Arabic term "*al-wasaṭiyya*," which connotes the idea of a "middle-way." In contemporary Muslim discourses, the term "*al-wasaṭiyya*" is frequently utilized by a particular group of religious scholars to describe their favored approach to Islamic law (*al-madrasa al-wasaṭiyya*).[27] I will refer to these scholars as "Wasaṭi."[28]

Like Salafis, Wasaṭis also demand a direct return to the sacred texts. However, contrary to Salafis, they reject the notion that literalism is the only legitimate form of textual interpretation. In the place of literalism, Wasaṭis incline toward subjectivist pluralism. Every juristic opinion is viewed as having a claim to validity (*kull mujtahid muṣīb*).[29] This is the case even if it runs contrary to the letter of the sacred texts (as well as the opinions of the four legal schools). Interpretations that depart from the letter of the texts are typically justified on the argument that the original rulings were not intended to apply to present-day conditions. Nevertheless, two important qualifications need to be made, lest Wasaṭism appear more radical than it really is. All Wasaṭi jurists hold that the rules of ritual worship (*ʿibādāt*) and family law partake of a special juristic status. Subjectivist pluralism is not to be tolerated in matters of either type. Secondly, Wasaṭi jurists are not a uniform group. The most liberal Wasaṭis limit traditional legal interpretations to ritual and family law, holding that in all other areas European-style legislation is more suited to modern conditions. Although conservative Wasaṭis respect their liberal counterparts, they believe that traditional rulings are applicable far more broadly.

I should stress that labels like "Traditionalist," "Salafi," and "Wasaṭi" are only meant as helpful guideposts. In reality, the groups in question are not rigidly defined. Wasaṭis in particular are very hard to pin down. It is very common for Wasaṭis to partially identify with Traditionalism. In some cases (albeit less often), there are Wasaṭis who incline toward Salafism. Over the course of their lives, scholars may shift between these three overarching perspectives.

## III. GOVERNMENT FEARS OF ISLAMISM

Egyptian proponents of a European modernity have long viewed traditional understandings of religion as an impediment to national progress. In the first half of the twentieth century it appeared to many Egyptians that a deep and irreversible decline in religion was underway. Nevertheless, the 1970s marked the

[27] See al-Qaraḍāwī 2006:155; al-Qaraḍāwī 1999:233; Zeghal 2007:107–130.

[28] Although such scholars embrace "*wasaṭiyya*," they generally do not refer to themselves using the adjective "*Wasaṭi*."

[29] In the modern period this medieval legal maxim has taken on a new meaning.

beginning of an "Islamic Awakening" (*al-Ṣaḥwa al-Islāmiyya*) in which the general Egyptian populace displayed signs of renewed commitment to religious values. The public resurgence of religious discourses has served to greatly intensify the perceived danger of religion in the eyes of Westernized Egyptian elites. Visible religious commitment is seen as chipping away at the legitimacy of the regime and its orientation. Furthermore, sporadic acts of anti-regime violence at the hands of religious militants during the 1980s and 1990s have been taken as proof that Islamic commitment is something which must be tightly regulated, lest it explode into bloody insurrection.

Westernized Egyptian elites (who generally identify as liberal) have long tended to view the populace at large as culturally backward and dangerously inclined toward religious fanaticism. Although they do not oppose "Islam" per se, forms of Islam which are not consistent with modernization along Western lines are perceived as deeply threatening. Based on this perspective, most Egyptian liberals backed the military's forcible dissolution of the Islamist government elected immediately after the 2011 revolution.

State-controlled education has long been seen as a key tool for countering Islamic perspectives perceived as dangerous to the regime.[30] Ḥusayn Kamāl Bahāʾ al-Dīn, Minister of Education from 1991 to 2004, states: "the first aspect of a new educational policy is that education is an issue of national security."[31] Schooling must inculcate understandings of religion which do not engender hostility to the regime and its goals. At the heart of these efforts is an ongoing campaign to transform the character of religious scholarship.

The Egyptian government ensures that all state-controlled institutions of religious education subscribe to Wasaṭism, the most important of these being al-Azhar followed by the Dār al-ʿUlūm. In managing the doctrinal content of Islamic education, different considerations must be balanced. On the one hand, the state desires religious legitimation for its Westernization/modernization projects. Instilling respect for Western liberal values helps accomplish this goal. On the other hand, pushing educational content too far in a liberal direction risks discrediting Egyptian religious institutions and squandering the considerable prestige they presently command both at home and abroad. Once discredited, these institutions can no longer be utilized by the state to legitimate its policies. An absence of credibility encourages individuals to seek religious knowledge from sources unaffiliated with the regime and beyond its control.

The late Mubārak regime balanced matters as follows. All state educational institutions were obliged to embrace a Wasaṭi identity. Traditionalism was tolerated on the margins, while Salafism was barred outright as too radical. In the interests of preserving al-Azhar's credibility, the professors with whom students were in day-to-day contact commonly endorsed moderate to conservative versions of Wasaṭism. However, top positions were allocated to very liberal Wasaṭis. Good examples are the late Shaykh al-Azhar Muḥammad Sayyid Ṭanṭāwī (d.2010)

[30] See B. Cook 2000. [31] Quoted in Herrera 2006:29.

and recent state Muftī Alī Jumʿa (who served 2003–2013). Generally speaking, the outlook of the personnel at al-Azhar becomes more liberal as one moves up the administration. By structuring matters thus, the state assures itself the loyalty of those at the highest levels while working to maintain al-Azhar's overall authority.

## IV. AL-AZHAR AT PRESENT

In order to understand al-Azhar as it exists in the early twenty-first century, there are two points which merit attention at the outset. The first is that even though the mosque of al-Azhar still exists, it is no longer the center of religious education. The bulk of the lessons which it once housed were transferred outside its walls several decades ago. Teaching at al-Azhar currently takes place in separate buildings erected over the course of the twentieth century. The second point which requires attention pertains to al-Azhar's status as a "university." Although al-Azhar is commonly described as a university, it is better conceptualized as a far-reaching network of government-run educational institutions, many of which enroll non-university students.

To grasp the overall Azhar system, it is best to begin by examining the situation of students before they go to university. Within Egypt, free primary and secondary education is provided by the state. The vast majority of children are taught in public schools, although the option of private instruction is available for those who can afford it. Government-provided public education at all levels is bifurcated into two parallel systems: national schools and religious schools. The existence of two parallel systems is a legacy of nineteenth-century modernization efforts, where European-style institutions were constructed alongside the traditional religious establishments of learning.

Roughly 80 percent of the public schools in operation belong to the national system. They are overseen by the Ministry of Education. By contrast, the religious schools are under the administration of al-Azhar. They are known as "Azhar institutes" (*al-maʿāhid al-azhariyya*). Malika Zeghal estimates that in the early 1970s the institutes enrolled around 90,000 students. A decade later the number had ballooned to 300,000. By the beginning of the 1990s there were over a million, with the total reaching 1,300,000 in the early years of the twenty-first century. The institutes accept both boys and girls, although they receive instruction at separate sites.[32]

Both the national school system and the Azhar institutes share a general curriculum of non-religious subjects.[33] Islam is granted a limited place in the national system. Out of 30 hours a week that students spend in class, 2 to 3 are devoted to religious instruction.[34] The distinguishing mark of the Azhar institutes is that Islamic subjects receive more extensive attention. Part of this

[32] Zeghal 2007:110. [33] Herrera 2006:26. [34] B. Cook 2000:481–482.

involves intensive study of the Qur'an. By the time they graduate from the institutes some students have memorized the Qur'an in its entirety. Others have acquired a degree of familiarity verging on memorization.

The graduate of an Azhar institute may proceed directly to advanced religious studies at the university level, starting with a four-year Azhar undergraduate degree (*al-līsāns*). Upon completion of the undergraduate program, qualified students may be accepted to pursue master's (*al-mājistīr*) and then doctoral degrees (*al-duktūrāh*). Unlike their counterparts from the Azhar institutes, the products of the national school system are presently barred from university studies at al-Azhar.[35]

Certain exceptions aside, just as the graduate of a national school may not continue on at al-Azhar, the graduate of an Azhar institute may not enroll at one of the national public universities. Consequently, not only is Egyptian education bifurcated into two corresponding multilevel systems, but crossovers between these systems are generally not allowed.

However, it is important to note that while the products of the Azhar institutes may only study at al-Azhar University, they are not required to pursue further specialization in religion. At the university level, al-Azhar incorporates both religious and non-religious faculties. Examples of the latter include Commerce, Medicine, Engineering, and Agriculture. Nevertheless, it is only the students who enroll in the specifically religious faculties that will eventually receive recognition as formally trained religious scholars.

To my knowledge, the latest publicly available comprehensive statistical manual detailing Azhar university education dates from 2008. It states that taken together, al-Azhar's religious and non-religious faculties total 62 in number,[36] and are distributed over 16 of Egypt's 27 territorial districts (*muḥāfaẓāt*). The largest concentration of faculties is in Cairo, which has 21.[37]

Since 1962 al-Azhar has offered higher education to women as well as men. The faculties are divided by sex. There are 43 faculties for men, serving about 270,000 students.[38] There are 19 faculties for women, serving about 130,000 students.[39] This gives a total of 400,000 students.

Oftentimes, multiple faculties are clustered together on a single campus. Yet some campuses are home to no more than one faculty. Thirty-six of the 62 faculties are devoted to religious studies, the remainder being dedicated to non-religious subjects. Of these 36, 26 are for men and 10 are for women.[40] The total number of students pursuing religious studies is about 270,000 (15,000 of which are foreign).[41] Altogether, they account for around 70 percent of the student population.[42]

[35] There are some limited exceptions to this principle.

[36] There are also five branch divisions in addition to these faculties. See Al-Azhar University (Official Manual) n.d.:20.

[37] Manual n.d.:20 [38] Manual n.d.:61,64 [39] Manual n.d.:62, 64.

[40] Manual n.d.:58. But women also have four branch divisions in addition.

[41] Manual n.d.:80–81. [42] Manual n.d.:65.

Without getting too involved in the precise administrative distinctions, I note that the religious faculties (*al-kulliyyāt al-islāmiyya*) are divided among five specializations. First, there is specialization in the Arabic language. Second, there is "*Uṣūl al-Dīn*," which might be translated "religious foundations." This specialization encompasses the study of theology, Hadith reports, and Qurʾanic exegesis. Third, there is law. Whereas specialization in law centers on the study of the Sharīʿa, there are also classes offered on the Egyptian legal system in general, the bulk of which is Western in origin. Fourth, there is a division specializing in missionary activity (*daʿwa*). Fifth, there is a division of general studies. Although within the other four divisions students receive some exposure to the full range of religious disciplines, all have a specialized focus not present in general studies.

While al-Azhar includes a total of 36 religious faculties, these vary in both age and prestige. The university's three oldest faculties were established in 1930, housed in new buildings constructed alongside the al-Azhar mosque. These three initial faculties were all religious in character, and each of them still exists today. One of these faculties is dedicated to the Arabic language, another to *Uṣūl al-Dīn*, and the last to Sharīʿa. All three are male. The two faculties of *Uṣūl al-Dīn* and Sharīʿa are the most prestigious of all al-Azhar's religious programs and are perceived as being the foremost heirs to its ancient heritage. All of the other faculties, both religious and non-religious, are located elsewhere, distant from the ancient mosque. None date before the 1960s. My fieldwork at al-Azhar University centered primarily (though not exclusively) on the Faculty of Sharīʿa.

## V. AL-AZHAR MOSQUE AT PRESENT

As noted previously, in the 1930s arrangements were made to move study-circles out of al-Azhar mosque. For decades they were forced to convene elsewhere, continuing on at other less prominent venues. Some met in the ancient mosques scattered around al-Azhar. Others were conducted in the homes of *shaykhs*. In the mid-to-late 1990s, government permission was given to revive study-circles within the al-Azhar mosque. Presently, the al-Azhar mosque serves as the center of a broader network of study-circles in old Cairo. Students who attend study-circles at the al-Azhar mosque frequent these other venues as well. These students are disproportionately foreign in origin (i.e., non-Egyptian). Although the vast majority of al-Azhar University students do not participate in the study-circles, most study-circle attendees are simultaneously enrolled at the university.

Whereas all of the instructors at al-Azhar University and the Dār al-ʿUlūm are Egyptians, teaching at the mosque is divided between an Egyptian majority and a foreign minority. Foreign instructors have trained in countries where premodern styles of learning have been disrupted less severely than in Egypt. Unlike at al-Azhar University and the Dār al-ʿUlūm, teaching at the mosque is strongly (perhaps predominantly) Traditionalist rather than Wasaṭi in orientation.

Given the frequency with which I will make reference to the al-Azhar mosque, it will be useful to provide a description from my fieldnotes:

> *The ancient mosque of al-Azhar is located in the heart of old Cairo amongst countless other grime-caked medieval buildings. The mosque is built out of large stone blocks, ranging in color from whitish-gray to yellowish-brown. Its high sidewalls are overtopped by five towering minarets and several domes of different sizes. These structures are irregularly scattered over the roof of the mosque, commemorating various chapters in its complex architectural history.*
>
> *In the middle of the mosque is a large rectangular open-air courtyard. The floor of the courtyard is fashioned out of smooth white marble with shades of gray. Constructed along the edges of the courtyard are the mosque's roofed-over areas. The roofing extends to cover the edges of the courtyard itself, forming a portico which stretches around its sides. On three sides the portico is separated off from the inner area of the mosque by large heavy dark wood screens. Within the mosque, a combination of screens and stone walls partition space into room-like sections of varying sizes. The walls inside are usually dull white. Red carpeting covers the marble floors. Interspersed throughout the entire area are innumerable slender marble pillars. They range in color from gray to white. The area below the mosque's high ceilings is traversed by wooden beams from which lamps and electric fans are hung.*
>
> *Above the ceilings in some areas are second and third stories. These contain a little over one hundred small residential rooms.*[43] *The rooms are arrayed along long wooden corridors. Some overlook the mosque's courtyard, others overlook the streets alongside the mosque. In the past each room lodged multiple students of religious studies. The last of these left around 1997,*[44] *joining the great majority of other students who had been relocated decades earlier. The rooms in the mosque now lie vacant. The stairwells leading up to them have been shut-off.*
>
> *After several decades in which study-circles were barred from assembling in the mosque, they were revived in the mid-to-late 1990s. The study-circles themselves tend to be scheduled around the prayers, operating throughout the week. Paper timetables are posted on a wooden board located near the courtyard. The study-circles usually last between one to three hours. Distributed in different areas of the mosque, I never witnessed more than four or five being held simultaneously. Oftentimes, the number was less. At any rate, even though the mosque is enjoying a revival, it is clear that there are far fewer classes these days than in al-Azhar's premodern past. Even when the study-circles are at their busiest, the vast majority of mosque space is either empty or being used for other activities.*
>
> *The size of the study-circles is highly variable, ranging from fewer than 10 students to 70 or more. Some gatherings attract hundreds, although these tend not to meet regularly. The sessions I frequented tended to have between 20 to 30 students. When females did attend, they were never more than a few in number. The men ranged in age from the early 20s to the early 40s. Two-thirds to three-quarters had beards. Perhaps between one-third and one-half wore jallābiyya-robes. About half of those with jallābiyya-robes also wore traditional caps*

[43] A custodian working at the mosque told me that there are 116 rooms.
[44] This is according to what I was told by a custodian working at the mosque.

*and head coverings. The remainder of those present were clothed in casual Western attire, wearing long pants along with button-down shirts or T-shirts. A few wore traditional caps.*

*In the larger circles teachers sit on chairs with cushions and speak into microphones. In smaller circles, teachers may dispense with microphones and sit on the floor. It is increasingly common for lessons to be recorded using a small digital camera mounted on a tripod. Recorded lessons may then be posted on the internet or broadcast on satellite television.*

*All of the study-circles are informal and open to the public. They have become something of a tourist attraction. Visitors to the mosque peek through the wooden screens into areas where classes are being held. Some are bold enough to enter and spend a few minutes sitting on the outer edges of the study-circles. The teachers simply disregard their presence.*

## VI. THE DĀR AL-ʿULŪM AT PRESENT

Earlier on, I noted that graduates of the ordinary national schools system are not permitted to pursue university-level Islamic studies at al-Azhar. So where do they go if they wish to specialize in religious subjects? In terms of recognized degree-granting institutions, they have one primary option. This is study at the Dār al-ʿUlūm. As mentioned previously, the Dār al-ʿUlūm was founded in 1892 in an attempt to reform religious learning outside of al-Azhar. It combined courses in traditional religious disciplines with new subjects drawn from a European-style curriculum. Teaching methods and administrative organization were also established on a Western model. The goal was to produce students grounded in the religious disciplines but familiar with modern non-religious forms of knowledge as well. Graduates were expected to serve in the state school system as teachers of the Arabic language.

Initially, the Dār al-ʿUlūm operated independently. However, in 1945 it was incorporated into Cairo University. Upon incorporation, the Dār al-ʿUlūm was transformed from a teacher-training institute into the home of Cairo University's faculty of Arabic and faculty of Islamic studies.[45] As part of the university it offers undergraduate, master's, and doctoral degrees. Previously an all-male institution, in the early 1950s the Dār al-ʿUlūm opened its doors to women as well. Although the overriding goal of the Dār al-ʿUlūm is no longer to produce language teachers for the state school system, its program in Arabic has a stronger reputation than its program in Islamic studies.

From the time of its founding, the Dār al-ʿUlūm has been seen as a hybrid institution striving to combine the traditional Islamic learning of al-Azhar with the modern European learning characteristic of Cairo University. Even though the Dār al-ʿUlūm is technically part of Cairo University, it is regarded by its other faculties as a citadel of conservatism. By contrast, al-Azhar is inclined to view the Dār al-ʿUlūm as too liberal. These perspectives persist to this day, and can be traced back

[45] See Aroian 1983:2, 43, 64.

to the beginning of the twentieth century.[46] Unlike their counterparts from al-Azhar, Dār al-ʿUlūm graduates do not have any special dress. Another difference is that those with doctoral degrees will usually be referred to with the honorific "Doctor" (*duktūr*) rather than "*Shaykh.*" Nevertheless, the differences between al-Azhar and the Dār al-ʿUlūm should not be exaggerated. Both see themselves as sharing a common tradition. Furthermore, not only is there a constant exchange of ideas between the two institutions, but a sizable minority of graduate students at the Dār al-ʿUlūm hold undergraduate degrees from al-Azhar's religious faculties. This is a major exception to the general rule which bars crossovers between the Azhar system and the ordinary national education system.

Similar to what is the case at al-Azhar, Wasaṭism is more or less the only perspective represented at the Dār al-ʿUlūm. The official 2010–2011 Dār al-ʿUlūm handbook (*dalīl*) opens by announcing its orientation. The Dār al-ʿUlūm is said to aim at a "multifaceted scholastic program and a creative synthesis blending authentic tradition (*al-aṣāla*) with modernity (*al-muʿāṣara*). Such is in order to preserve the Arabic-Islamic identity, to keep pace with the movement of progress (*al-taqaddum*) across the world, and to generate appropriate conditions for Arab-Islamic culture to participate in communication and discussion with others within a framework of Wasaṭism and moderation (*fī iṭār al-waṣaṭiyya wa-l-iʿtidāl*)."[47]

It is important to recognize that while al-Azhar and the Dār al-ʿUlūm are officially committed to Wasaṭism this does not mean that the student body at either institution is uniformly Wasaṭi. At both al-Azhar and the Dār al-ʿUlūm there are Wasaṭi majorities, followed in size by Traditionalist and Salafi minorities. Based on my limited experiences, Traditionalists appeared to outnumber Salafis at al-Azhar, while the reverse was true at the Dār al-ʿUlūm. Still, Salafis seemed to be rapidly gaining in number and prominence at each institution.

While second in importance to al-Azhar, the Dār al-ʿUlūm is a central part of Egypt's religious life. It is also one of the most respected and influential institutions of higher Islamic learning in the world. It produces a large number of graduates, though significantly less than the Azhar system. However, because statistics are kept confidential, further details are difficult to provide.

## VII. THE SOCIOECONOMIC LIVES OF RELIGIOUS SCHOLARS

In contrast to earlier periods in Egyptian history, formal training as a religious scholar rarely leads to lucrative employment opportunities or positions of substantial power and status. By the late nineteenth century, the well-to-do had begun to steer their children away from al-Azhar and from religious scholarship as a vocation.[48] At present, this trend is most pronounced in urban locales,

[46] See Reid 1990:35. [47] 2010–2011 Dalīl for Dār al-ʿUlūm 21. [48] Reid 1990:14.

especially among the middle and upper classes. On the other hand, the sizable number of students enrolled in the Azhar system shows that the sentiment in question is not a universal one.

In rural areas, religious scholars have had more success in preserving their traditional standing. Their meager earnings also have more purchasing power in the countryside than in the city. Al-Azhar enrolls a particularly large number of pupils from rural Upper Egypt, famed for its cultural conservatism and comparative isolation from Western cultural influences.

In present-day Egypt, the most promising career path is one which runs through private primary and secondary schools to private universities—the most esteemed of which are foreign. Yet this is prohibitively expensive for the middle and lower classes. Operating more or less free of charge, the non-religious national school system and its public universities are looked at as the second-best option. Interestingly, even within al-Azhar, the best students are attracted to the non-religious faculties. Thus, for the majority of students, religious specialization will only be pursued if their test scores are not high enough to gain access to prestigious non-religious faculties within Azhar such as Medicine, Pharmacy, and Engineering. The prestige of these faculties is directly linked to the job opportunities they open up. A common complaint is that whereas in the past only the best and brightest became religious scholars, right now such a status is reserved for failures incapable of succeeding elsewhere.

Because low test scores shunt students into Islamic studies, a substantial number of Azharis (especially undergraduates) see their trajectories as a result of circumstance rather than choice, and do not view themselves as exceptionally observant Muslims. In the course of my research I came across many such individuals, recording descriptions in my fieldnotes. Consider the following example:

> *Ṭalḥah is a 20-year-old undergraduate student at al-Azhar's Faculty of Sharīʿa. He memorized the Qurʾan by 13 with the assistance of private lessons from a* shaykh. *His family is originally from a small village outside of Tanta, to which they still have strong connections. His paternal grandfather was a Qurʾan-reciter, but was not educated at al-Azhar. Ṭalḥah's father is a secular-trained lawyer who relocated to Cairo before Ṭalḥah was born. His mother is a homemaker, although in her youth she worked at a company. Ṭalḥah has a brother and a sister. The brother was originally enrolled at al-Azhar, but left to study computer science at a private educational institute. The sister is still in primary school at one of the Azhar institutes.*
>
> *Lanky and tall, Ṭalḥah is clean-shaven. He likes to wear shorts and T-shirts. He is somewhat conflicted about his presence at the Faculty of Sharīʿa because he does not really see himself as a religious scholar. His parents simply enrolled him in an Azhar institute when he was younger and, through his studies, he eventually ended up in a religious faculty. He would have preferred to enter one of the more prestigious non-religious Azhar faculties if his grades had qualified him to do so.*

> *Ṭalḥah's true love is singing Arab pop. Given his talented voice he dreams of becoming a star, even if he knows such is highly unlikely. He also has a deep fascination with Western culture, longing for an opportunity to live in America or Europe. Alongside his religious studies he is intensively studying English. For a period he was enrolled at an English language institute. While there he became the boyfriend of a young female instructor of British nationality. He experienced many types of physical intimacy for the first time with his new girlfriend, but in the end they split up. One of the things they quarreled about was sex. He could not bring himself to have intercourse outside of marriage. She found this frustrating and annoying. "It doesn't make sense" she said. "How can you do all of these other things but not sex?" He had difficulty explaining to her that even though he was not scrupulous in his religious practice, there were still certain lines he could not cross.*

Egypt's educational system as a whole graduates far more students than the economy can support. The universities are frequently compared to factories graduating their immense output "into the streets." Most degree-holders are not able to support themselves with full-time employment in the fields in which they have trained. As a result, graduates must work part-time or full-time in other lower-status jobs. The typical Egyptian male is constantly on the lookout for additional sources of income; whether this means driving a cab, raising goats or chickens, engaging in small-time commerce, or serving as a middleman in arranging business transactions of various types. Students who have toiled through decades of education only to find low-status work outside of their specialization feel humiliated and betrayed. Concerns of this type were front and center in catalyzing the 2011 revolution.

Prior to the revolution, the Egyptian government was certainly conscious of the potential for unrest, and had spent decades trying to alleviate matters through a number of strategies. During the Mubārak era, economic liberalization was used to attract foreign investment and thereby spur more rapid job growth. Another key strategy was continuing earlier efforts to liquidate premodern kinship structures. From the standpoint of the state, these structures posed a significant danger in that they habituated citizens to value large family size. More children means a larger population and greater pressure on the government to supply jobs. In response, the state has waged a campaign through the schools and media to stigmatize older familial ideas as unhealthy and backward.[49] Such efforts have gone hand in hand with the promotion of late marriage and birth control.

These larger social developments have left their mark on indigenous religious scholars. Despite commitment to religious teachings which view premodern patterns of family life as legitimate, or even ideal, they themselves feel hard-pressed to realize them in light of prevailing economic realities. These realities are all the more acute for scholars, owing to their diminished earning prospects. As is common throughout society at large, the present generation of indigenous

[49] See K. Ali 2002; Abu-Lughod 2005.

male scholars tends to delay marriage into their mid-to-late 20s, taking spouses a few years younger. Marriages in which there is a significant age gap between spouses, or which produce more than two to three children, are becoming comparatively uncommon. While reliable statistics are hard to come by, only a very small minority of unions are polygamous—likely less than 10 percent. Overall, kinship patterns among religious scholars do not seem to differ significantly from those found among other segments of the population.

University specialization in religious studies can lead to a variety of different jobs, although there are differences depending upon whether a student graduates from al-Azhar or the Dār al-ʿUlūm.

Within Egypt, mosques of significant size are generally managed by the government's Ministry of Endowments (*Wizāra al-Awqāf*). The most important job within any mosque is that of the "Imam." The Imam's responsibilities include leading the five daily prayers[50] and delivering the weekly Friday sermon. He may also be asked to give public lessons and to answer religious queries. Government-run mosques only employ graduates of al-Azhar. In addition to being screened for their political views, applicants are tested on their religious knowledge. Only a fraction succeed in obtaining positions. Many of those chosen to serve as Imams are clean-shaven, and some even deliver their Friday sermons in suits and ties.

With the exception of being an official Imam, most other job opportunities are open to both graduates of al-Azhar and the Dār al-ʿUlūm. Employment may consist of teaching Arabic or Islamic studies at the primary or secondary school level. (University professorships are extremely scarce.) The highest-paying jobs are found abroad, especially in the Gulf countries. However, they are very difficult to come by. There is also the option of working in one of the countless bookstores specializing in religious titles. Frequent part-time jobs include teaching Qurʾanic memorization and editing Islamic books. A substantial benefit afforded by work in these fields is that it helps graduates maintain a connection with their religious expertise. The many graduates who must support themselves, either partly or wholly, through labor unrelated to religion, risk forgetting what they have learned and losing any claim they have upon scholarly status. For instance, I was surprised to find that one acquaintance, who I had assumed was simply a professional cabdriver, held a degree in religion from al-Azhar. He revealed that his brother, currently working on the family farm in Upper Egypt, also had such a degree. Neither of these individuals regarded themselves, or were regarded by others, as enjoying any special religious rank. Consider another example:

> *Ashraf has an undergraduate degree in religious studies from al-Azhar. A tall man, 47 years in age, he is calm and gentle in demeanor. Presently employed as a doorman at an elite residential tower located in Cairo, he wears a blue short-sleeve shirt and long pants to work every day. He is clean-shaven with a full head of shortly trimmed hair.*

[50] However, he is generally not present for all of them.

*Ashraf has been married for a little over 10 years. His wife is 36 and works as a homemaker. They have two sons and a daughter, aged 10, 7, and 4. The two older children are enrolled in the national school system. Ashraf is contemplating putting the youngest in an Azhar institute.*

*Ashraf's family is originally from the Upper Egyptian city of Sūhāj. His paternal grandfather was a weaver of mats. His father made a living trading in used construction materials. Moderately successful, his father was able to take three wives. These marriages produced seven sons and nine daughters. All of the sons currently work in non-religious professions. The daughters are homemakers.*

*After Ashraf spent a short period in a* kuttāb*, Ashraf's father enrolled him in an Azhar institute. Upon graduating from the institute he moved to Cairo to join al-Azhar's Faculty of General (Religious) Studies. For various reasons his graduation was delayed several years. When he finally finished his undergraduate degree, he had difficulty finding a job. Relying on skills that he had learned as a child, Ashraf began working in construction, specializing in building staircases. After a time doing this type of work, he eventually landed his present job as a doorman.*

*Although Ashraf learned the Qur'an by heart in his youth, such has now been largely forgotten due to lack of review. The lessons studied at al-Azhar have also become a distant memory. Ashraf no longer sees himself as a religious scholar, nor do those around him.*

Complex labor patterns make it extraordinarily difficult to sketch a satisfactory description of economic life as it exists for religious scholars. We must account for the fact that they derive income from myriad sources, some with no connection to their religious specialization. Furthermore, supplementary sources of income usually fluctuate in availability and expected yield. The data I give must therefore be looked at as highly impressionistic, especially because I was not permitted to undertake any kind of large-scale statistical survey. Most of the information I have has been pieced together from interviews. Based on these interviews I would surmise that monthly income for most scholars in 2010 fell within the range of 700 to 1,500 Egyptian pounds per month (at that time, one U.S. dollar equaled between 5 and 6 pounds). In Cairo, 700 pounds was seen as nearly impossible to live on. Then again, many scholars live in more rural areas. An income of 700 pounds was comparable to what might be earned in Cairo by a doorman, household cleaner, public schoolteacher, or wage worker in a shop. The amount of 1,500 pounds was widely perceived to be a very average salary. It was more comparable to what might be earned by a cabdriver, electrician, or lower-level administrative worker in a private corporation.

In 2010, the 700 to 1,500 pound income range was roughly equivalent to between 130 and 270 dollars per month. In Cairo, those positioned toward the upper end of this range were able, with family help, to shoulder the costs of marriage and two or so children. They could afford to reside independently of their parents, living in small apartments (perhaps two bedrooms and one bathroom). They would live in a low-cost neighborhood marked by an absence of Western food and clothing chains. Although paved streets and adequate trash-collection services would not be not guaranteed, electricity and running water could be taken for granted. A cell phone, a television, a computer, and a refrigerator would be within reach. A low-quality used car might even be possible. Money would be available to build a small library of religious texts, albeit one composed of low-cost Egyptian editions. Nevertheless, home internet, air conditioning, and savings significant enough to justify a bank account were the prerogative of other income brackets. Eating large amounts of meat would be associated with special occasions. Dining in Western restaurants, even fast-food chains, would be regarded as exorbitantly expensive. Daily fare would consist of low-cost foods like beans (*fūl*), pita-bread, falafel, and pasta (*kūsharī*), along with various dishes made from potatoes, rice, tomatoes, lentils, okra, and onions. These would be supplemented by modest quantities of chicken, fish, beef, goat, and lamb. Beverages would consist of soda and brown tea sweetened with sugar.

## VIII. STATUS DIFFERENTIALS AMONG RELIGIOUS SCHOLARS

Graduate students not only face more selective admission procedures, but also abundant post-admission obstacles which make it difficult to complete the degree program. Although the Dār al-ʿUlūm's graduate programs share many of the same characteristics, the challenges are greatest at al-Azhar. For instance, at al-Azhar's Faculty of Sharīʿa, annual tests are designed to fail a majority of the class, forcing graduate students to repeat one or more years. The expected length of theses also works to increase the difficulty of successfully completing a graduate degree. The Azhar M.A. usually takes a minimum of four years, and requires a public defense. The PhD also requires multiple years, although not necessarily as many as the MA.

In terms of age, MA students seem to usually range from the mid-20s to early 40s. PhD candidates are obviously older. All but the youngest graduate students are married. In Egypt, like many other parts of the Arab world, it is customary not to delay pregnancy. Thus, students with spouses also have one or more young children to take care of. While foreign graduate students often receive some kind of financial assistance from their home countries, their Egyptian counterparts, with the rarest of exceptions, receive no educational aid. As a result, they must balance graduate studies with the need to work enough to support a family. The inability to study full-time adds years upon years to the process of getting an advanced degree. Moreover, because the degree will almost never lead to a professorship, there is no hope of offsetting present sacrifices with enhanced employment prospects in the future.

The significance which should be accorded to a graduate degree is not something on which all scholars are in agreement. As we will see, there are scholars who do not believe that graduate degrees confer authority unless they are paired with other types of learning. Indeed, some even go so far as to affirm that becoming a scholar is in no way dependent upon holding any kind of formal university degree, whether undergraduate or graduate. Nevertheless, in the eyes of the majority, attaining status as a serious religious authority requires some sort of university certification. Although nowadays the question of who merits the appellation "scholar" is a hotly debated one, my own usage of the term reflects the preceding view. References to formally trained scholars are meant to apply first and foremost to those who have pursued Islamic studies at either an undergraduate or graduate level at institutions such as al-Azhar and the Dār al-ʿUlūm. Nevertheless, I broaden this definition on certain occasions, especially where such is necessary to accommodate a figure who is widely recognized as a scholar despite not holding a university degree in religion.

# Section II

# Traditional Islamic Learning and Legal Doctrine

# 3

## Sharīᶜa, Sunna, and Ethics

In this chapter, I take up the key concepts of Sharīᶜa, Sunna, and ethics, clarifying their place in Islamic legal doctrine and religious learning. Although I focus on contemporary Egyptian religious learning, my analysis is meant to have a more general relevance. I will argue that the concepts of Sharīᶜa, Sunna, and ethics can best be understood in terms of the relationship between mind (i.e., mental attributes) and action. In explicating this view, I draw on insights from hermeneutic theory and practice theory.

### I. ISLAM, ETHICS, AND PRACTICE THEORY

The study of ethics is a major topic of interest within practice theory. More specifically, practice theorists are interested in the general notion of "virtue ethics" as developed in Aristotle's *Nicomachean Ethics*, and as elaborated by various twentieth century philosophers (e.g., Alasdair MacIntyre, Pierre Hadot, Martha Nussbaum).[1] Virtue ethics differs from the notions of morality which have come to dominate contemporary Western life. According to these notions, normative evaluation focuses exclusively on human action. Hence, actions can be judged good or bad. By extension, what makes a person good is that s/he performs good actions. Likewise, what makes a person bad is that s/he performs bad actions. Examples of good actions are actions which benefit others, reduce their pain, or respect their autonomy. Meanwhile, examples of bad actions are actions which harm others or infringe upon their autonomy. Virtue ethics puts forth a different perspective. Virtue ethics holds that normative evaluation may apply to human action (i.e., actions may be judged good or bad). However, for virtue ethics, normative evaluation focuses primarily on mental attributes (i.e., dispositions). Hence, some mental attributes are good while others are bad. By extension, what makes a person good is (primarily) that s/he has good mental attributes. Likewise, what makes a person bad is (primarily) that s/he has bad mental attributes.

For example, many contemporary Muslims would consider the following list of mental attributes good: a belief in God, a belief in racial equality, a desire to

[1] See MacIntyre 2008[1981]; Nussbaum 1986; Hadot 1995[1987].

The Anthropology of Islamic Law. Aria Nakissa.

protect one's children, a desire to wear clean clothes, an emotional feeling of disgust at the prospect of eating feces or pork, an emotional feeling of shame at the prospect of fornicating. Many contemporary Muslims would consider the following list of mental attributes bad: disbelief in God, a belief in white racial superiority, a desire to harm one's children, a desire to wear filthy clothing, an absence of disgust at the prospect of eating feces or pork, an emotional feeling of pride in fornicating. Proponents of virtue ethics often refer to good mental attributes/dispositions as "virtues" and bad mental attributes/dispositions as "vices."

Proponents of virtue ethics suggest that mental attributes can be conceptualized as "dispositions." This means that such mental attributes can be acquired through practice. However, it also implies a particular understanding of the acquisition process, which can be explained as follows. Every mental attribute is associated with a *typical pattern of behavior* (which consists in *actions*). Hence, skill in piano-playing (a mental attribute) is associated with the act of competently playing the piano (a pattern of behavior). Likewise, belief in the prophethood of Muḥammad (a mental attribute) is associated with the action of five daily prayers and the avoidance of alcohol (a pattern of behavior). For proponents of virtue ethics, in many cases, an individual may acquire a mental attribute by practicing the typical pattern of behavior (i.e., actions) associated with it.[2] Hence, one may acquire skill in piano-playing through the practice of piano-playing. Similarly, one may acquire belief in the prophethood of Muḥammad through the practice of five daily prayers and alcohol avoidance. By practicing the pattern of behavior associated with a mental attribute, one becomes habituated to it, such that the behavior comes to one "naturally," with minimal need for effort or reflection. Hence, by practicing piano-playing a person reaches the point where piano-playing comes to him/her naturally, such that s/he does it without effort or thought. For proponents of virtue ethics, it is only at this point that the person has fully acquired skill in piano-playing. As long as a person must exert effort and think about how to play the piano, s/he has not fully acquired the skill (i.e., mental attribute). Similarly, by practicing prayer and alcohol avoidance, one may become habituated to them, such that they come to one naturally with minimal need for effort or reflection. It is at this point that one fully possesses belief in the prophethood of Muḥammad. As long as a person must think about whether or not to pray, and as long as s/he struggles to pray, s/he has not yet fully acquired the belief. To call a mental attribute a "disposition" implies that to fully possess the mental attribute, one must be "disposed" (i.e., inclined) to perform the behavior associated with the attribute, with minimal need for effort or reflection.

Writings on virtue ethics often pay special attention to one particular type of mental attribute/disposition; namely, the "character trait." Examples of character traits include generosity, stinginess, courage, cowardice, and patience. An

[2] See Ross 2009:23–24.

individual with a character trait is inclined to perform the actions associated with that character trait. Hence, a person with the character trait of generosity is inclined to perform generous acts (e.g., giving to the poor), and a person with the character trait of cowardice is inclined to perform cowardly acts (e.g., fleeing the battlefield). Whereas some character traits are good (e.g., generosity, courage) others are bad (e.g., stinginess, cowardice). Although Aristotle offers a more complex treatment of character traits, I will not take his treatment up here.[3]

For Aristotle, the proper aim of ethics is to replace bad mental attributes/dispositions with good mental attributes/dispositions. This is to be done by adopting an appropriate regimen of practice. Thus, suppose that a man has the bad character trait of cowardice. For Aristotle, the man may replace this bad character trait of cowardice with the good character trait of courage through an appropriate regimen of practice. Hence, he may acquire the character trait of courage through the practice of courageous acts (e.g., performing repeated acts of courage on the battlefield).[4] He performs these acts until they come to him naturally, with minimal need for effort or reflection. It is at this point that he fully possesses the mental attribute/disposition of courage. Similarly, suppose that a man has a desire to keep all his wealth to himself. Such a desire is bad. By contrast, the desire to give to the poor is good. The man may acquire the good desire to help the poor through the practice of giving to the poor.

Foucault holds that Aristotle's ideas are useful for social analysis, and he integrates them into practice theory.[5] However, Foucault differs from Aristotle on some key points. For Aristotle, there are some mental attributes/dispositions which are objectively good and others which are objectively bad. Moreover, Aristotle is not interested in the range of practices which can be used to acquire mental attributes/dispositions. By contrast, Foucault emphasizes that different societies and historical periods have different opinions about which dispositions are good and bad. Additionally, Foucault emphasizes that different societies and historical periods use different types of practices to acquire mental attributes/dispositions. For Foucault, researchers should study "ethics" (i.e., virtue ethics) in different societies. This involves examining how different societies use different practices to instill the dispositions they deem good.

Foucault's approach has stimulated much recent anthropological research.[6] Hence, Asad and his students recognize that ethics has great relevance to the study of Muslim religiosity.[7] After all, Islam has a developed tradition of ethical thought. This tradition extends back into the medieval period and is deeply

[3] Hence, for Aristotle character traits are complex entities that consist in multiple mental attributes melded together. Thus, on Aristotle's view the character trait of courage cannot really be distinguished from the desire to act courageously, and from particular emotional feelings (e.g., calmness rather than fear on the battlefield).

[4] See Ross 2009:23–24.

[5] See Foucault 1990[1985]; also see Faubion 2011.

[6] See Laidlaw 2002; Zigon 2008; Lambek 2010; Faubion 2011.

[7] Asad 2003; Mahmood 2005; Hirschkind 2006; B. Silverstein 2011; Agrama 2012.

indebted to the ideas of Aristotle.[8] In fact, medieval Islamic thinkers often refer to Aristotle as the "first teacher" (*al-muʿallim al-awwal*). Asad and his students have shown that broadly Aristotelian ethical ideas continue to inform Muslim religiosity into the present.[9]

The work of Asad and his students has generally focused on modern lay Muslim piety in relation to contemporary Islamic social or political movements.[10] By contrast, I wish to concentrate my attention on formally trained religious scholars. It is certainly true that lay and scholarly religiosity overlap in significant ways. However, formally trained scholars conceptualize ethics within a broader doctrinal framework largely unfamiliar to lay Muslims. Moreover, scholarly training includes unique forms of ethical practice that do not have lay equivalents. Lay religiosity is particularly distant from that of Traditionalist scholars committed to the preservation of premodern Islamic pedagogy and legal doctrine. Due to the popular impact of religious reformism, most lay Egyptians consciously repudiate central elements of Traditionalism.

There are two other ways in which my treatment of Islamic ethics diverges significantly from the valuable work of Asad and his students. First, unlike Asad and his students, my treatment incorporates extensive Islamicist-style analysis of relevant Arabic textual sources. Second, and more importantly, my treatment moves beyond the conceptual framework of practice theory to incorporate key ideas from hermeneutic theory. Utilizing both hermeneutic theory and practice theory permits a more comprehensive account of the relationship between action and mental attributes in the context of ethics. Thus, whereas strictly practice theoretical treatments focus on how repeated action instills mental attributes (in the context of ethics), I will also consider how mental attributes are inferred from actions (in the context of ethics).

## II. ISLAMIC ETHICS

In the Islamic tradition, ethical thought is strongly associated with Sufism. But here some further clarification is necessary. Traditional Islamic scholarship encompasses several different fields of knowledge, including law, Qurʾanic exegesis, the study of Hadith reports, theology, and Sufism. Each field possesses a measure of distinctiveness in terms of its technical vocabulary, concepts, and styles of reasoning. However, throughout the premodern period these fields were taught together as parts of a broader integrated form of education. Indeed, the same is true today, at least among Traditionalist scholars. Consequently, these various fields cannot be understood separately. For instance, any attempt to analyze Islamic law or Sufism as an isolated field produces a partial and distorted view.

[8] See Sherif 1975; Hourani 1985; Fakhry 1994.

[9] See Mahmood 2005; Hirschkind 2006; Agrama 2012.

[10] See Mahmood 2005; Hirschkind 2006; B. Silverstein 2011; Agrama 2012.

Rather, Islamic law and Sufism must be analyzed together, and in relation to other fields like Qurʾanic exegesis, the study of Hadith reports, and theology.

Past generations of Islamicists posited a fundamental opposition between Islamic law and Sufism. However, more recent studies have rejected this view.[11] In the course of Islamic history, different varieties of Sufism developed. Some varieties of Sufism challenged or dispensed with standard Islamic legal teachings.[12] Nevertheless, most Sunni Muslim religious scholars endorsed forms of Sufism which strongly affirmed Islamic legal teachings. Indeed, in the premodern period, many (if not most) major legal authorities were devout practitioners of Sufism. Prominent examples include Abū Ḥāmid al-Ghazālī (d.505/1111), al-Nawawī (d.676/1277), Ibn Taymiyya (d.728/1328), and Ibn ʿĀbidīn (d.1252/1836). This fusion of law and Sufism was also present in eighteenth and nineteenth century Egypt, where it was embodied by major authorities like Aḥmad al-Dardīr (d.1201/1786) and Ibrāhīm al-Bājūrī (d.1277/1860).[13]

The same pattern still holds today among contemporary Traditionalist scholars. For such scholars, religious learning involves the study of texts on law and Sufism. Thus, understanding their views requires a closer look at these texts.

In addressing ethical matters, Islamic texts use a particular array of technical Arabic terms. Let us review some of the most important. First, there exist various terms which denote mental attributes/dispositions. Among the most general are "*awṣāf al-qalb*" and "*ṣifāt al-qalb*," which may be translated as "mental attributes" (literally: "attributes of the mind[14]").[15] Stable mental attributes are known as "*maqāmāt*" (often translated as "stations"). Meanwhile, transitory mental attributes are known as "*aḥwal*" (often translated as "states").[16] Examples of such attributes include certain belief in God (*īmān, yaqīn*),[17] emotional feelings of fear towards God (*khawf, taqwā*),[18] and emotional feelings of shame (*ḥayāʾ*) in disobeying God.[19]

Muslim scholars refer to mental attributes as "dispositions" when such attributes have been acquired through practice. Hence, Ibn Khaldūn (d.808/1406) asserts that a "disposition (*malaka*) is an ingrained [mental] attribute (*ṣifa rāsikha*) which is produced through doing an act and repeating it time after time until its form has been ingrained."[20] Similarly, al-Dabbāgh (d.696/1296) explains that stable mental attributes (*maqāmāt*) should be conceptualized as dispositions (*malaka*).[21] Ibn Khaldūn and al-Dabbāgh use the Arabic term "*malaka*" for disposition. Islamic understandings of "*malaka*" reflect Aristotelian ideas, and the

[11] See Algar 1976; Makdisi 1991 VII:129; Asad 2003:224. [12] See Ahmed 2016.
[13] See Sayyid-Marsot 1972:151; Heyworth-Dunne 1968[1939]:24.
[14] Later on, I will further explain the term of "*qalb*" in relation to mind.
[15] "*Iʿlam anna al-rajāʾ min jumla maqāmāt al-sālikīn wa aḥwāl al-ṭālibīn wa innamā yusammā al-waṣf maqāman idhā thabata wa aqāma wa innamā yusammā ḥālan idhā kāna ʿāriḍan sarīʿ al-zawāl . . . fa-kadhālika ṣifāt al-qalb tanqasim hādhi al-aqsām.*" Al-Ghazālī 2005:1488.
[16] Al-Ghazālī 2005:1488; al-Jurjānī 2004:72–73; al-Qushayrī 2001:91–92.
[17] Al-Sarrāj 1960:43; al-Qushayrī 2001:214–218.
[18] See Al-Sarrāj 1960:43–44; al-Qushayrī 2001:161–167, 141–146.
[19] Al-Sarrāj 1960:43–44; al-Qushayrī 2001:249–252. [20] Ibn Khaldūn 2010, 2:856.
[21] Hence Al-Dabbāgh (n.d.:67) states that a *maqām* is "*al-malaka al-thābita.*"

term is often translated as "habitus."[22] A related Arabic term is "*akhlāq*" (sing. "*khuluq*"). Islamic texts often refer to *akhlāq* as a type of *malaka*, and hence the word "*akhlāq*" may be translated as "dispositions."[23] "*Akhlāq*" may also be translated as "mental attributes." Hence, the famous Egyptian scholar and *Shaykh al-Azhar* Ibrāhīm al-Bājūrī (d.1277/1860) asserts that *akhlāq* are "inner [i.e., mental] attributes" (*al-awṣāf al-bāṭina*).[24] Islamic ethical writings probably invoke "*akhlāq*" more than any other word. Such writings also commonly mention the terms "*faḍīla*" (virtue) and "*radhīla*" (vice).

In the Islamic tradition, Ibn Miskawayh (d.421/1030) and Abū Ḥāmid al-Ghazālī (d.505/1111) are among the most influential proponents of virtue ethics. Both figures draw on Aristotelian ideas, especially with regard to the notion of dispositions/*akhlāq*. Ibn Miskawayh defines "*akhlāq*" as "a condition of the soul which impels it to its actions without thinking or reflection.[25] This condition is of two types. [The first] of the two is that which is natural, being from [one's] original temperament . . . [The second] of the two is that which is acquired through habituation and training."[26,27] Ibn Miskawayh's definition underlines two important features of *akhlāq*/dispositions. First, they are inclinations to exhibit particular forms of behavior in an automatic fashion, "without thinking or reflection." [28] Second, *akhlāq*/dispositions can be acquired through practice (i.e., "habituation and training").

Al-Ghazālī has similar ideas.[29] He notes that the term "*akhlāq*" does *not* refer to actions (*laysa al-khuluq ʿibāra ʿan al-fiʿl*).[30] Rather it refers to:

> a deeply-rooted condition of the soul from which [certain] acts issue forth with ease, without need for thinking or reflection.[31] If the condition is such that the acts which issue forth from it are beautiful and praiseworthy from the standpoint of the intellect and the divine law (*sharʿ*), that condition is called good *akhlāq*. [On the other hand] if the acts which issue forth are wicked, that condition which is their source is called bad *akhlāq*.[32]

Al-Ghazālī affirms that good *akhlāq* are obtained through practice. More specifically, when one desires to acquire specific *akhlāq*, one performs the type of actions associated with them. Al-Ghazālī remarks that in referring to:

> the acquisition of these [good] *akhlāq*/dispositions . . . I mean causing the self to perform the acts which are required by the desired disposition. (*iktisāb hādhihi al-akhlāq . . . Aʿnī bihi ḥaml al-nafs ʿalā al-ʿamāl allatī yaqtaḍīhī al-khuluq al-maṭlūb*). For

[22] Lapidus 1984:53–56; Messick 1993:19; Mahmood 2005:136–137. Also see Franz Rosenthal's comments Ibn Khaldūn 1967[1958], 1:lxxxiii–lxxxiv.

[23] Al-Rāzī 1981 30:81; Al-Dijwī:1981, 2:711–712.

[24] Al-Bājūrī 2001:17.

[25] "*Ḥāl li-l-nafs dāʿiya lahā ilā afʿāliha min ghayr fikr wa lā rawiyya.*"

[26] "*Al-ʿāda wa-l-tadrīb.*"

[27] Ibn Miskawayh 2006:30.

[28] Also see al-Iṣfahānī 2007:97.

[29] For a general overview of al-Ghazālī's ethical thought see Sherif 1975.

[30] Al-Ghazālī 2005:935.

[31] "*'Haiʾa fī al-nafs rāsikha ʿanha taṣdur al-afʿāl bi-suhūla wa-yusr min ghayr ḥāja ilā fikr wa-rawiyya.*"

[32] Al-Ghazālī 2005:934. Also see al-Jurjānī 2004:89.

> example, if one wishes to acquire for himself the disposition of generosity, then the path to this is to force himself to perform the actions of a generous person, and that consists in spending money. Then he continues to demand this of himself, and he forces himself to persist in it, struggling against himself until that [behavior] comes naturally and easily to him. He thereby becomes a generous person. Likewise, if one who is dominated by arrogance wishes to acquire for himself the disposition of humility, then his path is to persist in the actions of humble people for an extended period . . . All dispositions which are praiseworthy from the standpoint of the divine law are acquired in this way.[33]

Classic examples of *akhlāq* include character traits like patience (*ṣabr*), humility (*khusūʿ*), and gratitude (*shukr*).

In describing the acquisition of dispositions/mental attributes, Muslim religious scholars make constant reference to the "*qalb*." *Qalb* is sometimes translated as "heart," but this is misleading. In English, the heart is conceptualized as the seat of the emotions. However, for the majority of Arab Muslim thinkers, the heart is the seat of the entire mind.[34] On this view, an individual's "heart" (i.e., mind) contains his/her beliefs, desires, emotions, intentions, and character traits. The heart thereby brings together various mental processes, including emotion and cognition. In light of the preceding considerations, I will translate "*qalb*" as "mind/heart."

Muslim religious scholars frequently assert that practice shapes the mind/heart (*qalb*). By this, they mean that such practice instills the dispositions/mental attributes found in the mind/heart. For religious scholars, the aim of ethical practice is "purification of the mind/heart" (*tazkiya al-qalb*). A mind/heart is pure insofar as it contains good dispositions/mental attributes and has been purged of bad dispositions/mental attributes.

Thus, going back to the medieval period, religious scholars have promoted the notion that Muslims should seek to acquire good dispositions/mental attributes through an appropriate regimen of practice. But how does one identify which dispositions/mental attributes are good? Here the views of religious scholars are informed by a particular perspective on the Prophet. Such scholars hold that God tasked the Prophet with conveying His teachings to mankind. Moreover, such scholars also hold that the Prophet often conveyed these teachings through his example. Religious scholars I spoke with were fond of citing the following Qurʾanic verse: "In the Messenger of God (i.e., the Prophet) there is a good exemplar (*uswa ḥasana*) for you."[35] Because scholars see the Prophet as an exemplar, they hold that his specific dispositions/mental attributes are endorsed by God. The view of Muslim scholars may be contrasted with that of Aristotle. Aristotle associates good dispositions with an abstract ideal of human perfection. However, Muslim scholars equate good dispositions with the dispositions

[33] Al-Ghazālī 2005:940.

[34] The intellect (*ʿaql*) is viewed as a dimension of the heart rather than as a distinct and separate entity. Ibn Manzur 2003:v.7 463. Also see Ibn Taymiyya 2004, 9:303–304; Makdisi 1981:102.

[35] Qurʾan [33:21].

of a concrete historical figure; namely, the Prophet Muḥammad. In this way, the Prophet's distinctive dispositions/mental attributes come to define what count as good dispositions/mental attributes. Put differently, the Prophet's dispositions/mental attributes are seen as embodying human perfection.

Traditionalist scholars that I interviewed constantly emphasized the preceding point,[36] stressing that every good disposition, without exception, was concretely embodied in its fullest form by the Prophet. One of the modern texts taught at the Dār al-ʿUlūm speaks of the Prophet as "combining every noble disposition possessed by the prophets before him, such that with him and in him [good] dispositions became complete."[37] Because the Prophet represents pure human perfection, acquiring his dispositions becomes the ethical ideal.

In one of his most well-known treatises, the late Azhari scholar Muḥammad al-Ghazālī (d.1996) has the following to say about the relationship between Aristotelian and Islamic approaches to ethics:

> it was said to a Muslim scholar: "have you read the ethics of Aristotle (*adab al-nafs li-Ārisṭū*)?" [The Muslim scholar] said [in reply]: "Rather I have read the ethics of [Prophet] Muḥammad bin ʿAbdullah, peace and blessings be upon him . . . !"
>
> We have read the ethics of Aristotle and his like from among the philosophers. And we have also read the ethics of Muḥammad bin ʿAbdullah, peace and blessings be upon him. [As for] the ideals imagined and chosen by the ancient [philosophers], after [their] toil, we have found them perfect in some respects and imperfect in others. [On the other hand] we have found [an ethical ideal] transformed into a living reality, embodying perfection and the most luminous way of human life . . . That is the ethics of Muḥammad bin ʿAbdullah, peace and blessings be upon him.[38]

(Unless otherwise noted, all later references to al-Ghāzalī are to the famous medieval scholar Abū Ḥāmid al-Ghāzalī).

## III. PRACTICE, SHARĪʿA, SUNNA

Thus, religious scholars identify good dispositions/mental attributes with those of the Prophet. These dispositions are to be acquired through practice. But what form does such practice take? The short and simple answer is that these dispositions/mental attributes are acquired through practice of the Sharīʿa and adherence to the Sunna. However, to appreciate this answer it is necessary to clarify the concepts of Sharīʿa and Sunna.

Let us begin with Sharīʿa. We may say that the Sharīʿa consists in rules (as long as we do not define "rule" too narrowly). "Sharīʿa" is usually translated as "Islamic law." But this translation is misleading and reductive. Sharīʿa is, in

[36] For more on ideas of this type see Schimmel 1975:27, 272–273; Hoffman 1995:58–59, 236; Hoffman 1999.

[37] Al-Fāwī 2004:14.

[38] M. al-Ghazālī 1987:4.

a sense, "law." But it is also much more than "law." In the modern West, "law" refers to rules imposed by the state, but excludes rules of ritual and etiquette. By contrast, Sharīʿa not only includes rules imposed by the state but also rules of ritual and etiquette (which are not necessarily imposed by the state). Hence, Sharīʿa includes ritual rules related to prayer, fasting, and pilgrimage. Moreover, Sharīʿa includes rules of etiquette concerning how to eat and use the bathroom (e.g., eat with the right hand, do not urinate while standing). A Sharīʿa rule is known as a "*ḥukm*" (plural "*aḥkām*"). The Arabic term "*ḥukm*" literally means "judgment." In Islamic legal discourse, a *ḥukm* is God's judgment on a particular legal matter (typically an action). Hence, God has judged that prayer is obligatory and that drinking alcohol is prohibited. In other words, He has laid down a rule that prayer is obligatory and that drinking alcohol is prohibited. The totality of God's judgments (i.e., the totality of Sharīʿa rules) are known as the "*Aḥkām* of the Sharīʿa" (*Aḥkām al-Sharīʿa*).

Sharīʿa also differs from modern Western conceptions of law in its fundamental legal classifications. Put simply, modern Western law classifies in terms of a binary distinction between permission and obligation. Hence, a subject of Western law is permitted to do some things (e.g., express his/her political opinions). Such a subject is also obligated to do other things (e.g., pay taxes, refrain from murder). Like Western law, Sharīʿa permits Muslims to do some things (i.e., *mubāḥ*) and obligates them to do others (i.e., *wājib, ḥarām*). However, Sharīʿa includes an additional category. Hence, the Sharīʿa encourages particular actions, but does not obligate Muslims to perform them (i.e., *mustaḥabb, makrūh*). For instance, Muslims are obliged to pray five times a day. The Sharīʿa also encourages them to perform additional prayers, but it does not obligate them to do so (i.e., the additional prayers are *mustaḥabb*). Similarly, the Sharīʿa encourages Muslims to refrain from playing chess, but they are not obligated to refrain from it (i.e., playing chess is *makrūh*).[39] An individual is rewarded by God for doing what the Sharīʿa encourages. However, an individual is not punished by God if s/he does not do what the Sharīʿa encourages.

I have stated that the Sharīʿa consists in rules. Nevertheless, this idea requires further explanation. Hence, Asad (2003:205–256) suggests that the Sharīʿa cannot be reduced to rules, because it also prescribes particular dispositions/mental attributes. Let us take a close look at the issue raised by Asad.

Islamic legal texts from both the premodern and modern periods explicitly assert that one aim of the Sharīʿa is to promote acquisition of good dispositions (*makārim al-akhlāq*).[40] For instance, this view is articulated by the contemporary Moroccan Muslim legal scholar Aḥmad al-Raysūnī. Al-Raysūnī is an influential global figure, and during my research I saw him speak at al-Azhar's Hall of Muḥammad ʿAbduh. Al-Raysūnī holds that, under modern European influences, many Muslims have mistakenly assimilated the Sharīʿa to the Western concept

[39] This is a common, though not universal view.

[40] This is often addressed under the heading of "*taḥsīnāt*" in discussions of *Maqāṣid al-Sharīʿa*. See al-Shāṭibī 2004:223.

of "law." From this perspective, the Sharīʿa is essentially a set of legal rules imposed by the state.[41] Al-Raysūnī asserts that this is a deep mistake, emphasizing that the traditional concept of Sharīʿa is far more expansive. Al-Raysūnī notes that the traditional concept of Sharīʿa includes "belief in God" as well as "the acquisition of praiseworthy dispositions and manners" (*al-takhalluq bi-makārim al-akhlāq wa-l-ādāb*).[42]

Similar views are echoed in Sufi works. Thus, the distinguished Sufi Abū Naṣr al-Sarrāj (d.388/988) explains that mental attributes/dispositions are a fundamental element of the Sharīʿa. In laying out his position, he makes a distinction between "external actions" (*al-aʿmāl al-ẓāhira*) and "internal actions" (*al-ʿamāl al-bāṭina*). "External actions" are performed with the body (e.g., eating with the mouth, running with the legs, speaking with the tongue). Meanwhile, "internal actions" are performed with the mind/heart. An internal action consists in possessing a mental attribute. Hence, believing is an internal action. Desiring and feeling emotions are likewise internal actions. In fact, many Islamic texts equate possessing mental attributes with performing internal actions (i.e., *ʿamal al-qalb*).[43] Al-Sarrāj asserts that just as the Sharīʿa has rules which regulate external actions (e.g., an obligation to pray, a prohibition on drinking alcohol), it also has rules which regulate internal actions (e.g., an obligation to believe in God, an obligation to fear God). In other words, it has rules which require Muslims to possess some mental attributes but not others.

Al-Sarrāj emphasizes that there are, in fact, many Qurʾanic statements and Hadith reports which corroborate the view that Muslims are required to possess particular mental attributes/dispositions (e.g., belief in God, fear of God, patience, gratitude). Al-Sarrāj says:

> Knowledge of the Sharīʿa indicates and calls to [both] external actions and internal actions. External actions, like the actions of the limbs, such are [rules on] worship and [other] rules. For instance, [rules on] ablution, alms-giving, pilgrimage, *jihād*, and other things. These are [rules on] worship. As for [other] rules, they are [rules on] the *ḥadd* criminal punishments, divorce, the emancipation of slaves, sales, inheritance, retaliation, and other things. All of this concerns the external limbs which are the limbs of the body . . . As for internal actions, they are like the actions of the mind/heart, which are stable or transient mental attributes (*fa-ka-aʿmāl al-qalb wa hiya al-maqāmāt wa-l-aḥwāl*), like holding [Islamic tenets] to be true (*al-taṣdīq*), belief, certitude, truthfulness, sincerity, knowledge, trust, love, contentment, remembrance, gratitude, repentance, fear . . . for every external action and every internal action there is knowledge and legal understanding (*ʿilm wa fiqh*) . . . and there is evidence for the correctness of every external and internal action in the verses of the Qurʾan and the reports on the Messenger [i.e., Muḥammad].[44]

[41] Al-Raysūnī 2013:72 [42] Al-Raysūnī 2013: 72-73
[43] See, e.g., ʿĪsā 1993:28; Ibn Taymiyya 1982:59; Ibn Taymiyya 2004, 11:381–382.
[44] Al-Sarrāj 1960:43–44.

Al-Sarrāj's views persist among contemporary scholars with Traditionalist leanings. Hence, the noted Syrian Sufi Scholar ʿAbd al-Qādir ʿĪsā (d.1991) writes that the "legal obligations of the Sharīʿa" (*al-takālīf al-sharʿiyya*) are of two kinds: "rules (*aḥkām*) pertaining to external actions and rules (*aḥkām*) pertaining to internal actions."[45] Both kinds of rules involve "commands and prohibitions" (*awāmir wa nawāhi*). ʿAbd al-Qādir explains that God *commands* us to perform *external actions* such as prayer and pilgrimage while *prohibiting* us from *external actions* like killing and fornication. Likewise, God *commands* us to perform *internal actions* like humility and trust in God while *prohibiting* us from *internal actions* like disbelief, hypocrisy, and arrogance.[46]

For both al-Sarrāj and ʿAbd al-Qādir, the study of Sharīʿa is divided between two disciplines. Hence, the discipline conventionally referred to as Islamic law (i.e., *fiqh*), focuses on Sharīʿa rules pertaining to external actions. Meanwhile, the discipline of Sufism focuses on Sharīʿa rules pertaining to internal actions (i.e., mental attributes/dispositions). This perspective is illuminating, even though I do not endorse the idea that mental attributes should be conceptualized as "internal actions."

Based on the preceding evidence, it might be said that the Sharīʿa cannot be reduced to rules because it also prescribes mental attributes/dispositions. This is one possible way of describing things. However, drawing on al-Sarrāj and ʿAbd al-Qādir, I would prefer to say that the Sharīʿa consists of (at least) two types of rules. First there are rules on actions (e.g., obligation to pray, prohibition on alcohol). These are what ʿAbd al-Qādir refers to as "rules (*aḥkām*) pertaining to external actions." Second there are rules on mental attributes (e.g., obligation to believe in God, prohibition on arrogance). These are what ʿAbd al-Qādir refers to as "rules (*aḥkām*) pertaining to internal actions."

Notably, both rules on actions and rules on mental attributes can be equated with God's intentions/will. Thus, just as it is God's intention/will that Muslims pray, it is His intention/will that Muslims believe in the prophethood of Muhammad. Similarly, just as it is God's intention/will that Muslims refrain from drinking alcohol, it is His intention/will that Muslims not be arrogant.

Now, it would make little sense for God to legislate rules which cannot be obeyed. And when it comes to rules which prescribe mental attributes, obedience is somewhat complicated. After all, a person cannot simply choose to have a mental attribute in the same way that s/he can choose to perform an action (e.g., I cannot simply choose to have particular beliefs, desires, or character traits). But this is where the Sufi emphasis on practice becomes important. For a person can choose to undertake the practice needed to acquire the good mental attributes which God has commanded (and eliminate the bad mental attributes which God has prohibited). In this way, practice becomes the necessary means of obeying God's rules on mental attributes. Addressing this issue, al-Ghazālī remarks: "if *akhlāq* could not be changed [i.e., through practice] then [religious]

[45] ʿĪsā 1993:28. [46] ʿĪsā 1993:28.

commands, exhortations, and forms of discipline would be worthless, and the Prophet would not have said: "Make good your *akhlāq* (*ḥassinū akhlāqakum*).'"[47]

However, more needs to be said about the nature of the practice needed to acquire the mental attributes/dispositions prescribed by the Sharīʿa. In part, this practice consists in practice of the rules of the Sharīʿa. Hence by practicing (i.e., continuously obeying) Sharīʿa rules on actions (e.g., obligation to pray), one thereby acquires the appropriate mental attributes, and hence complies with the Sharīʿa rules on mental attributes (e.g., obligation to believe in God). Thus, al-Ghazālī states that acquiring good dispositions involves:

> the removal of all evil habits (*al-ʿādāt*) which the divine law (*sharʿ*) [i.e., Sharīʿa] identifies in detail, such that a person [comes to] hate them and avoid them as he avoids filthy things (*al-mustaqdharāt*). [It likewise involves a person] becoming accustomed to good habits and [coming to] desire (*yashtāq*) them so that he prefers them and takes pleasure in them."[48]

In other words, Sharīʿa rules prohibit particular actions (i.e., "evil habits"), and one can only acquire good dispositions/mental attributes if one complies with these prohibitions. Al-Ghazālī also states that a disposition is good if "the acts which issue forth from it are beautiful and praiseworthy *from the standpoint of the intellect and the divine law (sharʿ)* [i.e., Sharīʿa]."[49] Here al-Ghazālī indicates that the rules of the Sharīʿa are a criterion for determining which actions are beautiful and praiseworthy (i.e., good). One who practices the rules prescribed by the Sharīʿa acquires good dispositions/mental attributes.

There are many examples of how practice of Sharīʿa rules instills good dispositions/mental attributes. For instance, the Sharīʿa prescribes yearly almsgiving to the poor (*zakāh*). The Muslim who engages in such almsgiving acquires the good disposition of generosity (a character trait). The Sharīʿa bars men from wearing silk or gold. By adhering to this practice, Muslim men acquire the good disposition of humility (*tawāduʿ*).

The practice of Sharīʿa rules also instills the good disposition of belief (*īmān*) in God and the Prophet. During my fieldwork, scholars I interviewed often claimed that there was a strong relationship between Sharīʿa-compliant action (*ʿamal*) and such belief (*īmān*). In their view, a Muslim experiencing doubt (*shakk*) should seek to dispel it through worship and pious obedience to the Sharīʿa. It is through such behavior that one attains certainty (*yaqīn*) in the tenets of Islam.

Al-Ghazālī is well aware that belief is internalized through practice. Hence, he remarks that "persistent action in accordance with a belief" ("*al-muwāẓaba ʿalā al-ʿamal bi-mūjib iʿtiqādihi*") roots it in the soul and increases confidence (*ṭumaʾnīna*) in its truth. Al-Ghazālī states that the accuracy of his claim is confirmed by inner experience.[50]

The late *Shaykh al-Azhar* Muḥammad Sayyid Ṭanṭāwī (d.2010) expresses a similar view: "Verily God—the Highest—did not legislate the forms of worship

[47] Al-Ghazālī 2005:937. [48] Al-Ghazālī 1964:255. Also see al-Iṣfahānī 2007:97–99.
[49] Al-Ghazālī 2005:934. Also see al-Jurjānī 2004:89. [50] Al-Ghazālī 2004b:123.

with which He obligated His slaves, and which are among the pillars of Islam, without an aim. [Rather] God—the Highest—only legislated them to fix belief firmly in the soul (*li-tathbīt al-īmān fī al-nufūs*), to purify the heart, and to habituate man to adhere to good dispositions (*maḥāsin al-akhlāq*), praiseworthy attributes (*ḥamīd al-khiṣāl*), and beautiful habits."[51] Notice that Ṭanṭāwī refers to the rules of worship legislated by God, and asserts that they fix belief in the soul.

## IV. SHARĪʿA AND SUNNA

As mentioned previously, Muslim scholars use the word "Sunna" to refer to the totality of the Prophet's actions (including statements). Or, to be more specific, the word "Sunna" refers to the totality of the Prophet's *obedient* actions, as it is assumed that the Prophet always acted in accordance with Sharīʿa rules (i.e., he always obeyed them).

But Sunna has a second related meaning. The Prophet did not merely perform (obedient) actions in accordance with Sharīʿa rules. Rather, he performed these actions in a *repetitive* fashion. Hence, by virtue of his constant obedience to Sharīʿa rules, the Prophet repeatedly acted in accordance with these rules. For example, by virtue of his constant obedience to the rule mandating five daily prayers, the Prophet repeatedly performed the five daily prayers. By virtue of his constant obedience to the rule prohibiting alcohol, he repeatedly refused to drink alcohol.

Now, a repeated action is a practice, and repeated action in accordance with a rule is practice of that rule. Therefore, it may be said that the Prophet practiced Sharīʿa rules by repeatedly acting in accordance with them. This gives rise to the second related meaning of Sunna. Hence, religious scholars often use the term "Sunna" to refer to the *Prophet's practice of Sharīʿa rules*. Moreover, religious scholars assert that all Muslims should strive to "imitate" the Prophet (*al-iqtidāʾ bi-l-nabī*) by "following the [Prophet's] Sunna" (*ittibāʿ al-Sunna*).[52] In other words, Muslims are to take the Prophet as a model for how Sharīʿa rules should be practiced, and they are then to practice Sharīʿa rules in the way that the Prophet practiced Sharīʿa rules. A Muslim "follows the [Prophet's] Sunna" when s/he practices Sharīʿa rules (i.e., repeatedly acts in accordance with them), using the Prophet as a model. This means that there is a general equivalence between three ideas. The idea of "imitating the Prophet" is equivalent to the idea of "following the [Prophet's] Sunna," which is equivalent to the idea of "practicing Sharīʿa rules."

"Sunna" is actually a pre-Islamic Arab concept which denotes a normative practice laid down by a particular individual.[53] As a normative practice, a *sunna* was worthy of being followed by others. For instance, the normative practice

[51] Ṭanṭāwī 2004:215. [52] See, e.g., al-Shāfiʿī n.d.:88–89.
[53] See Bravmann:1972:139, 160–161, 173. Also see Hallaq 2005; Schacht 1965:29–30; Schacht 1967[1950] 70.

laid down by a tribal chief was his *sunna*. Later members of the tribe might then imitate the chief by following his *sunna*. The earliest Muslims took over these basic ideas and applied them to their Prophet. Hence, in an Islamic context, the Sunna came to mean the Prophet's practice of Sharīʿa rules. Later Muslims were then to imitate the Prophet by following his Sunna (i.e., practice of Sharīʿa rules).

Notably, for Muslim scholars, even very minor aspects of the Prophet's behavior are associated with Sharīʿa rules. Recall that the Qurʾan speaks of the Prophet as an exemplar (*uswa ḥasana*) to imitate.[54] Consequently, many scholars adopt a general principle which may be stated as follows: absent contrary evidence, whenever the Prophet performs an action there is a Sharīʿa rule requiring or encouraging performance of that action. Remember, that Sharīʿa rules may simply encourage actions without making them obligatory (i.e., such actions are *mandūb, mustaḥabb*).[55] Hence, the Prophet wore a turban, ate with his right hand, and wore a silver ring. For many scholars, this means that there are Sharīʿa rules encouraging Muslims to wear turbans, eat with their right hands, and wear silver rings. On such a view, when the Prophet wore a turban, he was practicing a Sharīʿa rule which encourages the wearing of turbans. Accordingly, practice of Sharīʿa rules (i.e., following the Sunna) entails close and detailed imitation of the Prophet.

Now, in practicing Sharīʿa rules by imitating the Prophet (i.e., following the Sunna), a Muslim thereby acquires the dispositions/mental attributes prescribed by the Sharīʿa. It can also be said that a Muslim thereby acquires the dispositions/mental attributes of the Prophet. This is because the dispositions/mental attributes prescribed the Sharīʿa are those possessed by the Prophet. Such is precisely why the Prophet is the ultimate ethical exemplar—because he possesses all of the dispositions/mental attributes prescribed by the Sharīʿa.

Traditionalist scholars often emphasize that one acquires the Prophet's dispositions by habitual, detailed, and meticulous imitation of the Prophet. By living every waking moment of one's life exactly like the Prophet, one aims to turn oneself into a living replica of the Prophet—acting, thinking, feeling, and perceiving the world in the same way he did. Religious authorities are clear on the fact that mimicry of the Prophet must extend to both one's "inner life" as well as to one's outer deeds. An agent's thoughts, emotions, and will must be tightly monitored and regulated so as to bring them in to line with those of the Prophet. Ibn Taymiyya (d.728/1328) remarks that whoever thinks that there is "a path to God other than through following Muḥammad—peace be upon him—inwardly and outwardly (*bāṭinan wa ẓāhiran*), and who does not follow him inwardly and outwardly, is a disbeliever."[56] Ibn Taymiyya thereby implies that just as there is an "outer Sunna" to be imitated with the actions of the body, there is also an "inner Sunna" to be imitated with the mind/heart.

[54] Qurʾan [33:21].

[55] This is why, in legal discourses, a third common meaning of "Sunna" is an action which is *mustaḥabb*.

[56] Ibn Taymiyya 1982:59. Also see Ibn Taymiyya 2004, 11:381–382.

These ideas are well illustrated in a recent television special devoted to the subject of Islamic ethics, featuring the Yemeni Traditionalist Ḥabīb ʿAlī al-Jifrī. While al-Jifrī is world-famous, he is especially prominent in Egyptian religious life. Al-Jifrī opens the special by emphasizing the need for Muslims to concretely embody the Prophetic exemplar, thereby enabling him to "live on in our dispositions and our thoughts, in our movements and stillnesses."[57] For al-Jifrī, proper ethics ensures that the Prophet is incarnated in each new generation of Muslims.

The preceding ideas are spelled out even more explicitly in a present-day educational treatise. "Islam makes its permanent exemplar (*qudwa*) the personality (*shakhṣiyya*) of its noble messenger [i.e. Muḥammad]—it makes [this personality] an exemplar which is renewed down through the generations—it is renewed in the [living] existence of human beings—[Islam] puts forth this exemplar in order for them to bring it into being within their very selves (*li-yuḥaqqiqūhā fī dhawāt anfusihim*)."[58]

Some scholars refer to the process of erasing the existing self in favor of a Muḥammadan form as "[self-] annihilation" or "*al-fanā.*'" Al-Qushayrī (d.465/1072), in his still popular *Risāla*, defines "[self-] annihilation" as the "disappearance of blameworthy attributes[59] [i.e., the disappearance of blameworthy mental attributes/dispositions]."[60] To appreciate the import of al-Qushayrī's statement, it must be remembered that blameworthy dispositions are conceived of as dispositions different from those of the Prophet. Hence, to reach for perfection by annihilating what is blameworthy in oneself is the same as annihilating one's difference from the Prophet. Tellingly, many contemporary Egyptian Sufis specifically speak of "annihilation in the Messenger [Muḥammad]" ("*al-fanā' fī al-Rasūl*").[61] Moreover, this conception can be traced back to the medieval period.[62]

Within premodern education, meticulous and constant imitation of the Prophet was viewed as a primary normative imperative. George Makdisi quotes a medieval text offering the following advice to students: "You should model your conduct on that of the early Muslims. Therefore, read the biography of the Prophet, study his deeds and concerns, follow in his footsteps, and try your utmost to imitate him. When you come to know his habits regarding food, drink, clothing, sleep, waking, sickness, medical treatment, enjoyments and the use of perfumes, and his relations with his Lord, his wives, his companions and his enemies, when you come to know this, and do ever so little of what you have learned, then you will be a completely happy person."[63] Ibn Ḥanbal (d. 241/855) is reported to have been so intensely desirous of imitating the Prophet that he refused to eat watermelon on the grounds that the Prophet had never done so.[64]

[57] "Yaḥyā fī akhlāqinā wa fī adhkārinā, wa fī ḥarakātinā wa sakanātinā." *Al-Shajra al-Ṭayyiba.* Episode 1. http://www.youtube.com/watch?v=aLAHoMnqDcA&feature=relmfu 6/7/12 (last visited Dec. 10, 2018).

[58] Jarrār 1997:24.

[59] "*Suqūṭ al-awṣāf al-madhmūma.*"

[60] Al-Qushayri 2006:145. For more on the concept of "*fanā*" see Schimmel 1975:47–48, 142–143.

[61] See Hoffman 1995:63, 140–141.

[62] Schimmel 1975:216, 378; Hoffman 1995:64–65; Hoffman 1999.

[63] Quoted in Makdisi 1981:89–90.

[64] Rippin 2006:95.

Intricate details about the Prophet's personal habits account for a large amount of the material in the six canonical collections of Hadith reports. Nevertheless, a conscious concern with the minutiae of Prophetic practice finds its most consummate expression in the *Shāmaʾil* of al-Tirmidhī (d.279/892). During my fieldwork, the *Shamāʾil* was being taught at al-Azhar mosque in one of the most prestigious study-circles. The text has been popular among Azhari scholars at least as far back as the eighteenth century,[65] and remains a favorite among those with a Traditionalist orientation.

The word "*shamāʾil*" means "dispositions" or "attributes."[66] Here the reference is to the beautiful dispositions and attributes of the Prophet. Roughly 150 pages in length, the text[67] consists in a collection of Hadith reports. Hadith reports are distributed among 56 sections. Each section deals with a particular aspect of the Prophet's appearance and behavior. Sections are devoted to: the Prophet's hairstyle, the way he combed his hair, the way he dyed his hair, how he applied kuhl to his eyes, his signet ring, his leather socks, his sandals, his sword, his turban, how he walked, how he leaned on his pillow, the type of bread he ate and how he ate it, his preferences in fruits, his use of perfume, his manner of laughing, his manner of joking, how he put himself to bed, and other such topics. The acute attention paid to the most minor aspects of the Prophet's appearance and behavior reflects the normative emphasis placed on detailed imitation of his Sunna.

## V. THE TWO ASPECTS OF THE CONCEPT OF SUNNA

The preceding analysis enables us to recognize that the concept of Sunna has two aspects. These two aspects can only be appreciated by drawing on both hermeneutic theory and practice theory.

The first aspect of the Sunna was addressed in chapter 1. It can be explicated as follows. The Sunna consists in the totality of the Prophet's actions. Each of these actions is a sign/effect of God's mental attributes. Consequently, it is possible to infer knowledge of God's mental attributes from the Prophet's actions as described in Hadith reports. Or, to put things differently, it is possible to infer knowledge of Sharīʿa rules from the Prophet's actions as described in Hadith reports (because knowledge of Sharīʿa rules is knowledge of God's mental attributes). Works of Islamic legal theory (*Uṣūl al-Fiqh*) focus on this aspect of the Sunna. Accordingly, such works assert that the Sunna is the second major source (*aṣl*) of knowledge about Sharīʿa rules (after the Qurʾan). This aspect of the Sunna can only be grasped through hermeneutic theory.

We now come to the second aspect of the Sunna, which can be explicated as follows. The Sunna consists in the Prophet's practice of Sharīʿa rules, and this

[65] Heyworth-Dunne 1939:48. Heyworth-Dunne also records that it has attracted three commentaries.

[66] See Al-Bājūrī 2001:17; Ibn Manẓūr 2003:v.5 195.

[67] Al-Tirmidhī 2008.

practice operates to instill specific mental attributes (namely, those mental attributes prescribed by the Sharīʿa). Hence, when Muslims follow the Sunna by practicing Sharīʿa rules (using the Prophet as a model), they acquire the mental attributes prescribed by the Sharīʿa. Sufi writings focus on this second aspect of the Sunna, which can only be grasped through practice theory.

Thus, to appreciate both aspects of the Sunna, it is neither sufficient to rely solely on hermeneutic theory or solely on practice theory. Rather, both currents of theory must be taken into account.

## VI. SHARĪʿA AND THE ROLE OF THE SUFI *SHAYKH*

I have stated that imitating the Prophet by practice of Sharīʿa rules (i.e., following the Sunna) is a means of acquiring good dispositions/mental attributes. But, it is not the only means. Traditionalist scholars often express the view that individuals naturally differ in terms of their dispositions. Thus, one individual is humble but does not have a strong belief in God. A second individual has a strong belief in God, but is very arrogant. Practice of Sharīʿa rules is one means of helping these individuals replace their bad dispositions with good dispositions. But, such practice alone may not suffice. At this point, a wise religious scholar may step in and prescribe additional rules, tailored to the specific needs of the individual. Sufi religious scholars (i.e., *shaykhs*) typically fulfill this role. Traditionalist scholars often compare the role of the Sufi *shaykh* to a doctor (*ṭabīb*), who prescribes special medicine as treatment (*ʿilāj*) for the diseases of the mind/heart (*amrāḍ al-qulūb*). Thus, the Sufi *shaykh* may advise the person with a weak belief in God to add specific forms of worship to his daily routine. For instance, the *shaykh* may require an extra hour of Qurʾan reading every day. The shaykh may also require that the person chant formulae praising God a specific number of times per day (*dhikr*). The shaykh's requirements thereby become a set of additional person-specific rules. By practicing these additional rules the first individual is able to strengthen his belief in God. Meanwhile, the shaykh may require that the second individual (who is arrogant) spend time quietly and humbly serving others. This becomes an additional rule for him. By practicing this rule, the second individual is able to replace his arrogance with humility.

To be sure, the assistance of a shaykh would not be necessary for a perfect individual who already has all of the good dispositions/mental attributes prescribed by the Sharīʿa. Yet, Sufis assert that such perfect individuals are rare or nonexistent. Hence, al-Ghāzalī claims that, generally speaking, every person has some bad dispositions/mental attributes (prohibited by the Sharīʿa). Consequently, every person needs Sufi training (administered by a qualified Sufi authority) until his/her bad dispositions/mental attributes have been replaced with good ones.[68]

[68] Al-Ghazālī 2005:23; ʿĪsā 1993:31.

Although the additional rules prescribed by a Sufi *shaykh* go beyond the standard Sharīʿa rules, they do not constitute a rejection of the standard Sharīʿa rules. Instead, they are meant to supplement standard Sharīʿa rules. They are meant to help specific individuals acquire the dispositions/mental attributes prescribed by the Sharīʿa. But while such a perspective is common among contemporary Traditionalist scholars, it is not necessarily endorsed by scholars from other groups. For instance, Salafis tend to view the prescription of additional rules by Sufis as an illegitimate form of innovation (*bidʿa*) and a usurpation of God's legislative authority.

## VII. THE DISPOSITIONS OF GOD AND THE PROPHET

As explained previously, Traditionalist scholars encourage Muslims to acquire the dispositions/mental attributes prescribed by the Sharīʿa through the practice of Sharīʿa rules. Moreover, these dispositions/mental attributes are identified with the dispositions/mental attributes of the Prophet. But the views of Traditionalist scholars have a second dimension. For such scholars, the Prophet's dispositions/mental attributes correspond, in large part, with the dispositions/mental attributes of God. Hence, God is kind, generous, and patient. Likewise, the Prophet is kind, generous, and patient. When God desires or loves something, the Prophet desires or loves the same thing. When God wills/intends something, the Prophet wills or intends the same thing. All of this has an important consequence. If the Prophet's dispositions correspond with those of God, then when the pious Muslim acquires the Prophet's dispositions s/he also acquires those of God. In other words, through practice of Sharīʿa rules, the pious Muslim comes to acquire both the Prophet's dispositions/mental attributes and God's dispositions/mental attributes. The outcome of this process is that the mind of the pious Muslim resembles both the mind of the Prophet and the mind of God.

In order to clarify the preceding ideas, let us return to the Sufi concept of "[self-] annihilation" (*al-fanāʾ*). For Sufis, such annihilation admits of different levels. One form of annihilation is the aforementioned "annihilation in the Messenger [Muhammad]." In this form of annihilation, the pious Muslim replaces his/her dispositions/mental attributes with those of the Prophet. Yet, for Sufis, this form of annihilation is simply a means to an even higher and more coveted form of annihilation. The second higher form of annihilation is referred to as "annihilation in God" (*al-fanāʾ fī Allah*). The pious Muslim achieves annihilation in God by acquiring the dispositions/mental attributes of God. The reason "annihilation in the Messenger [Muhammad]" is a means to "annihilation in God" is that the Prophet possesses (some) of God's dispositions. Hence, when one acquires the Prophet's dispositions/mental attributes, one also acquires God's dispositions/mental attributes.

While the idea of annihilation in God is found among modern Egyptian religious scholars, it is widespread in medieval texts as well.[69] Commenting on

[69] See Hoffman 1995; 1999.

the concept of "annihilation in God" in medieval Sufism, Annemarie Schimmel states:

> *Fana* [i.e., annihilation] is, in the beginning, an ethical concept: man becomes annihilated and takes on God's attributes—it is the place of the alleged *ḥadīth: takhallaqū bi-akhlāq Allāh*, "qualify yourself with the qualities of God," i.e., through constant mental struggle exchange your own base qualities for the praiseworthy qualities by which God has described Himself in the Koranic revelation.[70]

In fact, the Hadith report that Schimmel mentions is more accurately translated as "Acquire for yourselves God's dispositions (*akhlāq Allāh*)." Thus, according to this (controversial but famous) Hadith report, the Prophet is explicitly exhorting Muslims to acquire God's dispositions.

Al-Ghazālī takes up the theme of acquiring God's dispositions at some length.[71] Hence, al-Ghazālī describes a range of divine dispositions which human beings can and should seek to acquire. For instance, al-Ghazālī mentions that God possesses a number of character traits. God is kind (*Raḥmān*), just (*ʿAdl*), generous (*Karīm*), grateful (*Shakūr*), wise (*Ḥakīm*), forgiving (*ʿAfuww*), and patient (*Ṣabūr*). For al-Ghazālī, the pious Muslim should also seek to become kind, just, generous, grateful, wise, forgiving, and patient.[72]

The notion that God's dispositions can be shared by human beings is also suggested by a famous description of the Prophet. This description is attributed to the Prophet's wife ʿĀisha. She says of the Prophet that: "His dispositions were the Qurʾan" (*kāna khuluquhu al-Qurʾān*). Ibn Rajab (d.795/1393) explains this as meaning that: "The Prophet took upon himself the manners of the Qurʾan and he acquired its dispositions (*yataʾaddab bi-ādābihi, wa-yatakhallaq bi-akhlāqihi*), so that he took pleasure in what the Qurʾan praised and despised what the Qurʾan condemned."[73] Now, for Muslims, God is the author of the Qurʾan. Hence, the dispositions of the Qurʾan are, in some sense, God's dispositions. Consequently, to assert that the Prophet's dispositions are those of the Qurʾan is to indicate that the Prophet possesses dispositions akin to those of God. Insofar as human beings can acquire the dispositions of the Prophet, they can also acquire dispositions akin to those of God.

In Sufi texts, "intention/will" and "desire" have a special place. Thus, these texts often assert that a pious Muslim can share in the intentions and desires of God. Here, two Arabic terms are particularly important. The first term is "*irāda*," which is used to denote intention/will. The second term is "*maḥabba*." *Maḥabba* can be translated as "desire," although it is more commonly translated as "love." For Sufis, intention/will (*irāda*) and desire/love (*maḥabba*) are tightly related to one another. Indeed, in some cases they are treated almost interchangeably. For instance, al-Qushayrī states that "desire/love . . . is intention/will" (*al-maḥabba hiya al-irāda*).[74] It is not surprising that Sufis recognize a tight relationship between desire/love and intention/will. After all, as explained

[70] Schimmel 1975:142 [71] Al-Ghazālī 1999:29–42. [72] Al-Ghazālī 1999:44–132
[73] Ibn Rajab 2004, 1:411–413. Also see Ṭanṭāwī 2004:217. [74] Al-Qushayrī 2001:348.

earlier, intention/will is a product of desire/love. Hence, if I form an intention to eat chocolate ice cream, this is because I desire/love eating chocolate ice cream.

With the preceding facts in mind, let us examine an oft-quoted statement from the early Sufi Dhū al-Nūn al-Miṣrī (d.245/859). He declares that the pious should aim to "desire/love (*tuḥibb*) what God desires/loves and to hate what God hates."[75] This reflects a basic Sufi notion; namely, that a pious Muslim's desires should match God's desires. Sufis hold that this matching of desires leads to a matching of wills/intentions. Al-Qushayrī refers to this condition as "correspondence" (*muwāfaqa*). It occurs when "the mind/heart agrees with what the Lord wills" ("*muwāṭaʾa al-qalb li-murādāt al-Rabb*").[76] Referring to this condition, Ibn Taymiyya speaks of "a mind/heart which has been taken possession of by a will/intention directed towards that which is desired/loved by God (*irāda mā yuḥibbuhu Allah*)."[77] Thus, for Sufis, the pious Muslim should strive to attain a state wherein s/he desires/loves what God desires/loves, and consequently wills/intends what God wills/intends.

Sufis hold that a pious Muslim attains such a state through ethical discipline involving practice of Sharīʿa rules. Hence, Ibn Taymiyya cites a number of textual proofs meant to establish that the sensibilities of pious men and the sensibilities of God may coincide. Among them is a famous Hadith report, where the Prophet quotes God as stating:

> there is nothing by which my slave draws near to Me, which is more beloved to Me, than [performing] that which I have obligated him to do. My slave does not cease drawing close to me through supererogatory acts of worship until I love him. [Note: supererogatory acts of worship are acts of worship which are encouraged, but not required, by the Sharīʿa]. And when I love him I become the hearing by which he hears, the sight by which he sees, the hand by which he grasps, and the foot by which he walks. . . ."[78]

Ibn Ḥajar (d.852/1448) mentions another version of the Hadith report wherein God adds that He likewise becomes "the mind by which he understands[79] and the tongue by which he speaks."[80] This Hadith report highlights two important points. First of all, a sort of correspondence is possible between God and a pious Muslim. In this state, the pious Muslim's entire self comes to be taken over by God. Second, the pious Muslim attains this state by "[performing] that which [God has] obligated him to do . . . and drawing close to [God] through supererogatory acts of worship." Put differently, the state is attained by habitual practice of Sharīʿa rules.

Therefore, Islamic ethical thought suggests that practice of Sharīʿa rules leads to a sharing of dispositions among God, the Prophet Muḥammad, and the pious Muslim. However, it should be noted that Muslim scholars differ over the extent

[75] Al-Sulamī 1986:18. Also see al-Ghazālī 2005:1696–1697.
[76] Al-Qushayrī 2001:350.
[77] Ibn Taymiyya 2004, 10: 472–473.
[78] This version of the ḥadīth is cited in Ibn Ḥajar 2004, 11:386. Ibn Taymiyya's version is slightly different. See Ibn Taymiyya 2004, 10:474.
[79] "*Fuʾāduhu alladhī yaʿqil bihi.*"
[80] Ibn Ḥajar 2004, 11:389.

and nature of such sharing. For instance, Ibn Taymiyya takes a restrictive view of this phenomenon. Hence, he holds that, in a sense, a pious Muslim can share in the desires/love and intentions/will of God.[81] Yet, Ibn Taymiyya does not claim that a pious Muslim can share in other dispositions of God. Al-Ghāzalī takes a more expansive view, suggesting that a pious Muslim can, in a sense, share in a wide range of God's dispositions.[82]

Insofar as practice of Sharīʿa rules produces a sharing of dispositions/mental attributes among God, the Prophet Muḥammad, and the pious Muslim, it produces a resemblance of minds among these figures. I will argue that this point has implications for the relationship between ethics and legal knowledge.

## VIII. ETHICS AND SHARĪʿA KNOWLEDGE

Premodern educational treatises constantly assert that there exists a relationship between seeking knowledge and purifying one's dispositions through pious practice of Sharīʿa rules. Ibn Jamāʿa (d.733/1333) states that a religious student's first obligation is:

> to purify his mind/heart of all corruption, filth, malice, jealousy, as well as every wicked belief and disposition, such that it is suited to receive and retain knowledge and to behold its precise meanings and the true nature of its mysteries. As some have said, truly knowledge is "the prayer of secret thoughts, the worship of the heart-mind, and the piety of the inner self." Just as prayer, which is the worship of the outer limbs, is not sound except upon purifying the outer self of filth and ritual uncleanliness, likewise, knowledge, which is the worship of the mind/heart, is not sound except upon purifying it of filthy attributes and the uncleanliness of evil and base dispositions.[83]

Al-Zarnūjī (fl.620/1223) likewise stresses the importance of piety in the learning process. "The more pious the student of knowledge is, the more beneficial is his knowledge, the easier it is for him to learn, and the more he gets out of it (*fawāʾiduhu akthar*)."[84]

The connection between knowledge and piety is considered to be so strong that sin undermines one's ability to retain information. Contemporary scholars make frequent reference to an anecdote concerning Imam al-Shāfiʿī (d.204/820), a scholar famed for his amazing powers of memory. The anecdote concerns al-Shāfiʿī during his student days. According to the story, one day al-Shāfiʿī was perplexed to find his powers of memory diminished. Not knowing the reason, he went to consult his *shaykh*, whose name was Wakīʿ. When informed of the problem, Wakīʿ told al-Shāfiʿī that he must have committed a sin. Prompted by his teacher's comments, al-Shāfiʿī began to reflect on his recent doings. He then recalled that he had inadvertently looked upon part of a woman's leg while she

[81] Ibn Taymiyya 2004, 10: 472–473. [82] Al-Ghazālī 1999. [83] Ibn Jamāʿa 2009:80.
[84] Al-Zarnūjī 2004:76.

passed in front of him. Realizing the truth of his teacher's words, al-Shāfiʿī enshrined the lesson in a poem. "I complained to Wakīʿ about the poorness of my memory. So he guided me to leaving my sins. He said to me that knowledge is light. And the light of God is not given to a sinner."

Remarking on the relationship between knowledge and ethics, one scholar told me: "The foundation of knowledge is fear of God (*taqwā*) and good dispositions. It is not abstract intelligence. That is only academic knowledge. Of course, intellect (*dhakāʾ*) and reason (*ʿaql*) have a function, but they are not a substitute for a moral upbringing. They only come into play once that upbringing is in place. I know of one person who had memorized the Qurʾan. But because of his bad ethics, God wiped it from his mind."

Almost every scholar I spoke with affirmed that Islamic knowledge is tied to internalizing proper dispositions (*akhlāq*). Having good dispositions was seen as beneficial in two respects. First, it encouraged one to apply one's knowledge. Second, and perhaps more interesting, was the assertion that good dispositions are required for understanding the Sharīʿa rules found in sacred texts. It was believed that increasing one's understanding required refining the dispositions through adherence to God's commands. Those I interviewed frequently cited the medieval maxim: "Whosoever practices what he knows, God gives him knowledge of that which he does not know (*Man ʿamila bi-mā ʿalima ʿallamahu Allah ʿilm mā lam yaʿlam*)."[85]

For many contemporary Traditionalist scholars, there is a particular process whereby purifying the dispositions yields knowledge. They explain that this process has three stages. The first is known as "*takhallī*" or "abandonment." It consists in disciplining the self by leaving off wicked behavior. The second is known as "*taḥallī*" or "adornment." Here one uses continuous imitation of the Prophet (i.e., practice of Sharīʿa rules) to instill in oneself his dispositions. This leads to the third stage of "*tajallī*" or "revelation." Once an individual has transformed himself into a replica of the Prophet, he is illuminated with knowledge from God.

One Azhari scholar I interviewed admitted that certain fields of knowledge could be mastered irrespective of a scholar's moral state, mentioning chemistry and physics as examples. Yet he cautioned that knowledge of Sharīʿa is not like these fields. When I asked him whether it was conceivable for a brilliant non-Muslim Orientalist to accurately interpret Sharīʿa rules, he responded that such was impossible in principle. Some other authorities to whom I posed the question offered similar replies, often being taken aback by the very suggestion that things could be otherwise.

In discussing the relationship between knowledge and ethics, the proof text that I heard cited most often was a verse from the Qurʾan which reads: "Fear God and He will give you knowledge (*wa-ttaqū Allaha wa yuʿallimukum Allah*)."[86] The medieval exegete al-Qurṭubī (d.656/1259) explains the verse as follows. "[This

[85] This maxim is found in a number of variants. This variant can be found in Ibn ʿĀbidīn 2000, 1:42.

[86] Qurʾan [2:282]. Also see Ibn ʿAbidīn 2000, 1:42. Muslim exegetes debate whether the grammar of the verse really allows for this particular reading.

is] a promise from God—the Highest—that He will give knowledge to whosoever fears Him. Which is to say that He will place in his mind/heart a light by which to understand that which is set before him . . . [it being] a criterion whereby to distinguish between truth and falsehood (*fayṣalan yafṣil bihi bayna al-haqq wa-l-bāṭil*)."[87] Al-Qurṭubī goes on to say that the message of this Qurʾanic verse is similar to another which reads: "if you fear God he will give you a criterion." ("*in-tattaqū Allaha yajʿal lakum furqānan*"[88]). Al-Qurṭubī explains the second verse as meaning:

> If the slave fears his Lord—and that is by following His commandments and avoiding His prohibitions [i.e., adhering to Sharīʿa rules], by leaving aside those matters of doubtful legitimacy owing to fear of falling into that which has been forbidden, by filling his mind/heart with sincere intention, and by filling his limbs with righteous deeds . . . [then in that case] God will provide him with a criterion whereby to distinguish between truth and falsehood.[89]

Thus, al-Qurṭubī believes that God places a "criterion" for understanding in a mind/heart which adheres to Sharīʿa rules. Al-Ghazālī likewise indicates that Sufi religiosity (including practice of Sharīʿa rules) gives a person access to a special type of knowledge, which he theorizes (at least partly) using ideas from Ibn Sīnā's Neoplatonic philosophy.[90] Admittedly, not all premodern scholars held such views. Hence, Frank Griffel draws attention to al-Ghazālī's illustrious Andalusian student Abū Bakr Ibn al-ʿArabī (d.543/1148). Parting ways with his teacher, Ibn al-ʿArabī rejects the view that pious practice of Sharīʿa rules provides access to a special type of knowledge. Ibn al-ʿArabī's stance is similar to some other Andalusian scholars of his day.[91]

Nevertheless, on the whole, premodern religious scholars do assert a relationship between ethics and religious knowledge. Moreover, this position is still endorsed by contemporary Traditionalist scholars. Some contemporary Traditionalist scholars hold that good ethics are an absolute requirement for the proper interpretation of Sharīʿa rules. Meanwhile, others hold that good ethics are not an absolute requirement, but that they provide a boost to interpretive abilities.[92] In reality, these two positions blend into one another, and some scholars waver between them. Consider, for example, the views of the famous contemporary Azhari authority Yūsuf al-Qaraḍāwī. Addressing the role of ethics in legal interpretation, he states:

> perhaps a sinful person (*al-ʿāṣī*) can attain the ability to [competently] interpret legal texts (*rutbat al-ijtihād*) if he fulfills its scholarly requirements (*shurūṭahu al-ʿilmiyya*) . . . however, it is to be mentioned here that a person who does not fear God—may He be exalted—and does not fear his accountability [before God], [that person] will rarely be given success in correct [interpretation]. And it is worried

[87] Al-Qurtubī 2010, 2:346. [88] Qurʾan [8:29]. [89] Al-Qurtubī 2010, 4:340.
[90] Griffel 2009:66–71. [91] Griffel 2009:66–67.
[92] It could be argued that al-Ghazali falls into this category. See al-Ghazālī 2000:342, but also his claims about ethics-based mystical knowledge in *Iḥyāʾ ʿUlūm al-Dīn*.

> that the darkness of his sinfulness will blot out the light of legal understanding (*fiqh*) in his mind/heart. For this reason, God—may He be exalted—said: "O you who believe, if you fear God he will give you a criterion" [Qurʾan 8:29].

Al-Qaraḍāwī goes on to explain that "for this reason we find statements of the Prophet—peace be upon him—and his Companions after him which call attention to the importance of worship, fear of God, and righteousness among those who undertake legal interpretation."[93]

Other scholars take an even stricter stance on the relationship between ethics and legal interpretation. Thus, one of those I interviewed during my fieldwork was a 60-year-old professor at al-Azhar's Faculty of Sharīʿa. Responding to my queries about ethics, he remarked:

> In Islam there is a fundamental connection between knowledge and dispositions (*akhlāq*). If a person is evil it will undermine his ability to properly interpret the law. He will be led to produce wicked rulings that correspond to his wicked desires. His opinions will reflect his sinful dispositions. It is said in a poem: "If knowledge is not encompassed by noble dispositions (*shamāʾil*) that elevate it, then it is an instrument for failure (*maṭiyyat al-ikhfāq*)."

## IX. THEORIZING ETHICS AND LEGAL KNOWLEDGE

How are we to understand the relationship between ethics and knowledge of Sharīʿa rules? I would suggest that this relationship can be understood on two levels. The first level involves the mental attribute of skill. The second level involves the mental attributes of desire and emotion.

Let us begin with the first level. Ethics requires practice, which enables learning through practice. Hence, Islamic ethics requires practice of Sharīʿa rules. This enables learning knowledge of Sharīʿa rules through practice. For instance, the Muslim who practices the Sharīʿa rules of prayer learns knowledge of Sharīʿa rules on prayer. Knowledge of Sharīʿa rules learned through practice is a skill (i.e., knowledge of how to competently apply the Sharīʿa rules).

As noted earlier, learning through practice has a number of noteworthy features. First, while some forms of knowledge can adequately be learned through texts or bare observation, there exist other forms of knowledge which can only adequately be learned through practice (e.g., knowledge of how to ride a bike, or how to speak Arabic). Second, knowledge learned through practice is largely unconscious and intuitive. Consequently, it is difficult (or impossible) to adequately express such knowledge verbally (i.e., in words).

I would suggest that knowledge of Sharīʿa rules is a form of knowledge which can only be adequately learned through practice. As such, it is natural that religious scholars associate learning knowledge of Sharīʿa rules with ethics. For

[93] Al-Qaraḍāwī 1999:63–64.

ethics enjoins practice of Sharīʿa rules, and such practice is needed to adequately learn Sharīʿa rules. As we will soon see, religious scholars also associate knowledge of Sharīʿa rules with intuition. Such intuition is conceptualized as a special form of understanding which God grants to the pious. Once again, views of this type are not surprising. After all, where Sharīʿa rules have been learned through practice, the resulting knowledge of Sharīʿa rules will be largely unconscious and intuitive. Thus, Ibn Taymiyya recognizes that knowledge of Sharīʿa rules can be unconscious, intuitive, and hence resistant to verbal articulation. Speaking of such knowledge, he remarks that "not everyone is capable of expressing [in verbal form] the knowledge (*al-maʿānī*) present in his mind/heart."[94]

This brings us to the second level of analysis required to understand the relationship between ethics and knowledge of Sharīʿa rules. Here we must move beyond the mental attribute of skill, and consider mental attributes of desire and emotion. I begin by further clarifying how practice of Sharīʿa rules instills desire and emotion. I then examine how such mental attributes relate to the proper interpretation of Sharīʿa rules.

As we have seen, practice can instill mental attributes like desire and emotion. For instance, a woman may initially have no desire to eat shrimp or play chess. However, through the practice of eating shrimp she develops a desire to eat shrimp, and through the practice of playing chess she develops a desire to play chess. Indeed, she also develops emotional feelings of pleasure. Hence, even though she found shrimp disgusting when she was a little girl, she now takes great pleasure in eating shrimp. In other words, through practice she has developed a taste for shrimp. Likewise, even though she found playing chess boring when she was little, she now takes great pleasure in playing chess (as a result of practice).

Muslim religious scholars suggest that practice of Sharīʿa rules produces particular forms of desire and emotion. Hence, the Muslim who practices Sharīʿa rules develops a desire to practice (i.e., obey) these rules. Indeed, s/he comes to experience practice of these rules as pleasurable. This general line of analysis builds on the *Nicomachean Ethics*, where Aristotle argues that a person who is habituated to a practice comes to desire it and experience it as pleasurable.[95]

Let us return again to a previous quote by al-Ghazālī. He asserts that acquiring good dispositions involves "the removal of all evil habits (*al-ʿādāt*) which the divine law (*sharʿ*)[i.e., Sharīʿa] identifies in detail, such that a person [comes to] hate them and avoid them as he avoids filthy things (*al-mustaqdharāt*). [It likewise involves a person] becoming accustomed to good habits and [coming to] desire (*yashtāq*) them so that he prefers them and takes pleasure in them (*yatanaʿʿam bihā*)."[96] Al-Ghazālī explains that the ideal is to reach a state wherein one always "experiences pleasure in obedience [to the Sharīʿa] (*istildhādh al-ṭāʿa*) and experiences disgust in disobedience (*istikrāh al maʿṣiya*)."[97]

[94] Ibn Taymiyya 2004, 10:476–477. [95] Ross 2009:23–27. [96] Al-Ghazālī 1964:255.
[97] Al-Ghazālī 1964:256. Also see al-Ghazālī 2005:940–941.

For al-Ghazālī, "good habits" involve practice of Sharīʿa rules (by obeying these rules). Through the practice of Sharīʿa rules one comes to desire practice of these rules, and even comes to take pleasure in this practice (i.e., in obedience). This is why al-Ghazālī states that one "experiences pleasure in obedience." Moreover, by practicing Sharīʿa rules, one practices abstaining from actions which contravene the Sharīʿa (e.g., gambling, fornication). Through the practice of abstaining from such actions one develops a desire to avoid them, and a hatred for them. Indeed, one comes to experience an emotional feeling of disgust toward them. This is why al-Ghazālī states that one "experiences disgust in disobedience."

Similar ideas are echoed by other scholars. Hence, al-Rāghib al-Iṣfahānī (d. early 5th/11th C) writes that Sharīʿa-compliant ethical practice requires man to do two things: "[1] To abandon evil habits such that he causes himself to hate them. He avoids vices as a means to [acquiring] virtues. [2] To accustom himself to good habits such that he causes himself to prefer them and enjoy them."[98]

To sum up, pious practice of Sharīʿa rules imparts particular desires and emotions. These mental attributes are located in the mind/heart. Muslim religious scholars hold that one may appeal to a pious mind/heart as a criterion of legal interpretation. This is technically known as "seeking rulings from the mind/heart" (*istiftāʾ al-qalb*).[99] Nevertheless, jurists are clear that the procedure in question is only trustworthy when exercised by individuals who live in accordance with Sharīʿa rules. To ignore these rules is to commit sin, which kills off the mind/heart. A dead mind/heart cannot be appealed to in order to distinguish right from wrong and the legally permissible from the prohibited. Al-Ṭabarī (d.310/923) mentions a Hadith report in which the Prophet says: "When the believer commits a sin, a black spot appears on his mind/heart. If he repents and gives up [that sin] and seeks forgiveness, his mind/heart will be polished [and the sin wiped away]. [However] if the sin increases, [the size of the black spot likewise] will increase until it overwhelms his mind/heart." The Hadith report goes on to say that the Prophet associated this process with Verse [83:14] from the Qurʾan. Speaking of evildoers, the verse in question asserts that "what they have acquired [through their deeds] has left a stain on their mind/hearts."[100] Discussing the verse, al-Ṭabarī mentions a number of opinions indicating that when a mind/heart is overwhelmed with the sins it "dies away," "blackens," and becomes "blind."[101]

It is frequently asserted that the guidance provided by the mind/heart is intuitive in nature, and cannot be expressed in words. There are a variety of terms for such guidance. These include "*dhawq*," [102] "*ilhām*,"[103] "*kashf/mukāshafa*,"[104] and "*firāsa*."[105] I will speak of such guidance as "pious intuition."

[98] Al-Iṣfahānī 2007:101. [99] See al-Mansī 2005.

[100] Al-Ṭabarī 2010, 11:440. Also see Ibn Kathīr 2005, 8:319–320. Similar verses include Qur'an [61:5], [4:155], [2:7].

[101] Al-Ṭabarī 2010, 11:441–442. Also see Ibn Kathīr 2005, 8:320; al-Qurṭubī 2010, 10:214–216.

[102] See Madkūr 2010. Also see al-Jabartī n.d., 1:15.

[103] See, e.g., Ibn Taymiyya 2004, 10:470–478; al-Anṣārī 2002, 2:410–411; al-Kinānī 2005:87–211. For more on this matter see al-Zarkashī 2007: v.4 400–403.

[104] See Trieger 2012. [105] Ibn al-Qayyim 2005: j.2 388–398; al-Qusahyrī 2006:380–392.

The strong linkage among knowledge, ethics, and pious intuition was impressed upon me through my conversations with an Azhari scholar named *Shaykh* Maḥmūd. In order to provide a richer picture of these interactions, I reproduce an excerpt from my fieldnotes:

Shaykh *Maḥmūd is in his mid-30s. Of rural origins, he is heavy-set with a long brown beard. He attributes his light skin tone to distant Turkish ancestry. On his mother's side he is descended from a recently deceased* Shaykh *al-Azhar. He has a daughter from his first wife, who passed away. He recently remarried, taking his deceased wife's sister as a spouse.*

Shaykh *Maḥmūd usually wears a jallābiyya-robe when in the vicinity of his home. He opts for slacks and long-sleeve button-down shirts for classes at the university. Every Friday he circulates among various small mosques delivering the weekly sermon. On these occasions he wears the special garb of an Azhar graduate.*

*Unlike the vast majority of his contemporaries, the* shaykh *has invested substantial efforts in memorizing texts. In addition to the Qurʾan, he has committed to memory both the Minhāj of al-Nawawī (about 600 pages) as well as the Saḥīḥ of al-Bukhārī (roughly 1,300 pages).*[106] *The* shaykh *received his bachelor's degree from al-Azhar's Faculty of Sharīʿa. He had begun his MA in the same program when he was asked by national security to work as an informant. His refusal led to his expulsion from al-Azhar. After a period of time studying abroad in India he returned to Egypt and enrolled as an MA student at the Dār al-ʿUlūm. He attended a number of graduate courses which I was auditing, and it was here that I made his acquaintance.*

*The* shaykh *was not wealthy, living in a small inexpensive two-bedroom apartment located on the desert outskirts of Cairo. His building was located in the midst of a cluster of new low-cost residential complexes, most of them still under construction. The lack of paved roads and lighting made the area dangerous after dark. The* shaykh *used the little money he had to amass a sizable private collection of religious books. He also managed to afford a cheap laptop computer and a cell phone.*

Shaykh *Maḥmūd was extraordinarily learned. Among his neighbors, he was also renowned for his deep piety. Given his distinguished attainments, I asked the* shaykh *whether there was any relationship between knowledge and ethics. He responded:*

*"Yes, there is a strong relationship between the two. In Islamic law, a jurist must seek rulings from his mind/heart (istiftāʾ al-qalb). This has been elucidated in the Hadith report recounting the story of Wābiṣa.*

*Wābiṣa went to the Prophet, whereupon the latter said: 'you came to ask about righteousness and sin.' [Wabisa] said: 'yes.' Then the Prophet put his fingers together and struck his chest [i.e. the place of the mind/heart] with them. He said three times: 'O Wābiṣa seek guidance from yourself, seek guidance from your mind/heart.' 'Righteousness is that in which the soul finds peace, in which the mind/heart finds peace. Sin is that which causes discomfort in the soul and hesitation in the chest even if people repeatedly give you an opinion [in favor of its legitimacy].'*

106 The number of pages is highly variable depending on the edition. Accordingly, the above figures should not be used to make precise comparisons between the lengths of texts.

> *On the basis of this Hadith report it is clear that the jurist is guided by his mind/heart. But the mind/heart can only be trusted if it has been purified through ethical living. Those of wicked character cannot properly engage in juristic reasoning because corrupt mind/hearts (qulūb fāsida) produce corrupt legal opinions (fatāwā fāsida). Consider that in reading a text the scholar may be faced with a number of different possible interpretations. What enables him to select the correct one? He must rely on the guidance of his mind/heart to decide which opinion has most weight (tarjīḥ). The reason that a corrupt jurist issues corrupt rulings is that he cannot weigh correctly, because his heart is diseased.*

Thus, *Shaykh* Maḥmūd addresses the situation of a religious scholar whose mind/heart has been "purified through ethical living" (i.e., practice of Sharīʿa rules). Such a scholar may "seek rulings from his mind/heart." It would seem that for such a scholar, emotional feelings of pleasure and disgust are a guide in interpreting Sharīʿa rules. Consider that, through practice of Sharīʿa rules, the scholar now experiences pleasure when obeying Sharīʿa rules and disgust at disobeying them. Suppose that this scholar is not sure about whether a particular action is prohibited by the Sharīʿa. If he looks upon the action as pleasurable, then such is evidence that it is permitted. By contrast, if he experiences disgust toward the action, then such is evidence that it is prohibited. I think that this line of analysis can be used to understand the Hadith report quoted by *Shaykh* Maḥmūd. In the Hadith report, the Prophet states: "Righteousness is that in which the soul finds peace, in which the mind/heart finds peace. Sin is that which causes discomfort in the soul and hesitation in the chest." Now "righteousness" accords with Sharīʿa rules. Meanwhile, "sin" contravenes Sharīʿa rules. Based up the Prophet's statement, a person knows which acts accord with Sharīʿa rules ("righteousness") and which acts contravene Sharīʿa rules ("sin"), based on emotional feelings. Hence, a positive emotional feeling (e.g., peace, pleasure) indicates that an action is permitted by Sharīʿa rules. By contrast, a negative emotional feeling (e.g., discomfort, disgust) indicates that the action is prohibited by Sharīʿa rules.

Notably, Maḥmūd utilizes the technical legal term "*tarjīḥ*" in expressing his views. "*Tarjīḥ*" is the act of judging one interpretation stronger than others.[107] *Tarjīḥ* comes into play when a scholar is not sure about how the Sharīʿa views a particular action. For instance, do Sharīʿa rules permit this action or prohibit it? In such a situation, the scholar first seeks guidance by consulting the relevant textual sources (e.g., the Qurʾan, the Hadith reports). However, he may find that these texts are open to multiple possible interpretations. For instance, on one interpretation, Sharīʿa rules permit the action. Yet, on another interpretation, Sharīʿa rules prohibit the action. The scholar makes *tarjīḥ* in judging one interpretation stronger than the other. For Maḥmūd, pious intuition constitutes a valid form of evidence on the basis of which to make *tarjīḥ*. This basic idea finds expression in a large number of medieval texts.[108] For instance, al-Sarakhsī

[107] Also see Chapter 5 in Hallaq 2001.

[108] For an extensive discussion of this matter see al-Kinānī 2005:87–211.

(d.483/1090) argues that pious intuition is a valid form of evidence when making *tarjīḥ*. He states: "when [the jurist] performs *tarjīḥ* based on pious intuition[109] [thereby giving precedence] to one [of a number of possible interpretations, it is to be accepted that] he has established the rule with a [valid form of] legal evidence (*dalīl sharʿī*)."[110] In support of this idea, al-Sarakhsī cites two statements attributed to the Prophet: "The believer sees with the light of God" and "The intuition (*firāsa*) of the believer does not err."[111]

*Tarjīḥ* is also addressed in a particular passage written by Ibn Taymiyya. This passage is well known among contemporary Egyptian religious scholars, and a number of scholars referenced it when explaining to me the relationship between ethics and knowledge.

In the passage, Ibn Taymiyya argues that the intuition (*ilhām*) of a righteous scholar is a valid form of legal evidence:

> When a mind/heart filled with fear of God (*taqwā*) performs *tarjīḥ* in accordance with its will/intention (*irāda*), such is [considered] a religiously legitimate form of *tarjīḥ* (*tarjīḥ sharʿī*) . . . [Consider the case of] whosoever has a heart which has been taken possession of by a will/intention directed towards that which is desired/loved by God (*mā yuḥibbuhu Allah*), along with a hatred of that which is detested by God. If, with respect to a particular matter, he does not know whether it is desired/loved or hated by God, and he sees that his heart desires/loves it or hates it, this serves as a method of *tarjīḥ* for him. It is akin to receiving information from someone who is more likely to tell the truth than to lie.
>
> Performing *tarjīḥ* based on this information, in the absence of other selection criteria [qualifies] as *tarjīḥ* on the basis of a religiously legitimate form of evidence (*tarjīḥ bi-dalīl sharʿī*). Generally speaking, when [the legal interpreter] believes it is probable that one of two possibilities is more beloved to Allah and His Messenger, this is *tarjīḥ* on the basis of a religiously legitimate form of evidence. Those who categorically deny intuition (*ilhām*) as a [valid] method have erred, as do those who consider it to be a valid method in an unqualified sense [i.e. by following their intuition irrespective of contrary textual indicants].[112]

Thus, Ibn Taymiyya is speaking about a Muslim whose mind/heart desires/loves what is desired/loved by God and hence wills/intends what God wills/intends. It is clear from the context of the passage that the pious Muslim's mind/heart has attained this state through practice of Sharīʿa rules. Therefore, Ibn Taymiyya is saying that a person whose mind/heart has been purified through practice of Sharīʿa rules can use his desires as a guide in interpreting Sharīʿa rules. Suppose, for instance, that a scholar does not know whether Sharīʿa rules prohibit smoking cigarettes or oral sex. He first seeks an answer from textual sources (e.g., the Qurʾan, Hadith reports). Yet these texts are ambiguous. They can be interpreted as permitting cigarettes and oral sex. Alternatively, they

109 "*[R]ajjaḥa aḥadahā bi-nawʿ firāsa.*"
110 Al-Sarakhsī 1993, 2:15–16.
111 Al-Sarakhsī 1993, 2:14.
112 Ibn Taymiyya 2004, 10: 472–473.

can be interpreted as prohibiting cigarettes and oral sex. Consequently, he is forced to decide between these contrary possible interpretations (i.e., perform *tarjīḥ*). Hence, the scholar consults his own desires. He finds that he has a desire to smoke cigarettes. However, he has no desire to engage in oral sex, and experiences disgust at the prospect of such an action. Moreover, he knows that by virtue of practicing Sharīʿa rules, he has come to desire what God desires. Therefore, he decides that Sharīʿa rules permit cigarettes but prohibit oral sex.

To recapitulate: the relationship between ethics and knowledge of Sharīʿa rules can be understood on two levels. The first level involves the mental attribute of skill. Hence, through the practice of Sharīʿa rules an individual acquires knowledge of Sharīʿa rules (i.e., skill in applying them). Such knowledge is largely intuitive and unconscious. The second level involves the mental attributes of desire and emotion. Hence, through the practice of Sharīʿa rules an individual acquires particular desires and emotional feelings (i.e., pleasure, disgust). The individual may use these desires and emotional feelings as guides in interpreting Islamic texts and understanding Sharīʿa rules.

## X. ETHICS AND LEGAL JUDGMENT

I now wish to describe a few instances of religious scholars issuing legal rulings. Nevertheless, while ethnographic observation is helpful, there are limits to how far it can be used to probe the impact of pious intuition on such rulings. For while it is easy to observe the ethical practices whereby the dispositions underlying pious intuition are instilled, it is not possible to observe the intuition itself. Rather such intuition is hidden in the "heart," and hence invisible to the ethnographer. Moreover, as a species of embodied knowledge, intuition cannot be explicitly verbalized into words that the ethnographer can record.

Contemporary Muslim scholars are constantly asked to supply legal rulings. Aside from the tiny fraction who work as judges, the overwhelming majority of requests come outside a courtroom setting. Ordinary Egyptians feel entitled to demand rulings free of charge from scholars whenever they see them. Scholars who teach at universities or mosques are typically approached for rulings after class. It is also common for scholars to be approached after communal prayers at the mosque. Some religious authorities circulate their phone numbers, and are contacted in this manner.

Scholars I observed were confronted with a wide variety of questions. Some were fairly simple and straightforward legal issues. Illustrative examples include a farmer who wanted to know how to calculate religious alms on agricultural produce, and a young man who asked whether his prayer was invalidated by mispronouncing the Qurʾan. On the other hand, there were also many queries involving emotion-laden personal problems embedded in highly complex fact situations. In cases of this type, legal questions frequently blurred into more general requests for spiritual counsel and advice on how to manage social relationships.

As I was sitting with one *shaykh*, we were approached by an unmarried female university graduate in her late 20s. She wore a purple veil and a black abaya. Her father was deceased and she had several sisters. The girl began to cry as she described how her older sisters were ruining the family's reputation in the village where they lived. Not only were they using drugs, but one of them had begun an extramarital relationship with a local boy. All of this had begun to influence the girl's younger sisters. She asked the *shaykh* whether she should flee the corrupting environment of the village household and start a new life in Cairo. Would it be sinful to abandon her younger sisters? After almost an hour of discussion, the *shaykh* recommended that she move to Cairo, giving her the phone number of a pious woman who could help her find work. However, he insisted that she should visit her village home periodically so as to be a positive influence in her sisters' lives.

The aforementioned case raises a number of legal issues. For instance, Islamic law encourages family members to look after one another's moral welfare. Moreover, there are restrictions on an unmarried woman's ability to live on her own. At the same time, matters of this type are regulated by nebulous guidelines that allow much room for juridical discretion. Where there is great scope for discretion, the additional guidance provided by pious intuition would appear to be particularly important.

Even in situations where more detailed textual guidance was available, I noticed that scholarly reasoning was not simply a matter of rigidly applying preexisting doctrine. Consequently, despite the amount of time I had spent studying such doctrine myself, I was often unable to accurately predict a particular scholar's rulings.

During my fieldwork a dispute arose between a divorcing couple with whom I was personally acquainted. The dispute centered on custodial rights over a young child. The couple was religiously observant and wanted a proper Islamic solution. I believed that one of the two sides had clear religious sanction for its demands, and I made my opinion clear. I contacted a Traditionalist *shaykh* I knew (the aforementioned *Shaykh* Maḥmūd), and asked that he confirm to the couple the correctness of my views. In order to make things easy for the *shaykh*, I presented him with extensive textual research that I had done, showing that my opinion had virtually unanimous support from the major authorities. For me, technical doctrinal analysis demonstrated that this was an open-and-shut case. The *shaykh* himself took a different position. He wanted to acquaint himself with the unique details of the individual case at hand and use mediation to arrive at a practical solution. In his eyes, technical doctrine provided a general framework for addressing legal matters, but did not always contain straightforward solutions to specific real-life problems.[113]

[113] Also see Rosen 1989; Hallaq 2009:164–176.

Reformist scholars stress the importance of convincing laypersons to accept their rulings by providing explicit verbalized justifications (*adilla*). By contrast, the *shaykh* believed that laypersons lacked the training to understand and should therefore simply defer (*taqlīd*) to scholarly opinion. For Traditionalists, rulings are based (in part) on intuition shaped through the specialized regimen of ethical discipline characteristic of scholarly training. Such intuition cannot, by its very nature, be articulated or explained verbally.

Traditionalists recognize that intuition may lead different scholars to different opinions. In their view, this is natural. They point out that during the Prophet's life, he himself was willing to tolerate alternative solutions to legal problems as long as certain limits were not transgressed. Interestingly, in evaluating the acceptability of a given opinion, scholars do not limit their attention to its content. They also scrutinize the moral character of its source. To be fully trustworthy, opinions must be issued by scholars characterized by scrupulous piety (*waraᶜ*). One Azhari scholar I spoke with related an anecdote concerning two of the world's foremost living legal authorities: Muḥammad Sa'īd Ramaḍān al-Būṭī and ᶜAbdullah bin Bayya. According to this account, al-Būṭī had come to be concerned by some of the rulings recently issued by his counterpart bin Bayya. These rulings struck al-Būṭī as overly permissive, so he went to pay bin Bayya a visit. When al-Būṭī walked in upon bin Bayya he found him earnestly worshipping God through the recitation of verbal formulae (*dhikr*). Impressed by bin Bayya's worship, al-Būṭī's fears were allayed. Even though he personally did not agree with bin Bayya's rulings, once he ascertained the piety of their issuing source he knew they were worthy of respect. This anecdote illustrates the role of ethics in determining which opinions acquire credibility within Islamic law.

# 4

# Acquiring Knowledge through Companionship (*Ṣuḥba*)

A distinctive feature of premodern Islamic learning was its lack of formal institutional structure. For instance, Jonathan Berkey describes education in medieval Cairo as "fundamentally informal, flexible, and tied to persons rather than institutions."[1] Daphna Ephrat depicts a comparable situation in eleventh century Baghdad. Emphasizing the "marginality" of "any form of organization," Ephrat asserts that learning operated primarily through individual teacher-disciple relationships.[2]

Admittedly, the lack of formal institutional structure found in medieval Arab learning did not necessarily persist into the Ottoman period. Indeed, at the time of the Napoleonic invasion, Egyptian learning had begun a move toward more institutional structure.[3] Still, there was no fundamental break with older models. Egyptian learning certainly did not resemble modern Western education.

If education revolved around informal relationships, how were such created and maintained? Here studies have drawn attention to the aforementioned pedagogy of "companionship" (*ṣuḥba/mulāzama*).[4] In companionship, a student and a religious scholar (i.e., *shaykh*) enter into a long term personal relationship. The scholar often adopts the student into his household as a type of personal servant (i.e., *khidma*).[5] Scholar and student spend their time eating together, worshipping together, and traveling together. The student is expected to continuously observe (*mushāhada*) and imitate (*iqtidāʾ*) the scholar. Meanwhile, the scholar takes on the role of a fatherly teacher, and is expected to continuously monitor and correct (*taʾdīb*) the student's behavior (i.e., *tarbiya*). In this way, the student

[1] Berkey 1992:18. Also see Makdisi:133, 145–146; Ephrat 2000:75; Hallaq 2009:138.

[2] Ephrat 2000:85. Also see Chamberlain 1994:87. Also see Chapter 2 in Chamberlain 1994; Chapter 3 in Hallaq 2009. For a criticism of these views as too extreme see Stewart 2004.

[3] Ottoman influences played an important role in increasing institutionalization. On the other hand, Egyptian educational institutions retained a character different from those in Anatolia. For more on the comparatively institutional character of Ottoman education see Hallaq 2009:155–158; Ahmed and Filipovic 2004); El Shamsy 2008:104–105. For a recent work on Islamic learning in the Arab lands under Ottoman rule see Burak 2013.

[4] Berkey 1992:34; Hallaq 2009:137–138. Also see Makdisi 1981:128–129; Chamberlain 1994:118–122; Ephrat 2000:81–85; El Shamsy 2008:100–101.

[5] See Chamberlain 1994:116–118; El Shamsy 2008:101. Also see Hallaq 2009:138.

The Anthropology of Islamic Law. Aria Nakissa.

acquires knowledge of Sharīʿa rules. As we will see, the pedagogy of companionship persists to this day among Traditionalist scholars at al-Azhar.

The present chapter examines the pedagogy of companionship. However, this pedagogy must be situated in relationship to the broader phenomenon of Islamic learning. As explained previously, in many cultural, legal, and religious traditions, knowledge of rules is learned through a combination of methods. Three of the most important methods are: (1) learning through texts, (2) learning through observation, and (3) learning through practice. Such methods operate together in an integrated fashion because they all contribute to a coherent overall picture of a mind (and, in many traditions, knowledge of rules is knowledge of a mind).

The pedagogy of companionship does not focus on learning through texts. Rather, it combines the methods of learning through observation and learning through practice. Insofar as companionship involves learning through observation it is best explicated using insights from hermeneutic theory. As explained earlier, hermeneutic insights can be applied to companionship in the following way. In the Islamic tradition, religious scholars (ideally) obey God by acting in accordance with His rules/intentions. In other words, religious scholars (ideally) practice Sharīʿa rules, thereby imitating the Prophet and following the Sunna. Since religious scholars act in accordance with God's rules/intentions, their actions are effects (and hence signs) of God's rules/intentions (e.g., God intends that Muslims pray five times a day, and as an effect, religious scholars pray five times a day). Given this situation, God's mental attributes can be inferred from the obedient actions (including statements) of religious scholars. Hence, if a religious scholar refuses to smoke cigarettes, we might infer that it is God's will/intention that Muslims refrain from smoking cigarettes. It may further be inferred that God desires to protect human health and that God believes/knows that smoking is harmful to human health. In companionship, a student constantly observes the obedient actions of his *shaykh* (who is a religious scholar). From these actions, the student infers God's intentions/rules, as well as the desires and beliefs upon which these intentions/rules are based. In other words, by observing the *shaykh*'s actions (i.e., the *shaykh*'s practice of Sharīʿa rules), the student infers knowledge of Sharīʿa rules.

To be sure, the *shaykh*'s actions are not the student's only source of knowledge about Sharīʿa rules (God's mental attributes). After all, God's statements in the Qurʾan, Hadith reports on the Prophet's actions, and reports on the actions of past scholars are also sources of knowledge about Sharīʿa rules. These are all effects/signs of God's mental attributes, just as the obedient actions of the *shaykh* are effects/signs of God's mental attributes. In synthesizing a coherent overall picture of God's mind (i.e., mental attributes), the student will take account of all effects/signs of God's mental attributes.

The pedagogy of companionship also involves learning through practice. Insofar as companionship involves learning through practice it is best explicated using insights from practice theory. As explained earlier, practice theoretical insights can be applied to companionship in the following way. In companionship, the student does not merely observe his *shaykh* to learn knowledge of Sharīʿa rules. The student is also expected to obey these rules himself by practicing them. This involves imitation. Hence, the *shaykh* practices Sharīʿa rules. The student imitates the *shaykh* by practicing the same Sharīʿa rules. Moreover, we will see that the student practices such rules under the watchful eye of the *shaykh*, such that the *shaykh* corrects the student when the student makes a mistake in practicing Sharīʿa rules. For instance, if the student smokes cigarettes, the teacher verbally or physically disciplines the student. In this way, the student learns that there is a Sharīʿa rule prohibiting cigarettes (i.e., that it is God's intention that Muslims refrain from smoking cigarettes). Being exposed to the discipline of the *shaykh*, the student continuously refines his knowledge of Sharīʿa rules (and God's mental attributes). The student likewise continuously adjusts his practice of Sharīʿa rules, for his practice of Sharīʿa rules is based on his knowledge of Sharīʿa rules. It is in this sense that the student gains knowledge of Sharīʿa rules through practice. And it is possible to refer to such knowledge as a skill (i.e., the student knows how to competently apply Sharīʿa rules). As we will see, Muslim scholars associate the pedagogy of companionship with acquiring knowledge of Sharīʿa rules in the form of a skill.

As indicated previously, in companionship, learning through practice cannot be analyzed separately from learning through observation. This is because the student's practice is based upon observing the actions of his *shaykh*. More specifically, the student observes the *shaykh* perform an action (e.g., refrain from cigarette smoking). The student must then infer God's rule/intention from the action (e.g., it is God's rule/intention that Muslims refrain from smoking cigarettes). *It is only after the student has inferred the rule/intention that he can act in accordance with the rule/intention* (i.e., *practice the rule/intention).* I emphasize this point, because practice theorists[6] habitually overlook the fact that the practice of rules (often) requires (hermeneutic) inference of mental attributes from observed actions.

One more remark is in order. To fully appreciate the pedagogy of companionship, we must also attend to its ethical dimension. Hence, the preceding chapter explained that Muslim scholars associate the practice of Sharīʿa rules with the acquisition of various dispositions/mental attributes prescribed by the Sharīʿa. As we will see, since the pedagogy of companionship entails the practice of Sharīʿa rules, it is also tied to the acquisition of dispositions/mental attributes prescribed by the Sharīʿa.

## I. KNOWLEDGE AS A CRAFT

To grasp the educational model underlying companionship it is necessary to examine classical Muslim writings describing the learning of crafts through

[6] E.g., Bourdieu, Asad.

apprenticeship. In premodern times knowledge of the Sharī'a was conceptualized as a "craft" (*ṣināʿa*).[7]

Ibn Khaldūn (d.808/1406) gives an extensive treatment of this issue in his *Muqaddima*. For Ibn Khaldūn, knowledge of a craft exists in the form of a disposition (*malaka*), which he defines as a mental attribute acquired through practice.[8] Although there are many types of disposition/mental attributes, Ibn Khaldūn is largely interested in skills. Hence, his idea is that through the practice of making swords or speaking Arabic one acquires knowledge of how to make swords or speak Arabic, and such knowledge exists in the form of a disposition/skill.

Thus, Ibn Khaldūn's account of craft-learning centers on knowledge in the form of a disposition. He distinguishes this disposition-based type of knowledge from knowledge which can be expressed and communicated in words. Accordingly, Ibn Khaldūn rejects the idea that a disposition can be acquired from written texts. Rather he holds that a disposition can only be acquired with the help of a teacher ("*lā budda . . . min al-muʿallim*").[9]

For Ibn Khaldūn, a disposition can be acquired from a teacher in two ways. First, there is instruction through direct observation ("*naql al-muʿāyana*"). This involves teaching by example. The teacher executes the practice associated with the disposition in front of the student, so that the latter can observe and imitate him.[10] For instance, the teacher might execute the practice of sword-making or Arabic-speaking in front of the student, so the student can observe it and imitate it. The second mode of instruction mentioned by Ibn Khaldūn is teaching by words ("*naql al-khabar wa al-'ilm*"). It is not clear exactly what he intends here. He may mean that the teacher actively directs the student's practice through comments, instructions, and the citation of relevant texts (e.g., texts on sword-making or Arabic speaking). Alternatively, he may simply mean that the teacher offers comments, instructions, and text citations without overseeing the student's practice. This would still differ from book learning in that a teacher (unlike a book) can answer questions and discuss matters with the student.

In any event, Ibn Khaldūn stresses that of the two methods, teaching by example is superior. It transmits knowledge "more comprehensively and fully (*awʿab wa-atamm*)," producing a disposition that is "more complete and deeply rooted (*akmal wa-arsakh*)."[11]

The fact that the student takes his knowledge from a teacher means that the disposition acquired is a replica of the teacher's.[12] In other words the teacher transmits his dispositions to the student, such that the student comes to possess the same dispositions.

[7] Mitchell 1991:82; Messick 1993:104. Also see, e.g., al-Taftāzānī n.d., 1:30; al-Zarnūjī 2004:64; al-Dihlawī 1398h: 21; Lapidus 1984.

[8] Ibn Khaldūn 2010, 2:856. [9] Ibn Khaldūn 2010, 2:856.

[10] On the importance of bodily imitation in Islamic learning see Chamberlain 1994:123.

[11] Ibn Khaldūn 2010, 2:856.

[12] Ibn Khaldūn says: "the skill of the student and the habitus that he acquires in the craft is commensurate with the quality of the instruction [he receives] and the habitus (*malaka*) possessed by the teacher." Ibn Khaldūn 2010, 2:856.

Ibn Khaldūn sees his schema as applying to all varieties of crafts. Like other premodern Muslim scholars, he views knowledge of Sharīʿa rules as one such craft.[13] Given that it is a craft, transmitting knowledge of Sharīʿa rules means transmitting dispositions through practice.

The pedagogy of companionship operates as a mechanism for the transmission of dispositions within the framework of craft-apprenticeship outlined by Ibn Khaldūn. Thus, for Ibn Khadun, in craft-apprenticeship, a student directly observes a teacher and imitates the latter's practice of the craft until he acquires knowledge of the craft in form of a disposition. In companionship, a student directly observes a religious teacher and imitates the latter's practice of Sharīʿa rules until he acquires knowledge of Sharīʿa rules in form of a disposition (or multiple dispositions). Nevertheless, we will see that companionship has a number of other distinctive features.

## II. COMPANIONSHIP

Muslim religious scholars trace the basic idea of companionship back to the life of the Prophet. Hence, it is held that the earliest converts to Islam shared in a form of companionship with the Prophet. Indeed, such is reckoned as their defining characteristic. Hence, the first generation of Muslims is known as the "Companions" (*al-Ṣaḥāba*).[14] Muslim sources portray the more senior Companions as having passed one to two decades constantly participating in the daily life of the Prophet, rarely leaving his side.[15] This meant spending their days with him in his home, praying with him in the mosque, traveling with him on journeys, and riding by his side in wars. During these activities, the Companions constantly observed the Prophet and made a conscious effort to imitate his behavior (i.e., follow his Sunna). In the process of spending their lives together, the Prophet formed intimate personal bonds with his Companions.

In the view of (Sunni) Muslim scholars, the companionship of the early Muslims is an ideal model of learning. Such learning does not merely involve observing and imitating a religious authority. It also involves forming a personal bond with the religious authority and sharing in his mundane everyday affairs over an extended period of time. Because the Companions learned from the Prophet in this way, they are recognized as having a unique level of religious knowledge not possessed by later generations. The Prophet's closest and oldest Companions are seen as the most knowledgeable. Many such figures intermarried into the Prophet's family and become part of his extended household. The

[13] Ibn Khaldūn 2010, 3:948.

[14] For a discussion of how the term "Companion" is understood in legal discourse see Jumʿa 2004:7–38. Companionship is taken to be an attribute that admits of many different degrees. The longer the amount of time spent with the Prophet, the higher one's level of companionship. See Ibn Taymiyya 2004, 20:298.

[15] Also see Makdisi 1981:129.

first four Caliphs and the Prophet's wives fall into this category. For this reason, they are considered to be paramount legal authorities in (Sunni) Islam.

## III. COMPANIONSHIP AMONG LATER SCHOLARS

Later generations patterned their educational methods on those ascribed to the first Muslims. The select senior students of a religious scholar (*shaykh*) were called his "Companions" ("*Aṣḥāb*"),[16] and they strove to share in his life the same way that the original Companions had shared in the life of the Prophet. Although the constant company of students could grate on a teacher's nerves, it was seen as a necessary part of the learning process. Al-Ājurī (d.360/970) counsels the teacher "not be become impatient with his companions due to the large amount of [their] companionship (*li-kathra ṣuḥba*)," assuring him that his labor will be rewarded by God.[17] Ibn Jamāʿa (d.733/1333), an educational authority constantly cited by scholars both past and present, offers similar advice to students. Enduring companionship is necessary and beneficial. "The length of [the period of] companionship [with a teacher] must not make you feel as though you have had enough. [The teacher] is like a date-palm. You wait for the time at which something from it falls to you."[18] In premodern times, companionship could involve students regularly dining with their teachers or even living under the same roof. Personal bonds were often cemented by a marriage between the student and one of the teacher's daughters.[19]

Muslim biographical dictionaries bear witness to the importance of companionship, routinely singling it out as a central element of a scholar's life history. Al-Jabartī's (d.1825) famous dictionary is no exception. Depicting scholarly life in Egypt, the entries highlight how *shaykhs* living around the time of Napoleon's invasion took their knowledge through companionship (*mulāzama*). The companionship spoken of by al-Jabartī admits of various degrees. The highest is called "general" or "complete" companionship ("*mulāzama kulliyya*"[20]). It is clear that for al-Jabartī, companionship is not merely limited to the taking of academic information. For instance, describing the life history of one *shaykh*, he records how he "gained admission to the inner circle of his teacher's companions and took upon himself his [teacher's] dispositions (*Ṣāra min khāṣṣa mulāzimīhi wa-takhallaqa bi-akhlāqihi*),"[21]

A particularly vivid illustration of companionship can be found in a passage wherein al-Jabartī recounts the life of his father Ḥasan, a religious authority of some prominence:

> [Ḥasan] viewed busying oneself with matters unrelated to knowledge as pointless. Whenever a student came to him, he was delighted. He devoted himself to [that

[16] Berkey 1992:34; Chamberlain 1994:121–122; Ephrat 2000:81; Hallaq 2009:137–138. Also see Makdisi 1981:92–93; Makdisi 1991: 239.

[17] Al-Ājurī 1985:31.

[18] Ibn Jamāʿa 2009:96.

[19] Hallaq 2009:137. Also see Ephrat 2000:83.

[20] See, e.g., al-Jabartī n.d., 1:118; 3:109, 145.

[21] Al-Jabartī n.d., 3:47.

> student], encouraged him, and treated him hospitably— especially if he was a foreigner. Oftentimes, he invited a student to discourse with him at his [home], and [the student] became one of his household. There were some who resided [with him] for twenty years. They slept and woke up [there], and they did not burden themselves with anything related to their daily living—even washing their clothes. And this was not [regarded as] wearisome or annoying [by Ḥasan].

Al-Jabartī continues on to describe how Ḥasan interacted with his closest students as if they were "his children." Two in particular are said to have virtually never left his side. To keep his students from getting bored, Ḥasan would mix his teaching with other lighter pursuits. He entertained pupils with jokes and stories, and would recite poetry to them.[22]

Another glimpse into companionship as it existed in this era is provided by the Englishman Edward Lane. Lane spent a substantial amount of time in Egypt, being a near contemporary of al-Jabartī. He describes the earliest phases of companionship, focusing on younger pupils:

> A sheykh who had studied in the Azhar, if he had only two boys, son of a moderately rich fellah, to educate, lived in luxury. His two pupils served him, cleaned his house, prepared his food, and though they partook of it with him, were his menial attendants at every time but that of eating: they followed him whenever he went out, carried his shoes (and often kissed them when they took them off) on his entering a mosque, and in every case treated him with the honor due to a prince.[23]

Lane's portrait of companionship in nineteenth-century Egypt is generally consistent with what Jonathan Berkey has found in the earlier Mamluk period. Berkey writes:

> In all respects a student was expected to behave towards his *shaykh* as a dutiful son to his father. His responsibilities extended to: physically shielding his *shaykh* from pressing crowds of people, approaching him only with clean clothing, clipped nails, and trimmed hair, and without unpleasant bodily odors, caring for his teacher's children and descendants, and, as a virtual member of his extended family, visiting the dead *shaykh*'s tomb.[24]

The descriptions offered by Lane and Berkeley highlight an important feature of companionship. In companionship, a student often offers himself as a sort of personal servant to the teacher (*khidma*).[25] By doing so, the student seeks to convince the teacher that his constant company will be helpful rather than burdensome.

It is easy to see the benefits that a system of this kind afforded teachers. But students were highly motivated to participate as well. Because knowledge was seen as being transmitted by companionship, constantly sharing in the intimate company of a teacher was the surest means of staking a claim to his epistemic

22 Al-Jabartī n.d., 1:458–459. 23 Lane 2005[1836]: 215. 24 Berkey 1992:36
25 See Chamberlain 1994:116–118; El Shamsy 2008:101. Also see Hallaq 2009:138.

authority and status. Being chosen as the companion of a famous *shaykh* provided a path to the top of the scholarly hierarchy. Al-Zarnūjī records an illustrative anecdote about a scholar "who was the chief religious authority in Marw, and whom the Sultan respected to the utmost degree. He used to say: I have only come into possession of this status by serving the master (*bi-khidma al-ustādh*) [Abū Zayd al-Dabūsī]. . . . I used to serve him and cook his food for thirty years, not eating from it at all.[26]

Because a *shaykh* could only have a few close companions (even if he had many students), being accepted to personally serve a prominent *shaykh* was among the most coveted and vied for of honors. In premodern times, a *shaykh*'s blood relatives often received preference. For this reason, religious authority was often tightly linked to specific families. Another means of gaining the privilege in question was by exhibiting exceptional intellectual and moral gifts. The right opportunity might present itself at various phases of a scholar's career. If contemporary practice is any indication, being taken as a companion by a famous *shaykh* was an attractive proposition even for established scholars in their 30s and 40s.

For a Traditionalist minority of modern Egyptian scholars, companionship retains its prized status. One distinguished Azhari scholar in his mid-30s spoke of how, with the assistance of some well-placed associates, he had been offered the privilege of leaving his graduate studies in Egypt to become the personal servant of a leading authority in Syria. Although a number of personal and political reasons prevented him from going abroad at present, he emphasized that it was his most ardent desire to do so as soon as he was able. When I asked him what he hoped to learn, he replied that companionship revolves around observation. "A student must pay attention to the smallest details of his teacher's behavior. If someone comes to question his *shaykh*, the student cannot merely focus on the answer given. He must also scrutinize how the *shaykh* reacts to the type of question. Does he smile, frown, or keep silent? It is by paying attention to these details that the student learns how to react to questions himself."

In the first months of my research my own relationship with this scholar began to develop in the direction of companionship, even though I did not recognize it at the time. We began sharing meals multiple times a week. We would spend entire days together, going to mosques, visiting bookstores, and discussing Islamic doctrine. The *shaykh* was relatively poor, considering the prices at Kentucky Fried Chicken to be exorbitantly expensive. But his impecuniousness did not prevent him from being as generous as he was able. In addition to food, he gifted me various books. He even offered me the key to his house, letting me know that I could sleep there overnight if I needed to. He never asked for anything in return, and constantly refused the financial assistance I tried to offer him. One of his neighbors confided in me that he was secretly a "big Sufi" master who concealed his saintly status from others. Anyhow, I began to feel

[26] Al-Zarnūjī 2004:27.

that all of our time together was detracting from my research. How was I supposed to probe the nature of Islamic learning if I was wasting my days and nights sharing in the mundane everyday affairs of a *shaykh*? These misguided sentiments on my part, combined with personal circumstances in the *shaykh*'s own life, caused us to drift apart.

My interactions with another Azhar scholar named Shaykh Karīm offer further insight into companionship as practiced by contemporary religious authorities. In order to provide a richer picture of these interactions, I reproduce an excerpt from my fieldnotes:

> *Shaykh Karīm is about sixty years of age. He holds an undergraduate degree from al-Azhar's Faculty of Sharīʿa. Barrel-chested, with a thick pepper-grey beard, the* shaykh *dresses in a robe and knit cap. He serves as custodian of a lodge located close to al-Azhar mosque, rarely leaving the premises.*
>
> *The lodge is located on the ground floor of an apartment building. The doorway of the lodge opens up on to a dusty unpaved alleyway. The lodge itself consists of two floors—one above ground and the other below. Each is rectangular in shape, the size of a large living room. There is pale green wall-to-wall carpeting. Much of it is covered over by thick red oriental rugs. The lodge's inner walls are plain white, adorned with photographs of contemporary religious personalities. Guests sit upon rectangular brownish-yellow cushions arrayed on the floor against the sides of the walls. There are no couches or tables.*
>
> *The lodge is used for assorted religious functions. Most importantly, it hosts study-circles taught by scholars affiliated with al-Azhar. (Shaykh Karīm himself does not teach). The study-circles meet seven days-a-week. On Fridays and Wednesdays there is only one study-circle. On Tuesday there are six. On other days there are two, three, or four. The study-circles are scheduled around the prayer times and take place on the bottom floor. They are open to the public, but most attendees are students enrolled at al-Azhar University.*
>
> *Prominently displayed on one of the walls is a framed photograph of Shaykh Karīm's own teacher, after which the lodge is named. A graduate of al-Azhar, he was one of Egypt's most eminent religious authorities. He passed away a little over a decade ago. Shaykh Karīm's eyes would light up and he would begin smiling whenever he spoke about his teacher.*
>
> *"My* shaykh *was a very special man. The thing that I loved about him was that his inside (bāṭin) was like his outside (ẓāhir). Both were so pure. Sometimes you find a person whose external behavior is good, but you do not know what he has inside of him.*
>
> *My* shaykh *had such a love of the poor. He constantly gave them money. He used to own a three-story building. But he gave it away in charity, moving into a smaller apartment. The* shaykh *also had a severe and courageous temperament. Despite his forcefulness [and hence political dangerousness] even the head of national security was obliged to respect him, and used to kiss his hand. Do you know Gamāl ʿAbd al-Nāṣir? He was a real tyrant. All the tyrants we have in the Arab world right now, like Ḥusnī Mubārak and Bashār al-Asad, are ʿAbd al-Nāṣir's pupils.*[27] *Well, one day the* shaykh *climbed the pulpit and shocked everyone around*

[27] This was spoken after the revolution had toppled Mubārak and while Asad's regime in Syria was facing serious unrest.

*him by fearlessly denouncing 'Abd al-Nāṣir, saying: 'a donkey has taken over the country.' After that the* shaykh *was put in jail, where he was locked-up alongside prostitutes. Eventually he was let out. But his time in jail only increased his stature in the eyes of the people.*

*As a child I lived in the same neighborhood as the* shaykh*. That is how I got to know him. When I was ten years old I began studying with him. Two days a week we would meet for private lessons in his home. On other days he would preside over public study-circles at various mosques. Some other young pupils and I would follow the* shaykh *around wherever he taught.*

*The* shaykh *taught me many things about proper learning. He used to say, 'whoever takes knowledge from books has taken the devil as his* shaykh*'. He taught us that not only every book, but every single word, must be read over with a teacher to ensure correct understanding.*

*The* shaykh *developed a personal relationship with me. For us, lessons were mixed with eating together and talking about our personal affairs. I saw the* shaykh *daily and remained his pupil for forty years until his death. He was like my father, and gave me my upbringing (tarbiya). He taught me in accordance with the example (qudwa) of the Prophet, who instructed those around him by forming bonds of companionship (ṣuḥba) with them."*

A further example of present day companionship among senior scholars was reported to me secondhand by a student at al-Azhar. It concerns an internationally renowned scholar over 50 years of age. This scholar had succeeded in obtaining permission to spend months at a time every year with an even more famous *shaykh*. Companionship in this case involved the less senior of the two traveling around the world with his mentor and humbly serving him. The student who reported this to me was granted the opportunity to have dinner with the two, speaking mostly with the less senior *shaykh*. When I asked him to describe what he had taken away from these conversations he reported how the *shaykh* had talked about his mentor's dietary preferences, and the need to make sure that the latter's yogurt was seasoned with just the right amount of sugar.

Although concern with minutiae of this type may seem odd, it is very much at the core of companionship. Earlier on, we saw that Muslim scholars have long demonstrated an intense preoccupation with the smallest details of the Prophet's practice. Because the *shaykh* serves as a living replica of the Prophet, the minutiae of his practice are likewise viewed as worthy of attention.

## IV. SONS AND FATHERS

Within the practice of companionship, the relationship between scholar and student is seen as being akin to that between father and son.[28] Al-Qābisī (d.403/1012) describes the teacher as "the one whose manners are copied, the supervisor who restrains [students] from that which is inappropriate, and the one who likewise undertakes to force upon them that which is beneficial. In all of this, he

[28] Berkey 1992:36–37; Chamberlain 1994:110; Ephrat 2000:83; Hallaq 2009:137.

guides them with what benefits them. Such does not prevent him from treating them with good kindness and compassion, for he is to them but a substitute for their fathers."[29] Ibn Jamāʿa advises the teacher that "he must take a concern in the affairs of the student and treat him the way he treats the most beloved of his children, in terms of compassion, sympathy, and kindness towards him."[30] The contemporary Azhari Ṭalʿat Muḥammad ʿAfīfī affirms that "it is necessary for the teacher to develop a relationship of love and affection with his students, exactly like that of a father."[31] For ʿAfīfī, this involves giving them moral counsel, inquiring into their personal and monetary problems, assisting them from one's own financial resources where possible, and visiting them in their homes.[32] In present day Traditionalist circles, even scholars who are very advanced in age refer to their *shaykhs* as their "spiritual" fathers,[33] speaking of them with the deepest tenderness and affection.

As "father" and "son," teacher and student opened up the intimacies of their lives to one another. The teacher took charge of the student's upbringing. The student submitted himself to fatherly advice and care. The fact that students were commonly entrusted to the care of *shaykhs* while still young boys helped invite such relationships. The tendency to conceptualize students as sons was also reinforced by the fact that knowledge frequently circulated in scholarly families where pupils learned at the feet of their actual fathers or close blood relatives.[34] In eighteenth century Egypt, ties of blood are known to have played an important role in education.[35]

Premodern *shaykhs* viewed shaping their "sons'" dispositions (*akhlāq*) as among their chief responsibilities—perhaps the most important. Ibn Jamāʿa opens his treatise on education by citing a Qurʾanic verse praising the Prophet for possessing virtuous dispositions ("*innaka la-ʿalā khuluq ʿaẓīm*").[36] In doing so, he signals that acquiring proper dispositions lies at the heart of the learning process. Ibn Jamāʿa then proceeds to mention a number of quotations which affirm that the behavior and manners taught by teachers are of greater importance than their lessons in doctrine. He cites one statement wherein a father exclaims: "O my son, I prefer that you know one unit of good manners than that you learn seventy units of [religious] knowledge." He quotes another father saying: 'O my son, take as your companions (*iṣḥab*) the jurists and the scholars; learn from them and take their manners. That is more beloved to me than much [knowledge of] *ḥadīth* reports."[37]

Writing around 1900, future *Shaykh al-Azhar* al-Ẓawāhirī states that certification as a scholar must not be given to those of poor character regardless of their intellectual abilities. "None must obtain it except those of noble dispositions, even if their knowledge does not rise above a middling grade."[38] The Azhari Yūsuf

[29] Al-Qābisī 1986:128. [30] Ibn Jamāʿa 2009:69. [31] ʿAfīfī 2005:48.
[32] ʿAfīfī 2005:50–51. [33] Also see ʿAfīfī 2005:48; Khafājī 1987, 2:120.
[34] See, e.g., Berkey 1992:169. [35] See Heyworth-Dunne 1939:36.
[36] Qur'an [68:4]. Ibn Jamāʿa 2009:27. [37] Ibn Jamāʿa 2009:28.
[38] Al-Ẓawāhirī 1904:58.

al-Dijwī (d.1948) approvingly quotes the maxim: "our need for a small amount of [good] manners is greater than our need for an abundance of knowledge."[39] Even today, Traditionalist authorities often remark that the student must concern himself with taking a *shaykh*'s manners (*adab*) before taking his knowledge.

## V. THE STRUCTURE OF COMPANIONSHIP

The preceding sections provide an overall sense of what is involved in companionship. However, at this point, I wish to take a closer look at three key features of companionship. First, I will examine how companionship involves the method of learning through observation (i.e., observation of a living *shaykh*). Second, I will examine how companionship involves the method of learning through practice (i.e., the student imitates the practice of the *shaykh*). Third, I will examine how *shaykhs* utilize punishment as a means to ensure that student practice is consistent with the Sharīʿa.

## VI. COMPANIONSHIP AND LEARNING THROUGH OBSERVATION

The first component of companionship consists in learning through observation of the actions of a living *shaykh*. We have already come across the idea of learning through observation in Ibn Khaldūn, where he emphasizes that it is a more effective means of teaching than verbal communication. This view is standard in Islamic legal texts. Al-Ījī (d.756/1355) states: "Directly observing a practice clarifies it better than being informed about it. For that reason it is said in the widely-known adage: 'A report is unlike seeing with one's own eyes.'"[40] Al-Ījī notes that the Prophet himself taught various religious practices by performing them in front of others. Hence, the Prophet "clarified prayer and pilgrimage through his [nonverbal] actions (*bayyana al-ṣalāh wa-l-ḥajj bi-l-fiʿl*)."[41]

The importance of learning through direct observation is frequently broached in juristic discussions concerning the Prophet's Companions. They are accorded paramount epistemic status on account of having directly witnessed the Prophet's practice of Sharīʿa rules (i.e., the Sunna).

A very ancient and rudimentary expression of this view can be traced to Imam Mālik (d.179/795). Mālik explains the authoritative nature of the Companions' knowledge as follows: "the Prophet—peace be upon him—was present in their midst. They were present as the revelation was sent down. He ordered them and they obeyed him. He laid down the *Sunna* and they followed it. [This continued] until [the Prophet] died."[42] Here Mālik highlights the fact that the Prophet was

[39] Al-Dijwī 1981, 2:532. [40] "*Laysa al-khabar ka-l-muʿāyana.*" [41] Al-Ījī, 3:125.
[42] Quoted in Abū Zahra 2002:265.

personally present among the Companions, giving them firsthand knowledge of the revelation. They learned the Sunna from him, and this process continued over time until the Prophet's death. Mālik's own comments are fragmentary, but they are expanded upon by later writers.

Explaining the unique status of the Companions' opinions, Ibn al-Qayyim (d.751/1350) foregrounds the significance of direct observation. The longer it is done, the greater its epistemic value. For Ibn al-Qayyim, the Companions' views are:

> based on [knowledge] of the context within which [the Prophet's] speech was given, or on [knowledge] of the totality of matters understood by [the Companions], attributable to the length of time they had [spent] watching the Prophet—peace and blessings be upon him—his deeds, his situations, his life, and hearing his speech, and their knowledge of his aims, and their witnessing the sending down of the revelation, and their watching [the Prophet] interpret it by means of his actions, such that [with respect to the rule in question, the Companion is able to] understand that which we ourselves do not understand.[43]

Speaking of the Companions, al-Sarakhsī (d.483/1090) states:

> their opinions are stronger than those of others, because they directly witnessed the manner in which the Messenger of God—peace and blessings be upon him—made clear the [appropriate] rules for [different] events and likewise they witnessed the conditions in which the divine texts were revealed as well as the causes which occasioned changes in the rules. For these reasons their opinions are to be given more weight than those who have not directly witnessed any of these things.

Al-Sarakhsī proceeds to affirm a substantial epistemic gulf ("*al-tafāwut*") separating the people of his era from the generation of the Companions, rebutting the notion that both are equal in knowledge. Justifying his view, he stresses that the Companions "[directly] observed (*shāhadū*) the circumstances of he to whom the revelation was sent down [i.e. the Prophet] and [directly] took knowledge from him orally (*samiʿū minhu*). These things have only come to us in the form of textual reports transmitted through [the Companions] and a textual report [on something] is not like directly seeing [it]."[44] Al-Sarakhsī not only values direct witnessing, but explicitly privileges it over purely textual knowledge.[45]

In these texts, we see that the Companions acquired a special knowledge of Sharīʿa rules through direct observation of the Prophet's practice of Sharīʿa rules (i.e., the Sunna). In acquiring knowledge in this manner, the Companions set an example for later generations. On the other hand, later generations cannot observe the Prophet practice of Sharīʿa rules (Sunna). Instead, they observe the practice of their teachers (who follow the Sunna). Thus, while the Companions learned the Sharīʿa rule mandating five daily prayers by seeing the Prophet pray

[43] Ibn al-Qayyim 2004, 4:406. [44] Al-Sarakhsī 1993, 2:108–109.
[45] Also see Al-Ghazālī 2004a, 1:29; al-Shātibī 2004:670.

five times a day, later generations learn the Sharīʿa rule mandating five daily prayers by seeing later religious scholars pray five times a day.

One Traditionalist scholar I spoke with quoted an anecdote wherein a student is asked whether the Prophet wore trousers. The student's response was not to look for the answer in any book. Instead, he approached his *shaykh*, who was known for his strict adherence to the Sunna. When he entered upon his *shaykh* he found the latter wearing trousers. Returning to the questioner, the student replied that, given what he had seen from his *shaykh*, the Prophet also wore trousers. The preceding anecdote not only conveys the epistemic value of direct observation, but also reflects the idea that latter-day *shaykhs* precisely transmit the Prophetic Sunna in living form.

Here it is worth re-emphasizing an important hermeneutic insight mentioned earlier. Schutz asserts that it is possible to (unconsciously) infer mental attributes from texts. Yet, Schutz holds that one may (unconsciously) infer far more information about mental attributes by observing actions over a span of time (1967[1932]:139–214; Schutz and Luckmann 1973:16–17, 61–68). This idea is important for understanding the role of observation in companionship. Thus, suppose that a Muslim student observes his *shaykh*'s actions over a sustained period of time (e.g., the student sees how the *shaykh* fasts during Ramadan, how the *shaykh* prays, which clothes are worn by the *shaykh*). From observing many thousands (or millions) of the *shaykh*'s actions, the student constructs an increasingly detailed model of God's mind through unconscious inferences. As noted earlier, these inferences not only relate to God's intentions, but also to His desires and beliefs. Thus, if a student sees his *shaykh* avoid gazing at the faces of women (e.g., in the street), he not only infers that God intends/wills that Muslim men avoid gazing at the faces of women. The student also infers that God desires to prevent extramarital sex, and that God believes that gazing at the faces of women leads to extramarital sex. Once again, as emphasized by Schutz, unconscious inferences produce an enormous but (largely unconscious) stock of knowledge. Hence, by observing the actions of their *shaykhs*, students come to possess an enormous but largely unconscious knowledge of God's mind.

For Muslims scholars, observation is closely tied to acquiring dispositions. Accordingly, Islamic texts assert that a *shaykh* may mold the dispositions of his students by putting himself forth as an example to be observed. Thus, the medieval scholar Ibn Jamāʿa asserts that if a scholar is righteous, students can "acquire good dispositions and manners from him."[46] This requires constantly mirroring his behavior. The student must "follow the way [of his *shaykh*], observing his habits with respect to knowledge and religion, imitating his movements and his stillnesses in acts of worship and other affairs, copying his manners and not leaving off imitating him."[47] I think Ibn Jamāʿa is saying something along the following lines. The *shaykh* practices Sharīʿa rules, thereby acquiring the dispositions prescribed by the Sharīʿa. The student directly observes the *shaykh*'s

[46] Ibn Jamāʿa 2009:89. [47] Ibn Jamāʿa 2009:92.

practice of Sharīʿa rules. The student then imitates the *shaykh* by practicing these same Sharīʿa rules. In practicing these Sharīʿa rules the student also acquires the dispositions prescribed by the Sharīʿa. In this way the student has acquired the same dispositions as the *shaykh* (i.e., those prescribed by the Sharīʿa).

It is not only medieval scholars who emphasize the value of direct observation. Similar ideas can also be found in the modern period.[48] The late *Shaykh al-Azhar* Muḥammad Sayyid Ṭanṭāwī (d.2010) emphasizes the importance of direct observation, with specific reference to the goal of acquiring dispositions:

> Beautiful dispositions are not produced from mere speech alone, but rather are only produced, in their most perfect and superior form, by means of a beautiful model, a good exemplar, and [the exhibition of] praiseworthy manners. . . . The Prophet was, among his Companions, the most elevated example of the dispositions he preached. He implanted these sublime dispositions in his Companions by the excellent way he lived his life before he implanted them through speaking in terms of legal rulings and sermons.[49]

## VII. DIRECT WITNESSING AND BARAKA

When scholars speak about the value of direct observation, their attention is not restricted solely to the visible. Rather, they are concerned with the totality of contextual sensory data available to one who is physically present while a practice is performed. A full understanding of this issue requires exploring the relationship between learning through companionship and the acquisition of "*baraka*."

While the precise nature of "*baraka*" is a disputed matter, most Traditionalist Muslim scholars conceive of it as a kind of supernatural force containing God's blessings.[50] A defining feature of *baraka* is the fact that it, along with its blessings, can be transferred through physical proximity. Although *baraka* may reside in any number of places, its paradigmatic locus is a righteous scholar. God endows the scholar with *baraka* owing to his piety. Those wishing to share in this *baraka* can do so by keeping close physical proximity to the scholar, directing their vision toward him, and even touching him.[51] In contemporary Egypt, kissing a *shaykh*'s hand upon his entrance or exit from a religious gathering is one common way of seeking *baraka*.[52] Another is kissing or rubbing prayer mats on a scholar's grave.[53]

*Baraka* is linked to blessings of various types, such as health, abundant children, and material prosperity. However, among scholarly circles it is very tightly

[48] See, e.g., Ḥasb Allah 1997:5; al-Dusūqī 2009:26

[49] Ṭanṭāwī 2003:219–220. Also see ʿAfīfī 2005:36, 42.

[50] For references to "*baraka*" in contemporary Egypt see, e.g., Hoffman 1995:4, 92; J. Johansen:1996:9, 53.

[51] Hoffman 1995:95–96.

[52] Also see al-Jabartī n.d., 1:446.

[53] See J. Johansen 1996:155–156.

connected to the acquisition of knowledge, which is considered to be one of God's greatest blessings.[54] In fact, many of the scholars I interviewed associated taking a *shaykh*'s *baraka* almost exclusively with taking his knowledge. On this view, by virtue of close physical proximity to a scholar, God supernaturally blesses a student with enhanced understanding of the Sharīʿa. It is at this point that seeking *baraka* and learning through companionship begin to merge into one another. Both result in the acquisition of knowledge through close physical proximity. The difference is that whereas the *baraka* route is supernatural, companionship (including its element of direct observation) operates in a manner intelligible to reason.

Muslim scholars believe that the two methods are intertwined. Thus, al-Shāṭibī refers to:

> a special characteristic that God—the Exalted—has placed between the teacher and the student, witnessed by all those who devote themselves to knowledge and to scholars. How many times does a student read about a matter (*masʾala*) in a book, memorizing it and repeating it in this mind, but [nevertheless] not understanding it? Then when it is directed to him by a teacher, he understands it immediately and acquires knowledge of it by virtue of the [teacher's] presence. This understanding is either acquired through contextual data related to the situation, which is not supernatural in nature (*bi-amr ʿādī min qarāʾin aḥwāl*), and which clarifies the problem for the student in an unexpected way. Or perhaps [the understanding] is acquired through supernatural [assistance] (*bi-amr ghayr ʿādī*), which God gifts to the student while he is present before the teacher and while he is in clear need of what is bestowed upon him.[55]

Hence, al-Shāṭibī recognizes that the physical presence of scholars can generate knowledge through means both ordinary and supernatural. The former revolve around "contextual data related to the situation," whereas the latter hinge on a direct blessing from God. This is an implicit reference to *baraka*.

Other scholars are more explicit. Ibn al-Ḥājj (d.737/1336) asserts that the student of religious knowledge:

> should not neglect visiting the saints and the pious. Through looking upon them God brings dead hearts to life as He brings the earth to life through a heavy rain shower. It is by them that constricted chests find relaxation, and by looking upon them that difficult matters become easy . . . It is necessary to hasten to look upon them and take their *baraka*. This is because by looking upon one of them [the student] acquires what is perhaps impossible to describe with respect to understanding and ability to memorize, as well as other things.[56]

Mayyāra (d.1071/1662) records an anecdote about Ibn Surayj (d.306/918), a founding figure of the Shāfiʿī school famous for the sharpness of his intellect. Ibn Surayj was passing by the lessons of the Sufi master Junayd, whereupon

[54] Also see Chamberlain 1994:122.
[55] Al-Shāṭibī 2004:56.
[56] Ibn al-Ḥājj 2008, 1:j.2 118.

he was struck by the force of the latter's words. Subsequently, Ibn Surayj kept the constant company of Junayd ("*ṣaḥabahu wa-lāzamahu*"). Immediately after mentioning Junayd's companionship, the anecdote continues to describe how this process boosted Ibn Surayj's already scintillating intellectual capacities to new heights. "When [Ibn Surayj] spoke about general [religious] principles and specific [religious] rules he dazzled the minds [of those who heard him]. He said: 'this is due to the *baraka* from sitting with Abū al-Qāsim al-Junayd.' "[57]

Sometimes the medium for supernatural transmission of knowledge is spoken of as "light" (*nūr*) rather than *baraka*. The two terms are often used more or less interchangeably. One *shaykh* explained to me: "knowledge is light, and this light is not contained in written lines. Rather it is located in the heart, passing from one scholar to another through personal instruction." This is a very common view of medieval origins.[58] References to light are associated with various types of "internalized" religious knowledge. For instance, once memorized, sacred texts are seen as being stored in the heart in the form of light. Nevertheless, light in the heart is an image primarily linked to knowledge spontaneously received from God. Contemporary scholars often quote Mālik as saying: "Verily knowledge is not the abundance of [memorized] texts (*kathra al-riwāya*). It is only a light which God places in the heart." The preceding quote functions to underline the importance of virtuous dispositions. This is because it is believed that God only fills a heart with light once it has been cleansed through the removal of evil dispositions.

A scholar with light/knowledge in his heart is capable of radiating it (*ishrāq*) onto those in his physical proximity. Addressing this phenomenon, al-Shāṭibī writes:

> When [present] before [the scholars], there is revealed to the student what is not revealed in their absence. For students, the light [of a teacher] remains with them in proportion to the extent that they remain following their teacher, behaving before him with proper manners, and imitating him. This path is beneficial in all cases.[59]

Ideas of this general type were deeply rooted in eighteenth and nineteenth century Egyptian religious life. Praising righteous scholars, al-Jabartī speaks of how "their light is derived from the lamp of Muḥammadan prophecy (*mishkāh al-nubuwwa al-muṣṭafawiyya*)."[60] He proceeds to chronicle the transmission of this light among the learned of his era. Of one student, he recounts that "light appeared upon him from the companionship [of this teacher]."[61] In a neighboring entry he writes of a scholar who "made companionship with [a teacher whose] light he acquired."[62]

[57] Mayyāra 2007:22.

[58] For a general discussion of knowledge as light in the Islamic tradition see Chapter 6 in Rosenthal 2007.

[59] Al-Shāṭibī 2004:56.

[60] This quote has been slightly altered. Al-Jabartī n.d., 1:16.

[61] Al-Jabarti n.d., 3:108.

[62] Al-Jabarti n.d., 3:109. See also al-Jabarti n.d., 1:125.

Within some Sufi circles, the conception of knowledge as light has been worked out in ways that, while highly controversial, are nonetheless interesting for our purposes. The doctrinal developments in question posit that the Prophet Muḥammad himself is literally an entity crafted from light, who then radiates light from his being on to those in his presence.[63] Such is referred to as the "Muḥammadan light" (*al-nūr al-Muḥammadī*).[64] One incident commonly cited in support of this belief[65] pertains to an interchange between the Prophet and his wife ʿĀʾisha. A contemporary Egyptian Sufi author describes it as follows:

> Āʾisha, mother of the believers—may God be pleased with her—was in her home in the dark and a needle had dropped from her hand. [Then the Prophet] entered upon her. When [he] —peace and blessings be upon him—entered, his great light radiated (*ashraqa*) upon to her, and his *baraka* settled upon her so that she saw the needle owing to the glow of his light, and the light in her heart increased by witnessing his radiance.[66]

The same author explains that the light transmitted between latter-day Islamic scholars is traceable to that initially radiated by the Prophet Muḥammad.[67]

All of this raises the following question: Is the light which is passed on to be conceptualized as *deriving from* the Prophet, or does it, in some sense, *literally constitute* the Prophet himself? After all, if the Prophet is himself light, he can be seen as radiating himself into each successive generation of scholars, literally indwelling in their mind/hearts. Some contemporary Egyptian Sufis use suggestive language that can be read either way. For instance they state that the Prophet is "living in our mind/hearts" (*ḥayyun fī qulūbina*). Sitting in groups, they will address the Prophet, repeatedly chanting: "you are in us" (*anta fīnā*). The ambiguity of such language may be intentional. By using it they avoid publicly committing themselves to the controversial claim that the Prophet is actually dwelling within them.

Once again, we see the symmetry between rationally intelligible and supernatural approaches to knowledge transmission. In the former, practicing companionship allows the student to transform himself into a replica of the Prophet by receiving the appropriate manners and dispositions from a *shaykh*. The Prophet can then be said to "live on" in the form of the student. In the more supernatural approach, physical proximity to a *shaykh* provides access to the Prophet's light—something not readily distinguishable from the Prophet himself. When this light enters the mind/heart so does the Prophet, enabling the latter to mystically live on in the student.

Efforts to acquire *baraka* and light from scholars center on engaging the senses. Such is attested in premodern texts and continues among Traditionalist circles into the present. It is most apparent at Sufi gatherings, held in mosques

[63] Ibn Sabʿīn 2007:159–162.

[64] On the notion of "Muhammadan light" in general see Schimmel 1975:214–227 and in a modern Egyptian contexts see Hoffman 1995:54–68; J. Johansen 1996:123–128.

[65] Also see J. Johansen 1996:124. [66] Ibn Sabʿīn 2007:159. [67] Ibn Sabʿīn 2007:179.

or at more private venues. These are highly variable in size, with the more public sessions drawing hundreds or even thousands.[68] Different types of gatherings appeal to people of different social backgrounds. Oftentimes they are attractive to laypersons of poorer and/or rural backgrounds, and may be occasions for ecstatic manifestations of piety. Among scholars there seems to be a preference for small, somber, and intimate sessions, composed largely of *shaykhs* and advanced students. The smaller sessions I attended were not in mosques. They took place in less conspicuous venues like lodges, and attracted somewhere around 20–50 people. They generally lasted between three to five hours, though some were shorter.

Whether large or small, leadership for a gathering falls to one or more of the *shaykhs* in attendance. *Shaykhs* position themselves to make their actions as visible as possible to other attendees. For instance, if food is served the *shaykhs* might all sit together at the front of the room, eating from the same plate and demonstrating various detailed forms of dietary etiquette. Alternatively, they might sit upon chairs or cushions, reciting the Qurʾan and poetry praising the Prophet.[69] They lead the gathering in making remembrance (*dhikr*) of God through the repetition of verbal formulae. In the course of doing so, they conspicuously express various emotional-mystical states through facial expressions, breathing patterns, bodily posture, and modulations of the voice. Meanwhile the audience stares at them as intensely as possible, striving to take in everything they see. Reflecting the state of technology, many individuals accentuate their efforts by holding out video cameras and cell-phone recording devices, focusing them upon the *shaykhs*. This behavior is reflected in the maxim: "looking upon the face of the *shaykh* is a form of worship (*ʿibāda*)."

During the sessions, people will seek to get as close to the *shaykhs* as possible. Those nearest to a *shaykh* often huddle around him to make direct physical contact. During or after the session, individuals come forward to pay their respects, taking the opportunity to hold a *shaykh* in an extended embrace and kiss his cheeks. In one session, I watched as an aged *shaykh* sat on a chair invoking God with his hands raised, palms-upturned, to the sky. While he was doing so, a religious student placed his torso against the *shaykh*'s lower leg and his elbows on the *shaykh*'s knee. The *shaykh* continued on with his invocations, as the student imitated him, raising his own hands in the same way. In another less scholarly gathering someone handed the presiding *shaykh* a can of soda from which he took a sip. The can was then passed around to others so they could drink from it as well. The aim was to permit them to touch and taste what the *shaykh* had touched and tasted.

All of these acts are seen as a means of acquiring *baraka* and light from the *shaykhs*, including the blessings of knowledge. But they are also seen as a method for acquiring knowledge through companionship in the mode of direct observation. Echoing al-Shāṭibī, gatherings of this kind evince a belief that deep sensory

[68] Also see Chapter 9 in J. Johansen 1996. [69] Al-Būṣīrī's Burda is the favorite.

engagement is capable of producing knowledge in both rationally comprehensible and supernatural ways.

## VIII. COMPANIONSHIP AND LEARNING THROUGH PRACTICE

I now wish to take a closer look at how companionship involves learning through practice (i.e., repeated action). Here the student imitates the teacher's practice of Sharīʿa rules, thereby acquiring the same dispositions as the teacher.

One of the many present-day texts critical of the increasing tendency to take knowledge from books rather than from scholars draws attention to a passage found in the writings of Ibn Khaldūn. In it he explains why it is necessary to spend time with *shaykhs*.[70] "The reason for [spending time with *shaykhs*] is that a man acquires their knowledge and their dispositions, their doctrinal schools and their virtues, sometimes through teaching and dictation, and sometimes through imitation and instruction by practice (*muḥākatan wa-talqīnan bi-l-mubāshara*); except that to acquire dispositions through practice makes them more firmly rooted and deeply ingrained."[71]

Thus, Ibn Khaldūn associates learning with spending a lengthy duration of time with *shaykhs*. Lengthy duration is an important part of companionship for two reasons. First, the longer a student spends with a *shaykh*, the longer he can directly observe the *shaykh*. Schutz would suggest that this provides more opportunities to infer mental attributes. The second reason has to do with the principle of repetition. The longer a student spends with a *shaykh*, the longer he imitates the *shaykh* (i.e., the longer he repeats the actions of the *shaykh*). The longer an act is repeated, the higher the number of total repetitions. And the higher the number of total repetitions, the more deeply instilled is the associated disposition.

Lengthy companionship was an important element of Egyptian scholarly life on the eve of the Napoleonic invasion. Recall that al-Jabartī describes some of his father's students as passing 20 years with him. The importance of a long period of companionship is something which finds emphasis in present-day Traditionalist circles as well. This is well illustrated in an interview I had with a popular teacher at al-Azhar mosque. The teacher began by asserting that "religion consists in [pious] dispositions (*al-dīn al-khuluq*)," citing a well-known Hadith report in which the Prophet states: "I have only been sent to perfect noble dispositions." The teacher explained that acquiring these dispositions required an extended period of companionship. As proof, he noted that the Prophet had only begun promulgating laws many years after his mission had begun. Before that, he had spent over a decade preparing the way by imparting virtuous dispositions through companionship. The teacher also referenced

[70] Al-Ghurbānī 1999:39–40. [71] Ibn Khaldūn 2010, 3:1120.

an anecdote wherein a student of Mālik states that he passed 20 years in his company—two in order to take his knowledge, and the remainder to take his dispositions (*akhlāq*) and manners (*adab*).[72] He continued on to say that this emphasis on spending years acquiring dispositions had served as the backbone of Muslim learning throughout the centuries until the West came and destroyed the traditional system. He then excused himself, sat down alone in an empty corner of the mosque in which we were speaking, and began quietly weeping.

I also encountered these ideas at a small Sufi gathering featuring an older scholar in his seventies. Confined to a wheelchair, he had a short beard and was attired in the special Azhari garb. All eyes turned to the *shaykh* as he recounted how he had acquired his knowledge. Rather than focusing on institutional degrees, he spoke of how he had spent his whole life in the company of various *shaykhs*. One of them was his father, a Shāfiʿī scholar who had performed 45 years of companionship with an even more senior authority. The *shaykh* said that his own education actually began with his mother. She was a scholar in her own right, affiliated with the Mālikī legal school. The *shaykh* said he had profited from hearing her cite Hadith reports and other sacred knowledge while still in her womb. His mother's status had allowed him to maintain intimate and continuous presence with a scholar from conception. For him, the process of companionship started before he was born.

Another illustration of these ideas can be found in the writings of Usāma al-Sayyid, a rising Azhari Traditionalist scholar in his late 30s. Al-Sayyid teaches in al-Azhar mosque. He owes much of his own fame to being the companion of a leading Egyptian religious authority.

Al-Sayyid lays out his views in a short educational pamphlet entitled: "Towards a Grand Renewal: The Salient Features of the Azhari Approach." For al-Sayyid, traditional Azhari learning is founded on an extended period of companionship. He states that for:

> the children of [the traditional Azhari] approach, none will put himself forth [as a qualified scholar] except after receiving knowledge from the scholars and keeping their company for an extended period (*al-ṣuḥba al-ṭawīla*) . . . and if you ask one of them: "how long have you kept the company of your *shaykh* or your *shaykhs*?" he will mention to you that he kept their company a long time, until he came to grasp and understand from them the [correct] method of understanding and the means of gaining access to knowledge. This is opposed to other approaches [where the transmission of knowledge] is broken and interrupted. [Here] one of their adherents puts himself forth without keeping the company of scholars. If you ask one of them: "how long have you kept the company of your *shaykh*?" He will mention to you that he [only] kept his company a limited number of hours (*ṣaḥibahu sāʿāt maʿdūda*). How [then] is it possible for him to have obtained knowledge and how is it that his understanding can be trusted?"[73]

[72] This anecdote was told to me by other scholars in a number of variant forms.
[73] Al-Sayyid 2010:4.

The practice of companionship is not limited to a specific span of time. Premodern texts often speak of a teacher's companions remaining with him until his death. The idea that companionship can (or even should) continue on indefinitely is related to a more general belief that learning should be continuous. It is customarily described as extending "from cradle to grave" (*min al-mahd ilā al-laḥd*).[74] One oft-cited maxim states: "The scholar is a scholar only so long as he sees himself as ignorant. If he sees himself as a scholar he has become ignorant."[75] Writing of Egypt in the early nineteenth century, Edward Lane notes how some students "remain all their lifetime studying in the Azhar, and aspire to be ranked among the higher ʿUlama [scholars]."[76]

The ideal of constant learning is linked to the belief that one should always maintain oneself in a companionship relationship with a higher-ranking *shaykh*. According to this perspective, every *shaykh* must always have a *shaykh* above him, no matter how old or distinguished he is. Seeking to gain further insight into this practice, I once asked a Traditionalist scholar whether it was really true that even aged and eminent authorities still submitted to higher *shaykhs*. To press the point, I specifically named a distinguished teacher in his 70s, with a prestigious study-circle in the vicinity of al-Azhar mosque. I was told that the teacher does in fact still have a *shaykh*, and I was even given a name.

Understanding these views can be difficult for those accustomed to Western forms of education, where learning has a specific endpoint marked by "graduation." The existence of this endpoint allows participants in the educational system to be divided into two opposed categories: learned individuals who have graduated and not-yet-learned individuals who are still students.

In traditional Islamic learning there is no point at which a student graduates. Even after assuming teaching responsibilities, religious figures typically still attend the study-circles of others. The status of individuals in this system is relational in nature. Absolute categories do not exist. Any scholar is more knowledgeable than some and less knowledgeable than others. The former he should teach and the latter he should learn from.

## IX. PUNISHMENT IN COMPANIONSHIP

I now wish to examine how religious authorities utilize punishment as an element of companionship. In companionship, the teacher has a responsibility to oversee the student's "upbringing" (*tarbiya*). This involves continuously monitoring the student's practice of Sharīʿa rules. When the student performs an action which is not in accord with Sharīʿa rules, the *shaykh* must correct the student. Such often entails some sort of punishment or discipline (*taʾdīb*). By correcting the student through punishment, the *shaykh* helps refine the student's knowledge of Sharīʿa

[74] See Aḥmad Shalabī 1999:307.

[75] See Ibn al-Ḥājj 2008, 1:j.1 65; Ibn Jamāʿa 2009:53.

[76] Lane 2005[1836]:214.

rules. Moreover, the *shaykh* uses punishment to compel the student to practice Sharīʿa rules. By being compelled to constantly practice Sharīʿa rules, the student acquires knowledge of Sharīʿa rules in the form of a disposition (i.e., skill). Furthermore, the student acquires the other various dispositions prescribed by the Sharīʿa (e.g., generosity, patience, certain belief in God).

Premodern scholars held that teachers should employ punishment from an early age. Such punishment began with a student's entry into the *kuttāb*. The *shaykh* supervising children in the *kuttāb* was known as the "*muʾaddib*" or "discipliner."[77]

Ibn al-Ḥājj (d.737/1336) explains that the job of the discipliner is to "make [the students] follow the Sunna and to teach them the rules their Lord has placed upon them in the same way that he teaches them the Qurʾan."[78] The discipliner puts special stress on the foundational obligation of prayer. Students are trained to stop whatever they are doing and make the prescribed supplications whenever they hear the call to prayer. The discipliner gradually teaches them how to make ablutions and pray. He habituates them to praying communally in the mosque at the designated times.[79]

While punishment is present at all stages of traditional Islamic learning, it is particularly intense at the level of the *kuttāb*. This is due to the widespread belief that ethical reform is most efficacious in the early years. Ibn ʿAbd al-Barr (d.463/1071) illustrates the point by quoting poetry: "The discipliner can reform the disposition (*mayl*) of a boy. [But] discipline does not profit the gray-haired." He also cites the maxim: "Clay can only be given an impression when moist."[80]

Successful teaching in the *kuttāb* meant frequent recourse to punishment.[81] On the milder end of the spectrum, Ibn al-Ḥājj mentions sanctions such as frowning, harsh words, and threats. Harsher punishments include humiliation and beatings. Still, he asserts that punishment should not transgress the proper limits. Sanctions should only be used to the extent necessary. Where the teacher resorts to physical discipline, he should not utilize overly harsh implements and must avoid severe beating. Brutality is not consistent with the moral code of a Qurʾan teacher. Ibn al-Ḥājj laments that some of his contemporaries cross the appropriate boundaries.[82] Ibn Ḥajar al-Haytamī (d.974/1566) complains that he was the victim of excessive physical punishment while a student at al-Azhar, even though he still affirms that corporal punishment is in the best interests of children.[83] Once authorized by parental permission, al-Haytamī states that the teacher may employ punishment in response to "any bad disposition that expresses itself in action."[84]

77 See, e.g., Ibn al-Ḥājj 2008, 1:j.2 286.
78 Ibn al-Ḥājj 2008, 1:j.2 286. Also see Ibn al-Ḥājj 2008, 1:j.2 284.
79 Ibn al-Ḥājj 2008, 2:284. On learning to pray in the *kuttāb* also see Heyworth-Dunne 1939:6.
80 Ibn ʿAbd al-Barr 2006:96–97.
81 Relevant here is Ibn ʿAbd al-Barr 2006:97.
82 Ibn al-Ḥājj 2008, 1:j.2 285. Also relevant is Ibn al-Hajj 2008, 1:j.2 292.
83 Jackson 2004:25–28.
84 "*ʿAlā kulli khulqin sayyʾin ṣadara minhu.*" Jackson 2004: 26. Notice my translation differs slightly from Jackson's.

In eighteenth century Egypt, discipliners made frequent use of palm-sticks to keep order.[85] Within contemporary Egyptian popular culture, stringent discipline is stereotypically associated with old-fashioned *kuttāb* learning. Egyptian films and television shows regularly portray teachers as wielding sticks and referring to their students as "donkeys." At the same time, traditional *kuttāb* methods are widely seen as imparting a mastery of the Qurʾan and the Arabic language otherwise unattainable. Scholars I spoke with sometimes explained a person's skillfulness in these fields by smiling and saying that he was raised by a bad-tempered *shaykh* with a big stick.

During a journey to a rural area outside of Ṭanṭā, I had the opportunity to interview a contemporary *kuttāb* teacher. In his 30s, he had a beard and wore a *jallābiyya*-robe. He repeatedly asserted that his job revolved around the physical discipline he was empowered to administer, remarking: "In the *kuttāb* the *shaykh* is the only law, and the government law does not apply." As I asked him about his teaching methods, he kept expressively flipping his wrist while snapping his fingers to indicate that he handed out beatings. The *shaykh* then brought out some kind of wooden punishment apparatus used to keep order and ensure that students were memorizing their lessons. (Although the 50–80 children learning with him clearly feared it, they also began giggling as he took it out and described his methods). At the same time, the *shaykh* acknowledged that corporal punishment had its limits. It was better to expel overly recalcitrant students than to constantly beat them.

## X. PUNISHMENT AT LATER AGES

When children left the *kuttāb* to join study-circles at the mosque or madrasa, physical discipline receded into the background in favor of more subtle methods of character formation. Ibn Jamāʿa urges the teacher to "monitor the condition of students with respect to their manners, their being guided, and their dispositions—both inner and outer."[86] The teacher performs his task by means of "good advice and tenderness, not with severity and arbitrariness. He intends by that to give [the pupil] a good upbringing and improve his dispositions (*ḥusn tarbiyatihi wa-taḥsīn khuluqihi*) . . . [the teacher] disciplines him such that he takes on the most sublime manners and encourages him to [to take on] the most pleasant dispositions. He enjoins upon him habits which accord with the Sharīʿa."[87] In assuming the role of the students' caretaker, the *shaykh* should strive to fulfill their needs, spending from his own pockets so long as his finances permit him to do so without difficulty.[88]

[85] Heyworth-Dunne 1939:4. On the moral function of *kuttāb* discipline also see Heyworth-Dunne 1939:6. Also see Eickelman 1985:62–63.

[86] Ibn Jamāʿa 2009:75.

[87] Ibn Jamāʿa 2009:69.

[88] Ibn Jamāʿa 2009:75. Also see Al-Ājurī 1985:34–35.

The notion that religious learning must integrate an ethical component remains a standard, if muted, theme in modern educational treatises. One instance can be found in the writings of Ṭalʿat Muḥammad ʿAfīfī. A prominent television personality, ʿAfīfī was formerly dean of al-Azhar's Faculty of Missionary Activity (*Daʿwa*). ʿAfīfī asserts that:

> work in the field of teaching is not a profession wherein a person [simply] earns what suffices him [i.e. monetarily] without care for anything else. Rather it is a [religious] mission (*risāla*) which the teacher carries upon his shoulders . . . If he neglects to give a [moral] upbringing (*tarbiya*) to students, and only pays attention to what furthers his personal interests, then verily God—the Highest—will interrogate him about that and take him to account. The Messenger of God—peace be upon him—spoke truly when he said: "Every one of you is a shepherd and every one of you is responsible for his flock."[89]

[89] ʿAfīfī 2005:38.

# 5

# The *Sanad*

Any account of traditional Islamic learning must center on what is variously called the "*sanad*," the "*isnād*," or the "*silsila*." Subtle technical matters aside,[1] it is possible to think of these terms as synonymous, denoting the concept of a linked chain of religious scholars extending through time. The chain exists for the purpose of transmitting knowledge. Consider the following chain: Prophet Muḥammad—Ibn ʿUmar—Nāfiʿ—Mālik—Ibn al-Qāsim. Excepting the origin of the chain in the Prophet Muḥammad, each link consists of a scholar who plays two roles in the transmission of knowledge. On the one hand, he is the direct student of the individual who immediately precedes him in the chain. On the other hand, he is the direct teacher of the individual who immediately follows him in the chain. For the sake of simplicity, one may think of chains as operating in a temporal order wherein the teacher is always older than his student and predeceases him. Take knowledge of how to pray. How is this knowledge transmitted from the Prophet to Ibn al-Qāsim (who lived about two centuries after the Prophet's death)? It is held that this knowledge has been passed from the Prophet through each link in the chain, eventually reaching Mālik and then being directly transmitted from him to Ibn al-Qāsim. Muslim scholars emphasize that the value of the "*sanad*" is crucially dependent upon its being interlinked (*muttaṣil*) with no breaks or gaps (*inqiṭāʿ*). Additional names are added to the end of the chain as knowledge is transmitted to new generations. William Graham observes that for premodern Muslims the *sanad* "came to function . . . as the authoritative mechanism of transmission of all learning and scholarship."[2]

Why does traditional Islamic learning place so much value on the *sanad*? Such has not been an easy question to answer. Western scholars have long viewed the *sanad* as an "unusual phenomenon"[3] whose precise functions are unclear.[4]

The first step in addressing the enigmatic character of the *sanad* is to ask what types of knowledge are passed through it. The most obvious consists in

[1] For a technical discussion of the relationship between the terms "*sanad*" and "*isnad*" see Abū Ghuddah 1992: 14–15. For a treatment of "*silisila*" see Graham 1993: 514–518.

[2] Graham 1993:510. Also see Abū Ghudda 1992:34–38; Abū Ghudda 2008:143–152.

[3] M. Cook 1997: 510.

[4] In a lengthy article (1997) addressing previous Islamicist scholarship, Michael Cook ultimately concludes that the *sanad* system can only be explained as a historical "residue of Rabbinic Judaism" (1997:510, 520–521). Although many Islamicists would not agree with this particular explanation, providing a satisfactory alternative has proven difficult.

The Anthropology of Islamic Law. Aria Nakissa.

knowledge of texts. Premodern scholars put great emphasis on receiving religious texts through a *sanad*. They were hostile to the notion of simply coming into possession of texts by purchasing them or copying them from a manuscript library (*wijāda*).[5] A text needed to be received directly from a scholar who had likewise received it from another scholar in an unbroken chain extending back to that text's original author.[6] Being passed from one trustworthy scholar to another helped guard against the misattribution or alteration of transmitted material. Where a text was not procured through a *sanad*, doubt was liable to be cast on its authenticity as well as the owner's understanding of its contents.

Within the Western Islamicist literature, the *sanad* is looked at primarily as a mechanism for preserving textual authenticity. Such is indeed the function which overwhelmingly preoccupies Muslim religious scholars specializing in the study of Hadith reports. This is hardly surprising given that Muslim Hadith scholarship is concerned with authenticating textual reports containing information about the Prophet. Yet it would be a mistake to presume that concerns of this sort have the same prominence in other Islamic disciplines (e.g., law, Sufism). Within these other disciplines (as well as within the discipline of Hadith scholarship itself), the *sanad* undoubtedly has functions besides that of authenticating texts. However, such have been obscured owing to the fact that Islamicist research on the *sanad* has focused on Muslim Hadith scholarship.[7]

## I. THE *SANAD* AND COMPANIONSHIP

The *sanad* must be situated in relationship to the broader phenomenon of Islamic learning. As explained previously, knowledge of rules is acquired through a combination of methods, including: (1) learning through texts, (2) learning through observation, and (3) learning through practice. I suggest that the *sanad* bears a relationship to each of these three methods. Hence, the *sanad* is clearly tied to the method of learning through texts. After all, the *sanad* is a mechanism for faithfully transmitting texts, and Muslims acquire knowledge of Sharīʿa rules by studying such texts. I suggest that the *sanad* is also tied to the methods of learning through observation and learning through practice. This is because the *sanad* is intertwined with the pedagogy of companionship, which combines learning through observation and learning through practice. In explaining these ideas, I wish to turn back to the concept of Sunna.

We have seen that *sunna* is originally a pre-Islamic Arab concept. Sunna denotes a normative practice laid down by a particular individual.[8] As a normative practice, a *sunna* is worthy of being followed by others. For instance, the normative practice laid down by a tribal chief was his *sunna*, and this *sunna* was to be

[5] See Abū Ghudda 1992:34. Also see Ibn al-Ṣalāḥ 1989:358–360. [6] Abū Ghudda 1992:34.

[7] See, e.g., Robson 1978; Schacht 1967[1950]; Motzki 2002. Also see Ephrat 2000:82.

[8] See Bravmann:1972:139, 160–161, 173. Also see Hallaq 2005; Schacht 1965:29–30; Schacht 1967[1950] 70.

followed by later members of the tribe. The pre-Islamic Arabs were nonliterate. Hence, they did not transmit knowledge of *sunna* through written texts. Rather, they transmitted such knowledge using the methods of learning through observation and learning through practice. Thus, tribesmen might observe the normative practice (i.e., *sunna*) of the chief, and then imitate him by performing this practice themselves. In doing so, they followed his *sunna*. This can be seen as a kind of proto-companionship. The first generation of tribesmen would then transmit the chief's *sunna* to the second generation. Tribesmen from the second generation would learn the *sunna* by observing and imitating the first generation. This process would continue down through the ages, naturally giving rise to an unbroken *sanad*. This unbroken *sanad* began with the chief. The chief transmitted knowledge of his *sunna* to the first generation, which transmitted it to the second generation, and so on. Accordingly, I suggest that the notion of *sanad* is implicit in the pre-Islamic concept of *sunna*.

As noted previously, with the rise of Islam, *sunna* comes to be identified with the practice of the Prophet—or more specifically, the Prophet's practice of Sharīʿa rules. By extension, knowledge of the Sunna become knowledge of Sharīʿa rules (i.e., knowledge of how to competently apply these rules). This knowledge is transmitted through the pedagogy of companionship. Hence, the Prophet practices Sharīʿa rules (this is his Sunna). The first generation of Muslims (i.e., the Companions) observes and imitates the Prophet, thereby acquiring knowledge of Sharīʿa rules. The first generation follows the Sunna by practicing these Sharīʿa rules. The second generation then observes and imitates the first generation, thereby acquiring knowledge of Sharīʿa rules. The second generation also follows the Sunna by practicing these rules. Once again, this process continues down through the ages, naturally giving rise to an unbroken *sanad*, wherein knowledge of Sharīʿa rules originates with the Prophet, then is transmitted to the first generation, then is transmitted to the second generation, and so on.

The above-described scheme also has implications for the transmission of dispositions. As explained earlier, the practice of Sharīʿa rules instills a particular set of dispositions, associated with the dispositions of the Prophet. The Companions observed and imitated the Prophet by practicing Sharīʿa rules. By practicing Sharīʿa rules, the Companions thereby acquired the Prophet's dispositions. Then, the second generation observed and imitated the Companions, by practicing Sharīʿa rules. By practicing Sharīʿa rules, the second generation also acquired the Prophet's dispositions. The process in question was repeated in every subsequent generation. In this way, the Prophet's dispositions were also transmitted in an unbroken *sanad*.

Hence, the *sanad* is not only a mechanism for faithfully transmitting texts. It is also intertwined with the pedagogy of companionship, which functions to transmit knowledge of Sharīʿa rules and associated dispositions.

The preceding vision of learning continues to be championed by contemporary Traditionalist scholars. Consider the views of ʿAbd al-Fattāḥ Abū Ghudda (d.1997), an eminent Azhari scholar of Syrian origin. Extolling the importance of the *sanad*, he writes that:

> among the most important special characteristics of the Muḥammadan nation is that of the *sanad*[9] in the transmission of the purified Sharīʿa and its sciences, from the early generations (*salaf*) to the later ones (*khalaf*). [In the past] the *sanad* was the first condition in every form of transmitted knowledge, even if [that being transmitted was no more than] a single word. Through the *sanad* the later generations took from the early ones, and the following generations took from those before them. [By virtue of the *sanad*] God the Highest blessed the Muslim nation with the preservation of the texts of the Sharīʿa and its sciences until they became deeply rooted and protected against change and alteration . . . .[10]

As part of a larger work criticizing the modern proclivity for acquiring knowledge from books rather than through a *sanad*, Abū Ghudda selected out and republished an extended passage from a medieval legal treatise written by Abū Isḥāq al-Shāṭibī (790/1388).[11] The passage in question has become something of a rallying point for proponents of premodern learning techniques.[12] In it, al-Shāṭibī argues that learning requires knowledge be passed from generation to generation through companionship in the form of an unbroken *sanad*, and that such has always been the foundation of Muslim education.

Al-Shāṭibī explains that practice of companionship ("*mulāzama*") was the:

> "manner of the pious first generations" ("*kāna sh'an al-Salaf al-Ṣāliḥ*"). In support of this contention, he explains that "the first [instance] of [companionship] was the companionship of the Companions, may God be pleased with them, with the Messenger of God—peace be upon him—with them taking from him his words and deeds, and their depending on what came from him, whatever it was, and however it was, and whether or not they understood the meaning he intended by it . . . This [i.e. taking knowledge through companionship] became like a principle for those after them. The second generation of Muslims committed themselves to [taking knowledge] from the Companions in the same way that [the Companions] had taken it from the Prophet—peace be upon him—until they became knowledgeable and attained the peak of perfection in the Sharīʿa sciences."[13]

For al-Shāṭibī, the way that knowledge is passed down through the ages is that each generation imitates its teachers. Accordingly, al-Shāṭibī states that among the requirements of mastering the Islamic sciences is "imitating and taking the manners of he from whom one takes knowledge (*al-iqtidāʾ bi-man akhadha ʿanhu, wa-l-taʾaddub bi-adabihi*), as you know from the Companions' imitation of the Prophet—peace be upon him—and the second generations' imitation of the Companions, and so forth in every generation."[14]

Scholars that I interviewed expressed similar ideas. One Azhari authority explained things to me as follows: "The dispositions and manners of any scholar

[9] Actually he uses term "*isnād*" rather than "*sanad*" here and elsewhere.
[10] Abū Ghudda 1992:11. Also see Abū Ghudda 1992:9, 15–16, 23–24, 29–30,77.
[11] See Abū Ghudda 1992:150–153.
[12] I have come across it on multiple occasions. See e.g., al-Ghurbānī 1999:35–39.
[13] Al-Shāṭibī 2004:55. [14] Al-Shāṭibī 2004:56.

living today have no other origin than his teacher. And his teacher took them, in turn, from his own teacher and so on, extending all the way back to the Prophet in an unbroken chain. Every generation acquires its dispositions by imitating its immediate predecessor. But the dispositions passed down ultimately have their origin in the Prophet. Scholars are the inheritors of the prophets (*al-ʿulamāʾ waratha al-anbiyāʾ*), and part of this inheritance consists in dispositions."

These points can be used to further elucidate the concept of "annihilation" (*al-fanāʾ*). Introduced earlier, "annihilation" refers to the alteration of a subject's dispositions (*akhlāq*) through Sharīʿa-compliant ethical practice. Recall that annihilation admits of different levels. At the top-level is "annihilation in God." Below this is "annihilation in the Prophet," which is undertaken as a means to annihilation in God. After all, God and the Prophet share the same dispositions. In Sufi thought there is a third level of annihilation called "annihilation in the *shaykh*."[15] Annihilation in the *shaykh* is properly understood as a means to annihilation in the Prophet, and ultimately to annihilation in God. This is because just as the Prophet's dispositions match those of God, the *shaykh*'s dispositions match those of the Prophet. The *shaykh* has the Prophet's dispositions because they have been transmitted to him through an unbroken *sanad*. Annihilation in the *shaykh* involves acquiring these dispositions from the *shaykh* by imitating him.

## II. THE *SANAD* AND THE LIMITATIONS OF LEARNING THROUGH TEXTS

Going back to Aristotle's *Nicomachean Ethics*, it has been argued that not all forms of knowledge can be adequately learned through texts. Rather, some can only adequately be learned through observation and practice. This is, of course, a major theme in practice theory. Such a perspective is also advocated by premodern Muslim scholars, including Ibn Khaldūn (d.808/1406).

Recall that Ibn Khaldūn conceptualizes certain types of knowledge (including Sharīʿa knowledge) as "crafts."[16] Knowledge of a craft exists in the form of a disposition. Such knowledge cannot be acquired from texts. Rather it must be acquired from a living teacher.[17] Acquiring such knowledge from a living teacher typically involves observing him and imitating his practice.[18]

Ibn Khaldūn links his perspective to the concept of the *sanad*. Hence, after emphasizing that knowledge must be acquired from an instructor, Ibn Khaldūn states that "for this reason, with regards to every type of knowledge and craft, the people of every place and generation give consideration to the fact that the *sanad* [through which] instruction [is passed] extends to famous teachers."[19]

[15] See Hoffman 1999; Hoffman 1995:140–141, 202–204; Schimmel 1975:216, 386–387.

[16] Mitchell 1991:82; Messick 1993:104. Also see, e.g., al-Taftāzānī n.d., 1:30; al-Zarnūjī 2004:64; al-Dihlawī 1398h: 21.

[17] Ibn Khaldūn 2010, 2:856.

[18] On the importance of bodily imitation in Islamic learning see Chamberlain 1994:123.

[19] Ibn Khaldūn 2010, 3:925.

Ibn Khaldūn's statement can be explained as follows. The student receives his knowledge from an instructor. The quality of the knowledge received by the student will depend upon the quality of the knowledge possessed by the instructor. Therefore, if the instructor's knowledge is deficient, the student's knowledge will also be deficient. For example, suppose that an instructor has deficient knowledge of the Arabic language, such that he makes many mistakes with regards to grammar and vocabulary. The student who learns Arabic from this instructor will also possess a deficient knowledge of the language.

How then, can the student ensure that the instructor's knowledge is adequate? Here the student must confirm that the instructor received his knowledge through an unbroken *sanad* extending back to a "famous teacher" whose knowledge is well established. It is not sufficient for the instructor to take his knowledge from a teacher whose knowledge is flawed or doubtful—for that will make the instructor's own knowledge flawed and doubtful. Moreover, it is not sufficient for the instructor to take his knowledge from texts—for that will make the instructor's knowledge deficient. After all, texts do not suffice to adequately transmit knowledge. Rather, the instructor must learn the knowledge of the famous teacher through practice. This might happen in one of two ways. First of all, the instructor might learn directly from the famous teacher. In this case, the instructor imitates the practice of the famous teacher. Second of all, the instructor might learn directly from a student of the famous teacher. The instructor imitates the practice of the student of the famous teacher on the assumption that the student's practice comes from the famous teacher. In a similar way, the instructor could learn from a student of a student of the famous teacher, and so forth. In all of these situations, the instructor takes his knowledge through an unbroken *sanad* extending back to the famous teacher whose knowledge is well established. The preceding points allow us to see that Muslim emphasis on an unbroken *sanad* derives (largely) from a belief that written texts alone cannot serve as an adequate vehicle for the transmission of knowledge (i.e., knowledge in the form of dispositions).

Where knowledge of Sharīʿa rules is concerned, there is no doubt that the "famous teacher," which Ibn Khaldūn requires to be at the origin of the *sanad*, is none other than the Prophet himself. Among Islamic scholars, it is the Prophet's knowledge of Sharīʿa rules which is passed down from generation to generation.

Ibn Khaldūn's belief that craft knowledge of *any* type (religious or non-religious), consists in dispositions which must be transmitted through a *sanad* recurs repeatedly in Muslim writings.[20] A legal epistle authored by al-Dihlawī (d.1762) provides an instructive example. Al-Dihlawī stresses that Sharīʿa knowledge has always been passed from generation to generation in an unbroken chain. "The Muslim nation has agreed to depend on the early generations (*salaf*) regarding knowledge of the Sharīʿa. The second generation depended on the Companions [i.e., the first generation]. The third generation depended on the

[20] See Eickelman 1978:492.

second. In this manner, the scholars of each generation depend on those before them." Al-Dihlawī goes on to explain that every craft (including Sharīʿa knowledge) is passed through the generations by keeping the company of living teachers. "All crafts, like knowledge of Arabic morphology, knowledge of Arabic syntax, medicine, poetry, blacksmithing, carpentry, and goldsmithing cannot be easily acquired by anyone except through constantly being in the presence of those who know them (*mulāzama ahlihā*)."[21] It is noteworthy that half of the crafts to which al-Dihlawī compares Sharīʿa knowledge (blacksmithing, carpentry, and goldsmithing) have no textual component at all. The remainder may integrate texts to some extent, but are in no way reducible to them.

In an Egyptian context, the notion that the *sanad* works to transmit dispositions is well illustrated in a religious certificate (*ijāza*) written in the late nineteenth century by two-time *Shaykh al-Azhar* Shams al-Dīn al-Inbābī.[22] Al-Inbābī states: "In both old times and new, the great scholars, notables, and teachers of this [Muslim] nation have been deeply concerned with taking knowledge through an unbroken *sanad*, whether or not it consists in a craft (*al-ṣināʿa*) or in *ḥadīth* reports."[23] Observe that al-Inbābī not only associates the *sanad* with the transmission of crafts, but also makes a distinction between transmitting crafts through the *sanad* and transmitting Hadith reports through the *sanad*. Here craft knowledge (which exists in the form of dispositions) is explicitly singled out as separate from knowledge of Hadith reports (which exists in the form of texts). The *sanad* operates as a conduit for both.

A contemporary Egyptian manifestation of the same general conceptual scheme can be found in the writings of Usāma al-Sayyid, a rising Azhari scholar introduced in the previous chapter. In one pamphlet, he lays out what he considers to be the defining characteristics of traditional Azhar education.

According to al-Sayyid, "the first component" is "possession of an unbroken *sanad* with respect to the transmission [of texts], with respect to understanding [these texts], and with respect to ethical purification" ("*ittiṣāl sanadihi, riwāytan, dirāyatan, wa-tazkiyatan*").[24] The conception of *sanad* referenced by al-Sayyid is clearly inconsistent with the assumption that it functions only for the "transmission [of texts]" (*riwāya*). On the contrary, there is express mention of the fact that the *sanad* also relates to the understanding of these texts as well as to the process of "ethical purification." It is this second element on which I would like to concentrate. "Ethical purification" (*tazkiya*) is a technical term referring to the acquisition of good dispositions and the elimination of bad ones. When al-Sayyid refers to a *sanad* in ethical purification, what he means is taking one's dispositions from a scholar who has received his own dispositions through an unbroken chain extending back to the Prophet Muḥammad.

21 Al-Dihlawī 1398h:20–21.
22 He may not have been *Shaykh al-Azhar* at the time he wrote this *ijāza*.
23 Collected in Khafājī 1987, 2:108.
24 U. al-Sayyid 2010:4. This particular phrase is not unique to al-Sayyid. For instance it is also used by the popular Yemeni traditionalist Ḥabīb ʿAli al-Jifrī. See, e.g., http://www.alhabibali.com/ar/library/cat/101/ accessed 10/22/2011.

While Western scholars of Islamic law have generally ignored the transmission of the Prophet's living practice and dispositions among later generations, it has received some attention as an element of Sufi practice. Vincent Cornell quotes a late sixteenth century Sufi text from Morocco which reads: "May God be favorable to the saints . . . *who by their words and acts* have transmitted the principles of the religion, and who, by the exactness of their transmission, have preserved them from all alteration" [emphasis mine].[25] Cornell goes on to observe that because the Sufi *shaykh* has faithfully transmitted the practice of the Prophet in living form, he becomes an embodied representation of the Prophet to those around him.[26]

The idea that present-day Islamic authorities, Sufi or otherwise, have succeeded in preserving the practice of Sharīʿa rules (Sunna) may appear to entail an obvious contradiction. Living scholars exhibit different practices. How is it conceivable that this range of practices be attributable to the Prophet Muḥammad? When I confronted Traditionalist scholars with this query they noted that there is some difference of opinion in how Sharīʿa rules are understood. Such is reflected in the existence of the four Sunni legal schools (*madhāhib*). Each legal school has a distinctive understanding of the Sharīʿa rules, and hence members of each school practice these rules differently. One *shaykh* I interviewed recounted the fact that even the Prophet's Companions differed to some degree in their understanding of Sharīʿa rules and how they lived their lives. He then cited a well-known Hadith report in which the Prophet remarks: "My Companions are like stars—whomever you imitate you will be rightly guided." Hence, even though the Prophet's Companions differed, this did not *in itself* imply that they had abandoned the practice of Sharīʿa rules (Sunna). Consequently, any one of them was worthy of imitation, even if he differed from his counterparts.

Another reason scholars differ is simply human imperfection. One Azhari scholar explained to me: "One of Imam Mālik's students spent a year recording his dispositions and his manners. Why? Because they were those of the Prophet, and Mālik had inherited them through the Companions. The dispositions of any *shaykh* are traceable to the Prophet who embodied the dispositions of the Qurʾan. On the other hand, the Prophet was perfect, and it is too difficult for any one of us to replicate his perfection. But we try to imitate as much of it as we can. Because it is impossible to encompass the totality of the Prophet's dispositions, each living scholar successfully embodies some elements of his character but not others. This leads to differences between scholars."

With the partial exception of Sufism, why have Western Islamicist scholars found it so difficult to appreciate that the *sanad* functions to transmit dispositions rather than merely to transmit texts? One factor is undoubtedly the manner in which textually oriented Islamicists study Sharīʿa. Such Islamicists attempt to acquire mastery of the Sharīʿa simply by reading over written materials. They

[25] Cornell 1983:77.

[26] Cornell 1983:79, 82. For a similar analysis focused on medieval Palestine see Ephrat 2008:99–101. For the same idea in a modern Egyptian context see J. Johansen 1996:59.

do not imitate the personal habits of those who teach them these materials. Indeed, they would regard the very suggestion that they should do so as bizarre. Given their training, Islamicists are inclined to view this method of dealing with Islamic texts as normal and natural, rather than as highly idiosyncratic and foreign to traditional Islamic learning. But misunderstandings of this type also owe their causes to deeper factors such as Western "language ideology"—an issue to which we will now turn.

## III. WRITTEN TEXTS AS A MEDIUM FOR THE TRANSMISSION OF KNOWLEDGE

Islamicist scholarship recognizes that during the first two centuries after the Prophet's death, knowledge of Sharīʿa rules was largely learned through practice. Put differently, each new generation learned how to follow the Sunna (i.e., practice of Sharīʿa rules) by observing and imitating the previous generation.[27] However, it is typically supposed that this form of learning died out once the Prophet's teachings were inscribed in written compilations of Hadith reports. Having recorded the Sunna, Muslims thenceforth relied on written texts.[28] They no longer learned how to follow the Sunna by observation and imitation.

But as we have seen, Traditionalist Muslim scholars hold that throughout history, and up until this day, knowledge of Sharīʿa rules is transmitted through practice. In other words, up until this day, people still learn how to follow the Sunna (i.e., practice Sharīʿa rules) through observation and imitation. Why do many Islamicists insist otherwise? Here it is useful to draw on the linguistic anthropological concept of "language ideology."[29] To put matters in very simple terms, a language ideology consists in a set of assumptions about what language is and how it operates. Anthropological research on language ideologies has established that they vary widely from culture to culture.[30] Hence, in trying to isolate the language ideology (or range of language ideologies) found among premodern Muslim scholars, we cannot assume that they are similar to those found in the contemporary West. Indeed, it would be a startling coincidence if they were the same. After all, it is widely recognized that contemporary Western notions of language have been thoroughly transformed by exposure to

[27] See, e.g., Schacht 1965:29–30; Dutton 1999:1-5; Hallaq 2005:102–112, 196–202; El Shamsy 2013.

[28] Schacht 1965:34–35; El Shamsy 2013:220–226. Also relevant are M. Cook 1997:521–523; Schoeler 2006:129. Hallaq has recently signaled the need for a "major revision" of this view, noting that even in later ages the Sunna persisted as a "*lived* legal ethics and legal morality"(emphasis in original). Hallaq 2009:171–172. Nevertheless, although Hallaq is clearly aware that any such revision must take due account of the ethical nature of traditional legal education (Hallaq 2009:137–138), he declines to elaborate these ideas, consigning his brief comments to a footnote. See Hallaq 2009:172 ft.46.

[29] See Silverstein 1976; 1979. Also see Woolard and Schieffelin 1994.

[30] Hymes 1977:12–14; Woolard and Schieffelin 1994:55. As regards Muslim societies in particular see Messick 1993:24–25.

print and electronic mass media[31]—phenomena which are obviously absent from premodern Muslim history.

A defining feature of contemporary Western language ideologies is their tendency to assume that all knowledge is possible to express and communicate in words, including written words (i.e., texts). Accordingly, such ideologies conceive of writing as an ideal and more or less self-sufficient vehicle for the transmission of knowledge over time. Consequently, these ideologies customarily assume that the introduction of writing inevitably leads to the decline, and eventual replacement, of other ways of transmitting knowledge.[32] Nevertheless, the assumption of such universal evolutionary routes has been undermined by myriad studies establishing that different societies react to the introduction of writing in different ways.[33] With this in mind, it cannot be taken for granted that efforts to record the Sunna in writing after the Prophet's death precipitated the end of transmission through practice. Why couldn't transmission by practice have continued to exist side by side with writing?[34] Craig Calhoun has observed that such patterns of dual transmission existed not only in premodern Muslim societies but in their Indian, Chinese, and European counterparts as well.[35]

Automatically foreclosing the possibility of dual transmission would only make sense if Muslims believed writing itself to be a sufficient medium for transmitting knowledge. Nevertheless, it has been noted that such contemporary Western perspectives are "exactly the reverse" of premodern Muslim views.[36] While Muslim authorities freely acknowledge the value of writing, they emphatically reject the notion that written texts *alone* suffice to convey religious knowledge.[37] Therefore, premodern Muslim scholars used written texts to transmit knowledge, but also insisted on using non-textual methods of knowledge transmission, like learning through observation and learning through practice.

[31] See Goody 1977; Eisenstein 1979; Ong 1982.

[32] See Goody 1977; Ong 1982.

[33] See, e.g., Kulick and Stroud 1999; Messick 1993:24–25; Woolard and Schieffelin 1994:65–67. Also see Chamberlain 1994:134–135.

[34] It should be noted that transmission by practice is distinct from oral transmission. The question of oral transmission in Islam has been explored by drawing parallels to the Jewish concept of "Oral Torah." For recent discussions of this issue, see Chapter 5 in Schoeler 2006; M. Cook 1997.

[35] Calhoun 1993:79.

[36] See M. Cook 1997:438. Also see Mitchell 1991:150.

[37] For a discussion of this matter in relation to early Islamic history see, e.g., Chamberlain 1994:133–151; Cook 1997; Heck 2002a; Schoeler 2006. For a focus on later ages see Mitchell 1991:150–154; Robinson 1993; Green 2010.

# 6

# Taking from the Mouths of *Shaykhs* (*Mushāfaha*)

The present chapter looks at how written texts are used in traditional Islamic learning. However, before proceeding further, a few words about the relevant anthropological literature are in order.

Recall that early anthropological scholarship was methodologically committed to the study of nonliterate "primitive" societies. As such, it paid little attention to writing. Nevertheless, recent decades have seen writing attract increasing anthropological interest. A distinguishing feature of anthropological scholarship on writing is that it has sought to situate specific forms of writing within broader patterns of social practice (e.g., scientific laboratory research, international human rights activism, academic assessment exercises, bureaucratic state governance).[1]

Anthropological scholarship on writing has both strengths and weaknesses. One significant weakness is that it neglects hermeneutic theory. By extension, it neglects the process whereby people infer a coherent overall picture of a mind from signs/effects of mental attributes, which are often recorded in written texts. Hence, in the Islamic tradition, such signs/effects include God's statements in the Qurʾanic text, textual Hadith reports on the Prophet's actions, and textual reports on the actions of past religious scholars.

But anthropological scholarship on writing also has some noteworthy strengths. Such scholarship highlights two important points about writing. First, not only do distinct social groups use writing in distinct ways, but specific forms of writing often play a fundamental role in generating and maintaining these groups. Thus, the social bonds tying together group members are commonly sustained through the circulation of written artifacts like letters, petitions, novels, academic articles, newspapers, and business cards. Hence, when examining specific forms of writing, it is necessary to ask what types of social bonds they create.

This brings us to the second point. Recent anthropological scholarship on writing has challenged the tendency to treat material objects as passive instruments manipulated by human agents. Rather, it has stressed that such objects

[1] See Latour and Woolgar 1986; Riles 2001; Brenneis 1994; Strathern 2006; Hull 2012.

The Anthropology of Islamic Law. Aria Nakissa.

influence and shape social practices. This is perhaps most obvious with respect to high-tech objects like computers and robots. However, it is also true of more ordinary written materials. The formatting and design of such materials work to elicit particular types of responses from human agents, thereby shaping, in distinct ways, practices of reading, organizing information, communicating, and the like. Hence, when examining specific forms of writing, it is necessary to ask how they shape social practices.

The present chapter builds on these two points. Accordingly, it is argued that the written texts used in traditional Islamic learning are designed in a manner which promotes the pedagogy of companionship, thereby creating social bonds between *shaykhs* and their pupils. This being said, let us take a closer look at the distinctive way written texts are integrated into Islamic learning.

## I. *MUSHĀFAHA* AND ORALITY

A defining feature of traditional Islamic learning is its attitude toward orality. Premodern educational treatises stress that to understand a text requires reading it aloud in the presence of a scholar.[2] Independent reading is condemned in the harshest terms. Ibn Jamāʿa quotes one authority as saying: "Among the greatest calamities is to make a book into one's *shaykh*."[3] Ibn Jamāʿa himself adds: "Knowledge is not to be taken from books, and doing so is among the most harmful of corrupt acts (*min aḍarr al-mafāsid*)."[4]

Present-day Traditionalist scholars are fond of quoting a rhyming maxim which states: "Whosoever takes his book as his *shaykh* errs more often than he is correct." (*Man akhadha shaykhahu kitābahu fa-khaṭʾuhu akthar min ṣawābuhu*). At one gathering, I witnessed a *shaykh* read out the following lines of poetry: "Whoever takes knowledge from a *shaykh* orally (*mushāfahatan*). He is prevented from deviance and misguidance. And whosoever takes knowledge from pages (*ṣuḥuf*). In the eyes of the people of knowledge, it is as if his knowledge does not exist." A common term of abuse for one who studies by private reading is "*ṣuḥufī*"[5]—related to the Arabic word "*ṣaḥīfa*," which means page.[6] Traditionalist authorities constantly warn those around them never to trust the opinion of a *ṣuḥufī*, and deny that such individuals have any claim to scholarly status.

The process of properly receiving knowledge from a teacher orally is known as "taking from the mouths of *shaykhs*" (*al-ahkdh min afwāh al-mashāyikh*). It is also commonly referred to by the Arabic term "*mushāfaha*." The practice in question has varied both over different periods and across different geographical areas. Nevertheless, there are also overarching continuities which have exerted a defining influence on the character of traditional education.

[2] Berkey 1992:25. [3] Ibn Jamāʿa 2009:90. [4] Ibn Jamāʿa 2009:105.
[5] Also pronounced "saḥafī." [6] See Al-Ghurbāni 1999:19–21 and Schoeler 2006:59.

## II. TEXTS RATHER THAN COURSES

To understand how taking from the mouths of *shaykhs* operates, attention must be given to the larger educational system in which it is embedded. In the contemporary West, learning is organized in terms of topic-based courses (e.g., "Introduction to Chemistry," "Modern French Literature," etc.). Teachers are tasked with giving students a mastery of the course topic. The material is typically conveyed through a combination of lectures and readings from different texts. Upon completing this material, students may pursue more specialized knowledge by enrolling in more advanced courses.

Traditional Islamic learning is organized around texts rather than topic-based courses. To be sure, texts are usually related to specific topics. But students do not conceptualize their educational histories as a series of courses. Rather they speak of a series of texts. To learn a text entails proceeding through it in a linear fashion—ideally from beginning to end. There is no breaking away from the text in favor of readings from other sources on the same subject. Moreover, although a teacher may offer comments upon a text, his lectures are not a substitute for it. In other words, the teacher cannot excuse students from reading over particular passages by explaining the subject matter with which they deal. The specific words of the text must be covered. The teacher may add to them. But he may not subtract from them.

Mastering a field (e.g., law, grammar, theology) involves progressing through the various texts with which it is associated. Traditional learning does not proceed within the framework of a fixed curriculum. Still, there remain general ordering principles. Now, as in the past, those who participate in study-circles recognize that different texts are suitable for students at different levels of knowledge. Some are appropriate for beginners, whereas others should only be taken up by intermediate or advanced students. Common patterns emerge for attaining mastery in specific fields. These patterns are constantly evolving over time, and also differ by geographical region. Hence, patterns in Egypt are distinct from those in Morocco and Yemen. Even within a single region, there may be several different alternatives, varying in terms of the texts covered and/or the order in which they are covered. It is the responsibility of students to choose a workable pattern. In present-day Egypt, choices are largely dictated by which texts the available teachers are covering.

## III. MEMORIZATION

Traditional Islamic learning places great emphasis on memorization.[7] Memorization admits of numerous degrees. For scholars whom I interacted with, to "memorize" a text could mean a variety of different things. At the highest

[7] For a description of memorization in the medieval period see Makdisi 1981:99–102.

level of memorization, a scholar can produce the entirety of the text, word-by-word. Upon being supplied part of a phrase located anywhere in the text, he can immediately produce the remainder of the phrase. He can also produce the phrase which immediately preceded it. At a lower level of memorization, a scholar can produce the entire text, but only in a linear sequence. To recall the material he must start at the beginning of a chapter or some other fixed unit. At an even lower level, a scholar can only produce the text after hearing it recited, or after reviewing it in written form. Still lower levels of memorization consist in the ability to passively recognize the exact wording of the original text upon hearing it.

Because memorization admits of so many levels, it is not always apparent what is meant when it is said that a scholar has "memorized" a particular text. For some texts (such as the Qur'an), references to memorization are typically understood as referring to the higher levels. But with respect to most texts, things are usually less clear. Scholars in different geographical regions often have different expectations concerning which texts should be memorized and how deeply they should be memorized. Such differences are nothing new, being attested in premodern times as well.[8]

Keeping a text memorized (especially at the higher levels) is only possible by constantly repeating it, either to oneself or others.[9] Absent repetition, the text will gradually descend down to lower levels of memorization. Eventually it may be forgotten. The amount of repetition necessary to preserve a text depends on the age at which it was initially memorized. One ancient authority is reported to have said: "as for what I have learned in my youth, it is as if I can see it [written] on parchment or paper."[10] A *shaykh* I spoke with cited the following rhyming maxim: "Whosoever takes knowledge while he is young, it is akin to engraving in stone. Whosever takes knowledge after becoming older, it is akin to writing on the surface of water." This maxim is also attested in medieval sources.[11]

Those I interviewed insisted that intensive exercise of memory skills during one's youth also made it easier to acquire and preserve new texts later in life. It is for this reason that traditional Islamic education begins with memorizing the Qur'an in the *kuttāb*. The skills built up by memorizing the Qur'anic text can then be drawn on throughout later stages of education.

Notably, although Muslim scholars emphasize the importance of memorization, this does not prevent them from relying on written materials as well.[12] This may seem surprising, given the common Western assumption that memory and writing operate as two opposed alternatives. Yet in premodern Muslim societies, writing and memory were utilized together as part of a single process.[13] While scholars strove to keep material in memorized form, they also constantly checked the texts they had memorized against written versions. Such prevented

[8] Eickelman 1985:58. [9] Also see Makdisi 1981:128. [10] Ibn ʿAbd al-Barr 2006:95.
[11] See Ibn ʿAbd al-Barr 2006:94. Also see Ibn ʿAbd al-Barr 95 and Ibn al-Ḥājj 2008, 1:j.2 296.
[12] See Makdisi 1981:104–105. [13] See Chapter 1 in Schoeler 2006, especially p.41.

errors from creeping in.[14] Still, despite the acknowledged value of writing, its proper role was understood to be that of a memory aid. It could not substitute for the memorized version of the text. Hence, learning a text always necessitated receiving it from a *shaykh* who had memorized it rather than simply taking it from the pages of a book.

In eighteenth century Egypt, students began their higher studies at al-Azhar upon reaching puberty. Before then they had completed memorization of the Qurʾan, probably finishing somewhere between the ages of 9 to 13.[15] Many had memorized several additional texts as well.[16]

At present, large feats of memorization are rare in Egypt, even among scholars who are consciously Traditionalist in orientation. The decline of memorization has been brought about by modernizing educational reforms. Contemporary Egyptian students at al-Azhar's religious faculties struggle to fully memorize the Qurʾan itself. Prior to enrolling at the university, time spent at the Azhar institutes has usually enabled them to internalize most or all of the Qurʾan at a low level of memorization. During their four undergraduate years, Egyptian students gradually memorize the entirety of the Qurʾan at a high level. Their progress is ensured through periodic tests. Foreign students at al-Azhar are held to far lower standards. Although requirements vary by nationality, the undergraduate degree often requires memorizing no more than 4/30ths of the Qurʾan while the master's degree only requires 6/30ths. At the Dār al-ʿUlūm, neither Egyptians nor foreigners are obliged to memorize the entire Qurʾan. To graduate with a master's degree from the Department of Sharīʿa only requires 5/30ths. The doctorate requires 10/30ths.

Most current students at al-Azhar memorize no texts besides the Qurʾan and a very small number of Hadith reports. A Traditionalist minority, disproportionately foreign in origin, devotes more energy to memorization. Yet, even among them, few texts other than the Qurʾan (around 600 pages) are memorized at a high level. Those texts which are memorized tend to be shorter in length than the Qurʾan. On a number of occasions, I had the opportunity to personally test scholars on their memorization. The largest texts presented to me were longer than the Qurʾan but still under 1,000 pages. Some scholars I spoke with claimed to know individuals who had memorized much larger works, even if such feats were admittedly very rare.

## IV. THE *SANAD* AND THE *IJĀZA*

In traditional learning, a teacher is only entitled to transmit a text if he has received it directly from another scholar. As noted previously, the transmission of texts revolves around the concept of *sanad*. All texts must be received through

[14] In this sense, "memorization" in Muslim societies operated in a manner substantially different from various other cultures; see, e.g., Ong 1982:57–67.

[15] See, e.g., Naṣr 2009:140; Sedgwick 2009:2. [16] Heyworth-Dunne 1939:36.

an unbroken chain. Where the Qurʾan and Hadith reports are concerned, the *sanad* always extends directly back to the Prophet Muḥammad. In the case of other texts, the *sanad* must extend back to their author. For instance, a book on jurisprudence by Imam al-Shāfiʿī requires a *sanad* extending back to al-Shāfiʿī. Nevertheless, there is another sense in which even a text of this type is seen as ultimately extending back to the Prophet. In the eyes of Muslim scholars, al-Shāfiʿī acquired his knowledge through an unbroken chain originating with the Prophet.[17] Because his book is a product of that knowledge, it can be thought of as having an indirect *sanad* linking it to the Prophet.

In traditional learning, an individual who wishes to take a text from a scholar, and thus to add his name to the *sanad* of transmission, must first secure that scholar's "permission" or "*ijāza*." This permission may take verbal form. It may also be recorded in writing, furnishing durable evidence that an individual has acquired a text legitimately. *Ijāzas* do not have a standardized form. Still, certain elements are common. A written *ijāza* often bears the sign or seal of the issuing *shaykh*. It frequently lists the names of every individual in the *sanad* of the *shaykh* through whom a text is being received. Contemporary *ijāzas* for very early texts may include lists of names which total over 20 in number.

## V. THREE MODES OF TRANSMISSION

How does a teacher decide whether or not to give a student an *ijāza* for a specific text? In traditional Islamic learning, there are three possibilities. Let us consider them in turn.

Ideally an *ijāza* is not issued until after the performance of what is known as "*samāʿ*" ("audition"). In *samāʿ* the *shaykh* recites the text to students orally, word-by-word. *Samāʿ* is the paradigmatic model for the practice of "taking from the mouths of *shaykhs*."

When reciting a text, a teacher may do so either directly from memory or by reading from a book. While some premodern *shaykhs* are said to have relied on the former method,[18] I never witnessed it myself. All the teachers I saw read from books. In theory, even reading from a book still relies on memory—for the *shaykh* is supposed to check the book against his memory to ensure its accuracy. Such was indeed important in premodern times, when all texts were handwritten in manuscript form. Memory provided a valuable means of guarding against scribal errors and omissions. In any event, at present, teachers only dictate from standardized printed editions, and are thus little concerned with problems of this type.

An *ijāza* may also be issued after the performance of what is known as "*qirāʾa*"[19] ("reading"). *Qirāʾa* differs from *samāʿ* in that it is the student rather than the

[17] Consequently, Muslim authors supply full unbroken *sanads* linking the legal knowledge of later jurists directly to the Prophet. For an example see al-Kawtharī 2004:67–68.

[18] See, e.g., Makdisi 1981:100.

[19] Or "ʿarḍ."

teacher who orally recites the text being taught. The student may either recite the text directly from memory or read from a written version. In either case, the oral recitation occurs in the presence of a teacher, putting the latter in a position to check over what is being recited and correct any mistakes. *Qirāʾa* sessions are usually not limited to the teacher and the student reciting the text. Other students will also be in attendance, simply listening. *Qirāʾa* functions as a substitute for *samāʿ*. Although *samāʿ* is generally regarded as superior to *qirāʾa*, the difference between them is not a great one, and many scholars view them as equivalent in value.[20]

The need to read texts aloud, evident in both *samāʿ* and *qirāʾa*, is associated with (although not reducible to) the peculiar properties of the Arabic script.[21] The Arabic script can be (and usually is) written in such a manner that only the consonants are recorded. The vowels linking these consonants must be inferred by the reader. For instance, the words "*kataba*" (he wrote), "*kutiba*" (it was written), and "*kutub*" (books) are all recorded identically as "k-t-b." Contextual cues must be used to identify which of these words was intended by the author, and hence how the text should be pronounced. At times, the cues are ambiguous, leading to doubts concerning the proper meaning/pronunciation of the consonantal text. An oral recitation of the text eliminates these doubts by explicitly articulating the proper vowelling.

Performing *samāʿ* or *qirāʾa* guarantees that the student possesses a reliable copy of the text being taught. If the student lacks the text altogether, he may write it down word-by-word as it is recited in the lesson, thereby creating his own version. In the manuscript era, when cheap printed books were not available, producing written texts in this way was an important component of student life. Even in cases where a student already possessed a written copy of the text, going through it word-by-word in the presence of a teacher provided an opportunity to authenticate its contents. Modern use of standardized printed editions is liable to blind us to how important this issue was in the past. To ensure that an edition is reliable, we simply look for the printed seal of a credible publishing house. To appreciate the concerns of premodern scholars, it is helpful to consider the anxiety we might experience in citing textual material from random internet pages. Certainly this anxiety would not be lessened if we were depending on this material for our religious salvation.

A third mode of textual transmission is known as "*munāwala*."[22] Unlike *samāʿ* and *qirāʾa*, *munāwala* does not qualify, in any straightforward sense, as taking from the mouths of *shaykhs*. In *munāwala* the teacher issues an *ijāza* for a text without first demanding the performance of *samāʿ* or *qirāʾa*. The student is left to read the text independently.[23] A teacher will only permit *munāwala* if he is certain

[20] See Schoeler 2006:30 and Ibn ʿAbd al-Barr 2006:413–417.

[21] Messick 1993:26 and Schoeler 2006:59.

[22] In Egypt, *munāwala* is usually referred to simply as "ijazā." So rather than saying: "this was taken by *munāwala*," it will be said "this text was taken by *ijāza*."

[23] Ibn ʿAbd al-Barr 2006:417–420.

that the student has access to a copy whose authenticity admits of no doubt. In theory, the teacher must additionally be convinced that the student's past education has prepared him to understand the text on his own. Ibn ʿAbd al-Barr remarks that "permission [for *munāwala*] is only acceptable for someone who is masterful and skillful in the craft, and who knows how to receive knowledge of it through *munāwala*."[24] It was assumed that the only way for a student to achieve such a status was by having already learned other texts through either *samāʿ* or *qirāʾa*. In other words, *munāwala* was never supposed to operate alone. Rather, it was only legitimate if used as a supplement to *samāʿ* and *qirāʾa*. Despite universal agreement that *munāwala* is inferior to *samāʿ* and *qirāʾa*, it is in wide use today among Traditionalist scholars. It also seems to have been extensively practiced in late premodern Egypt.[25]

At first glance, it may appear that *shaykhs* give out *ijāzas* for *munāwala* indiscriminately. During my fieldwork, I witnessed some *shaykhs* give out *ijāzas* of this type to gigantic crowds of students of whom they have no personal knowledge. Moreover, these *ijāzas* were for hundreds of texts rather than a single text. Such grants of *munāwala* were usually given after *samāʿ* or *qirāʾa* of a single short text (or part of a short text). Sometimes they were given after performing group worship (e.g., *dhikr*) together for a few hours.

When I expressed my confusion regarding these practices scholars informed me that *ijāzas* for *munāwala* could mean very different things according to context. For instance, the mass granting of *ijāzas* that I had witnessed was not intended to convey scholarly authority. Rather, it was simply done for the sake of *baraka* ("*al-ijāza li-l-baraka*"). Students sought *baraka* by receiving permission to attach themselves to a *sanad* of scholars stretching back to the Prophet. The Prophet's *baraka* was believed to run through this chain.[26] (The idea of granting apparent scholarly certification for non-scholarly purposes is hardly foreign to the West, as is obvious in the conferral of honorary degrees.)

In reality, it is not only *ijāzas* for *munāwala* that admit of different types. As we shall soon see, all *ijāzas*, even those based on *samāʿ* and *qirāʾa*, can mean radically different things depending on the circumstances in which they are received.

At present, students may acquire different parts of a single text in diverse ways. It is common for a teacher to go over part of the text through *samāʿ* or *qirāʾa*, and allow the remainder to be taken through *munāwala*. A teacher may also cover a single text in its entirety by *samāʿ* or *qirāʾa* and then give students *ijāzas* to take all of the other texts he knows by *munāwala*. These transmission practices extend back into the late premodern period, and perhaps even earlier.[27]

Once a scholar has an *ijāza* for a text he may transmit it to others, issuing them *ijāzas* himself, and thereby permitting the extension of the text's *sanad*. While

[24] Ibn ʿAbd al-Barr 2006:419–420.

[25] I base these conclusions partly on *ijāza* manuscripts I looked at in al-Azhar's library. But it is supported by printed *ijāzas* as well. See, e.g., Khafājī 1987, 2:104–122; al-Fādānī 2008.

[26] Relevant here is Ibn Jamāʿa 2009:67.

[27] I base these conclusions partly on *ijāza* manuscripts I looked at in al-Azhar's library. But it is supported by printed *ijazas* as well. See, e.g., Khafājī 1987, 2:104–122; al-Fādānī 2008.

ordinary *ijāzas* concern specific texts, some also confer general permission to teach law and/or issue legal opinions.[28] How these latter types of *ijāzas* function is a controversial matter into which we will not enter here.[29]

There is no upper limit to how many *ijāzas* an individual may possess. The more *ijāzas*, the better. In maximizing the number of *ijāzas*, a student may go through the same text with different teachers, taking a separate *ijāza* from each of them.

## VI. *MATNS* AND COMMENTARY

We have already seen that traditional Islamic learning stresses memory, and that memory skills are exercised from youth. Still, the ability to memorize depends upon more than the mnemonic capacities of the scholar. It is also tied to the properties of the text to be memorized. Here the two most important characteristics are (1) the size of the text, and (2) whether or not it is versified. The shorter a text is, the easier it is to memorize. Similarly, a versified text in poetic form is easier to retain than prose.

After the eleventh century, Islamic learning came to revolve around a type of text known as a "*matn*" (or "*mukhtaṣar*")[30].[31] Late premodern Egypt was no exception.[32] *Matns* are designed for ease of memorization. They are short in length[33] and often versified. Traditionalist scholars are fond of a rhyming maxim which states: "Whosoever memorizes the *matns*, acquires the fields of knowledge."

A *matn* is meant to serve as a basic text. Its content consists in an overview of a particular field of knowledge. There are *matns* dedicated to law, theology, grammar, and the like. In some cases, a *matn* may restrict its attention to a particular subfield. Hence, while some *matns* seek to summarize the law as a whole, there are also works limited to the rules associated with prayer or inheritance (e.g., *al-Akhḍarī, al-Raḥbiyya*). The *matn* provides a sort of a mental outline to which the scholar can refer when dealing with a particular topic. An outline of this type is crucial in a field such as law, where rituals or transactions may consist in multiple ordered steps and require the fulfillment of myriad conditions. The only scholars I have ever met who can answer detailed legal questions without first consulting books are those who have memorized *matns*. Notably, traditional Islamic education works on the assumption that a scholar should be able to respond immediately to the queries he receives in the mosque and other venues. Al-Ẓawāhirī quips that those who lack adequate memorization skills should not be called "scholar," deserving instead the title "scholar of reviewing

[28] See Makdisi 1981:148–152.

[29] See, e.g., Stewart 2004.

[30] Although the terms "*mukhtaṣar*" and "*matn*" are largely interchangeable and often refer to the same texts, the two concepts are different. When I use the word "*matn*," what I mean more precisely is a "*matn mukhtaṣar.*"

[31] Hallaq 2009:138. Also see Messick 1993:18.

[32] Heyworth-Dunne 1939:6.

[33] Ibn Khaldūn 2010:v.3 1109; Messick 1993:21.

[source materials]" (*ʿālim al-murājaʿa*). He advises them not to leave the public libraries lest it causes them to lose their knowledge.[34]

To provide an idea of the size of *matns*, let me mention some of those I came across in a contemporary study-circle at al-Azhar mosque. In his mid-30s, the teacher was a Mālikī of Algerian origin. He was currently a master's student at al-Azhar University, having previously studied in Mauritania. His study-circle was exceptional for the wide range and high number of *matns* covered. These included (from shortest to longest): *al-Sullam al-Munawraq* in logic (about 10 pages), *Alfiyya ibn Mālik* in grammar (about 50 pages), *Marāqī al-Suʿūd* in legal theory (about 50 pages), *Jamʿ al-Jawāmiʿ* in legal theory (about 100 pages), and *Mukhtaṣar Khalīl* in Mālikī law (about 300 pages). These sizes are very loose estimates, given that the printed texts differ significantly in format and pagination. Nevertheless, they suffice to give a general idea of length. With the exception of *Marāqī al-Suʿūd*, all of the texts mentioned were utilized at al-Azhar during the eighteenth century.[35] While many of these *matns* may not seem particularly small, it should be kept in mind that the more extensive works in these various fields commonly run thousands of pages in length.

Where *matns* are concerned, the drive for concision leads to the omission of as much excess verbiage as possible. Consequently, a finished *matn* typically has the appearance of an ordinary work whose sentences have been whittled down to a string of key words. Some are unexplained technical terms. Others elliptically allude to more detailed doctrine. Ibn Khaldūn observes that the drive for maximal concision makes *matns* difficult to understand.[36] These difficulties are only magnified by the unconventional linguistic contortions needed to put *matns* into verse. One Azhar professor explained to me that *matns* are characterized by "impossibility [to understand] and obscurity" (*iʿjāz wa ilghāz*).

The obscure structure of the *matn* means that, by its very nature, it requires a commentary to be apprehended.[37] In recognition of this fact, authors of *matns* sometimes penned commentaries to go with them. Yet, in most cases, commentary was provided by other scholars. It is worth going into this point in some depth.

In traditional learning, when a teacher transmits a text he does not limit himself to its contents. Rather, an essential part of the transmission process consists in commentary. As the teacher goes through a text, he comments on it as needed. In *samāʿ*, where he himself is reciting the text, he pauses after every line (sometimes after every word) to add commentary. In *qirāʾa*, where the text is being recited by a student, the teacher interjects at appropriate points. The student enables him to do this by reciting at a slow pace,

[34] Al-Ẓawāhirī 1904:74.

[35] For an extensive list of *matns* used at al-Azhar prior to the reforms see Heyworth-Dunne 1939:42–65.

[36] Ibn Khaldūn 2010, 3:1109.

[37] Messick 1993:33–34.

immediately stopping when the *shaykh* begins to speak. The stream of remarks supplied by the *shaykh* contributes to the oral dimension of textual transmission and reinforces the idea that proper learning necessitates taking from the mouths of *shaykhs*.

Commentary on *matns* admits of different types. There are three levels. Where a teacher comments directly upon a *matn*, the result is called a "first-order commentary" (*sharḥ*). A basic aim of a first-order commentary is to "unpack" the *matn* by restoring the clarity lost in compressing it into memorizable form.[38] Every line in the *matn* is systematically explained. The commentary may be limited to what is minimally needed to understand a word or phrase, but it may go significantly beyond that. Oftentimes, the first-order commentary of a famous *shaykh* is written down by his students so as to preserve it for future generations. In this case, it may itself become the object of further commentary. Such "second-order commentary" (*ḥāshiya*) usually focuses on specific portions of the first-order commentary that require additional exposition. If written down, a second-order commentary may also become the subject of further commentary. "Third-order commentary" (*taqrīr*), like second-order commentary, focuses on particular points in need of supplementary explanation. Many of the works which have come down to us from late premodern Egypt originated in this fashion.[39] They are direct products of the pedagogical practices characteristic of taking from the mouths of *shaykhs*.

In the premodern period *matns* were memorized at a high level. Even today, such continues in some areas of the Muslim world. Generally speaking, memorization is less intense when it comes to commentaries. However, scholars I spoke with told me that practices vary by geographical region. It was claimed that in some regions outside of Egypt (e.g., Yemen and Mauritania) first-order commentaries, and even second-order commentaries, are memorized at a high level. I was not in a position to verify such assertions.[40] At any rate, memorization practices of this type play no significant role among contemporary Egyptian scholars.

Messick observes that in the early years of Islamic education there is a greater emphasis on memorization and a greater dependence on instruction from teachers. As a student progresses, each of these things becomes less central. This overall pattern is reflected in the type of texts studied at each stage of learning.[41] A student begins by memorizing *matns*. He starts with basic *matns*, gradually moving on to longer and more detailed ones. As a student increases in knowledge, less time is spent on memory-intensive texts like *matns*. Efforts are redirected toward commentaries and other types of texts which demand little or no memorization. Such include histories, literary works, collections of legal opinions, dictionaries, assorted treatises, and so forth. Like other works, these

[38] See al-Ẓawāhirī 1904:148–149.

[39] See Heyworth-Dunne 1939:66.

[40] For more on the question of memorizing commentaries see Messick 1993:87–88.

[41] See Messick 1993:84–92.

texts must be taken through a *sanad* with an *ijāza*. Nevertheless, those who are advanced in learning will become eligible to receive them, possibly en masse, by *munāwala*. This enables students to read more broadly, and to do so at a pace of their own choosing. An advanced student will still seek to acquire knowledge by *samāʿ* and *qirāʾa*. Yet the significance of *munāwala* will increase.

A defining characteristic of taking from the mouths of *shaykhs* is the (by present standards) extremely slow rate at which texts are covered. This slowness derives from several factors. First of all, students must devote a great deal of time to memorizing the texts being studied. Second, in learning a text, the student does not merely cover the text itself, but is also obliged to sit through *shaykhly* commentary. The word-length of the commentary is usually many times that of the text itself. Third, when proceeding by *samāʿ* or *qirāʾa*, the student is limited by the amount of text which the teacher covers in class. The student is not assigned portions of the text to read independently at home. A student's only "homework" consists of memorizing and trying to understand those segments of text which the teacher has already recited word-by-word.

It is difficult to estimate the precise rates at which teachers moved through texts in late premodern Egypt. Presumably, such would have varied not only according to the type of text, but also according to a specific teacher's pedagogical style. While those who currently teach using traditional methods may not operate at the same pace as their predecessors, their practices still offer a helpful illustration of the slowness with which texts are covered.

The lessons I attended almost all dealt with either *matns* or first-order commentaries, usually lasting between one and two hours. Where *matns* were involved, the teacher never covered more than a single page in a session, and sometimes was only able to make it through two lines. In the case of first-order commentaries, the most I ever saw covered was six pages. Ordinarily, the amount covered was closer to two pages, but sometimes did not exceed a single sentence. At al-Azhar's Faculty of Sharīʿa, in those classes I attended where traditional commentary methods were used, teachers only made it through approximately 15–30 pages per semester.

For those who currently use traditional methods, finishing a single moderately sized volume can take two to three years. Large multivolume works may consume five to eight years. Speaking with reference to al-Azhar toward the end of the nineteenth century, ʿAbduh mentions a long text requiring eight years to complete.[42] Obviously the more time spent acquiring a specific text, the less time which can be devoted to others. As a result, in traditional learning, reading widely is not emphasized. More stress is put on thoroughly mastering a limited amount of material.[43]

42 ʿAbduh 2006, 3:152. For related remarks see al-Ẓawāhirī 1904:151.

43 See Green 2010:245.

## VII. TAKING FROM THE MOUTHS OF *SHAYKHS* AND COMPANIONSHIP

Receiving texts by taking from the mouths of *shaykhs* provides a number of educational advantages not available to those who simply purchase books and read them independently. Recent studies have highlighted the benefit of having a teacher present to offer commentary and answer questions.[44] An aspect that has received less attention is the relationship between taking from the mouths of *shaykhs* and companionship.

During my fieldwork, I often asked scholars why they considered orality so important. Their responses repeatedly foregrounded its linkage to learning in the physical presence of a *shaykh*. Having a *shaykh* present not only allowed him to provide commentary, but also to transfer knowledge through companionship.

Recall that the practice of companionship involves directly observing and imitating a *shaykh*'s practice of Sharīʿa rules over an extended period of time. Taking from the mouths of *shaykhs* generates circumstances conducive to this type of relationship. The obligation to hear a text from a *shaykh* necessitates being in his physical presence, thereby enabling direct observation of the *shaykh*. Moreover, when a student is in the physical presence of the *shaykh*, the *shaykh* can use discipline/punishment to ensure that the student is properly imitating his practice of Sharīʿa rules. Finally, because it takes so long to proceed through a text, the student must remain with the *shaykh* for an extended period. As a result, the student must directly observe and imitate the *shaykh*'s practice of Sharīʿa rules for an extended period. By contrast, independent reading does not entail the physical presence of a *shaykh* at all. Consequently, it does not involve directly observing and imitating a *shaykh*'s practice of Sharīʿa rules over an extended period. In this sense, independent reading is the antithesis of companionship.

Premodern educational treatises continually link taking from the mouths of *shaykhs* with companionship, contrasting it with independent reading. For instance, Ibn Jamāʿa counsels aspiring students to select a teacher who has himself "had much discussion with a trustworthy *shaykh* of his era and passed a long amount of time in his company (*ṭūl ijtimāʿ*). [The student must not choose] someone which has taken his knowledge from paper, and is not known to have performed companionship (*ṣuḥba*) with skilled *shaykhs*."[45] Notice that Ibn Jamāʿa contrasts the *shaykh* who has performed companionship with the man who has taken his knowledge from books.

Further examples can be found in contemporary educational treatises. One text, dedicated entirely to criticism of independent reading, contains a chapter entitled "Encouragement to Take Knowledge from the Mouths of Scholars." The chapter quotes two ancient authorities, each urging students to acquire dispositions through companionship. The first authority cited states: "Narrating from scholars and sitting with them is more beloved to me than much legal knowledge

[44] See, e.g., Mitchell 1991; Messick 1993; Schoeler 2006.

[45] Ibn Jamāʿa 2006:90.

because it is the manners of the people and their dispositions." The second authority states: "O my son, go to the jurists and scholars. Learn from them and take from their manners, dispositions, and guidance. Verily that is more beloved to me than [learning] many *ḥadīth* reports."[46]

The author of another modern educational treatise says: "some students believe that by reading books they will become scholars, and that they are not in need of studying with scholars and taking from them, and this is a grave error (*khaṭ' fāḍiḥ*)."[47] In support of this claim, the author cites two lines of poetry attributed to Imam al-Shāfiʿī: "My brother you will not acquire knowledge other than through six [things]. I will inform you of their details with a list. Intelligence and desire and effort and competence. *And the companionship of a teacher and a long period of time.*"[48] [emphasis mine].

The eminent Azhari ʿAbd al-Fattāḥ Abū Ghudda (d.1997) explains that taking knowledge from books rather than through oral transmission means "the impossibility of acquiring [knowledge from the] good and righteous example (*al-qudwa*) [of a living person] by smelling[49] him, sitting with him, hearing him, and looking upon him, [such that his example] embodies the virtuous dispositions (*tujassim al-faḍā'il*) and implants [within the student] their imitation and endears [their imitation to him]." Abū Ghudda then immediately cites a Qur'anic verse which states: "In the Messenger of God there is a good exemplar for you."[50]

In the preceding passage Abū Ghudda describes the learning process with words that have sensory connotations, and expressly draws attention to the fact that the teacher literally "embodies" the virtues being taught. The teacher's bodily presence communicates a rich array of sensory data which then enables the learning through "imitation" characteristic of companionship. Mere textual representations provide nothing of this kind. Unlike a living exemplar, a book cannot be imitated bodily. Abū Ghudda indicates that the teacher serves as a surrogate for the Prophet's own bodily presence. He subtly signals the equivalence between teacher and Prophet by citing the Qur'anic verse enjoining imitation of the Prophet, even though he is technically speaking about imitating latter-day *shaykhs*.

At the beginning of my research, I was unaware of any connection between oral instruction and the transmission of dispositions through companionship. However, my attention was drawn to this linkage by a particular event, which I recount in my fieldnotes:

> *It was a Tuesday at al-Azhar's Faculty of Sharīʿa. I was studying with a cohort of master's students specializing in legal theory. Many of them lived in the countryside, only visiting Cairo for the purpose of attending classes. Students petitioned their teachers to keep the number of days they were required to be in the city to a minimum. Accordingly, the six or so*

[46] Al-Ghurbānī 1999:33.

[47] Karzūn 2008:74.

[48] Karzūn 2008:75

[49] This can also be translated "drawing near"; however, the rest of the phrase implies that the olfactory connotation of this word is intentional.

[50] Abū Ghudda 1992:146.

*classes they were taking for the semester were squeezed into two days per week. These classes included: (1) General Fiqh Maxims (al-Qawāʿid al-Fiqhiyya), (2) the Historical Development of Islamic Legal Theory, (3) Ḥanafī Legal Theory, (4) Non-Ḥanafī Legal Theory, and (5) the Overarching Goals of Sharīʿa Legislation (Maqāṣid al-Sharīʿa). There was also a required European language course. Each weekly class ran a little under two hours. The two days when classes were held were something of a marathon. Today four classes were scheduled, among them Ḥanafī Legal Theory.*

*Starting at 11:00 a.m., the Ḥanafī Legal Theory Class was held in a classroom on the fourth floor of the building occupied by the Faculty of Sharīʿa. Stuffy, dusty, and in poor repair, the room's windows were kept open to compensate for the lack of air conditioning. Doing so made audible the murmur of traffic from the busy street below. The walls of the classroom were painted a bluish-white hue, their lower-portions being streaked with dirt. The floor was constructed of dingy gray and white ceramic tiles.*

*Most of the area inside the classroom was taken up by old wooden furniture, much of it accidentally splotched with drops of white paint. The rear part of the room was being used to store several cabinets and bookcases. The middle was occupied by a mass of creaky brown wooden desk-chairs. Their ancient age was indicated by the fact that the desk-component of each unit had a small hole for use as an inkwell. The desk-component was attached to the chair from beneath, leaving the sides open and unobstructed.*

*The design of the desk-chairs allowed the individual units to be packed together in a row, forming one long unbroken bench with one long unbroken desk before it. Each row was placed against the row immediately in front of it as well as that immediately behind it, with no space in-between. The lack of space made it somewhat difficult to maneuver. To fill the rows, students had to first sit partially and then scoot in unison across the long benches that had been formed. A great deal of noise was produced by the resultant scuffing of wood against the floor.*

*At the front of the class was a sizable scraped-up pale green wooden table, behind which the teacher sat. To the rear of the teacher's chair was a large rectangular dry-erase board built into the wall. There were five rows of student seating in front of the teacher's table, each consisting of about 10 desk-chairs. The first row was placed up against the front of the table, directly in contact with it. Smaller rows of desk-chairs were placed up against the tables' left and right sides. There were a total of about 30 students in the class—only enough to fill about half of the available seats. They occupied the front-most rows to the maximum extent, leaving those closer to the rear of the classroom empty.*

*In his 60s, the teacher of the class was known for being a bit old-fashioned and exceptionally stringent on matters of student comportment. His lessons consisted in line-by-line commentary on a famous medieval Ḥanafī text authored by Ṣadr al-Sharīʿa. While delivering his commentary, he demanded the full and unwavering attention of those present. The gaze of every student was to be riveted on the physical body of the teacher and every ear was to be fixed on his words. While teaching he would periodically draw to an abrupt stop. He would then pick out a student, demanding that he reproduce word-for-word the last sentence out of his mouth. If the student hesitated or simply paraphrased he was forced to rise from his seat and stand for 20 minutes.*

*The teacher was very sensitive about the distractions posed by cell phones. One day, preparing to take notes on the day's lesson, I made the mistake of taking out my cell phone to consult the digital calendar and record the date. The instructor responded by rebuking me for my inattentiveness, telling me that I was to keep my focus on him and that by observing him and listening to his instructions I was to imitate his "manners" (adab) and thereby instill in myself his "dispositions" (akhlāq). Although I was puzzled by what he had said, it struck me as important, so I proceeded to write down his comments in my notebook. While I was doing so, he chastised me again. "Stop writing and pay attention to me. Don't you know that what I am teaching you is not found in books!"*

By his remarks, the teacher sought to make me more attentive to the type of knowledge he was transmitting. Rather than concentrating exclusively on words and texts, he wanted me to concentrate on his embodied example as well.

I would now like to relate the preceding points to traditional Islamic learning. Islamicists typically assume that the study of Sharīʿa is by nature a fundamentally textual endeavor. From this perspective, even if it is conceded that companionship is associated with the process of textual transmission, it will be imagined that it is simply "tacked on" as a secondary phenomenon. However, the impetus to automatically concede texts this type of supremacy stems from Western language ideology and its fetishization of writing. Beliefs of this type cannot be projected on to premodern Muslim scholars.

Describing educational life in medieval Damascus, Michael Chamberlain writes: "When young people mastered a text with a *shaykh*, or attended a lecture, or 'served' as in his ṣuḥba [companionship], the subject matter of education—the texts they studied—was in some respects arbitrary . . . When some books were read more often than others, it was because these were the books that the *shaykhs* carried, and that they themselves in turn passed on." Implicitly referencing Bourdieu's work on the habitus, Chamberlain affirms that what was most important was not so much the content of the texts themselves but rather "the latent 'curriculum' which permitted the young to incorporate bodily norms, ritual competencies, and performative techniques. . . ."[51] Chamberlain's analysis suggests that acquiring dispositions through companionship was not merely an accidental by-product of the transmitting texts. Rather, textual transmission derived much of its own significance from the fact that it provided an occasion for acquiring dispositions through companionship. It is for this reason that Chamberlain considers the content of transmitted texts to be of secondary importance. Brian Silverstein draws similar conclusions in the context of contemporary Turkish Sufism.[52]

Walter Ong's work suggests that premodern Muslim perspectives on learning are generally characteristic of societies where knowledge is transmitted orally rather than by writing. In such cultures individuals tend to learn by "observation and practice with only minimal verbalized explanation."[53] Ong observes

[51] Chamberlain 1994:151. [52] See B. Silverstein 2011:143–154. [53] Ong 1982:43.

that cultures dominated by writing (e.g., the modern West) evince a different orientation, placing emphasis on acquiring information through the abstract "study" of "stated truths" (i.e., explicit writing).[54]

Islamic texts function as nodes binding students and teachers together in companionship relations, and this function is reflected in the structure of such texts. Recall that the compressed and (frequently) versified structure of the *matn* makes it exceedingly difficult for a student to read on his own. Rather, he needs the continuous commentary of a teacher, which in turn necessitates the continuous physical presence of a teacher. This presence is the basis of companionship. Therefore, the structure of the *matn* works to enjoin companionship and bar private reading. Accordingly, al-Shāṭibī portrays texts as being "locked," asserting that it is only scholars who hold the "keys" needed to open them.[55]

The acute obscurity of the *matn* works to instill in students the broader notion that reading is too difficult to be done independently. When I spoke with more traditionally oriented scholars about reading, I was surprised at how often this view was expressed. Whereas my default assumption was that texts were inherently transparent and that reading was a simple task, they kept insisting that reading was difficult and required the assistance of a *shaykh*. As proof, they cited their experiences with *matns*.

If it were true that traditional education centered primarily on texts rather than relations of companionship, one might expect Muslim authors to depict knowledge as deposited in books. Yet they are very explicit that it resides in men. Knowledge is acquired by passing time with men, not books. One modern treatise dedicated to criticizing independent reading cites a Hadith report wherein the Prophet is reported to have said: " 'Take knowledge before it disappears." The people then ask "O Prophet of God, how can knowledge disappear whilst we have the book of God [i.e. the Qurʾan]." Upon hearing this the Prophet gets angry, recounting how the sacred texts of the Jews and the Christians have not benefited them. He then twice repeats the phrase "Verily the disappearance of knowledge is the disappearance of the people who possess it."[56] Al-Shāṭibī makes a similar point by quoting a Hadith report wherein the Prophet asserts that the way God makes knowledge disappear is by causing the death of scholars. For al-Shāṭibī such is proof that knowledge is transmitted through living men and that it "is necessary to have a teacher" (*lā budda min al-muʿallim*).[57] Significantly, this is the exact same expression which heads the section in Ibn Khaldūn's *Muqaddima* where he explains that learning consists in acquiring dispositions through imitation.[58]

[54] Ong 1982:8–9. To be precise, in the preceding passage the oral cultures referred to by Ong have no knowledge of writing at all. Yet, Ong also asserts that orality admits of different levels, and that the "mind-set" characteristic of purely oral cultures may be preserved in part even after the introduction of writing. See Ong 1982:11. He indicates that this is true in Arab Muslim societies. See Ong 1982:20, 26.

[55] Al-Shāṭibī 2004:57.

[56] Al-Ghurbānī 1999:14. Also see al-Ājurī 1985:17–19.

[57] Al-Shāṭibī 2004:54.

[58] Ibn Khaldūn 2010, 2:856.

The preceding points are nicely illustrated in an interview I had with a contemporary Azhari scholar in his mid-30s. When not studying for his master's degree, he divided his time between teaching in traditional study-circles and working as an administrative clerk at the Faculty of Sharīʿa. He explained to me that knowledge is stored in teachers. This is why it must be taken through a proper *sanad*. Individuals who are book-learned and lack a *sanad* must be avoided, as must book learning itself. "If there is a *shaykh* without a *sanad* do not take knowledge from him. Be careful about the *sanad*, because the *sanad* is the religion. The proper method of Azhari learning is expressed in a poem: 'The honor of the sciences is obtained from their [human] masters. Without them, books have no honor. Among Azharis, knowledge is a gem passed between them through inheritance. It is taken in a chain from recognized and honest persons.'"

The conception of knowledge being deposited in men rather than books is clearly tied to practices of memorization. Remember that the authoritative version of a text is that which has been memorized. The inscribed page is nothing more than a memory aid. The fact that knowledge is only truly present in men rather than books justifies the view that it can only be taken from men rather than books.

The notion of written texts as a memory aid must be understood in a broad sense. Therefore, it is not merely the case that Muslim scholars consult written texts as a means to preserve the texts they have memorized (e.g., the Qurʾan, various *matns*). Scholars also consult written texts as a means to preserve their proper practice of Sharīʾa rules (i.e., the Sunna). The living practice of Sharīʾa rules (i.e., Sunna) is the authoritative form of knowledge—but this knowledge is kept fresh and precise by consulting written texts as an aid.

## VIII. INDEPENDENT READING AND HERESY

Traditionalist scholars I spoke with strongly associated private reading with heresy.[59] A widely circulated expression holds that whosoever takes his book as his *shaykh* has taken the devil as his *shaykh*. One premodern scholar goes a step further, saying: "whoever has no *shaykh* has no religion, and whoever has no teacher has taken the devil as his Imam."[60]

Present-day Traditionalist authorities are fond of citing a particular passage by the medieval jurist al-Shāṭibī in support of their views.[61] The passage expounds the value of taking from the mouths of *shaykhs* primarily in terms of companionship.

[59] The premodern Catholic Church is known to have endorsed similar views. See Eisenstein 1979:334.

[60] Quoted in A. Shalabī 1999:211.

[61] I have come across this passage multiple times; see, e.g., Abū Ghudda 1992:150–153; Al-Ghurbānī 1999:35–39.

Al-Shāṭibī explains that a student who wishes to attain mastery in a field of knowledge must have:

> *shaykhs* who have given him an upbringing in that science, in order that he acquires it from them and makes companionship with them. [This is] so he is suited to take on their attributes as they relate to that [science]. Such was the way of the pious early generations (*salaf*). The first [instance] of [companionship] was the companionship of the Companions . . . This [i.e. taking knowledge through companionship] became like a principle for those after them. The second generation committed themselves to [taking knowledge] from the Companions in the same way that [the Companions] had taken it from the Prophet (saw), until they became knowledgeable and attained the peak of perfection in the Sharīʿa sciences. It suffices you [as proof] for the validity of this principle that you do not find a scholar famous among the people for dispensing knowledge unless he [himself] had a [living] exemplar [from which he learned] who was famous for the like in his [own] era.
>
> Rarely is there found a deviant sect or an individual opposed to the Sunna, except that he [has not performed companionship with a *shaykh*]. For this reason Ibn Ḥazm al-Ẓāhirī has been condemned, because he did not take [knowledge] from *shaykhs* through companionship and did not take upon himself their manners. Those scholars firmly rooted [in knowledge] such as the four Imams and their like [had an approach] opposite this.[62]

In al-Shāṭibī's eyes, heretical opinions and opposition to the true Sunna arise from not taking knowledge through companionship. He associates such deviance with independent reading. This is why he singles out Ibn Ḥazm for criticism. In the Islamic tradition, Ibn Ḥazm is notorious for having taken his learning through private reading.[63]

Al-Shāṭibī is hostile to private reading because it encourages people to believe that they can acquire knowledge of Sharīʿa rules by exclusive reliance on the method of learning through texts. Yet, al-Shāṭibī does not accept that texts alone suffice to adequately transmit such knowledge. Rather, anyone who wishes to acquire this knowledge must also utilize the methods of learning through observation and practice, which are combined together in the pedagogy of companionship. The technique of taking from the mouths of *shaykhs* is important because it ensures that whenever a student receives a text, he also partakes in companionship.

## IX. *IJĀZAS* REVISITED

At this point, I would like to briefly revisit the issue of *ijāzas*. Earlier on, I suggested that regardless of whether it is attained through *samāʿ*, *qirāʾa*, or *munāwala*,

[62] Al-Shāṭibī 2004:55.

[63] For more on this issue see Melchert 1997:189–190.

an *ijāza* does not have a fixed value. On the contrary, the value of an *ijāza* depends upon the circumstances surrounding its acquisition. We are now in a better position to appreciate why this is the case.

Present-day Traditionalist scholars ascribe radically different values to different *ijāzas*. If an individual has passed time with recognized authorities and has a demonstrated mastery of the religious sciences, then his *ijāzas* carry weight. The value of his *ijāzas* is further enhanced if they have been issued in the context of an extended relationship of companionship. Owing to their recognized significance, contextual facts of this type are often explicitly recorded in *ijāzas* themselves. This is true for those issued in the premodern period as well as today.[64]

An individual who possesses the necessary scholastic qualities, and has received his *ijāza* for a text under favorable circumstances, is regarded as a legitimate teacher of that text. Students come to learn it from him and to take it through his *sanad*. By contrast, students have little interest in studying with a teacher lacking these attributes, even if he has *ijāzas* received through *samāʿ* or *qirāʾa*. Irrespective of whether such a teacher can accurately convey the wording of the text itself, he is not in a position to supply trustworthy commentary or serve as an exemplar in a companionship relationship.

For a student to take knowledge from such a figure would be to undercut his own authority. This is because scholars establish their authority by presenting their *ijāzas* with the associated *sanads*. A *sanad* containing a figure without an established reputation (*majhūl*) is worthless. Now, as in the past, the need to establish that one's knowledge has been taken from credible authorities fuels the ongoing creation of elaborate biographical dictionaries. These dictionaries record the names of every new generation of scholars, allowing authorities to prove that all those present in their *sanads*, from beginning to end, have established reputations.

Without denying the possible existence of exceptions, it is doubtful whether premodern *ijāzas* were less variable in value.[65] Rather, the authority they represented was also highly dependent on the circumstances in which they were received. As we will see, understanding this point is necessary to appreciating the impact of the modern introduction of standardized degrees.

[64] For published examples see e.g., Khafājī 1987, 2:102, 109; Stewart 2004:68.
[65] See Berkey 1992:22; Chamberlain 1994:88–89. But also see Stewart 2004.

# Section III

# A New Perspective on Islamic Legal Doctrine

# 7

# The Structure of Islamic Legal Thought

In this chapter I address the overall structure of Islamic legal thought, and explain how it relates to Islamic learning. I link my analysis to ideas and practices found at al-Azhar University, al-Azhar mosque, and the Dār al-ʿUlūm.

In previous chapters, I have argued that knowledge of Sharīʿa rules can be conceptualized as knowledge of God's mental attributes (i.e., His intentions, as well as the beliefs and desires on which these intentions are based). In developing this line of analysis, I have relied heavily on ideas from hermeneutic theory. In the present chapter, I will further refine such ideas by drawing on recent work in "planning theory." "Planning theory" is an abbreviated name for what is known as the "planning theory of intention" or the "planning theory of agency." Planning theory is a leading approach in the philosophy of action. Since the 1980s, it has been developed in the writings of prominent philosopher of action Michael Bratman.[1] Although planning theory has yet to make a mark on anthropology or Islamicist history, it has already begun to impact legal scholarship through the influential recent work of Scott Shapiro and Richard Ekins.[2]

Bratman is a direct student of the prominent philosopher of action and hermeneutic theorist Donald Davidson. Accordingly, Bratman's work builds on hermeneutic ideas set forth by Davidson. Bratman's work is especially helpful in thinking about intentions, and how they relate to beliefs and desires. Meanwhile, Shapiro and Ekins have highlighted the relevance of Bratman's work on intentions to the analysis of legal rules. Bratman's ideas are complex, and there is no room here to review them in a precise and detailed manner. Rather, I will provide a simplified outline of planning theory based (roughly) on these ideas. I will then draw on these ideas to elucidate the overall structure of Islamic legal thought.

Admittedly, this chapter develops a line of analysis foreign to works of Islamicist history and anthropology. Although Islamicist scholarship recognizes that Islamic legal thought is centrally concerned with intentions (i.e., God's will/intentions), such scholarship tends to assume that the concept of intention is relatively simple and straightforward. Utilizing planning theory, I will challenge this assumption, explaining how intentions have a complex but intelligible

[1] See Bratman 1987; 1999; 2007; 2014; also see Holton 2009; Vargas and Yaffe 2014.

[2] See Shapiro 2002; 2011; Ekins 2012.

structure. Moving a step further, I will show how Sharīʿa rules (as God's intentions) have a complex but intelligible structure—one that has been hitherto overlooked by Islamicist scholarship. While Islamicist historians have at least acknowledged the necessity of seriously engaging with Islamic legal thought, anthropologists have avoided such engagement. I think this is a mistake, for an anthropologist cannot understand Islamic institutions (e.g., educational institutions, legal institutions) absent a serious engagement with Islamic legal thought. One must ask why people in these institutions have come to understand God's intentions (i.e., Sharīʿa rules) in a particular way. What is the reasoning behind their views? One cannot comprehend the reasoning of (religiously knowledgeable) Muslims without comprehending Islamic legal thought. That being said, let us turn to planning theory.

## I. PLANNING THEORY AND INSTRUMENTAL RATIONALITY

Planning theory builds on the notion of instrumental rationality advocated by hermeneutic thinkers like Weber and Davidson. Recall that, according to this notion, the totality of an individual's beliefs and desires cause him/her to form intentions. More specifically, an individual forms an intention to perform a particular action based on the strongest of his/her desires and in light of all his/her beliefs about the world. This intention then causes the person to perform the corresponding action.

Bratman holds that the preceding Davidsonian notion of instrumental rationality is partially correct. However, he insists that it is overly simplistic. For Bratman, a more sophisticated view requires a more complex analysis of intentions. Bratman suggests that intentions have several key characteristics which merit attention. I will focus on two of these characteristics: (1) intentions are partially instrumentally rational and partially arbitrary/non-rational, and (2) new circumstances can prompt individuals to abandon and reform their intentions.

Bratman's analysis of intentions is directly relevant to the analysis of rules.[3] To the extent that rules are intentions, it follows that they possess the two characteristics mentioned previously. In other words, (1) rules are partially instrumentally rational and partially arbitrary/non-rational, and (2) new circumstances can prompt individuals to abandon and reform rules. We will see that these characteristics give rules (including Sharīʿa rules) a significant capacity to guide behavior in complex circumstances. Such an analysis of rules breaks sharply with practice theory. As noted previously, practice theory does not conceptualize rules as intentions. Rather, it identifies rules with the literal meaning of verbal statements. Because practice theory does not see rules (including Sharīʿa rules) as intentions, it cannot appreciate how rules are partially instrumentally rational and partially arbitrary/non-rational, and it cannot appreciate

[3] See Shapiro 2002; Ekins 2012.

how new circumstances prompt individuals to abandon and reform rules. Consequently, practice theory embraces an overly simplistic understanding of rules—one which underestimates the capacity of rules to guide behavior in complex circumstances.

## II. INTENTIONS/RULES ARE PARTIALLY INSTRUMENTALLY RATIONAL AND PARTIALLY ARBITRARY/NON-RATIONAL

Let us begin by considering how intentions and rules are partially instrumentally rational and partially non-rational. After explaining this point, I will show how it illuminates Sharīʿa rules.

### A. Buridan Problems, Instrumental Rationality, Non-rationality

Bratman points out that individuals must act in a world where different options are equally desirable. A problem of choosing between multiple equally desirable options is commonly known as a "Buridan problem."[4] Hence, I confront Buridan problems when I have no preference between calling my mother at 7:00 p.m. and 8:00 p.m., between living in London and living in Dubai, or between studying medicine and studying engineering. In all of these cases, I desire each of the alternative options equally. Now, if I desire two options equally, then my beliefs and desires do not provide grounds to choose between them. Put differently, my choice between the options cannot be explained in terms of the standard model of instrumental rationality. For such a model operates on the principle of pursuing one's strongest desire in light of one's beliefs. But in this case, there is no single strongest desire. Rather there are multiple options desired with equal strength.

One common response to Buridan problems is to suppress them. This is typically done by positing that, in reality, a human being always desires one option more strongly than another, even if such a desire is unconscious and highly idiosyncratic. For instance, even if I don't think I have a preference between calling my mother at 7:00 p.m. and 8:00 p.m., in reality, at an unconscious level, I more strongly desire one option (e.g., to call at 8:00 p.m.). By extension, even if I don't think I have a preference between calling my mother at 7:37 p.m. and 7:38 p.m., in reality, at an unconscious level, I more strongly desire one option (e.g., to call at 7:37 p.m.). Similarly, if I walk into a supermarket and see 100 identical boxes of Cheerios cereal, I may think that I don't prefer one more than another. Yet, I will unconsciously prefer a particular box (i.e., the box that I end up purchasing). Such desires are, of course, highly idiosyncratic, for it is not apparent why someone should desire to call at 8:00 p.m. rather than 7:00 p.m., or at 7:37 p.m. rather than 7:38 p.m. Similarly, it is not apparent why someone would

[4] Named after the famous philosophical problem of Buridan's ass.

desire a particular box of Cheerios cereal (Is it because one box is a millimeter closer than another box? Or because the box is directly in one's line of sight? Is there any empirical evidence for this?). Practice theory suppresses Buridan problems by positing that each individual has a collection of unconscious and highly idiosyncratic desires which s/he acquired through practice. Such desires are part of his/her distinctive habitus.[5]

Rather than suppress Buridan problems, Bratman deals with them directly. Accordingly, in Bratman's view, it is really possible for a person to have no preference between calling his/her mother at 7:00 p.m. and 8:00 p.m., or between living in London and living in Dubai. Bratman asserts that Buridan problems are ubiquitous and that they are a fundamental feature of human life. Hence, any account of human action and practical reasoning must take them into account.[6] In adopting this stance, Bratman breaks with both Weber and Davidson.

For Bratman, the phenomenon of intention is the key to dealing with Buridan problems. In his view, intention serves as a mechanism for choosing between equally desirable options. For instance, suppose that I must choose between the options of calling my mother at 7:00 p.m. and 8:00 p.m. I do this by forming an intention to call my mother at 7:00 p.m. This is my choice (i.e., decision). Once I have formed the intention to call my mother at 7:00 p.m., this intention then causes me to perform the action of calling my mother at 7:00 p.m.

For Bratman, resolutions to Buridan problems are always, in some sense, "non-rational" or "arbitrary." This is because there are no grounds for choosing one option over another. In other words, an individual's beliefs and desires cannot serve as the basis for a choice. Hence, it is arbitrary that I choose (via intention) to call my mother at 7:00 p.m. rather than 8:00 p.m.

Bratman's views involve a revision, rather than a rejection, of Davidson's understanding of intentions. Hence, Bratman agrees with Davidson that an individual forms an intention based on the totality of his/her beliefs and desires. Yet, Bratman insists that an intention cannot be explained exclusively in terms of an individual's beliefs and desires. Rather, an intention is, to an extent, based upon a non-rational/arbitrary choice.[7] This implies that intentions generally have two dimensions. To some extent, a given intention is instrumentally rational, explicable in terms of beliefs and desires. Yet, to some extent, an intention is non-rational/arbitrary, being inexplicable in terms of beliefs and desires.

For Bratman, an individual may intend that s/he performs an action. For instance, I may intend to call my mother. However, Bratman argues that an individual may also intend that another person performs an action.[8] Bratman, Shapiro, and Ekins indicate that this phenomenon is particularly important where there exist relations of authority.[9] For instance, a general may form an intention that his troops bomb a particular factory. In such a situation, were the troops to bomb the wrong factory, the general might respond: "That is not what I intended you to do." Likewise, a mother may form an intention that her child

[5] See Bourdieu 1977; 1984. [6] See Bratman 1987. [7] See Bratman 1987.
[8] Bratman 2014:60–64. [9] Bratman 2014:60; Shapiro 2011; Ekins 2012.

study medicine, and a teacher might form an intention that his/her students read a particular book.

Shapiro and Ekins suggest the aforementioned phenomenon is relevant to the analysis of rules.[10] Hence, in many cases, where an authority figure lays down a rule, it is his/her intention that people act in a particular way. For instance, a king may intend (i.e., will) that his subjects refrain from dumping toxic waste in the ocean. Of course, the king might not intend to bind his subjects by this rule in all circumstances. For instance, he might say: "it is not my intention to prevent my subjects from dumping toxic waste in the ocean under emergency circumstances (e.g., where they must dump the waste in order to protect their lives)."

Bratman, Shapiro, and Ekins hold that an intention may be shared by multiple individuals.[11] For instance, two people can share an intention to paint a house. Shared intentions are also relevant when it comes to rules. Thus, members of a legislature may form an intention that citizens refrain from dumping toxic waste in the ocean. This shared intention is a rule. As mentioned previously, in many legal, cultural, and religious traditions, rules are referred to as the "will" of the legislature, the people, or the ancestors. Such rules may often be treated as shared intentions (e.g., the shared intentions of the legislature, the people, the ancestors).

Shapiro and Ekins do not claim that rules must always be conceptualized as intentions. Rather, they merely provide a way of understanding how, in some important cases, rules may be conceptualized as intentions.

Insofar as a rule is conceptualized as an intention, then that rule will be partially instrumentally rational and partially non-rational/arbitrary (i.e., partially explicable in terms of beliefs and desires, and partially inexplicable in terms of beliefs and desires). For instance, suppose that a king lays down a penalty of 40 lashes for dumping toxic waste in the ocean. The king's rule may be regarded as partially instrumentally rational and partially non-rational/arbitrary. Hence, we may say that the king desires to protect the animals and plants which live in the ocean. Moreover, he believes that toxic waste will kill these animals and plants. Based on his belief and desire, the king forms an intention/rule that his subjects (or his judges) punish with 40 lashes those who dump toxic waste. This is the king's "will." But even though the king's intention/rule can be explained partially in terms of his beliefs and desires, it is also partially non-rational/arbitrary. Thus, the king may have no preference between a 40-lash penalty and a 50-lash penalty. On the positive side, the 40-lash penalty is more lenient. However, on the negative side it will have less of a deterrent effect. Meanwhile, the 50-lash penalty is less lenient, but it will have more of a deterrent effect. In this situation, the king views both penalties as equally desirable, but is forced to make an arbitrary/non-rational choice between them. As a result, he lays down a rule with a 40-lash penalty.

[10] Shapiro 2002; 2011; Ekins 2012.

[11] Bratman 2014; Shapiro 2002; Ekins 2012.

Because practice theory equates rules with the literal meaning of verbal statements, it cannot account for the fact that rules are partially instrumentally rational and partially non-rational/arbitrary. After all, while notions of instrumental rationality and arbitrariness apply to intentions, they do not apply to the literal meaning of verbal statements.

There is, however, an additional layer of complexity when it comes to Bratman's treatment of intentions, and the treatment of rules put forth by Shapiro and Ekins. This complexity can be explicated in terms of means and ends. When an individual forms an intention, s/he chooses an end, and s/he also chooses a suitable means to realize that end. For instance, visiting China is an end. Purchasing a plane ticket to China is a means to this end. Losing weight is an end. Jogging is a means to this end.

Buridan problems exist both with respect to ends and with respect to means. This can be explained as follows. For a person there are equally desirable ends. The person, must choose between these ends in a non-rational fashion. This is done through intention. Moreover, once a person has chosen a given end, s/he must also choose a means to realize this end. However, there are equally desirable means to realize the end. The person must choose one of these means in a non-rational fashion. This is also done through intention.

Here an example will be helpful. Suppose that John has a desire to visit China and an equally strong desire to visit India. These two desires are ends. But he must make a non-rational choice between them (assuming that he lacks time to visit both countries). Hence, John chooses by forming an intention to visit China. Next he must choose a means to realize this end. Thus, suppose there exist three airline companies selling tickets to China. Company "A" sells a standard ticket for $500. Company "B" also sells a standard ticket for $500. There is no difference in quality between the tickets sold by Company "A" and Company "B." Meanwhile Company "C" sells a higher quality ticket (e.g., better food, larger seats), but charges $600—a higher price. John finds each of these ticket options equally desirable. This is because there is no significant difference between the tickets offered by Company "A" and Company "B." John also finds the ticket from Company "C" equally desirable, for the additional benefits of this ticket (i.e., its higher quality) are counterbalanced by its higher cost. Ultimately, John must make a non-rational choice between the three tickets. Therefore, he forms an intention to purchase his ticket from Company "B." In this way, John has chosen both an end (visiting China) and a means (purchasing a ticket for Company "B"), by forming intentions.

It is possible to speak of John as having two intentions. Hence, he has an intention to visit China and he also has an intention to purchase his ticket from Company "B." However, these intentions fit together into a coherent "plan." A plan can be thought of as an end and a means for realizing that end. For Bratman, intentions fit together into plans (which is why he endorses a "planning theory of intention").[12] Rather than speaking of John as having two intentions (which

[12] See Bratman 1987.

fit together into a plan), we could speak of John as having one *composite intention*. For instance, we could say: John intends to purchase a plane ticket from Company "B" (the means) in order to realize his desire to visit China (the end). Here we speak of John as having one intention, but we mention both the "means component" and then the "end component" of that intention. I will refer to such an intention as a "composite intention."

Furthermore, I will refer to the end component of a composite intention as an "intended end." An intended end is always a desire to be realized (e.g., John's desire to visit China). Meanwhile, I will refer to the "means component" of a composite intention as an "intended means." Hence, we may say that John intends to purchase a plane ticket from Company "B" (the intended means) in order to realize his desire to visit China (the intended end). In fact, Bratman, explains that intentions can take highly complex composite forms, wherein an individual chooses multiple intended means to realize an intended end (i.e., each means is a step toward the realization of the end).[13] However, for the sake of simplicity, I will not take up these more complex composite forms of intention.

If intentions have a composite form, and (some) rules are intentions, then it follows that (these) rules also have a composite form. Let us return to the king who lays down a rule which stipulates a penalty of 40 lashes for dumping toxic waste in the ocean. The king desires to protect the animals and plants which live in the ocean. The king equally desires to preserve the freedom of his subjects to act as they please on the ocean. However, the king cannot realize both of these desires simultaneously, for if his subjects are left free their actions will harm the animals and the plants. Hence, the king must make a non-rational choice between these desires. He chooses his desire to protect the animal and plants by forming an intention to protect the animals and plants. It can be said that realizing this desire is his end. But the king must now choose a means to realize his end. As mentioned previously, there exists the option of laying down a 40-lash penalty for dumping toxic waste. There also exists the option of laying down a 50-lash penalty. The king finds both of these options equally desirable, and must make a non-rational choice between them. He chooses the 40-lash penalty, by forming an intention that his subjects (or his judges) punish those who dump toxic waste with 40 lashes. We could say that the king actually has one composite intention with a "means component" and an "end component." Hence, it is the king's intention that his subjects lash those who dump toxic waste 50 times (the intended means) in order to realize his desire to protect the animals and plants which live in the ocean (the intended end). We can also say that the king's rule has a composite form.

To sum up, planning theory builds on the notion of instrumental rationality, which holds that an individual forms an intention based on the totality of his/her beliefs and desires. Yet, an intention cannot be explained exclusively in terms of an individual's beliefs and desires. Rather, an intention is, to an extent, based

[13] See Bratman 1987.

upon non-rational/arbitrary choice. An individual must make a non-rational choice between desires which are equal in strength. In other words, s/he must choose between equally desirable ends. Moreover, once s/he has chosen an end (the intended end), s/he must make a non-rational choice between equally desirable means of realizing that end (the intended means). It is through composite intentions that these non-rational choices are made. Significantly, (some) rules can be conceptualized as composite intentions.

I suggest that Sharīʿa rules are best conceptualized as God's *composite intentions*. God's composite intentions are partially instrumentally rational in that they are based on the totality of God's desires and beliefs/knowledge. However, God's composite intentions, like all composite intentions, are also partially non-rational.

## B. Sharīʿa Rules

Existing scholarship overlooks the fact that Sharīʿa rules (as God's composite intentions) are both partially instrumentally rational and partially non-rational. However, this fact is of fundamental importance in grasping the structure of Islamic legal thought.

Let us first consider how Sharīʿa rules are (partially) instrumentally rational. One of the most important terms in Islamic legal discourse is "*maṣlaḥa*." A *maṣlaḥa* is a "benefit" (*manfaʿa*), understood as something which brings pleasure (*ladhdha*). The opposite of a *maṣlaḥa* is a *mafsada*. A *mafsada* is a "harm" (*maḍarra*), understood as something which brings pain (*alam*).[14] In Islamic legal discourse, there are constant references to benefit/*maṣlaḥa* and harm/*mafsada*.

Both premodern and modern Muslim scholars reject the idea that God laid down Sharīʿa rules for no purpose (*ʿabathan*), or for the purpose of benefiting Himself. Rather, scholars generally hold that God laid down Sharīʿa rules in order to benefit mankind.[15] This is one of the reasons that God is considered to be a kind and benevolent being (*al-Raḥmān*).

Premodern Muslim legal scholars worked to develop a theoretical framework capable of explaining how Sharīʿa rules benefit mankind. Some of the most prominent figures associated with this effort include al-Juwaynī, al-Ghazālī, Ibn ʿAbd al-Salām, al-Qarāfī, Ibn Taymiyya, Ibn al-Qayyim, and al-Shāṭibī. The framework developed by these figures is referred to as the theory of "*Maqāṣid al-Sharīʿa*."[16] "*Maqāṣid al-Sharīʿa*" can be translated as the "Intended Aims of the Sharīʿa."

According to the theory of *Maqāṣid al-Sharīʿa*, Sharīʿa rules produce two types of benefits for human beings: "worldly benefits" (*maṣāliḥ dunyawiyya*) and "otherworldly benefits" (*maṣāliḥ ukhrawiyya*). Worldly benefits relate to the pleasures and pains experienced in this world. Otherworldly benefits relate

[14] See al-Ghazālī 2000:174; al-Ījī 2000: 320; al-Būṭī 2005:37–38. For a more general discussion of *maṣlaḥa* see Opwis 2010.

[15] See Emon 2010.

[16] See al-Raysūnī 2006; Emon 2010; Opwis 2010.

to those experienced in the Hereafter. In the context of this framework, jurists divide Sharīʿa rules into two general categories. First, there are rules pertaining to family law, commercial law, and criminal law (i.e., *muʿāmalāt*). These rules are primarily concerned with securing worldly benefits. Second, there are rules of ritual worship (*ʿibādāt*) (e.g., prayer, fasting). These rules are primarily concerned with securing otherworldly benefits. Hence, prayer and fasting do not aim at worldly pleasure. Rather, their function is to bring people closer to God (*taqarrub*).[17] Having a close and loving relationship with God is seen as immensely valuable in itself. Moreover, individuals who build a close relationship with God will be rewarded with Paradise in the Hereafter. By contrast, sinners will be subject to the torments of Hell. For these reasons, individuals secure an otherworldly benefit (i.e., salvation, closeness to God) through the performance of ritual worship.

In accordance with the theory of *Maqāṣid al-Sharīʿa*, Muslim scholars constantly emphasize that Sharīʿa rules exist to benefit humankind in this life and the next. Thus, al-Ghazālī states: "the Messengers were only sent [by God] for the sake of human benefits in the Hereafter and in this life (*li-maṣāliḥ al-khalq fi-l-dīn wa-l-dunyā*)."[18] Similarly, Ibn al-Qayyim states: "Verily the Sharīʿa is founded upon human benefits in this life and the next."[19]

The basic theory of *Maqāṣid al-Sharīʿa* is a standard element in medieval Islamic legal works. Nevertheless, most jurists do not explore this theory in depth. One notable exception is Abū Isḥāq al-Shāṭibī (d.1388), author of a treatise known as *The Concordances* (*al-Muwāfaqāt*). *The Concordances* offers an extensive analysis of the theory of *Maqāṣid al-Sharīʿa*. Although *The Concordances* only received limited attention in the premodern period it was rediscovered and popularized around the beginning of the twentieth century. ʿAbduh and Riḍā played a key role in this process.[20] For them, al-Shāṭibī's ideas were useful in responding to common Western criticisms of Islam, which depicted Sharīʿa rules as irrational and antithetical to human welfare.

In the law classes I attended at al-Azhar University and the Dār al-ʿUlūm, no doctrinal issue received more attention than the theory of *Maqāṣid al-Sharīʿa*. In their lectures, professors constantly emphasized that Sharīʿa rules function to secure human benefits. Indeed, they hold this principle to be the foundation of Islamic legal theory itself (*Uṣūl al-Fiqh*), believing that it receives its definitive expression in *The Concordances*.

At al-Azhar University, *The Concordances* is used as the capstone text for graduate students specializing in legal theory. Employing traditional Islamic pedagogical methods, professors read out the text line-by-line, stopping after every few words to supply explanatory commentary.

*The Concordances* itself is approximately 1,000 pages. In the two semesters devoted to its study, al-Azhar professors can only cover a small fraction of the total.

17 Ibn ʿAbd al-Salām 2004:75.
18 Al-Ghazālī 1971:162. Cited in Emon 2010:132–133. Also see Ibn Khaldūn 2010, 2:569.
19 Ibn al-Qayyim 1423h, 4:337.
20 See Johnston 2007:161–162.

For this reason they choose to concentrate on a particular section entitled "The Book of the Intended Aims" (*Kitāb al-Maqāṣid*). The name is appropriate because the section is devoted to explaining how Sharīʿa rules must be looked at as a means to realize particular aims. Al-Shāṭibī identifies these aims as related to human welfare. He opens *The Book of the Intended Aims* by stating: "Sharīʿa rules have only been legislated for the sake of human benefits[21] (*waḍʿ al-sharāʾiʿ innamā huwa li-maṣāliḥ al-ʿibād*)."[22]

Discourse on the theory of *Maqāṣid al-Sharīʿa* constantly invokes a dichotomy between "means" (*wasāʾil*) and "ends" (*maqāṣid*). This is best understood as follows. God has chosen to realize a particular set of desires. Each of these desires is a desire to benefit humankind in a particular way (e.g., God's desire to protect property, God's desire to preserve human life). The desires that God has chosen to realize are His intended ends (*maqāṣid*). God has also chosen a particular set of Sharīʿa rules (*aḥkām al-Sharīʿa*). These Sharīʿa rules are His intended means (*wasāʾil*). Hence, it can be said that God forms intentions/Sharīʿa rules (intended means) in order to realize His desires to benefit humankind (intended ends). Thus, the Arabic expression "*Maqāṣid al-Sharīʿa*" refers to the desires that God has chosen/intended to realize through the legislation of Sharīʿa rules.

What is the proof that Sharīʿa rules are legislated for the benefit of humankind? Here Muslim scholars claim that abundant evidence is provided by God's statements (in the Qurʾan), the Prophet's actions (described in Hadith reports), and the actions of early Muslims scholars (described in reports).[23] These are all considered signs/effects of God's mental attributes. As explained earlier (with reference to hermeneutic theory) Muslims scholars ask which set of mental attributes (i.e., beliefs, desires, and intentions) would God need to have in order to cause these signs/effects. For instance, which set of beliefs, desires, and intentions would God need to have in order to cause Him to utter the statements found in the Qurʾan? Which set of beliefs, desires, and intentions would God need to have in order to cause the Prophet and later scholars to perform the obedient actions which have been recorded in reports? In carrying forth the analysis Muslim scholars presume the notion of instrumental rationality. Hence, they presume that God forms intentions based on the totality of His desires and beliefs.

For example, consider God's statement in the Qurʾan: "Amputate the hand of the thief." Which desires, beliefs, and intentions would have caused God to utter this statement? Muslim scholars draw attention to the protection of property (*māl*), which is a human benefit (*maṣlaḥa*).[24] It is inferred that God *desires* to secure this benefit for mankind. It is also inferred that God believes (i.e., knows) that the amputation penalty will deter theft. The preceding desire and belief cause God to form the intention that Muslims amputate the hands of thieves. Or, if we want to be more precise, we could say that God has formed a composite

[21] Literally, "the benefits of the slaves." [22] Al-Shāṭibī 2004:219–220.
[23] Shalabī 1947:14–93; al-Ghazalī 2000:179; al-Shāṭibī 2004:220–223.
[24] Al-Ghazālī 2000:174; al-Shāṭibī 2004:222.

intention. God has chosen/intended to realize His desire to protect property (the intended end). Moreover, he has chosen/intended that Muslims amputate the hands of thieves as a means to this end. Consequently, we may say that it is God's intention that Muslims amputate the hands of thieves (the intended means) in order to realize His desire to protect property (the intended end). This intention then causes God to utter the statement "Amputate the hand of the thief." Notice that the preceding line of analysis confirms that God legislates Sharīʿa rules for human benefits. After all, God legislated the amputation penalty out of a desire to protect property (which benefits humans).

Consider another example. For Muslim scholars, human beings benefit from known patrilineal kinship bonds (*nasab*).[25] More specifically, it is assumed that when people know they are related by blood, they are inclined to love and support one another. This phenomenon is known as "kinship solidarity" (*ʿaṣabiyya*), and it is discussed extensively in the famous medieval sociological work of Ibn Khaldūn.[26] For instance, if a father knows that he is related by blood to a child, he will be inclined to love that child, to support him or her financially, and protect him or her. Similarly, members of a tribe are inclined to care for one another, support each other financially, and defend each other. Thus, ties of blood/kinship are a benefit to human beings, because they provide love, support, and protection. Various Sharīʿa rules exist to protect kinship bonds. Hence, Sharīʿa rules ban extramarital sex (*zinā*), Sharīʿa rules ban polyandry (while allowing polygyny), and Sharīʿa rules restrict interaction between the sexes. These Sharīʿa rules are established in the Qurʾan, the Hadith reports, and reports concerning the actions of early Muslim scholars.

Extramartial sex is banned because it undermines kinship bonds by bringing paternity into doubt. In other words, if a woman gets pregnant after having sexual relations with multiple men, the identity of the child's father will be unknown. By extension, the identity of the child's paternal relatives will be unknown (e.g., the paternal grandfather, the paternal uncles, half-brothers and sisters born to the father). As a result, neither the father nor the broader circle of paternal relatives will be inclined to offer the child affection and support. A similar logic underlies Sharīʿa rules which ban polyandry while permitting polygamy. Women are banned from having multiple husbands (polyandry) for this brings paternity into doubt. By contrast, men are permitted to have up to four wives (polygyny), for this does not bring paternity into doubt. Analogous concerns are reflected in Sharīʿa rules restricting interactions between the sexes. According to these rules, a man and a woman are forbidden to meet together alone unless they are married or related by blood. It is assumed that if an unmarried man and woman meet together alone, they may be tempted to engage in extramarital sex.

In making sense of these rules, Muslim scholars begin with the Qurʾan, Hadith reports, and reports concerning the actions of past Muslim scholars. They then

25 See al-Ghazalī 2000:174.

26 Ibn Khaldūn 2010, 2:479–483.

infer God's mental attributes in accordance with the notion of instrumental rationality. Thus, God states in the Qurʾan that extramarital sex is forbidden.[27] It is inferred from this that God desires to protect patrilineal kinship bonds (*nasab*).[28] It is also inferred that God believes/knows that extramarital sex undermines kinship bonds by bringing paternity into doubt. God's belief and desire cause Him to form a (composite) intention that Muslims refrain from extramarital sex (the intended means) in order to realize God's desire to protect patrilineal kinship bonds (the intended end). This intention then causes God to state that extramarital sex is forbidden. Similarly, Hadith reports on the Prophet's actions record that he prohibited (unmarried and unrelated) men and women from meeting alone together.[29] It is inferred from this that God desires to protect patrilineal kinship bonds. It is also inferred that God believes/knows that men and women will be tempted to engage in extramarital sex if they meet alone. It is likewise inferred that God believes/knows that extramarital sex undermines kinship bonds by bringing paternity into doubt. Accordingly, God's desire and beliefs cause Him to form a (composite) intention that men and women refrain from meeting alone together (the intended means) in order to realize God's desire to protect patrilineal kinship bonds (the intended end). God then communicated this intention to the Prophet, which caused Him to prohibit men and women from meeting alone together (as is recorded in Hadith reports). Finally, there are reports on early Muslim scholars which record that they permitted polygyny while prohibiting polyandry. From these reports, it is inferred that God desires to protect patrilineal kinship bonds, and that God believes/knows that polyandry (as opposed to polygyny) undermines kinship bonds. God's desire and belief cause Him to form a (composite) intention that Muslims refrain from polyandry (the intended means) in order to realize God's desire to protect patrilineal kinship bonds (the intended end). God communicated this intention to the Prophet who then communicated it to later scholars. Later scholars were then caused to prohibit polyandry (but not polygyny) by their knowledge of God's intention to prohibit polyandry. This is reflected in reports on these scholars. The preceding line of analysis again confirms that God legislates Sharīʿa rules for human benefits. For these various rules are attributed to God's desire to protect patrilineal kinship bonds, which is a benefit for human beings.

When Muslim scholars assert that God desires to protect patrilineal kinship bonds, they do not simply consider one piece of evidence. Rather, they consider the various signs/effects of God's mental attributes found in the Qurʾan, the Hadith reports, and reports on past scholars. Or, to put things differently, they consider the various rules which can be inferred from these texts (e.g., the rule prohibiting extramarital sex, the rule prohibiting polyandry, the rule prohibiting men and women from meeting alone). Taken together, these rules all support a common conclusion; namely that God desires to protect patrilineal kinship bonds. Muslim jurists refer to this sort of analysis as "*istiqrā*."[30] "*Istiqrā*"

[27] Qurʾan [17:32]. [28] Al-Ghazālī 2000:174. [29] Muslim 1426h:610.
[30] Al-Shāṭibī 2004:220–223; also see al-Ghazālī 2000:179.

is an Arabic term that can be translated as "study" or "investigation." But in a legal context, such study has a specific character. In *istiqrāʾ*, a jurist examines the totality of relevant evidence (i.e., all the signs/effects of God's mental attributes, including those found in the Qurʾan, Hadith reports, and reports on the actions of past scholars). From the totality of evidence, the jurist infers the kinds of benefits/*maṣlaḥa* that God desires to realize through His legislation (e.g., protection of property rights, protection of patrilineal kinship bonds).

It is also possible to think of *istiqrāʾ* as follows. One takes the totality of the Sharīʿa rules revealed by the evidence. One then asks, which set of desires would motivate God to lay down these specific rules (i.e., form these specific intentions)? For instance, God has laid down (1) a rule mandating the amputation of the hand of the thief, (2) a rule banning extramarital sex, (3) a rule banning polyandry, (4) a rule permitting polygyny, and (5) a rule banning murder. One may infer from these five rules that God desires to protect property (*māl*), desires to protect patrilineal kinship bonds (*nasab*), and desires to protect life (*nafs*). However, it is worth emphasizing that this form of analysis necessarily attributes to God beliefs as well as desires, even if this is done tacitly. Hence, it can be argued that God would only seek to protect kinship bonds by banning extramarital sex if He believed (1) that extramarital sex tends to bring paternity into doubt, and (2) that fathers and paternal relatives are less inclined to offer affection and support to a child if they doubt that the child is related to them by blood. If God did not believe/know these things, His rule would no longer make sense from the standpoint of instrumental rationality. Keeping this in mind, it is possible to give a more precise description of *istiqrāʾ*. In *istiqrāʾ*, one begins with the total collection of Sharīʿa rules (i.e., God's intentions). One then asks which specific set of desires and beliefs would have caused God to lay down this total collection of rules (i.e., form this total collection of intentions). In this way, one arrives at a model of God's mind (i.e., His desires, beliefs, intentions). Moreover, one explains how God's rules derive from His desire to benefit mankind.

The theory of *Maqāṣid al-Sharīʿa* not only recognizes that God has many desires, it also holds that these desires differ in strength. In situations where God's different desires cannot be realized simultaneously, God weighs between them (*muwāzana*) and chooses to realize the desire that is strongest (*rājiḥ*).[31] Obviously, such a view is consistent with the notion of instrumental rationality, which presumes that individuals act to realize the strongest of their various desires.

For Muslim jurists, the relative strengths of God's desires are reflected in Sharīʿa rules. For instance, the jurists believe that drunkenness leads to a variety of harms. Hence, when a person is drunk, s/he is likely to get involved in conflicts and fights.[32] Consequently, sobriety (*ʿaql*) is regarded as benefit (*maṣlaḥa*) for human beings. In order to ensure such sobriety, God has laid down a Sharīʿa rule prohibiting the consumption of grape wine. On the other hand, God also desires to preserve human life (*nafs*), which is also a benefit for mankind. Notably,

[31] See al-Shāṭibī 2004:231–232.

[32] See Qur'an [5:91]; al-Zuḥaylī 2006, 1:575.

there are situations where it is not possible to both ensure sobriety and preserve human life. Thus, a woman dying of thirst might have a bottle of grape wine but no other fluids. God states that such a person is permitted to consume grape wine.[33] In other words, the Sharīʿa rule banning the consumption of grape wine admits of an exception in these circumstances. From this, it may be inferred that God's desire to preserve human life is stronger than His desire to ensure sobriety.

As a second example, recall how ʿUmar temporarily suspended the amputation penalty for theft during a famine where hunger was forcing people to steal for survival.[34] From ʿUmar's action, it may be inferred that God's desire to preserve human life is stronger than His desire to protect property. Accordingly, God did not intend to amputate hands (for the sake of protecting property) in a situation where people could only preserve their lives by stealing.

By studying the rules of the Sharīʿa in this way, Muslim jurists are not only able to determine which specific benefits (*maṣlaḥa*) God desires to realize (e.g., protection of property, ensuring sobriety), but jurists are also able to determine the relative strength of God's various desires (e.g., God desires to preserve life more strongly than He desires to ensure sobriety or protect property).

Based on the preceding form of analysis, the theory of *Maqāṣid al-Sharīʿa* lists out and ranks many of the benefits that God desires to realize for mankind. To this end, the theory of *Maqāṣid al-Sharīʿa* introduces a three-tiered ranking system. According to the ranking system, there are benefits of highest importance (*ḍarūriyyāt*), benefits of middle importance (*ḥājiyyāt*), and benefits of lower importance (*taḥsīniyyāt*).[35]

The benefits of highest importance are those which God most strongly desires to realize. The jurists hold that these benefits are five in number: (1) the protection of religion (*dīn*), (2) the preservation of life (*nafs*), (3) the protection of patrilineal kinship bonds (*nasab*), (4) the protection of material wealth (*māl*), and (5) the preservation of sobriety/reason (*ʿaql*). Some jurists also add the preservation of dignity/honor (*ʿird*) to this list.[36] Despite being on the same general tier, these high-importance benefits actually differ in weight, for God desires to realize some more than others. Thus, the preservation of life takes precedence over the protection of material wealth because God desires to preserve life more than He desires to protect wealth. Given considerations of space, there is no room to discuss specific benefits of middle and lower importance. However, the overall idea should be clear.

Regarding God's desires, one more point of clarification is necessary. God has specific desires to benefit humankind in particular ways (e.g., His desire to preserve life, His desire to protect patrilineal bonds). However, in the view of Muslim jurists, God also has a general desire to secure benefits for human beings (*jalb al-maṣlaḥa*). As indicated earlier a benefit (*maṣlaḥa*) is something which produces pleasure.[37] Nevertheless, matters are complicated by the fact that things

[33] See Qur'an [2:137], [6:145].
[34] See Biltājī 2006:214–223.
[35] Al-Ghazālī 2000:174–175; Al-Shāṭibī 2004:221–223.
[36] Shalabī 1947:282.
[37] See al-Ghazālī 2000:174; al-Būṭī 2005:37–38.

often produce both some measure of pleasure and some measure of pain.[38] For something to be considered a benefit it must produce more pleasure than pain. Hence, extramarital sex (*zinā*) produces pleasure. Yet, it produces pain as well, because it destroys patrilineal kinship bonds and the affection, support, and protection they provide. Since the pain (*mafsada*) produced by extramarital sex outweighs the pleasure, such sex cannot be considered a benefit.

In discussing these matters, Muslim jurists divide benefits into three classes.[39] The first class consists in benefits which are known to be desired by God, based on evidence from religious texts (i.e., *maṣlaḥa muʿtabara*). For instance, based on the Qurʾan and the Hadith reports it is known that God desires to protect patrilineal kinship bonds. The second class consists in benefits which are known not to be desired by God, based on evidence from religious texts (i.e., *maṣlaḥa mulghāh*). For instance, based on the Qurʾan and Hadith reports, it is known that sexual liberation is not desired by God. The third (and most interesting) class consists in benefits for which there is no clear evidence from religious texts (i.e., *maṣlaḥa mursala*). Such benefits are identified through human reason and experience. Reason and experience tell us something is a benefit if it produces pleasure (or it produces more pleasure than pain).[40] Examples include cures for diseases, roads which facilitate travel, and clean spaces free of filth and trash. It can be assumed that God desires these things. For instance, it can be assumed that God desires the invention of cures for diseases given that they provide the pleasure of health and remove the pain of disease. Presumably, the more pleasure something produces (for human beings), the more strongly it is desired by God.

Thus, the theory of *Maqāṣid al-Sharīʿa* represents a particular perspective on the fundamental nature of Islamic law. This perspective highlights the instrumentally rational character of Sharīʿa rules. After all, God has laid down these rules to realize the strongest of His desires in light of His beliefs/knowledge.

The notion that Sharīʿa rules are (at least partially) instrumentally rational is reflected in a number of other Islamic legal concepts. I will briefly mention two. Like the theory of *Maqāṣid al-Sharīʿa*, both of these concepts originate in the medieval period, but remain important today.

The first legal concept is expressed in the Arabic phrase "*taʿlīl al-aḥkām.*" The word "*taʿlīl*" is related to the term "*ʿilla*," which means a "cause" or a "reason." The word "*aḥkām*" means rules. "*Taʿlīl al-aḥkām*" refers to the process of clarifying the causes underlying God's rules. Muslim jurists emphasize that a proper understanding of the Sharīʿa requires clarifying the causes underlying Sharīʿa rules. For Muslim jurists, God's desire/aim (*gharaḍ*) to realize benefits for human beings (*jalb al-maṣlaḥa*) causes Him to lay down rules.[41] Accordingly, when one clarifies the cause of a given legal rule, one explains how a desire to realize a specific benefit caused God to lay down the rule. Take the rule mandating

38 Al-Shāṭibī 2004:231–232; Emon 2010:55–56.
39 See Shalabī 1947:281–296; al-Ghazālī 2000:173–174.
40 See Emon 2010 for a broader discussion of this issue.
41 For a discussion see Shalabi 1947:94–128.

amputation for theft. One clarifies the cause of the rule by explaining that God's desire to protect property (a benefit) caused Him to lay down the rule. Notice that this perspective views Sharīʿa rules as instrumentally rational (i.e., designed to realize desires).

The second legal concept is "*munāsaba*." "*Munāsaba*" is an Arabic term which means "appropriateness" with respect to the standards of rational behavior.[42] Muslim jurists assume that rational behavior consists in acting to secure desired benefits (*jalb al-maṣlaḥa*) and to prevent undesired harms (*darʾ al-mafsada*). Hence, Fakhr al-Dīn al-Rāzī (d.606/1209) explains that "appropriateness" means that something "suits the acts of rational beings" (*mulāʾim li-afʿāl al-ʿuqalāʾ*) with respect to securing benefits and preventing harms.[43] Muslim jurists hold that, as a general principle, God's legal rules exhibit "appropriateness," reflecting the standards of rational behavior. This means that God has not formulated rules in a random or haphazard fashion. On the contrary, God has designed His rules in order to secure desired benefits. Once again, this perspective implies that Sharīʿa rules are instrumentally rational.

To sum up: For both premodern and modern Muslim religious scholars, Sharīʿa rules are, at least partially, instrumentally rational. Nevertheless, such scholars recognize that Sharīʿa rules likewise have a significant non-rational dimension. In discussing this non-rational dimension, Muslim jurists frequently utilize the Arabic term "*taʿabbudī*." "*Taʿabbudī*" is derived from the word "*taʿabbud*," which denotes unquestioning submission to God.[44] When religious scholars describe a Sharīʿa rule as "*taʿabbudī*" they indicate that the rule cannot be grasped by human reason. As a result, individuals must accept and apply the rule in a spirit of unquestioning submission. Notably, when scholars assert that a rule cannot be grasped by reason, what they really mean is that it cannot be understood in terms of instrumental rationality.

Generally speaking, Sharīʿa rules are not *taʿabbudī* in an absolute sense. Rather, a given rule will have aspects that are instrumentally rational and aspects that are *taʿabbudī* (i.e., non-rational). Take the penalty for extramarital sex (*zinā*). To put things simplistically, an unmarried person who engages in extramarital sex is subject to a penalty of 100 lashes. In one sense, this rule is instrumentally rational, for it can be explained in terms of God's desires and beliefs. Thus, God desires to preserve patrilineal kinship bonds (*nasab*). Moreover, God (1) believes that doubtful paternity undermines kinship bonds, (2) believes that extramarital sex brings paternity into doubt, and (3) believes that lashes deter extramarital sex. Given God's desire and His beliefs, He lays down a rule mandating lashes as a penalty for extramarital sex. Nevertheless, for Muslim jurists, it is not clear why God has chosen a penalty of 100 lashes. After all, is not obvious why a 100-lash penalty is preferable to a penalty of 90 lashes or 105 lashes. Hence, this aspect of the rule is *taʿabbudī* (i.e., non-rational).[45] Indeed, the point can be pushed further. There are other ways to deter extramarital sex besides lashes. For instance, it

[42] For discussions of *munāsaba* see al-Ghazalī 1971:142–245; Shalabī 1947:239–277.
[43] Cited in Shalabī 1947:240. [44] See Katz 2013: 75–76. [45] Al-Zuḥaylī 2006, 1:673.

can be deterred by imprisonment or fines. It is not obvious why lashes are preferable to imprisonment or fines. Hence, the choice of lashes over imprisonment and fines may be regarded as *taʿabbudī* (i.e., non-rational).

It is easy to think of many other Sharīʿa rules with both instrumentally rational and *taʿabbudī* (non-rational) aspects. Rules of ritual worship (*ʿibādāt*) are a good example. As we have seen, for Muslim scholars, rules of ritual worship are closely intertwined with ethics and Sufism. Such rules have an instrumentally rational aspect in that they are designed to instill particular mental attributes. Rules of ritual worship also have a pronounced *taʿabbudī* aspect. Let us consider the Sharīʿa rules of prayer and fasting, which fall under the category of rules of ritual worship.

God has laid down a rule mandating five ritual prayers per day. These prayers take a specific form, involving particular bodily movements and verbal formulae. Hence, to pray, the Muslim must bow, prostrate, and recite the Qurʾan. The Sharīʿa rule mandating five ritual prayers per day requires that Muslims perform these prayers with the proper bodily movements and verbal formulae. How is the prayer rule to be understood? It can be said that God desires that Muslims believe in the tenets of Islam (i.e., He desires they possess this specific mental attribute). Moreover, God believes/knows that the performance of ritual prayers instills belief in the tenets of Islam.[46] In this sense, the prayer rule is instrumentally rational. On the other hand, it is possible to think of alternative rules which might be equally effective in instilling belief. Hence, God could have laid down a rule mandating 3 ritual prayers a day or a rule mandating 10 ritual prayers a day. Moreover, God could have changed the form of the prayer, stipulating a different set of bodily movements and verbal formulae. Given these alternative possibilities, it is not obvious why God laid down the existing prayer rule. In this sense, the prayer rule is *taʿabbudī* (non-rational).[47]

We now come to fasting. Thus, God has laid down a rule requiring Muslims to refrain from food, drink, and sex during daylight hours for the month of *Ramaḍān*. How is this rule to be understood? God accepts that Muslims have desires for worldly pleasures. However, God does not want these desires to be excessively strong. Rather He wants them to be weak. In other words, God desires that Muslims have weak desires for worldly pleasures. (Weak desire is a specific mental attribute). Moreover, God believes/knows that Muslims' desires can be weakened (*kasr al-shahawāt*) through the ascetic practice of renouncing worldly pleasures like food, drink, and sex.[48] In this sense, the existing fasting rule is instrumentally rational. On the other hand, there are many other rules that could be used to weaken Muslims' desires for worldly pleasures. Hence, God could have required Muslims to fast a month other than *Ramaḍān*. Or alternatively, He could have required them to fast both *Ramaḍān* and an additional month. Moreover, God could have required Muslims to refrain from food, drink, and sex during the night rather than during the day. Similarly, God could have required Muslims to

[46] This was discussed previously.
[47] See al-Zuḥaylī 2006, 1:673–674.
[48] See al-Ghazālī 2005:273–282.

refrain from sleep as well as food, drink, and sex, yet He did not do so. The point here is that God could have laid down any number of rules to weaken Muslims' desires for worldly pleasures. Nevertheless, He selected one specific set of rules. It is not obvious why these rules are preferable to an alternative set of rules. In this sense the existing fasting rules are *taʿabbudī* (non-rational).

To sum up, a proper understanding of Sharīʿa rules requires recognizing that they are partially instrumentally rational and partially non-rational. This is to be explained by the fact that Sharīʿa rules are intentions, and, as explicated by planning theory, intentions are partially instrumentally rational and partially non-rational.

In contemporary Egypt, religious scholars are obliged to grapple with both the instrumentally rational and non-rational dimensions of Sharīʿa rules. At present they play up the (instrumentally) rational dimension of Sharīʿa rules. This phenomenon is reflected in the increased emphasis placed on the theory of *Maqāṣid al-Sharīʿa* at al-Azhar and the Dār al-ʿUlūm. It is likewise reflected in the unprecedented popularization of al-Shāṭibī's work. Nevertheless, the non-rational dimension is always present as well. Thus, in the course of teaching Sharīʿa rules, conservative professors will often remark that obedience to these rules is a form of "worship" (*ʿibāda*). The notion of worship is most strongly associated with rituals like prayer, fasting, and pilgrimage which have a pronounced *taʿabbudī* aspect. Hence, when it is asserted that all Sharīʿa rules are worship, it is implied that all rules are akin to the ritual rules. This is because all rules involve unquestioning submission to God, which is not based on rational persuasion.

## III. NEW CIRCUMSTANCES CAN PROMPT THE ABANDONMENT AND REFORMATION OF INTENTIONS/RULES

According to planning theory, new circumstances can prompt individuals to abandon and reform their intentions (and rules). After explaining this idea, I will show how it helps illuminate the nature of Sharīʿa rules.

### A. Abandoning and Reforming Intentions

As mentioned previously, Bratman holds that human life is pervaded by Buridan problems. Hence, individuals constantly confront situations where different actions are equally desirable. Thus, I may have no preference between calling my mother at 7:00 p.m. or 8:00 p.m. Similarly, a king may have no preference between punishing those who dump toxic waste with 40 lashes or 50 lashes or 55 lashes. For Bratman, when an individual forms an intention, s/he makes a non-rational choice between equally desirable options.

Bratman recognizes that after a choice is made it can be abandoned. Or, to put things differently, after an intention is formed it can be abandoned. Thus, suppose I desire to inform my mother that I have a new job. Accordingly, I choose to call my mother at 7:00 p.m. by forming an intention to call her at 7:00 p.m. Yet, I could subsequently change my mind. Hence, I might simply abandon my intention to call her at 7:00 p.m. (with the result that I do not call her at all). Or I might abandon my intention to call her at 7:00 p.m. and form an intention to call her at 8:00 p.m. instead.

Nevertheless, Bratman realizes that abandoning an intention always has costs.[49] At the most basic level, such costs involve expending more time and mental effort on deliberation. However, depending on the circumstances, abandoning an intention may have other kinds of costs. As we will see, these costs can be very high where rules are concerned. At any rate, given the costs of abandoning intentions, Bratman holds that, all things being equal, individuals resist abandoning their intentions. Once an individual forms an intention, s/he typically treats the matter as settled, and does not consider changing his/her mind (i.e., abandoning the intention).

Still, new circumstances can prompt an individual to change his/her mind (i.e., abandon his/her intention). Recall that for Bratman, an individual's intentions are (partially) based on his/her desires and beliefs about the world. Yet, new circumstances may invalidate the beliefs upon which an intention is based. This may prompt the individual to abandon the intention. For instance, suppose that I desire to eat ice cream. Accordingly, I form an intention to visit "John's Ice Cream Shop" at 9:00 p.m. Or, to put things more precisely, I form a composite intention to visit John's Ice Cream Shop at 9:00 p.m. (the intended means) in order to realize my desire to eat ice cream (the intended end). This intention is based on a variety of beliefs. For instance, I believe that John's Ice Cream Shop has ice cream for sale. I believe that the shop will be open until 9:00 p.m. I believe that the ice cream will cost less than 10 dollars. I also believe that there is no other ice cream shop closer to my house than John's Ice Cream Shop. Yet, new circumstances may invalidate these beliefs. Hence, John's Ice Cream Shop might run out of ice cream, or it might close before 9:00 p.m., or it might raise the price of ice cream to 20 dollars per serving, or a new ice cream shop might open up which is closer to my house. In these circumstances, I may abandon my intention to visit John's Ice Cream Shop at 9:00 p.m. After all, the beliefs upon which this intention is based no longer hold true (i.e., these beliefs have been invalidated by new circumstances).

There are several categories of new circumstances which might prompt an individual to abandon an intention. Let us consider two of these categories. First, *an individual might abandon an intention because new circumstances make it excessively costly to realize the intended end.* For instance, if John's Ice Cream Shop raises the price of ice cream to 20 dollars per serving, I may abandon my intention to eat ice cream (the intended end). New circumstances make something excessively costly when they force an individual to sacrifice what is desired more strongly for what is desired less strongly. Hence, I may desire to eat ice cream, but I may desire 20 dollars more strongly. When the price of ice cream is raised

[49] See Bratman 1987.

to 20 dollars, I must sacrifice something I desire more (20 dollars) for something that I desire less (the ice cream).

Second, *an individual might abandon an intention because new circumstances reveal a more desirable alternative means of realizing the intended end.* For instance, perhaps a new ice cream shop opens up, and sells ice cream which is both cheaper and higher quality than that sold by John's Ice Cream Shop. Given the emergence of this alternative, I abandon my intention to visit John's Ice Cream Shop. Notice that, originally, visiting John's Ice Cream Shop was my intended means of realizing my desire to eat ice cream (my intended end). I have abandoned this intended means because there is now a more desirable alternative means of realizing my intended end (i.e., visiting the new ice cream shop).

Thus, there are (at least) two categories of new circumstances which may prompt an individual to abandon an intention. Both of them can be explained in terms of instrumental rationality. Hence, in each case, an individual initially forms an intention, seeking to pursue the strongest of his/her desires in light of his/her beliefs. Yet, new circumstances invalidate the beliefs on which the intention is based. Consequently, the individual abandons the intention.

But matters do not end here. Even after abandoning his/her initial intention, the individual will still seek to pursue the strongest of his/her desires in light of his/her beliefs. Yet, the individual will have new beliefs which reflect the new circumstances. This means that the individual will form a new intention based on these new beliefs.

For instance, suppose I desire to eat ice cream, and I believe that John's Ice Cream Shop is open at 9:00 p.m. Accordingly, I form an intention to visit the shop at 9:00 p.m. (the intended means) in order to realize my desire to eat ice cream (the intended end). But if I am told that the shop has a new schedule and now closes at 5:00 p.m., I will abandon my intention to visit at 9:00 p.m. I will then form a new intention in light of my new belief that the shop closes at 5:00 p.m. Thus, perhaps I form an intention to visit the shop at 3:00 p.m. or 4:00 p.m., thereby realizing my desire to eat ice cream (my intended end). This process illustrates an important principle; *namely new circumstances can prompt individuals to abandon and then reform their intentions.* Hence, in this case there is a new circumstance (i.e., John's Ice Cream Shop changes its schedule to close at 5:00 p.m.). The new circumstances prompt me to abandon my initial intention (of visiting the ice cream shop at 9:00 p.m.). After abandoning my initial intention I form a new intention (to visit the ice cream shop at 3:00 p.m.) in light of my new belief (that the ice cream shop closes at 5:00 p.m.). It will be noticed that both my initial intention and my new intention are formed in accordance with the principle of instrumental rationality (i.e., pursuing one's strongest desire in light of one's various beliefs). The key difference between the initial intention and the new intention is that the new intention incorporates new beliefs which reflect the new circumstances.

Consider another example. I form an intention to purchase ice cream from John's Ice Cream Shop (the intended means) in order to realize my desire to eat ice cream (the intended end). My intention is based on the belief that there do not exist other ice cream shops which sell higher-quality ice cream for lower prices. However, Beatrice's Ice Cream Shop then opens, and sells higher-quality ice cream for lower prices. This prompts me to abandon my intention to visit John's Ice Cream Shop. I will then form a new intention in light of my new belief that cheaper higher-quality ice cream is sold at Beatrice's Ice Cream Shop. Thus, I may form an intention to visit Beatrice's Ice Cream Shop. Once again, this situation illustrates the principle that new circumstances can prompt individuals to abandon and reform their intentions.

To sum up: Generally speaking, when an individual forms an intention, s/he considers the matter settled and does not abandon the intention. After all, abandoning an intention has costs. This means that individuals are resistant to abandoning their intentions. Nevertheless, such resistance can be overcome. Hence, new circumstances can prompt individuals to abandon and reform their intentions. This does not mean that new circumstances always prompt individuals to abandon and reform their intentions. For instance, the costs of abandoning an intention may be so high that an individual refuses to do so, even when faced with new circumstances. On the other hand, new circumstances raise the possibility that an individual might abandon his/her intentions.

## B. Abandoning and Reforming Rules

As we have seen, rules can often be conceptualized as the intentions of authority figures (e.g., God, the king, parliament). This means that the preceding analysis on the abandonment of intentions can also be applied to rules.

Earlier on, it was mentioned that abandoning intentions has costs. These costs are especially high where intentions are rules laid down by authority figures. Hence, when an authority figure abandons his/her intentions, s/he abandons (i.e., revokes) his/her rules. For instance, suppose that a king desires to protect the animals and plants which live in the ocean. Moreover, he believes that toxic waste will kill these animals and plants. Based on his beliefs and desires, the king forms an intention that his judges punish toxic waste dumpers with 50 lashes. This is the king's rule. The king might then subsequently change his mind and abandon this intention/rule. In other words, he might revoke the rule. As a consequence, there is no longer any penalty for dumping toxic waste. Yet, doing this has a heavy cost. By abandoning/revoking the rule, the king is no longer able to use the rule to realize his desire to protect the animals and plants.

It is possible to imagine a variation on this situation. Hence, perhaps as soon as the king abandons/revokes his initial rule, he then replaces it with another rule. For instance, after the king revokes the rule punishing toxic waste dumpers with 50 lashes, he replaces it with a rule punishing toxic waste dumpers with two years in prison. In other words, the king has abandoned the intention that his judges punish toxic waste-dumpers with 50 lashes and formed a new intention that his judges punish toxic waste-dumpers with two years in prison. In order to accomplish this change in rules, the king must expend resources in publicizing the new rule. This is a cost, albeit not necessarily a major one.

Nevertheless, it should not be assumed that rules can always be replaced in this way. Hence, in many legal, religious, and cultural traditions there is no simple or straightforward mechanism for the replacement of rules. The Islamic tradition falls into this category. According to the Islamic tradition, God communicated His rules to humankind through the Prophet Muḥammad. During the Prophet's life, God often proclaimed new rules and replaced older rules. For instance, God initially permitted wine drinking, but then forbade it.[50] Similarly, God initially ordered Muslims to pray in the direction of Jerusalem, but then later ordered them to pray in the direction of Mecca.[51] In both of these cases, God replaced one rule with another. The Prophet proclaimed these rule replacements after they were communicated to him through divine revelation. Nevertheless, according to the Islamic tradition, divine revelation came to an end when the Prophet died. Consequently, since the Prophet's death, there has been no simple or straightforward mechanism for replacing rules. This means that any effort to replace rules comes with heavy costs. Such efforts threaten to provoke disagreement and division within the Muslim community. Moreover, these efforts open the door to the gradual disintegration of the Islamic legal system into a heterogenous mass of subjective personal opinion.

This creates a complicated situation for Muslim religious scholars. Both in premodern and modern times, religious scholars have considered the possibility that God might abandon His intentions/rules in the face of new circumstances. This idea is articulated in a famous Arabic Islamic legal expression: "rules change in accordance with changes in time and place"[52] (*taghayyur al-aḥkām bi-taghayyur al-zamān wa-l-makān*).[53] This expression presumes that Sharīʿa rules were initially legislated in seventh century Arabia, and were based upon specific circumstances found in seventh century Arabia. Nevertheless, Muslim communities in other times and places have faced different circumstances. Thus, Muslim communities living in seventh century Arabia faced different circumstances than later Muslim communities living in thirteenth century Arabia or twentieth century Arabia. In other words, circumstances have changed over time (*taghayyur al-zamān*). Likewise, the circumstances of Muslim communities in Arabia are different from the circumstances of Muslim communities in Nigeria, Indonesia, or Spain. In other words, circumstances change according to place (*taghayyur al-makān*).

We might then say that changes in circumstances (tied to time and place) result in changes in rules. However, this is a simplification. For, in the view of Muslim jurists, *insignificant* changes in circumstances do not result in changes in rules. Rather, it is only *significant* changes in circumstances that result in changes in rules. The problem then becomes distinguishing significant changes

[50] See Qurʾan [5:90–91]. [51] See Qurʾan [2:144].
[52] Literally: "changes in rules in accordance with changes in time and place."
[53] Also see Chapters 4, 6 in Hallaq 2001.

in circumstances from insignificant changes. I do not believe that Muslim jurists have formulated a clear criterion for distinguishing significant from insignificant changes. Nevertheless, it is possible to elucidate some issues relevant to such a criterion.

Earlier, I noted that two types of new circumstances might prompt an individual to abandon an intention. First, *an individual might abandon an intention because new circumstances make it excessively costly to realize the intended end.* Second, *an individual might abandon an intention because new circumstances reveal a more desirable alternative means of realizing the intended end.* Where rules are intentions, new circumstances of either type might prompt the abandonment of rules. These ideas can be applied to Sharīʿa rules.

First, God might abandon (i.e., revoke) a Sharīʿa rule because new circumstances make it excessively costly to realize the intended end. This notion is reflected in a variety of medieval Islamic legal maxims. These maxims include: (1) "situations of necessity permit the prohibited" (*al-ḍarūrāt tubīḥ al-maḥẓūrāt*), (2) "hardship brings relaxation [of Sharīʿa rules]" (*al-mashaqqa tajlib al-taysīr*), and (3) "harm is removed" (*al-ḍarar yuzāl*).[54] For example, God desires to spread belief in the Islamic religion. Moreover, God believes that public affirmation of belief in Islam works to spread belief in Islam. Therefore, God has laid down a Sharīʿa rule which requires Muslims to publicly affirm their belief in Islam (the intended means) in order to realize His desire to spread belief in the Islamic religion (the intended end). However, new circumstances may bring persecution, such that Muslims are physically assaulted or killed for publicly affirming their belief. In these circumstances, there is an excessive cost for spreading belief in Islam through public affirmation. After all, God strongly desires to protect the bodies and lives of Muslims. But insisting that Muslims publicly affirm belief will come at the cost of realizing this desire. Consequently, in such circumstances, God will abandon/revoke the rule requiring Muslims to publicly affirm belief. In reality, God is making an exception to a general rule. Hence, Muslims are still obliged to publicly affirm belief, but there is an exception to this rule in circumstances of severe persecution. This example is standard in Islamic legal texts.[55]

Consider another example drawn from Islamic legal texts.[56] God desires to protect patrilineal kinship bonds. He believes that such bonds are undermined when unmarried men and women look at each other or touch each other (as such can lead to extramarital sex). Hence, God has laid down a rule prohibiting unmarried men and women from looking at each other or touching each other (the intended means) in order to realize His desire to protect patrilineal kinship bonds (the intended end). However, there may arise a class of doctors. In order to treat illnesses, these doctors must perform medical examinations which involve looking at and touching their patients (including their patients' private areas). Moreover, in a given region, there may only be doctors of one sex (e.g., male doctors). In new circumstances such as these, is a female permitted to go to a male

[54] See al-Suyūṭī 1983b: 76, 83–84.
[55] See al-Suyūṭī 1983b:84.
[56] See al-Suyūṭī 1983b:79.

doctor for medical treatment (which will involve him looking at and touching her body)? In such circumstances, God might abandon/revoke the Sharīʿa rule which categorically prohibits unmarried men and women from looking at and touching each other. In other words, God makes an exception for the women seeking medical treatment. After all, God desires to safeguard human health, and keeping the rule in place would come at the cost of realizing this desire. As we will see, this line of analysis has been utilized by Muslim jurists in both the premodern and modern periods, typically under the heading of *istiḥsān* or *istiṣlāḥ*.

We may now consider the second set of circumstances which might prompt the abandonment of rules. God *might abandon/revoke a rule because new circumstances reveal a more desirable alternative means of realizing the intended end of the rule*. For instance, in the Qurʾan, God lays down a rule requiring that Muslims obtain horses for war.[57] Yet, religious scholars hold that this rule must be interpreted differently under present-day circumstances. Today the rule requires that Muslims prepare for war by obtaining modern military technologies (e.g., tanks, aircraft, missiles) rather than horses.[58] How are we to understand this opinion? Let us return to the original Qurʾanic rule, which requires obtaining horses for war. Presumably God desires that Muslims acquire military power. Moreover, He believes that warhorses are an effective implement of war. Consequently, God forms an intention that Muslims prepare warhorses (the intended means) in order to realize His desire that Muslims acquire military power (the intended end). Now, in the seventh century (when the Qurʾan was revealed), it was correct to believe in the effectiveness of horses as an implement of war. However, at present, modern military technologies are far more effective implements of war. Accordingly, obtaining modern military technologies is a more desirable alternative means of realizing God's desire that Muslims acquire military power (the intended end). Given the existence of a more desirable alternative means, God abandons/revokes the rule that Muslims prepare horses for war. He then forms a new rule/intention that Muslims obtain modern war technologies. Hence, God has reformed the rule, maintaining the same intended end, but choosing a new intended means based on His belief that (under current circumstances) modern war technologies are the most effective implements of war. In this way, we see how new circumstances can engender the abandonment and reformation of rules/intentions. As we will see, this line of analysis has been utilized by Muslim jurists in both the premodern and modern periods, typically under the heading of *istiṣlāḥ*.

[57] Qurʿan [8:60]. [58] Riḍā 1368h, 10:68–71.

## IV. LANGUAGE AND THE PRINCIPLES OF ISLAMIC LEGAL INTERPRETATION: *ẒĀHIR AL-NAṢṢ, QIYĀS, ISTIṢLAḤ, ISTIḤSĀN*

Texts on Islamic legal theory (*Uṣūl al-Fiqh*), including those used in contemporary Egypt, emphasize the relationship between language and intentions. This is well illustrated in Fakhr al-Dīn al-Rāzī's (d.606/1209) massive legal theoretic work *al-Maḥṣūl*. Al-Rāzī opens the text by explicating the etymology of "*fiqh*," a classical term commonly used to denote "Islamic law." Al-Rāzī explains that "in its original linguistic signification, *fiqh* expresses [the idea of] grasping the intention (*gharaḍ*) of a speaker by means of his speech."[59] Islamic law is referred to as *fiqh* because it involves (among other things) grasping God's intentions from His statements in the Qurʾan. Al-Rāzī's equation of *fiqh* with the search for intentions behind language recurs frequently in other legal treatises.[60] As a consequence, Islamicist scholarship tends to assume that the discipline of Islamic law centers on the analysis of language.[61] I think that this view is mistaken, for, as I have argued, the discipline of Islamic law also involves the analysis of nonverbal actions (e.g., the reported actions of the Prophet, the reported actions of past Muslim scholars). Nevertheless, I recognize that the analysis of language is an important element in the discipline of Islamic law. Therefore, I will briefly address the analysis of language in Islamic law, and explain how it relates to the notion that knowledge of Sharīʿa rules is knowledge of God's intentions and the beliefs and desires on which these intentions are based.

Insofar as Islamic legal theory addresses the analysis of language, it focuses on God's statements as recorded in the Qurʾan and the Prophet's statements as recorded in the Hadith reports. These statements articulate rules. Hence, God states in the Qurʾan: "Amputate the hand of the thief." He likewise states: "Don't drink grape wine" (although this is a paraphrase).[62] Similarly, there is a Hadith report in which the Prophet states that it is forbidden to eat from gold and silver vessels.[63] Muslim jurists utilize four basic methods to interpret statements from God and the Prophet. First, there is strict adherence to the literal meaning of a statement (*ẓāhir al-naṣṣ*). Second, there is *qiyās*, which involves extending a rule through analogical reasoning. Third, there is *istiṣlāḥ*, which involves abandoning (and possibly reforming) a rule in light of new circumstances.[64] Fourth, there is *istiḥsān*, which involves making a limited exception to a rule in light of new/specific circumstances.[65] Let us examine each of these four methods in turn.

[59] Al-Rāzī n.d 1:78. [60] Yunis Ali 2000:1; also see al-Shāfiʿī n.d.:91–92.

[61] See, e.g., Yunis Ali 2000; Gleave 2012. [62] See Qurʾan [5:9091].

[63] Ibn Ḥajar 2008:56.

[64] For general discussion of *istiṣlāḥ* see al-Ghazālī 2000:173–180; al-Zarkashī 2007, 4:377–382; Shalabī 1947 268–277; Khallāf 2003:74–78; Abū Zahra 2002:313–345, al-Zuḥaylī 2006, 2:33–102.

[65] For general discussions of *istiḥsān* see al-Jaṣṣāṣ 2000, 2:339–355; al-Zarkashī 2007, 4:386–394; al-Ījī 2004, 3:575–577; Khallāf 2003:70–73; al-Zuḥaylī 2006, 2:17–32.

## A. *Ẓāhir al-Naṣṣ*

The first interpretive method is strict adherence to the literal meaning of a statement (*ẓāhir al-naṣṣ*). The literal meaning of a statement is its "explicit meaning" (i.e., its "wording," its "semantico-referential meaning"). Take God's statement in the Qur'an: "Don't drink grape wine." According to the literal meaning of this statement, God simply forbids drinking grape wine. God does not forbid drinking wine made from dates or smoking marijuana. After all, these things are nowhere mentioned in His statement.

If we strictly adhere to the literal meaning of God's statement, then we assume that His intention/rule coincides with the literal meaning of the statement. Hence, in stating "Don't drink grape wine" God's intention/rule is that Muslims are prohibited from drinking grape wine. However, they are not prohibited from drinking wine made from dates or smoking marijuana. (And indeed, some early Ḥanafī jurists were open to such an interpretation of God's statement).

## B. *Qiyās*

The second interpretive method is *qiyās*.[66] *Qiyās* involves extending a rule through analogical reasoning. In *qiyās*, we assume that God's intention/rule does not perfectly coincide with the literal meaning of a statement. Rather, it extends beyond the literal meaning of the statement. Hence, using *qiyās*, we could argue that when God states "Don't drink grape wine," His intention is not merely to prohibit drinking grape wine. Rather, His intention is to prohibit all intoxicants, including wine made from dates, and marijuana. In fact, this is the standard opinion of Sunni Muslim jurists.

But if God wanted to prohibit all intoxicants (rather than simply grape wine), why did He mention "grape wine" but not "intoxicants" in his statement? Juristic discussions of *qiyās* presume that sometimes God mentions a specific object as an example of a broader class of objects. Thus, grape wine is an example of a broader class of intoxicants. When God said: "Don't drink grape wine," He really meant "Don't drink things *similar to* grape wine" (i.e., "Don't drink things from the broader class of objects of which grape wine is an example"). This is like a rule which explicitly prohibits children from bringing "pistols" to school. A pistol is an example of a broader class of objects (i.e., deadly weapons). Such a rule can be read as implying a prohibition on children bringing any sort of deadly weapon to school (e.g., shotguns, machine guns, grenades).

We determine that God prohibits all intoxicants by inferring God's desires, beliefs, and intentions from the statement: "Don't drink grape wine." Hence, we infer that God desires to prevent conflicts and fights.[67] We also infer that God believes that drunkenness results in conflicts/fights. We then infer that God forms

[66] For general discussions of *qiyās* see al-Ghazālī 2000:280–341; al-Zarkashī 2007, 4:3–319; al-Ījī 2004, 3:279–550; al-Zuḥaylī 2006, 1:571–680.
[67] See al-Zuḥaylī 2006, 1:575.

an intention to prohibit all intoxicants (the intended means) in order to realize His desire to prevent conflicts/fights (the intended end). In discussing *qiyās*, Muslim jurists use the Arabic term "*ʿilla*" to designate the "intended means."[68] Meanwhile, jurists use the Arabic term "*ḥikma*" to designate the intended end.

In premodern Islamic law, *qiyās* is the most important method of interpretation. Through widespread use of *qiyās*, scholars elaborate a broader system of Sharīʿa rules which extends far beyond the literal meaning of God's statements in the Qurʾan and the Prophet's statements in the Hadith reports. By embracing *qiyās* Muslim scholars frequently depart from a strict literalist approach in legal interpretation.

## C. *Istiṣlāḥ*

The third interpretive method is *istiṣlāḥ*.[69] *Istiṣlāḥ* involves abandoning (and possibly reforming) a rule in light of new circumstances. The logic of this method was explained previously. Hence, God might abandon (i.e., revoke) a Sharīʿa rule because new circumstances make it excessively costly to realize the intended end. God might also abandon/revoke a rule because new circumstances reveal a more desirable alternative means of realizing the intended end of the rule.

Classic examples of *istiṣlāḥ* can be found in the actions of ʿUmar, the esteemed companion of the Prophet who assumed leadership of the Muslim community shortly after the Prophet's death. Thus, in the Qurʾan, God lays down a rule mandating the annual payment of alms (*al-zakāh*). These alms are used to help the poor. However, God also states that a portion of the alms should be distributed among new converts. This can be understood as follows. God desires to spread the Islamic religion. God believes that giving money to new converts will help retain converts and induce new conversions. Therefore, God forms an intention that money from the annual payment of alms is to be given to new converts (the intended means) in order to spread the Islamic religion (the intended end). During the Prophet's life, this practice was needed to help spread Islam. However, by the time ʿUmar assumed leadership of the Muslim community, the Islamic religion was already strong, well established, and spreading with ease. Hence, there was no longer any need to give money to new converts. In these new circumstances, ʿUmar cut off the payments to converts.[70]

At his time, ʿUmar saw that there were two means of spreading the Islamic religion. First, he could give money to new converts. Second, he could simply stand aside and let the religion spread by itself without giving money to new converts. For ʿUmar, the second means was more desirable for realizing the intended end of spreading the religion. After all, it saved unnecessary expenditure

[68] However, strictly speaking, the *ʿilla* is the set of characteristics which defines the broader class of objects addressed by the rule (e.g., the characteristic of being an intoxicant).

[69] For general discussion of *istiṣlāḥ* see al-Ghazālī 2000:173–180; al-Zarkashī 2007, 4:377–382; Shalabī 1947:268–277; Khallāf 2003:74–78; Abū Zahra 2002:313–345, al-Zuḥaylī 2006, 2:33–102.

[70] See, e.g., M. Shalabī 1947:37–38; Biltājī 2006:148–154.

from the annual payment of alms, such that ʿUmar could direct these funds to other worthy purposes (like helping the poor). In this way, ʿUmar reformed the rule in the Qurʾan, such that it no longer allocated money to new converts.[71]

Since *istiṣlāḥ* involves abandoning (and possibly reforming) a rule, it involves abandoning the literal meaning of the statements, from God and the Prophet, which express the rule. Hence, God states in the Qurʾan that new converts are to be given funds from the annual payment of alms. But ʿUmar does not abide by the literal meaning of this statement when he decides that, in light of new circumstances, funds should no longer be given to converts. Put differently, ʿUmar does not take a strict literalist approach in legal interpretation.

## D. *Istiḥsān*

The fourth interpretive method is *istiḥsān*.[72] *Istiḥsān* is given a range of competing and somewhat rough definitions in Islamic legal texts. However, *istiḥsān* is best conceptualized as follows. It involves making a limited exception to a rule in light of new/specific circumstances. Hence, as mentioned earlier, there is a general Sharīʿa rule prohibiting unmarried men and women from looking at each other or touching each other. However, there is an exception for a woman who visits a male doctor for medical treatment. Similarly, some jurists have argued that there is an exception to the prohibition on drinking grape wine where such drinking is necessary for medical treatment.[73] These are examples of *istiḥsān*. The logic of such opinions was explained previously. Thus, God might abandon (i.e., revoke) a Sharīʿa rule because new circumstances make it excessively costly to act on the rule.

In the view of Muslim scholars, ʿUmar's policies also provide examples of *istiḥsān*. Hence, in the Qurʾan God states: "Amputate the hand of the thief." However, recall that ʿUmar held the penalty to be inapplicable at a time of severe famine, when hunger was forcing people to steal. In this way, he made an exception to the rule.[74] It will be noticed that exceptions of this sort involve abandoning the literal meaning of the statements (from God and the Prophet) which express rules. Thus, the literal meaning of God's statement: "Amputate the hand of the thief" indicates that all thefts are to be punished with amputation (including in times of famine). ʿUmar does not abide by the literal meaning of this statement when he decides to suspend the amputation penalty in a time of famine. Once again, here we see that 'Umar does not take a strict literalist approach in legal interpretation.

I would note that, on a conceptual level, there is not always a clear distinction between *istiṣlāḥ* and *istiḥsān*. Hence, as noted previously, *istiṣlāḥ* involves abandoning and (possibly) reforming Sharīʿa rules. Meanwhile, *istiḥsān* involves

[71] Also see M. Shalabī 1947:48–56: Biltājī 2006:327–330.

[72] For general discussions of *istiḥsān* see al-Jaṣṣāṣ 2000, 2:339–355; al-Zarkashī 2007, 4:386–394; al-Ījī 2004, 3:575–577; Khallāf 2003:70–73; al-Zuḥaylī 2006, 2:17–32.

[73] See Ibn Nujaym 1999:65. Also see Hallaq 2001:140.

[74] Kamali 2013:325.

making an exception to Sharīʿa rules. However, it can be argued that when one makes an exception to a rule, one is abandoning and reforming the original rule. At any rate, what is most important, for our purposes, is recognizing how the logic of *istiṣlāḥ* and *istiḥsān* relates to intentions, desires, and beliefs.

## V. LITERALISM AND ISLAMIC LEGAL INTERPRETATION

To what extent can it be said that premodern Muslim scholars adopt a literalist approach to legal interpretation? Recent Islamicist studies have addressed this question with increasing sophistication.[75] In Islamic history, the transient Ẓāhirī legal school promoted a strict literalist approach.[76] Nevertheless, mainstream Sunni legal thought rejected a strict literalist approach, including all four legal schools (i.e., Ḥanafī, Mālikī, Shāfiʿī, Ḥanbalī). Thus, whereas the Ẓāhirī school repudiated the non-literalist interpretive method of *qiyās*, this method was adopted by the four legal schools. The Ḥanafī and Mālikī schools also adopted the interpretive methods of *istiṣlāḥ* and *istiḥsān*. The status of *istiṣlāḥ* and *istiḥsān* in the Shāfiʿī and Ḥanbalī schools is more controversial. However, it can be argued that both methods receive some measure of acceptance in each school.

There are two major reasons that mainstream Sunni thought rejected a strict literalist approach. First of all, Muslim scholars equate Sharīʿa rules with God's intentions. But, an individual's intentions often diverge from the literal meaning of his/her statements. Consequently, God's intentions cannot be reduced to the literal meaning of His statements. Second, later Muslim scholars were influenced by the example of the earliest generations, who were believed to have the highest level of knowledge on Sharīʿa rules. Thus, ʿUmar spent almost two decades as a close companion of the Prophet, acquiring knowledge of Sharīʿa rules directly from him. Yet, ʿUmar clearly rejected a strict literalist approach. Indeed, he even utilized the general forms of reasoning associated with *istiṣlāḥ* and *istiḥsān*. Accordingly, later Muslim scholars concluded that Sharīʿa rules should not be understood in terms of a strict literalist approach.

Although premodern scholars do not accept a strict "literalist" approach, they are inclined toward a "literalistic" approach which seeks to minimize departures from the literal meaning of scripture, even in the face of new circumstances. Thus, premodern scholars often strictly adhere to the literal meaning of scripture, especially in regard to rules of ritual worship (*ʿibādāt*). They are also often willing to extend rules through *qiyās*. This brings us to *istiṣlāḥ* and *istiḥsān*. In theory, *istiṣlāḥ* and *istiḥsān* could be used to justify many sweeping departures from the literal meaning of scripture. However, premodern scholars use *istiṣlāḥ* and *istiḥsān* only very sparingly. They are most comfortable using such methods to address severe hardships which imperil the lives, health, and safety of Muslims. Where severe hardships do not exist, premodern scholars typically

[75] See, e.g., Yunis Ali 2000; Gleave 2012.

[76] Melchert 1997:178–197.

avoid invoking *istiṣlāḥ* and *istiḥsān*. As we will see, with the coming of modernity, many religious scholars begin to countenance far more widespread and radical uses of *istiṣlāḥ* and *istiḥsān*.

Grasping these issues allows for a better understanding of the Islamic legal tradition. To further refine this understanding, I would like to consider several key concepts in the Islamic legal tradition: (1) *taqlīd*, (2) *ijmāʿ*, (3) the legal school (*madhhab*), and (4) *ijtihād*. I begin with *taqlīd*.

## VI. THE RATIONALE FOR *TAQLĪD*

In the view of premodern Muslim scholars, individuals with less knowledge about Sharīʿa rules must defer to individuals with more knowledge about Sharīʿa rules. In other words, the less knowledgeable are not entitled to put forth their own options about Sharīʿa rules. Rather, they should accept the opinions of the more knowledgeable. Such deference to those with more knowledge is known as *taqlīd*.[77]

*Taqlīd* has a pronounced temporal dimension. This is because premodern Muslim scholars hold that earlier generations are more knowledgeable than later ones. Ibn al-Qayyim states that "the closeness [of opinions] to the truth is in accordance with the closeness of those [who formulated them] to the era of the Messenger."[78] A corollary of this view is that since the dawn of Islam, knowledge has been in a steady state of decline. Al-Shāṭibī (d.790/1388) asserts: "The first generation's (*al-Ṣaḥāba*) mastery of the Sharīʿa sciences is unlike that of the second generation (*al-Tābiʿūn*). And that of the second generation is unlike those who succeeded them, and so on [goes the decline] until the present."[79]

As a general principle, because scholars from earlier generations are more knowledgeable, scholars from later generations should defer to them (through *taqlīd*). For example, if past scholars have asserted that Sharīʿa rules prohibit smoking marijuana, or permit a woman to visit a male doctor, then later scholars should defer to these opinions rather than putting forth their own opinions. The most knowledgeable generation is the first generation, followed by the second, then the third, and so on. Accordingly, the second generation should defer to the first. Meanwhile, the third generation should defer to both the first and the second, and so on.

However, deference to earlier scholars is not absolute, but rather admits of degrees. There are a variety of perspectives regarding the extent to which later scholars should defer to their predecessors. At one end of the spectrum, it is asserted that later scholars must defer to their predecessors' opinions even if they discover Hadith reports which appear to clearly contradict their predecessors'

[77] For traditional definitions of "*taqlīd*" see al-Ghazālī 2000:370; Ibn Qudāma 1994:205; al-Shawkānī 1994:391.

[78] Ibn al-Qayyim 2004, 2:j.4 384.

[79] Al-Shāṭibī 2004:57.

opinions. At the other end of the spectrum, it is asserted that later scholars are permitted (or even required) not to defer to their predecessors' opinions if they discover Hadith reports which appear to clearly contradict their predecessors' opinions.[80] In other words, in these circumstances, it is permitted (or even required) to abandon *taqlīd*.[81]

Western Islamicist scholars have had difficulty grasping the premodern Muslim view that Sharīʿa knowledge is in a constant state of decline. Such scholars generally presume that knowledge of Sharīʿa rules is learned through written texts. This seemingly puts later generations in a situation analogous to earlier generations. If earlier generations acquired knowledge of Sharīʿa rules by studying texts, then later generations should be able to acquire the same knowledge by studying the same texts. On such a view, knowledge of Sharīʿa rules should be stable, rather than declining. But if knowledge is not declining, and later scholars are not less knowledgeable than their predecessors, it becomes hard to understand why later scholars insist on deferring to their predecessors (through *taqlīd*). This line of reasoning has led Western Islamicists to propose alternative explanations for why later Muslim scholars insist on deference (i.e., *taqlīd*). Thus, some argue that such deference is a result of political-historical factors.[82] Others argue that deference makes life easier for later jurists by sparing them the trouble of having to derive rulings themselves.[83] Still others explicate deference as a means for securing stability or increased predictability in the operation of the legal system.[84] Without denying the partial validity of these explanations, they are not those offered by Muslim jurists themselves. Such explanations are problematic because they fail to adequately engage with the underlying epistemic foundations of premodern Sunni legal thought.

## VII. THE EPISTEMIC BASIS OF *TAQLĪD*

There are (at least) two reasons for premodern Muslim views on *taqlīd*. Both run contrary to the assumption that knowledge of Sharīʿa rules can be adequately learned from written texts that have been preserved over time. First off, premodern authorities hold that many (if not most) Hadith reports on the

[80] Ibn Taymiyya suggests that there may be reasons for not applying a Hadith report if it is not corroborated by the views of at some early scholars. See Ibn Taymiyya 2004, 20:247–252. On the other hand, Ibn al-Qayyim seems to require applying Hadith reports even absent corroboration of this type. See Ibn al-Qayyim 2004, 2:j.4 470–479. Also see Riḍā 2008:114–115.

[81] Between the most rigid perspectives and the most lax, there are a host of intermediary positions. These stipulate that whereas a contradictory Hadith report does not justify abandoning *taqlīd*, such is legitimate where additional conditions are fulfilled. See Ibn al-Ṣalāḥ 2009:81–82; al-Dihlawī 1398h:36–37.

[82] See Hallaq 1984:18; Hallaq 1986:134.

[83] Jackson 1996:172. Also see Calder 1996: 162–163.

[84] Fadel 1996; El Shamsy 2008:22; Ibrahim 2016.

Prophet were never permanently recorded in writing. Rather, they were collected by the early generations and preserved in memorized form, with the help of rudimentary notes. Only a fraction of the Hadith reports which circulated among early scholars (including the four Imams) were passed on to their successors. To give one illustrative example, Muslim sources state that the Hadith master al-Bukhārī (d.256/870) collected 600,000 Hadith reports. Of these, less than 8,000 were included in the famous compilation he left for later generations.[85] Speaking on this general issue, Ibn Taymiyya states:

> those who [lived] before the compilation of these collections of *ḥadīth* reports (*al-dawāwīn*) were far more knowledgeable than later generations about the *Sunna*. [This is] because much of what [the early generations] were acquainted with, and whose authenticity they were in a position to verify, has not come down to us [in a form whose authenticity can be verified] or has not come down to us at all. Their collections [of Hadith reports] were their chests [where the materials were memorized]. These contained multiple times (*aḍʿāf*) as much as what is found in [our] *collections* [of Hadith reports], and this is a matter which cannot by doubted by he who knows the issue.[86]

It is possible that not all premodern scholars shared this perspective.[87] Nevertheless, it seems to have been widespread. Indeed, views similar to those of Ibn Taymiyya are in evidence at al-Azhar into the early twentieth century. Thus, Rashīd Riḍā complains that in response to his criticisms of *taqlīd*, Azhar scholars respond that the founders of the legal schools had access to Hadith reports which are no longer extant.[88] Moreover, to this day, Traditionalist scholars still put forward these same arguments, emphasizing that the earliest jurists had access to a number of Hadith reports which "far exceeded those of the subsequently compiled collections [that have been transmitted to later generations]."[89] Thus, early scholars were acquainted with many Hadith reports that were never recorded in writing and passed on to later generations. Such implies that earlier scholars are more knowledgeable about Sharīʿa rules than later generations. From this perspective, it makes sense for later scholars to defer (through *taqlīd*) to their more knowledgeable predecessors.

Western scholars' difficulty in appreciating this point is largely due to the manner in which they acquire compilations of Hadith reports. Muslim authorities hold that compilations can only by properly understood if received through a *sanad*. This allows *shaykhs* to clarify their function and history. Because Western scholars obtain texts from bookstores and libraries, there is no one to tell them that such compilations are only understood to contain a portion of the Hadith

[85] See Azmi 1968:301–305. Here Azmi also makes the point that, contrary to what is often supposed, the fact that al-Bukhārī did not record a Hadith does not mean he believed it lacked evidential value.

[86] Ibn Taymiyya 2004, 20:238–239. Also see Ibn al-Qayyim 2004, 2: j.4 405–407.

[87] For an indication that al-Suyūṭī may have held a different position, see al-Suyūṭī 1983a:90.

[88] See Riḍā 2008:52.

[89] See Keller's comments in al-Nawawī 2002:134–135.

reports known to the early Muslims. The result is confusion regarding Muslim views on Hadith reports. This confusion then gives rise to misunderstandings of fundamental juristic doctrines like *taqlīd*.

The second reason that premodern Muslims endorse *taqlīd* relates to their views on learning. We have seen that for Muslim scholars (like Ibn Khaldūn), certain kinds of knowledge can only be adequately learned through practice. Written texts alone do not suffice. Notably, although written texts can be preserved unchanged over time, a practice cannot. Rather, a practice always gradually accumulates alterations, increasingly departing from the original.

Thus, the Prophet practiced Sharīʿa rules. This was his Sunna. The Companions directly observed and imitated the Prophet, thereby acquiring knowledge of Sharīʿa rules (through practice). But, while the Companions strove to imitate the Prophet to the best of their ability, they could not imitate him perfectly. Consequently, their practice of Sharīʿa rules was an imperfect copy of the Prophet's practice of Sharīʿa rules. By extension, their knowledge of Sharīʿa rules was not as precise or complete as the Prophet's knowledge. The second generation of Muslims then directly observed and imitated the Companions, thereby acquiring knowledge of Sharīʿa rules (through practice). But while the second generation strove to imitate the Companions to the best of their ability, perfect imitation was again impossible. Hence, the second generation's practice of Sharīʿa rules was an imperfect copy of the Companions' practice of Sharīʿa rules. By extension, the second generations' knowledge of Sharīʿa rules was not as precise or complete as the Companions' knowledge. In this way, we see that the practice of Sharīʿa rules is incrementally corrupted every time it is passed on to a new generation. Whereas the Companions have a direct but imperfect copy of the Prophet's practice of Sharīʿa rules, the second generation has an imperfect copy of an imperfect copy. Meanwhile, the third generation has an imperfect copy of an imperfect copy of an imperfect copy, and so forth. For example, the Companions' prayer (i.e., practice of the Sharīʿa rules on prayer) is closest to the Prophet's prayer. The prayer of the second generation is second closest, and so on. Because later generations acquire knowledge of Sharīʿa rules through increasingly corrupted practice, they have an increasingly corrupted knowledge of Sharīʿa rules. This implies that earlier generations possess an epistemic status that can never be rivaled by their successors. As a result, it is only rational for later generations to defer (through *taqlīd*) to earlier generations.

Premodern Muslim scholars emphasize that the first three (or so) generations possessed a particularly high level of knowledge of Sharīʿa rules (i.e., *Saḥāba*/Companions, *Tābiʿūn*/Successors, *Atbāʿ al-Tābiʿīn*/Successors of the Successors). These generations are referred to by the Arabic term "*Salaf*," which means "predecessors." When premodern Muslim scholars stress the need for deferring (through *taqlīd*) to earlier generations, they mean, first and foremost, deference to the *Salaf*.

## VIII. *TAQLĪD, IJMĀʿ*, AND THE LEGAL SCHOOLS

We are now in a position to examine the relationship of *taqlīd* to the legal schools. In examining this relationship, it is necessary to recapitulate several points made earlier, with reference to hermeneutic theory. Hence, it was noted that Muslim scholars aspire to knowledge of Sharīʿa rules, which is knowledge of God's mental attributes (i.e., intentions, beliefs, desires). Muslim scholars infer such knowledge from a number of sources, beginning with God's statements in the Qurʾan and the Prophet's actions as described in Hadith reports (these are signs/effects of God's mental attributes). But while some knowledge of Sharīʿa rules can be inferred from the Qurʾan and the Hadith reports, this knowledge is limited. After all, the Qurʾan and Hadith reports are open to various interpretations, and there are many legal questions which they do not explicitly address (e.g., "Is it permissible to smoke tobacco?," "Is it permissible for a woman to visit a male doctor?," etc.). This means that knowledge of Sharīʿa rules must be sought from other sources.

I have argued that the actions (including statements) of all later religious scholars are one such source. In other words, these actions are signs/effects of God's mental attributes from which knowledge of God's mental attributes (and hence Sharīʿa rules) can be inferred. This is because the actions of all later religious scholars are based on knowledge of Sharīʿa rules that has been transmitted through a *sanad* extending back to the Prophet. Hence, if any religious scholar refrains from smoking tobacco, it might be inferred that it is God's intention that Muslims refrain from smoking tobacco. It may further be inferred that God desires to protect human health and that God believes/knows that tobacco is harmful to human health.

Remember that inferring knowledge of God's mental attributes from the actions of religious scholars may be compared to inferring knowledge of a king's mental attributes from the actions of his subjects or inferring knowledge of a general's mental attributes from the actions of his soldiers. I would now like to expand on this point in a manner relevant to *taqlīd* and the legal schools.

The actions (including statements) of all religious scholars are a source of evidence on Sharīʿa rules. However, the strength of such evidence depends upon two key factors: (1) temporal priority, and (2) broadness of consensus.

Let us first consider the factor of temporal priority. This means that the actions of earlier scholars are stronger evidence than the actions of later scholars. Such is because the actions of earlier scholars are based on a better knowledge of Sharīʿa rules. Thus, the actions (including statements) of scholars from the first generation (the Companions) are stronger evidence than the actions of the second generation, and so on.

We now come to the second factor: namely, broadness of consensus. Thus, suppose that all scholars agree on a specific Sharīʿa rule (e.g., smoking marijuana is prohibited). In other words, they have a consensus on the rule. This consensus is reflected in their actions (including statements) (e.g., they all refrain from smoking marijuana; they all state that smoking marijuana is wrong). The fact that all scholars have a consensus on a rule is very strong evidence. Yet, universal consensus of this kind is rare. More often, there will exist some measure of disagreement (e.g., some scholars think smoking marijuana is prohibited while others think it is permitted). This disagreement is reflected in scholars' actions (including statements) (e.g., some smoke marijuana but others refrain from smoking it; some state that smoking marijuana is permitted but others state that it is prohibited). Although the actions of scholars are evidence, disagreement weakens this evidence. Hence, if some scholars refrain from smoking marijuana, their actions are evidence that marijuana is prohibited. But this evidence is weakened if other scholars do smoke marijuana. Such is comparable to the case of the general and his soldiers. If we see all the soldiers bombing civilian targets, their actions are strong evidence that it is the general's intention/plan that they bomb civilian targets. But this evidence is weakened if we see some soldiers refrain from bombing civilian targets.

On many legal issues, there is not an absolute consensus where every scholar agrees. Instead there is a broad consensus where most scholars agree (i.e., the "*jumhūr*"). As a general principle, the broader the consensus, the stronger the evidence. Thus, suppose that 99 out of 100 scholars agree that marijuana is prohibited. This is stronger evidence (that marijuana is prohibited), than a comparable situation wherein only 60 out of 100 scholars agree that marijuana is prohibited.

In premodern Islamic law, consensus is referred to as "*ijmā*ʿ." An ideal consensus would encompass all Muslims (or at least all Muslim scholars) throughout history. Yet a consensus of this type is usually elusive. For practical purposes, the strongest form of consensus that exists is an absolute (or broad) consensus by scholars from one of the earliest generations.[90] This form of consensus derives its special evidentiary strength from the factor of temporal priority (i.e., it is *early* scholars who agree). In works of Islamic legal theory, consensus is considered the third highest source (*aṣl*) of evidence on Sharīʿa rules after the Qurʾan and Hadith reports.

The notion of consensus presumes that the actions of scholars have strong evidentiary weight. For instance, suppose all scholars from the first generation agree that smoking of marijuana is prohibited. This agreement is reflected in their actions (including statements). Their actions then become strong/definitive evidence that smoking marijuana is prohibited.

A passage from the work of al-Ghazālī illustrates many of the preceding ideas. Al-Ghazālī states:

> The sources (*al-uṣūl*) [of evidence on Sharīʿa rules]: they are four: [1] The book of God the Almighty and Exhalted [2] the Sunna of the Messenger of God [3] the consensus of the Muslim nation (*Ijmāʿ al-umma*) and [4] reports on the Companions (*āthār al-Ṣaḥāba*). The consensus is a source in that it indicates the Sunna, so it is a source in

[90] I.e., *Ijmāʿ al-Ṣaḥāba, Ijmāʿ Ahl al-Madīna, Ijmāʿ Ahl al-Ḥaramayn, Ijmāʿ al-Miṣrayn.* See al-Zuḥaylī 2006, 1:489 (and more generally 465–580); al-Zarkashī 2007, 3:534. Also see al-Ghazālī 2005:24.

> the third rank. Likewise, is the report [on the Companions] (*al-athar*) for it also indicates the *Sunna*.[91]

Notice that al-Ghazālī asserts that both consensus and reports on the Companions are sources of evidence on Sharīʿa rules. This is because they "indicate the *Sunna*." When al-Ghazālī says that reports on the Companions indicate the Sunna, he means that the Companions follow the Sunna by practicing Sharīʿa rules. Consequently, we can infer Sharīʿa rules from their actions (as described in reports). The same holds for the Muslim nation more generally (or its scholars). Muslims follow the Sunna by practicing Sharīʿa rules. Where there is a consensus, Muslims practice the same Sharīʿa rules, and this is reflected in their actions (e.g., all refrain from smoking marijuana). Consequently, we can infer Sharīʿa rules from their actions (e.g., smoking marijuana is prohibited). Al-Ghazālī thereby presents one view (though not the only view) on how knowledge of Sharīʿa rules may be inferred from the actions of Muslims (including Muslim scholars).

With the preceding facts in mind, it is now possible to address the key concept of the legal school (*madhhab*). A legal school provides a *relatively complete, explicit, integrated, and coherent account* of the entire system of Sharīʿa rules. An account of this type is not provided in the Qurʾan or in the Hadith reports on the Prophet. Moreover, an account of this type is not provided by any religious scholar from the first and second generations.

Premodern jurists recognize that the legal schools only emerged around the time of the third generation, roughly two centuries after the Prophet's death.[92] The four Imams (i.e., Abū Ḥanīfa, Mālik, al-Shāfiʿī, and Ibn Ḥanbal) lived during the third generation (or slightly thereafter). Previous scholars had begun to explicitly work out Sharīʿa rules (*furūʿ*) and rudimentary principles of interpretation (*uṣūl*). But it was only in the era of the four Imams that these earlier efforts were developed into relatively complete, explicit, integrated, and coherent accounts of the entire system of Sharīʿa rules (i.e., legal schools). These accounts are largely similar, but exhibit some differences. Each account (i.e., legal school) enumerates the various Sharīʿa rules (*furūʿ*). Each account (i.e., legal school) likewise lays out a set of interpretive methods (*uṣūl*). As mentioned previously, such methods include adherence to literal meaning, *qiyās*, *istiṣlāḥ*, and *istiḥsān*.

In the era of the four Imams there were actually a number of other distinguished scholars who developed legal schools. While premodern jurists consider these schools to have been legitimate, they all eventually died out due to contingent historical factors.[93] It is only for this reason that Sunni Islam recognizes four legal schools rather than some other number.

[91] Al-Ghazālī 2005:24.

[92] A more full discussion of the emergence of the legal schools is not possible here. The process was gradual, and it certainly was not completed by the eponyms of the schools themselves. See Melchert 1997; Hallaq 2001.

[93] See al-Dihlawī 1398h:21.

The legal schools of the four Imams reflect the uniquely high knowledge of Sharīʿa rules possessed by the earliest generations. Because the Imams were more knowledgeable about Sharīʿa rules than later generations, these later generations are not entitled to introduce new legal schools. Rather scholars from later generations are required to defer (through *taqlīd*) to one of the four Imams by following his legal school. Al-Suyūṭī quotes Ibn Barhān as explaining: "The principles (*uṣūl*) of the [four] schools and their rules for evidentiary interpretation (*qawāʿid al-adilla*) are transmitted from the *Salaf*. Therefore, it is not permissible to introduce different [schools] in [later] ages."[94]

Moreover, later scholars may not claim to follow the legal school of the Prophet or the legal school of a scholar from the first or second generations. Admittedly, these individuals had the highest level of knowledge on Sharīʿa rules. Nevertheless, they never laid down legal schools. Thus, a passage repeated in the writings of both Ibn al-Ṣalāḥ (d. 643/1245) and al-Nawawī (d.676/1277) explains that no legal schools existed before the era of the four Imams:

> No one [may claim to] follow the legal school of an authority from among the Companions or from among the earliest Muslims [more generally] (*al-awwalīn*), even if [the earliest Muslims] were the most knowledgeable and of a higher rank than those after them. [This is] because [the earliest Muslims] did not occupy themselves with recording knowledge, or with the precise formulation of its principles and individual rules. None of them had a precise and refined established legal school. It was only those who came after them [in the era of the four Imāms] who undertook to do that...."[95]

I have said that each legal school provides a relatively complete, explicit, integrated, and coherent account of the entire system of Sharīʿa rules. It can also be said that each legal school provides a relatively complete, explicit, integrated, and coherent account of God's mind (i.e., His intentions, beliefs, and desires). This means that a legal school does not analyze Sharīʿa rules (i.e., God's intentions) as independent individual entities. Rather, it analyzes these rules/intentions as part of a coherent integrated whole. Because each legal school is a coherent integrated whole, premodern scholars were expected to commit themselves to the overall doctrine of one specific legal school. Such prevented them from haphazardly picking and choosing individual opinions from different legal schools. However, this policy did not necessarily preclude borrowing some opinions from other schools, if such was done carefully and sparingly (i.e., "*talfiq*").[96]

[94] Al-Suyūṭī 1983a:113.
[95] Ibn al-Salāḥ 2009:141–142; al-Nawawī n.d., 1:93–94. This passage is often cited elsewhere. See, e.g., Ibn Taymiyya 2008:319.
[96] See Krawietz 2002.

## IX. WHAT IS *IJTIHĀD*?

Finally, we come to the key topic of *ijtihād*. The concept of *ijtihād* is closely related to that of *taqlīd*. *Ijtihād* denotes the process whereby an individual infers Sharīʿa rules from relevant forms of evidence (e.g., Qurʾan, Hadith reports, *ijmāʿ*). By undertaking *ijtihād*, the individual independently formulates his/her own opinions about Sharīʿa rules. Meanwhile, as explained previously, *taqlīd* denotes deference to the opinions of others with more knowledge. When a person defers through *taqlīd*, s/he does not undertake *ijtihād*. Rather, s/he leaves *ijtihād* to the more knowledgeable individual and follows that individual's opinions. In traditional Sunni Islam, later scholars deferred through *taqlīd* to the four Imams by following their legal schools. Accordingly, in cases where the Imams had formulated an opinion, later scholars were required to follow this opinion rather than formulate an alternative opinion through *ijtihād*. However, this did not bar later scholars from undertaking *ijtihād* with respect to matters which had not already been addressed by the Imams.

The concepts of *ijtihād* and *taqlīd* have a key place in Western scholarship on Islamic legal history. Joseph Schacht's work is at the center of such scholarship. One of Schacht's most influential claims is that the development of Islamic law ground to a halt around the tenth century C.E. This is because jurists abandoned the practice of inferring Sharīʿa rules from relevant forms of evidence. Instead, they simply clung to the opinions passed down from their predecessors. In other words, they abandoned *ijtihād* in favor of *taqlīd* (i.e., the "closing of the gate of *ijtihād*"). On Schacht's view, the absence of fresh *ijtihād* meant that Sharīʿa rules could not be adapted to changing social conditions. Hence, even though jurists continued to write about Sharīʿa rules and teach them, premodern Muslim societies were forced to abandon these rules in practice. Consequently, Sharīʿa was reduced to a juristic mental construct divorced from social reality.[97]

Contemporary scholarship now recognizes that Schacht's claims about Islamic legal history are problematic.[98] Much of the credit for this recognition is due to Wael Hallaq, whose pioneering work over the past three decades has reoriented the Western study of Islamic law. Hallaq rejects Schacht's claim that Muslim jurists abandoned *ijtihād* in the tenth century. Rather, he points out that Muslim scholars continued to practice *ijtihād* throughout the premodern period. In doing so, they continuously adapted the Sharīʿa to changing circumstances, thereby ensuring that the Sharīʿa retained an important role in guiding premodern Muslim social life.

Hallaq has taken the lead in post-Schachtian efforts to theorize *ijtihād*. However, Hallaq's own understanding of *ijtihād* has evolved over time. In his early work, Hallaq highlights the role of creativity in Islamic law.[99] For Hallaq, "*ijtihād* is quintessentially a creative . . . activity."[100] One reason Hallaq stresses

[97] See Schacht 1965, especially 70–75. Also see Crone 1987.

[98] See Hallaq 1984; Johansen 1988.

[99] See, e.g., Hallaq 1984; Hallaq 1992; Hallaq 2001.

[100] See Hallaq 2001:21–22.

creativity in *ijtihād* is that it explains how jurists are able to adapt the law to changing social circumstances. Hallaq's emphasis on creativity must also be understood as a reaction to the Schachtian paradigm. Schacht's own account of Islamic legal history is shaped by ethnocentric Orientalist assumptions which hold that the Arab/Muslim "mind" lacks the creativity of its European counterpart. According to these assumptions, it is natural that Islamic law (a product of the Arab/Muslim mind) should lack creativity and therefore find itself incapable of adapting to changing historical circumstances. Drawing on Said's critique of Orientalism, Hallaq challenges assumptions of this sort.[101]

Hallaq's attack on Orientalist assumptions is warranted, and he is correct to emphasize that past jurists adapted the law to changing social circumstances. I would add that such adaptation can be understood, in part, in terms of the aforementioned process of *abandoning (and reforming) Sharīʿa rules in light of new circumstances.* Thus, jurists adapted Sharīʿa rules to changing circumstances by abandoning and reforming them in response to these circumstances.

However, taken by itself, the notion of "creativity" does not provide a full understanding of *ijtihād*. This is because the creative dimension of *ijtihād* is restricted in various ways, and these restrictions deserve attention. Hallaq himself is aware that these restrictions exist, and in his later work he develops a sophisticated approach to them. I wish to state this clearly because in my own writing I have not always given due attention to the subtlety of Hallaq's thought, thereby depicting his work in an unfairly simplistic manner.[102] In his later work, Hallaq explicates the relationship between *ijtihād* and *taqlīd*, clarifying some of the complex ways in which *ijtihād* is restricted by *taqlīd*. Hallaq (and others) have pointed out that *ijtihād* and *taqlīd* should not be conceptualized in terms of a simple binary distinction. Rather, Islamic legal reasoning often has a hybrid character which combines an element of *ijtihād* and an element of *taqlīd*.[103] I will offer some thoughts on this hybrid form of legal reasoning. However, my own analysis diverges from existing scholarship in that it is oriented by the hermeneutic ideas developed previously.

I wish to argue that *ijtihād* is essentially the hermeneutic process of inferring knowledge of God's mental attributes (and hence Sharīʿa rules) from signs/effects of God's mental attributes. I have argued that these signs/effects include: (1) God's statements in the Qurʾan, (2) the actions of the Prophet as described in Hadith reports, (3) the reported actions of religious scholars from the past, and (4) the observed actions of present-day religious scholars. Such signs/effects can be considered "evidence" of God's mental attributes (and hence Sharīʿa rules).

The concept of *ijtihād* that I have put forth can be related to the definition of *ijtihād* found in premodern legal texts. Thus, such texts define *ijtihād* as "exerting effort to attain [knowledge of] Sharīʿa rules" (*istifrāgh al-juhd fī darak al-aḥkām al-sharʿiyya*).[104] One attains knowledge of Sharīʿa rules by examining relevant forms of evidence (*adilla*).

[101] See Hallaq 2002. Also see Said 1994[1978].
[102] See Nakissa 2014b.
[103] See Calder 1996; Hallaq 2001; Ibrahim 2016b.
[104] Al-ʿUmarī 1986:24. Also see al-Ghazālī 2000:342.

Thus, I agree with premodern texts that *ijtihād* consists of the process of attaining knowledge of Sharīʿa rules. However, I go a step further by explicitly equating knowledge of Sharīʿa rules with knowledge of God's mental attributes. Moreover, I agree with premodern texts that one attains knowledge of Sharīʿa rules by examining relevant forms of evidence. However, I go a step further by adding that the evidence at issue consists in signs/effects of God's mental attributes.

The issue of evidence deserves further comment. Generally speaking, premodern jurists agree that relevant forms of evidence include the Qurʾan, the Hadith reports, and the consensus of the Muslim scholars (*ʿijmāʿ*). However, other forms of evidence are disputed. For instance, some jurists (but not others) assert that relevant forms of evidence include the statements of the Companions[105] and the consensus of early Muslim scholars in particular localities (i.e., *Ijmāʿ Ahl al-Madīna, Ijmāʿ Ahl al-Ḥaramayn, Ijmāʿ al-Miṣrayn*).[106]

At any rate, I would suggest that premodern debates on evidence can be misleading. Such debates often emphasize simple bright-line distinctions between what does and does not count as evidence. Nevertheless, if we consider the actual arguments found in premodern legal texts, matters are more complicated. Hence, in such texts, when jurists undertake *ijtihād* to determine Sharīʿa rules, they typically review the opinions of past Muslim scholars throughout history. When a jurist argues in favor of a particular position, he cites the opinions of other scholars who hold this position. Opinions from the earliest generations, and opinions with widespread support are given special emphasis. The fact that jurists cite the opinions of past scholars throughout history in support of their positions implies that these opinions have some measure of evidentiary value. In other words, the opinions of past scholars throughout history function as "evidence" in *ijtihād*. This is true even though theoretical discussions on *ijtihād* do not refer to such opinions as "evidence" (*adilla*). Therefore, I would maintain my claim that, in *ijtihād*, jurists infer knowledge of Sharīʿa rules from the reported actions (including statements) of past religious scholars.

I have also suggested that when jurists undertake *ijtihād*, they infer knowledge of Sharīʿa rules from the observed actions of present-day religious scholars. This claim may appear odd, but it is grounded in the structure of Islamic education. Premodern Muslim scholars hold that only competent individuals can undertake *ijtihād*.[107] A competent individual is one with a proper religious education, which necessitates performing companionship with a *shaykh*. As we have seen, companionship with a *shaykh* involves continuously observing his actions and inferring knowledge of Sharīʿa rules from them. Naturally, the student will later draw on this knowledge when he undertakes *ijtihād*. I admit that standard treatments of *ijtihād* found in premodern legal texts do not discuss knowledge acquired through companionship. But this is because they take such knowledge for granted.

[105] See, e.g., al-Ghazālī 2005:24.
[106] See al-Zuḥaylī 2006, 1:489; al-Zarkashī 2007, 3:534.
[107] Al-ʿUmarī 1986:57–117.

Just as *ijtihād* can be theorized in hermeneutic terms, *taqlīd* can also be theorized in hermeneutic terms.

Western Islamicist scholarship tends to conceptualize *taqlīd* in an overly simplistic manner. For such scholarship, deference (through *taqlīd*) to Imam al-Shāfiʿī is simply a matter of following the view of al-Shāfiʿī or the Shāfiʿī school. But determining the view of al-Shāfiʿī (or his school) is no easy task. Quite the opposite: it requires a hermeneutic process. I will refer to this as "the hermeneutic process of the legal schools."

The hermeneutic process of the legal schools simplifies *ijtihād*. This can be understood as follows. *Ijtihād* involves inferring knowledge of Sharīʿa rules from all relevant forms of evidence. However, *ijtihād* is immensely challenging. It may be simplified by focusing on some forms of evidence but excluding others.

It is commonly assumed that the process of inferring knowledge of Sharīʿa rules must focus on forms of evidence such as the Qurʾan and Hadith reports. But this is wrong. It is possible to infer a comparatively complete knowledge of Sharīʿa rules from the actions (including statements) of religious scholars, giving no attention to the Qurʾan or Hadith reports. Furthermore, it is possible to infer a comparatively complete knowledge of Sharīʿa rules from the actions (including statements) of religious scholars from one specific legal school. Indeed, a process of this type is found in traditional Islamic learning.

In traditional Islamic learning, students begin their legal training by studying a particular legal school. Such study does not focus on the Qurʾan and the Hadith reports. Rather, it focuses on scholars affiliated with the legal school. Scholars affiliated with a legal school include the school's founder and his later followers. For example, study of the Shāfiʿī legal school focuses on Imam al-Shāfiʿī, and later followers of al-Shāfiʿī (e.g., al-Buwayṭī, al-Ghazālī, al-Rāfiʿī, al-Nawawī). More specifically, study of a legal school focuses on reports on the actions (including statements) of scholars affiliated with the school. These reports are recorded in the legal texts of the school, which are studied by students of the school.

For example, study of the Shāfiʿī school focuses on reports on the actions (including statements) of Imam al-Shāfiʿī and his later followers. These reports are recorded in Shāfiʿī legal texts, which are studied by students of the Shāfiʿī school. By studying the actions (including statements) of scholars from a particular school, students acquire a comparatively complete knowledge of the entire system of Sharīʿa rules. However, this knowledge is, in a sense, "school-specific." Hence, a student who acquires knowledge of Sharīʿa rules based on studying the actions (including statements) of scholars affiliated with the Shāfiʿī school comes to possess a "Shāfiʿī understanding" of Sharīʿa rules. Deference (through *taqlīd*) to the Shāfiʿī school involves deference to a Shāfiʿī understanding of Sharīʿa rules. Similarly, deference (through *taqlīd*) to another school (e.g., Ḥanafī) involves deference to its understanding of Sharīʿa rules.

In Egypt, the preceding approach is followed by Traditionalists to this day. Elements of this approach have been covered already, but it will be helpful to add some further details. Thus, at al-Azhar mosque and related venues, Traditionalist students attend study-circles wherein they move through a series of legal texts consisting in *matns* and associated commentaries. Study-circles are coordinated by schedules that are circulated on the internet and posted on the walls of venues where study-circles are held. A given schedule commonly provides a list of texts, along with the name of the *shaykh* teaching each text, the days and times at which the text will be taught, the legal school associated with the text, and the level of student for which the text is appropriate. In the large majority of cases, the texts listed on schedules do not cater to advanced students. Rather they are appropriate for elementary and intermediate students. For instance, a schedule posted inside al-Azhar mosque includes entries like the following: "Book (*Kitāb*): *Manhaj al-Ṭullāb; Shaykh*: Hishām Kāmil; Time (*al-Mawʿid*): 10:00 a.m.; Level of the Book (*Mustawā al-Kitāb*): Intermediate (*Mutawassiṭ*); Subject (*al-Mādda*): Shāfiʿī *Fiqh*; Day (al-*Yawm*): Thursday."

The texts taught at al-Azhar and related venues are typically associated with the Mālikī, Shāfiʿī, and Ḥanafī schools (thereby excluding the Ḥanbalī school). These texts are familiar to Traditionalist scholars across the world. Mālikī students move through texts like *Matn al-Akhḍarī, Matn al-ʿAshmāwiyya, al-Durr al-Thamīn wa-l-Mawrid al-Muʿīn*, and *Risāla Ibn Abī Zayd al-Qayrawānī*. Shāfiʿī students move through texts like *al-Muqaddima al-Ḥaḍramiyya, Matn Abī Shujāʿ, Fatḥ al-Qarīb al-Mujīb*, and *Manhaj al-Ṭullāb*. Ḥanafī students move through texts like *Nūr al-Īḍāḥ, Mārāqī al-Falāḥ, Mukhtaṣar al-Qudūrī*, and *Fatḥ Bāb al-ʿInāya bi-Sharḥ al-Nuqāya*. The texts cited previously are considered appropriate for elementary and intermediate students. The most elementary of these texts describe the teachings of the school in a series of simple unequivocal statements. However, many of the texts for intermediate students report various statements from different scholars affiliated with a given school. For instance, the aforementioned Mālikī text, *al-Durr al-Thamīn*, reports statements from Mālikī authorities like Ibn al-Qāsim, Saḥnūn, and Ibn al-Ḥājib. Generally speaking, texts for intermediate students also include a small number of Qurʾanic verses and Hadith reports.

It is possible for some students to move beyond a school-specific understanding of Sharīʿa rules. Thus, traditional Islamic learning proceeds in stages. As students progress in their studies, they encounter more advanced legal texts (e.g., Ibn Qudāma's *al-Mughnī*, Ibn ʿĀbidīn's *Radd al-Muḥtār*, Ibn Rushd's *Bidāya al-Mujtahid*). Advanced texts introduce students to additional forms of evidence from which to infer Sharīʿa rules. These forms of evidence include (1) Qurʾanic verses, (2) Hadith reports, (3) reports on the Companions and other early scholars, (4) additional reports on scholars from within a given school (e.g., a Ḥanafī text will report on the full range of opinion within the Ḥanafī school), and (5) reports on scholars from other schools (e.g., a Ḥanafī text will report on Shāfiʿī and Mālikī scholars).

Advanced texts are distinguished from less advanced texts by their large size. Hence, it is not uncommon for an advanced text to be 10 or more volumes. One major reason that advanced texts are larger is that they contain additional forms of evidence. Because advanced texts are so large they are not taught with the frequency and regularity of less advanced works. As a result, they must often be read independently, either in whole or in part. (In theory, permission to read such texts might be given through *munāwala*). For example, Ḥanafī students are introduced to a wide range of evidence through advanced multivolume texts like al-Marghīnānī's *al-Hidāya* and al-Kāsānī's *Badāʾiʿ al-Ṣanāʾiʿ*. Similarly, Shāfiʿī students are introduced to a wide range of evidence through advanced multivolume texts like al-Nawawī's *al-Majmūʿ* and al-Rāfiʿī's *Fatḥ al-ʿAzīz*. Both *al-Hidāya* and *al-Majmūʿ* are texts that have been taught at al-Azhar mosque in recent years.

By familiarizing himself with an increasing range of evidence, a jurist gradually acquires an ability to undertake *ijtihād*, and thereby formulate an independent understanding of Sharīʿa rules. The jurist may then compare his independent understanding of Sharīʿa rules with the school-specific understanding of Sharīʿa rules. The question then becomes to what extent he will defer to the school-specific understanding. Such deference admits of different degrees. Thus, if he is strongly inclined to defer, he may hold to the school-specific understanding even if he believes there is compelling contrary evidence. Yet, if he is weakly inclined to defer, he may give precedence to his own opinion, even if there is also compelling evidence for the school-specific understanding. To the extent that the scholar defers, he affirms *taqlīd*. To the extent he gives precedence to his own opinion, he undertakes *ijtihād*. All of this means that he is engaging in a hybrid form of legal reasoning which combines an element of *ijtihād* and an element of *taqlīd*. Generally speaking, in premodern times, scholars were expected to be strongly deferential to their schools. However, scholars with great knowledge and status were given more leeway to formulate their own opinions. Nevertheless, even the greatest scholars of later generations were seen as inferior to the more knowledgeable scholars of the early generations. Hence, great later scholars were still bound by *taqīd*.

Admittedly, the preceding account of *ijtihād* and *taqīd* relies on some rather abstract hermeneutic ideas. Nevertheless, these abstract ideas enable a fine-grained analysis of traditional Islamic learning. For instance, I have tried to show how they enable us to understand the sequence and content of the specific texts currently taught at al-Azhar and related venues. Thus, with these hermeneutic ideas we can explain why intermediate texts are longer than elementary texts, why intermediate texts (unlike elementary texts) report various statements from different scholars affiliated with a given school, and why advanced texts contain more Qurʾanic verses and Hadith reports than elementary and intermediate texts.

# Section IV

# Modern Reform

# 8

# Reorganizing Time and Space

A key feature of learning in late premodern Egypt was that it was not restricted to specific times or places. Such is easiest to appreciate with respect to the pedagogy of companionship, which entailed a continuous informal melding of lives between teacher and pupil. Students ate, traveled, and prayed alongside their *shaykhs*. They also performed various acts of menial servitude like cooking, cleaning, and running errands. Mundane everyday activities of this sort could transpire in any number of places and were not regulated by a strict schedule.

The transmission of texts also lacked a rigid spatio-temporal structure. A *shaykh* was entitled to teach texts and issue *ijāzas* anywhere he pleased and according to whatever timetable he saw fit. He could teach a text to an individual or to a group. He could cover it quickly, holding lengthy sessions over consecutive days. He could also teach at a slower pace, giving shorter lessons scheduled periodically. Sessions might be held at the teacher's home, in a Sufi lodge, in a mosque, or even while traveling on a journey. Such flexibility remains a feature of learning among Traditionalist scholars to this day.

The existence of flexibility did not prevent the emergence of recurring patterns. The teacher's home was a common place for gatherings, especially with a *shaykh*'s most favored disciples. Nevertheless, the most popular venue was the mosque where the five daily prayers were performed communally. Holding study-circles in the mosque facilitated attending the prayers, an act to which great religious significance was ascribed.

As is common with Traditionalist study-circles today, those which operated in late premodern Egypt were scheduled around the prayer times. Heyworth-Dunne gives the following description:

> For teaching purposes the day was divided into five parts, the most important classes being held before sunrise to midday; *tafsir* [Qurʾanic exegesis] and *ḥadīth* were taught before sunrise and *fikh* [law] after the *fajr* prayers until the midday prayer. The three remaining parts of the day were used for other subjects with a preference for *nahw* [grammar], *balaghah* [rhetoric] and *usul* [legal theory] after midday until the *ʿasr* prayers, *hisab* [arithmetic] and other less important subjects after the *ʿasr* prayers until the *maghrib* and after *maghrib*, *mantik* [logic] and *hikmah*

> [philosophy]. The morning classes seem to have been much larger than those of any other part of the day.[1]

Based on his (somewhat bitter) personal experience as a student, Ṭaha Ḥuṣayn provides a similar description of al-Azhar as it existed at the very beginning of the twentieth century:

> After the dawn prayer came the study of *Tauhid*, the doctrine of divine unity; then *fiqh*, or jurisprudence, after sunrise; then the study of Arabic grammar during the forenoon, following a dull meal; then more grammar in the wake of the noon prayer. After this came a grudging bit of leisure and then, again, another snatch of wearisome food until, the evening prayer performed, I proceeded to the logic class which some sheikh or another would conduct.[2]

Scheduling study-circles around the prayers had at least two advantages. First, they were fixed times at which scholars were already gathering together in the mosque. Second, if lessons were not scheduled to commence and terminate around the prayers, there was the danger of a class running on during the prayers, thereby preventing students from attending. Such disregard for the communal prayer was reckoned impious.

## I. STUDENT FREEDOM AND THE STUDY-CIRCLE

Just as premodern *shaykhs* had few restrictions on how they taught, students had few restrictions on how they learned. As mentioned earlier, there were customary sequences of texts to proceed through in mastering various fields. Still, responsibility for moving through these texts was left up to students themselves. They were tasked with planning out a worthwhile course of study, and then locating and attending the study-circles necessary for its completion. When needed, advice was solicited from scholars and fellow students. But there was no bureaucratic apparatus charged with legislating study plans or monitoring student progress.

Since there was no required curriculum, there was no fixed schedule for its completion. Accordingly, schooling was not divided into "grades" meant to guarantee that every year students finished one portion of the overall curriculum in preparation for a more advanced portion the following year. As there was no need to ensure year-by-year progress in completing a curriculum, there were no regular tests. Lacking grades and tests, students of disparate ages and with different levels of knowledge often sat together in the same study-circles.

The absence of a mandatory curriculum not only removed the impetus to regulate student time, but also the impetus to regulate student placement in space. Foucault observes that a central feature of modern modes of power is the distribution of space. Whereas individuals who are clumped together irregularly

[1] Heyworth-Dunne 1939:65–66. [2] Cited in Reid 1990:13.

are difficult to count and supervise, fixing them in set geometric patterns helps expose them to the gaze of onlookers.[3] For instance, rows of chairs and desks make it easy for teachers to ensure that students are present for lessons and that they are paying attention to the instructor during class time. Nevertheless, because premodern *shaykhs* were not required to enforce a curriculum, dividing educational space for surveillance purposes was not a pressing concern. *Shaykhs* were not obliged to ensure that students were present at the site where a lesson was being taught, or that they were paying attention to the material.

In study-circles at al-Azhar, there were no rows of chairs and desks. Students sat on the floor wherever they could find an open space. Because the circles were open to the public, anyone, whether a student or not, was free to attend whichever lessons he pleased, leaving whenever he liked (or not coming at all).[4] If a student took his studies too lightly, he might lose his claim on financial aid from the Azhar endowments dedicated to support those pursuing an education.[5] Yet there was no threat of being "expelled" from a program, for no program existed.

Traditional study-circles at al-Azhar mosque and elsewhere continue to operate in the same "open" manner. It is common to see non-students (and even tourists) briefly seat themselves at the edge of study-circles, listening for a short while and then leaving. The teachers ignore them, focusing on their texts and the students sitting closest to them. This, in itself, points to an important feature of the study-circle format. Participants in the study-circle partake of different statuses vis-à-vis the teacher. These different statuses became apparent to me as I observed teacher-student relations in the study-circle. Those who sit closest to the teacher engage his attention most deeply. He knows when they are absent and when they are present. He interacts with them and asks them questions. He begins to develop relations with them outside of class. In some cases, when the "public" study-circle lesson ends, he invites them to spend further time with him, and perhaps to attend private sessions at his house. His familiarity with these students increases his willingness to write *ijāzas* for them and to vouch for their learnedness among other scholars. When a teacher sees a student who regularly attends his lessons seated far away, he will ask him to draw closer. A teacher's favorite students, those most eligible for companionship relations, usually sit immediately beside him. This particular custom can be traced to medieval times.[6] Students who sit on the outer edges and attend irregularly do not receive the same attention from the teacher. Knowing little about them, he is less willing to vouch for their scholastic abilities or issue them *ijāzas*. He will not form personal relationships with them, thereby denying them the elevated authority acquired through companionship.

The ease with which personal relationships may be developed with a teacher depends on the size of the study circle. The study-circles I attended at al-Azhar

[3] See Foucault 1995[1977]:143.
[4] See, e.g., al-Ẓawāhirī 1904:91–93, 118; Mitchell 1991:81–82.
[5] See Heyworth-Dunne 1939:36–37; al-Ẓawāhirī 1904:93.
[6] See Makdisi 1981:91–93; Melchert 2004.

and elsewhere were highly variable in size, ranging from fewer than 10 students to 70 or more. Now, as in the past, famous teachers regularly draw audiences in the hundreds.[7] However, most sessions I participated in tended to have between 20 and 30 students. Generally, medieval institutions of learning had endowments which provided support for no more than 20 students. Although additional students might also attend those institutions' study-circles, they would have to provide their own funding.[8]

The dynamics of the traditional study-circle differ greatly from those of the modern Western classroom, even when an equal number of attendees are present. In a large study-circle of a hundred students, only the small number of those sitting next to the *shaykh* are considered fully "present" and in a position to receive full "credit" for the lesson. Those who are further out possess a lower status, and may even be regarded as no more than onlookers. An individual who wishes to be fully present must regularly attend the lessons, moving as close to the *shaykh* as possible, until the latter gradually gains familiarity with him, and they begin a personal relationship. By contrast, in the Western classroom all attendees are equal. They are all fully "present" and will receive full "credit," leading to the same type of certification. Generally speaking, it is not essential for them to maintain deep personal relationships with their teachers.

In the late premodern period, Azhar students who neglected to form personal relationships with their *shaykhs* lost the capacity to stake claims to scholarly authority—particularly high-level authority.

## II. MAXIMIZING "EFFICIENCY" AND ELIMINATING "DISORDER"

Serious reforms at al-Azhar began in the later part of the nineteenth century. Proponents of reform perceived traditional education as woefully disorganized and inefficient. They based this judgment on a number of factors. One was the length of time that studies required. Lengthy study had been a characteristic feature of Islamic learning since medieval times.[9] Speaking of the late premodern period, Heyworth-Dunne observes that students joined al-Azhar upon reaching puberty. Those content with low scholarly status sometimes left after a stay of only two to three years. On the other hand, serious students spent an estimated 8 to 10 years completing the "general books." Additional time was allocated to more specialized knowledge.[10] Lane remarks that individuals aspiring to the highest levels of scholarship passed their entire lives studying at al-Azhar.[11] Addressing the situation of higher religious learning as it existed around 1900, future *Shaykh al-Azhar* Muḥammad al-Aḥmadī al-Ẓawāhirī speaks

[7] See A. Shalabī 1999:310–312.
[8] See Makdisi 1981:31; A. Shalabī 1999:310–312.
[9] See Makdisi 1981: 96–98.
[10] Heyworth-Dunne 1939:36–37.
[11] See, e.g., Lane 2005[1836]:214.

of students beginning no later than 15 years of age and remaining for at least 20 years.[12] Rashīd Riḍā also mentions a period of 20 years.[13] Speaking with reference to roughly the same period, Khafājī asserts that students spent no less than 15 years in their studies, and that they could go on indefinitely.[14]

A second apparent source of inefficiency was the informality of the entire learning process. Rather than being dedicated exclusively to "study," space at al-Azhar was being used for prayer, eating, sleeping, conversation, and play.[15] In other words, the mosque was permeated by "non-academic" personal interactions. During this period, many students actually resided in living quarters directly attached to the mosque, making it easy for their personal affairs to spill into the areas used for teaching.

A third apparent problem was the lack of standardized certification. After spending countless years at al-Azhar, a student had no official degree to show for his efforts. Rather, his chief accomplishments largely consisted in the personal relationships he had cultivated with various *shaykhs*. It was on these relationships that he based his authority and from which any *ijāzas* he had collected derived their value.

All of these putative sources of inefficiency are related to traditional Islamic learning's emphasis on learning through observation and practice using the pedagogy of companionship. It is companionship which requires that learning be spread over an extended period and that it involve sharing in mundane everyday activities. Companionship is also responsible for the emphasis given to cultivating personal relationships rather than acquiring official degrees. But if these features arise from the pedagogy of companionship (around which traditional learning is intentionally structured), then reformist claims asserting al-Azhar's "inefficiency" become problematic.

Western studies have been inadequately sensitive to the problematic nature of these claims. Such studies repeatedly emphasize that education at al-Azhar in this period was not only "grossly inefficient,"[16] but also permeated by "arbitrariness, nepotism, and corruption"[17] reflected in the fact that teachers "indulged in favoritism towards relations and friends."[18] Yet there is another way of looking at things. For premodern scholars, acquiring knowledge depended upon performing companionship within a framework of personal relationships. Because Western critics fail to appreciate this model of learning, such personal relationships can only seem extraneous or antithetical to proper education. For the critic, it is taken for granted that learning is formal and impersonal. Anything else can be dismissed as mere "arbitrariness, nepotism, and corruption."

Timothy Mitchell convincingly argues that the educational ideals embraced by Western critics derive from European schooling models characterized by

[12] Al-Ẓawāhirī 1904:106, 109. [13] See Riḍā 2008:56. [14] See Khafājī 1987, 2:178.
[15] See Mitchell 1991:81.
[16] Skovgaard-Petersen 1997:47–49. Also see Heyworth-Dunne 1939:404.
[17] Skovgaard-Petersen 1997:49. Also see Zubaida 1990:366–369; Eccel 1984:221.
[18] Heyworth-Dunne 1939:399.

particular modes of institutional discipline and bureaucratic organization. These models aim at maximizing "efficiency" through the precise division and regulation of space and time. A new generation of Egyptian government officials would be familiarized with these models in the early nineteenth century, often while students on educational missions to Europe. For them, traditional Islamic learning suddenly appeared to be in a state of complete "disorder."[19] As a consequence, reform was needed. Such reform would require eliminating the "inefficiencies" caused by the pedagogy of companionship.

The first step in combating inefficiency was laying down a mandatory fixed curriculum. Once a basic curriculum was in place, further efforts could be undertaken to boost educational efficiency by (1) increasing the speed at which students completed the curriculum, (2) decreasing the per-capita cost of completing the curriculum, and (3) maximizing the number of students completing the curriculum.

Overcoming resistance from within al-Azhar,[20] the government succeeded in promulgating an initial set of reforms in 1872. On the eve of these reforms, over 20 subjects were being taught at al-Azhar. The new regulations selected 11 of them to be made mandatory: legal theory (*Uṣūl al-Fiqh*), law (*Fiqh*), theology (*Tawḥīd*), Hadith reports, Qur'anic exegesis (*Tafsīr*), syntax (*Naḥw*), morphology (*Sarf*), and logic (*Manṭiq*), as well as the three sciences of rhetoric (*Maʿānī, Bayān, Badīʿ*). There was also a move to ensure that these subjects were taught using relatively standard texts.

The new curriculum went hand in hand with a new system of degrees to be issued by al-Azhar as an institution. A degree would henceforth only be received after passing an exam administered by a committee of *shaykhs*. The exam would test mastery of the fixed curriculum. The degree to be conferred was known as the "*ʿālimiyya*," since it was meant to certify its holder as a "scholar" (*ʿālim*). An individual without a degree would be barred from teaching in the mosque.[21]

Previously, students had gradually transitioned to the role of mosque teacher. A student began teaching when he felt ready and able. He established a new study-circle whose initial students consisted of a small number of prior acquaintances.[22] As his credentials and reputation grew he would gather a broader following, attracting ever more distinguished students.

It is important to remember that teachers, especially at the beginning of their careers, continued to attend the study-circles of others to boost their educational credentials. Studies of Islamic education have often used the term "peer learning" to describe the situation where those who are still students undertake to teach others.[23] Yet this term can be misleading, for the individuals involved may only be "peers" in the sense that they all still attend study-circles. Such does not imply they are equals. Depending on the gap between the parties in

[19] See Chapter 3 in Mitchell 1991. Also see Messick 1993:101–107.
[20] Skovgaard-Petersen 1997:45.
[21] See Heyworth-Dunne 1939:400–401; Gesink 2010:53.
[22] Heyworth-Dunne 1939:69.
[23] See Eickelman 1985:98; Messick 1993:89.

terms of age and knowledge, the more senior "student" may be more accurately characterized as the "*shaykh*" of his junior counterpart. Today it is possible to observe junior students sitting alongside more senior ones in the study-circles of high-ranking authorities. However, the juniors often refer to their senior counterparts as *shaykh*. The seniors sometimes have their own study-circles which the juniors attend as students. Remember, as we saw earlier, scholastic authority in traditional Islamic learning is relational rather than absolute.

In the premodern period a teacher aspiring to grow his study-circle needed the approval of established scholars. His circle would hold little appeal to students if it had been condemned or slighted by senior authorities. Shortly after a new teacher inaugurated his study-circle, it was customary for authorities to sit in, observing him and testing him with questions. If they were dissatisfied with his answers, his credibility would be undermined and he would be forced to halt his lessons.[24] One way that aspiring teachers ensured the approval of recognized scholars was by collecting *ijāzas* from them[25] and cultivating strong personal relationships with them. As long as a teacher enjoyed the sponsorship of high-ranking figures, his authority was difficult to bring into question. By the same token, scholars at the top of the educational hierarchy were able to keep their more junior colleagues in line by threatening to withdraw their sponsorship or speak out against them. Within some networks of contemporary Egyptian religious scholars, similar dynamics are still observable.

The new degree system heralded a fundamental change to this educational structure. It implied that an individual's basic status as a scholar was no longer essentially dependent upon personal relationships with individual authorities. Certification as a scholar was now to be conferred by an impersonal bureaucratic apparatus representing al-Azhar as an institution. This change drastically reduced the authority of individual scholars. They could no longer regulate the transfer of scholastic authority by refusing to take students as companions or to issue them *ijāzas*. Losing these powers also made it more difficult for *shaykhs* to submit pupils to regimens of ethical discipline.

In the wake of the reforms increasingly anonymous students began putting themselves forth to take degrees. This struck many Muslim authorities as a very dangerous development. Writing around 1900, al-Ẓawāhirī states: "Is it not astonishing that granting the status of scholar is being taken so lightly that it has reached the point that a student comes before the testing committee [to complete the test and take his degree], whilst being completely unknown? . . . without it being known whether he is from among the impious or from among the God-fearing?" Al-Ẓawāhirī continues on to state that these individuals "have not tasted ethical upbringing (*al-tarbiya*)" and that they simply wish to obtain official certification for the social status that comes with being a scholar.[26] He expresses disappointment that students are not getting to know their teachers personally, having the mistaken notion that "learning consists in people gathering around

[24] Heyworth-Dunne 1939:69.

[25] See Heyworth-Dunne 1939:67–68.

[26] Al-Ẓawāhirī 1904:70.

a *shaykh* who then delivers a lesson to all of them [as a group] without knowing them individually, and then [afterwards] they disperse."[27]

For al-Ẓawāhirī, the threat to the ethical dimension of Islamic learning is linked to the influence of new Western educational models employed in national government schools. He insists that certification as a scholar from al-Azhar must be different:

> Let no one imagine that the Azhar degree is like the degree in the government schools, for instance, which is given to every student with a talent in the fields of knowledge. For that is a technical degree centered [exclusively] upon knowledge. As for [the Azhar degree] it is a certification of religious leadership, wherein practice (*al-ʿamal*) must accompany knowledge (*al-ʿilm*).[28]

Al-Ẓawāhirī's concerns are also being expressed at a time when al-Azhar was witnessing an enormous increase in the student population. Premodern Muslim educational institutions had been able to foster personal relationships due to their small size. While gigantic by traditional standards, al-Azhar was tiny compared to a modern university. Around 1800, it was a place which was home to between 40 and 60 teachers along with between 1,500 and 3,000 students.[29]

The student population at al-Azhar rose drastically over the course of the 1800s as a result of the modernization policies initiated by Muḥammad 'Alī at the beginning of the century. Among these policies was the centralization of religious learning around large institutions such as al-Azhar and the Aḥmadī mosque in Ṭanṭā. Smaller institutions were closed as their endowment funding was redirected to various government projects.[30] By 1893 al-Azhar had swollen in size to the point where it accommodated 187 teachers and 10,451 students.[31] These changes steadily eroded the personal dimension of learning and helped reinforce the perception that the Azhar system was in a state of disorganized "chaos."[32,33]

These trends only intensified over the course of the twentieth century, fueled by astronomical population growth and the belief that al-Azhar should play a central role in government efforts at mass education. Already by 1917, the number of students at al-Azhar exceeded 20,000.[34] By 2008, al-Azhar University enrolled around 270,000 students pursuing religious studies alone.[35] With the rarest exceptions, students currently enrolled at al-Azhar University (as well as the Dār al-ʿUlūm) told me that they did not have personal relationships of any significance with their professors. This was not only true of undergraduates, but also of students in the master's and doctoral programs where there are smaller classes and fewer students per teacher. Students with a Traditionalist orientation typically regard the mass expansion of religious education very negatively. This is well illustrated in an anecdote I describe in my fieldnotes.

[27] Al-Ẓawāhirī 1904:91. [28] Al-Ẓawāhirī 72–73.
[29] Gesink 2010:41. Also see Heyworth-Dunne 1939:27–28.
[30] See Crecelius 1972:181–182; Gesink 2010:11–17. [31] Gesink 2010:124.
[32] See al-Ẓawāhirī 1904:89–90. [33] Gesink 2010:17, 124. [34] Khafājī 1987, 2:179.
[35] See *Jāmiʿat al-Azhar: 2007-2008* Official Manual:80–81.

*Shaykh Idrīs is in his 30s. He wears a short beard and a jallābiyya-robe. After completing his undergraduate degree at al-Azhar he spent five years attending traditional study-circles in Yemen. Currently he is doing an MA at the Dār al-ʿUlūm. We are meeting together in a medium-sized fourth-story apartment within walking distance from al-Azhar's Faculty of Sharīʿa. It has been converted into a lodge run by a Sufi authority with links to Yemen. In the reception room guests sit atop rectangular cushions arrayed on the floor alongside the walls.*

*I asked Shaykh Idrīs to compare between the different locales at which he had studied. He began by describing his time in Yemen. "In Yemen a teacher's general lessons may attract an audience of over 100 people. But the regular study-circles for serious students never exceed 20 or 25 individuals. Having a small number of students is important because a good teacher must get to know all his pupils personally and deeply, taking care to correct their manners and craft their dispositions. Yemeni shaykhs pay attention to how students wear their head-coverings and to proper sitting posture. They are successful in teaching because they practice their knowledge and provide a good example for students. A good example is very important in transmitting knowledge.*

*A* shaykh *of mine related to me a story. One day he was surprised when he came across a layman praying perfectly. My* shaykh *was so impressed that he himself decided to pray behind him. After the prayer had concluded, my* shaykh *asked the layman where he had learned to pray so perfectly. The layman responded that he used to pray behind a famous religious authority and that he had trained himself to imitate him. Such is evidence that seeing the prayer performed is more beneficial than reading about it in a book.*

*The Prophet taught his Companions in this way. By constantly keeping the Prophet's company and imitating him they took his attributes (ṣifāt), until his attributes became their attributes.*

*In Egypt, ethical upbringing (tarbiya) must be sought outside of the university. Professors not only do not care about forming personal relationships with their students, but they do not provide good ethical examples. Professors walk into the classroom and throw the class texts down on the desks behind which they sit [thereby indicating a reprehensible lack of respect for their sanctity]. They finish their lectures and then immediately leave, showing no interest in getting to know their students."*

Modern efforts to expand the scale of learning at al-Azhar have necessitated a fundamental reordering of educational space. Such spatial reordering is structured to correspond to curricular reordering. Between 1908 and 1911, al-Azhar's overall curriculum was elaborated in more detail and then distributed among three levels of education (elementary, secondary, and higher). Each level was to last four years. Ascending through the various grades of study required passing yearly exams.[36] In the coming years further divisions were made and studies were moved out of the mosque into newly constructed buildings. The lower levels of education would be taught in the Azhar Institutes. Meanwhile, university-level studies would take place at various faculties.

[36] See Gesink 2010:211–227; Khafājī 1987, 2:177–180.

The three oldest Azhar faculties were established in 1930, housed in new buildings constructed alongside the ancient Azhar mosque. One of these faculties is dedicated to the Arabic language, another to Uṣūl al-Dīn, and the last to Sharīᶜa. All three are male. The two faculties of Uṣūl al-Dīn and Sharīᶜa are the most prestigious of all al-Azhar University's religious programs. They are thought of as the foremost heirs to al-Azhar's ancient heritage. Since the 1960s over 30 additional religious faculties have been added to the al-Azhar system. All are housed in new buildings distant from the mosque.[37]

The Egyptian government's efforts to remap space devoted to religious education was not limited to al-Azhar. It also included the construction of alternative institutions, the most important being the Dār al-ᶜUlūm, founded in 1892. Before assessing the impact of these efforts, it will be helpful to take an inside look at the new facilities.

## III. AL-AZHAR'S FACULTY OF SHARĪᶜA

During my fieldwork I attended classes at al-Azhar's Faculty of Sharīᶜa (*Kulliyya al-Sharīᶜa wa-l-Qānūn*). Symbolizing its intellectual orientation, the Faculty is located facing the nearby Hall of Muḥammad ᶜAbduh. It is home to about 16,000 students, 3,000 of which are foreigners.[38] Prior to the revolution there was a police presence everywhere. Enclosed by a gate, entrance to the facility required presenting a permit. National security routinely reviewed university paperwork and was able to exert influence over the processes of admissions and graduation. Students suspected of "extremist" tendencies or unwilling to cooperate with security forces were exposed to damaging repercussions. These typically consisted in being denied access to faculty positions, higher degree programs, or final approval to graduate. For instance, one student I met completed writing his PhD dissertation, but was denied the degree at the last moment because his foreign country of origin had come to be seen as a security threat. Unsurprisingly, the first demands to be pressed in student demonstrations after the 2011 revolution were making al-Azhar completely independent of the government and removing the heavy police presence from around the university. Ultimately, these demands have been ignored.

The Faculty of Sharīᶜa faces the twin challenges of severe underfunding and overcrowding. Although these problems are endemic to Egyptian public education as a whole, they are probably more pronounced where religious studies are concerned. In basic architectural structure and layout, the Faculty of Sharīᶜa is modeled along the lines of a contemporary Western university. It is housed in a large five-story building: four above ground, one below. The building is around 80 years old, dusty, and in poor repair. A dearth of garbage receptacles means

[37] *Jāmiᶜat al-Azhar: 2007–2008* Official Manual:58.
[38] *Jāmiᶜat al-Azhar: 2007–2008* Official Manual:80.

that stray bits of refuse litter the hallways and bathroom floors. Computer technology plays only a marginal role in organization and administration. Information is stored and transmitted by paper. Test-results and class schedules (often handwritten) are posted en masse over the Faculty's dingy dirt-streaked walls. Important papers are exhibited behind sheets of glass built into large rectangular frames made of wood or aluminum. Dozens of these frames are attached along the hallway walls. Classrooms are of various sizes. Some contain long concrete benches, built into the floor. But most are crammed full of ancient movable wooden desk-chairs. There is no air conditioning. Relief from the Cairo heat is sought by opening windows and through sparing use of rickety electric ceiling fans. Foreign religious students from countries economically comparable to Egypt frequently express shock at the state of the Faculty's facilities, being struck by the incongruity between al-Azhar's preeminent reputation abroad and the actual conditions of the institution itself. These conditions are widely interpreted as proof of the contempt in which the national government holds religious scholars.

The call to prayer, emanating for the nearby al-Azhar mosque, is barely audible inside the building. Lectures are not scheduled around the prayers. Students who wish to pray must find time between classes. Some perform their worship in the few small rooms designated as prayer areas. Others crowd together on green plastic carpets temporarily rolled out in the hallways. There is little tolerance for tardiness caused by participating in group prayer. Teachers often lock classroom doors to prevent students from entering late. One professor explained: "Students must be taught the value of knowledge. They cannot be allowed to come late to class, because it shows disrespect for knowledge." On the other hand, not all professors have this attitude, and it is clear that some give exceptional priority to prayer and other traditional manifestations of religiosity. Consider the following profile I recorded in my fieldnotes.

*Shaykh Ḥasan is a professor at al-Azhar's Faculty of Sharīʿa. He is Wasaṭi in orientation. Fifty-two years old, he is partially bald. Individual gray hairs have begun to appear in his long black beard. When teaching at the university, he wears a suit and tie. He smiles frequently, and has a humble and gentle manner of speaking. There is a dark patch of discolored skin on his forehead—the mark of regularly prostrating in prayer. His aura could be described as saintly.*

*Shaykh Ḥasan grew up in a northern Egyptian village. Both his paternal grandfather and his father were farmers. He has two brothers and two sisters. His only wife has bore him five sons and no daughters. All of his children have come up through the Azhar system. One of his sons is studying in al-Azhar's Faculty of Medicine, a second in the Faculty of Commerce, and a third in the Faculty of Sharīʿa. His two youngest children are still in the Azhar institutes.*

*The shaykh began his education at six years old. After five years in a kuttāb, he joined an Azhar institute. He completed memorizing the Qurʾan around age 12 or 13. Upon finishing secondary school he moved to Cairo to enroll at the Faculty of Sharīʿa. He completed his undergraduate degree in four years, subsequently working as a teacher at an Azhar institute for six months. The shaykh then returned to the Faculty of Sharīʿa for his graduate studies. Because he was the top-ranked student in his undergraduate section, he received a modest scholarship. As a result, he did not have to pursue outside work. It took him five years to finish his master's degree. He then married, and after a brief delay, began on his doctoral work. The PhD degree took another five years. Shaykh Ḥasan has published five books. In addition to his work at the university, he teaches in traditional study-circles off campus.*

As in Western universities, classes at the Faculty of Sharīʿa vary in size and schedule. When I requested an official copy of the current curriculum plan I was given a guidebook published around 1987. According to the guidebook, undergraduates focusing exclusively on the study of Sharīʿa[39] are scheduled to spend around 23–25 hours per week divided among 8–9 courses. Students pursuing master's degrees are scheduled to spend around 14–16 hours per week divided among five courses. (There are no doctoral classes because the PhD degree is obtained by research alone.) Although the preceding schedule gives a flavor of what the curriculum is like, there have been substantial changes not accounted for in the guidebook. (This is particularly true regarding undergraduate study, where the course load appears to have been increased significantly.) Moreover, extraordinarily frequent class delays, teacher absences, and constant rescheduling make it difficult to say to what extent the hours officially allotted to classes are actually observed. Even when the teachers are present and classes are going on, there are huge numbers of student absences, particularly at the undergraduate level.

Most of the classes I attended were at the graduate level, lasting one to three hours and usually meeting once (sometimes twice) a week. There were usually 20 to 50 students present. The majority were Egyptian. Almost all students were in their mid-20s to mid-30s, with a small number in their early 40s. Just over half had beards, most of them short, but some more substantial in length. The rest were clean-shaven. Less than a quarter of the students wore *jallābiyya*-robes. About half of those that did wore head-gear as well. The remaining students dressed entirely in Western attire, consisting in long pants and shirts of various types. A few wore traditional caps with their Western clothing. As a general principle, Egyptian religious students, whether at al-Azhar or elsewhere, seem less inclined than their foreign counterparts toward beards and distinctly Islamic attire.

Undergraduate classes are generally larger than the graduate classes (often significantly so). The undergraduate classes I attended had between 100 and 150 students (though there are certainly other classes smaller than this). Between one-fifth and one-third of students had beards, almost always short. Around 10 percent wore *jallābiyya*-robes, often wearing Islamic head-gear as well. But the vast majority dressed in Western garb.

Eighty to 90 percent of the professors I saw wore suits and ties, with the remainder donning the special Azhari dress. Around half had beards, almost

39 Some students devote extensive time to the law of the Egyptian state in addition to Sharīʿa.

always short. The others were entirely clean-shaven, though some had moustaches. In terms of age, the younger professors were in their 40s and the older ones in their 70s or 80s.

The numerical figures given above reflect my own partial personal experience at the Faculty of Sharīʿa, and cannot serve as the basis for precise statistical generalizations. On the other hand, based on interviews and visits to other faculties, what I observed appears to be broadly reflective of university-level religious studies in the Azhar system as a whole.

## IV. THE DĀR AL-ʿULŪM

Now let us take a look inside the Dār al-ʿUlūm. I would like to begin with the profile of a professor that I recorded in my fieldnotes. The profile is useful because it provides the reader with a preliminary idea of how the faculty orientation at the Dār al-ʿUlūm differs from al-Azhar.

> *Professor ‘Azīz teaches Sharīʿa at the Dār al-ʿUlūm. Like other faculty, he is Wasaṭi in orientation. He is bald, with glasses and a moustache. He wears a suit and tie. Although 70 years of age, the professor has a youthful spirit. Jovial and lighthearted, he is enthusiastic about academic work and optimistic about what it can accomplish.*
>
> *Professor ʿAzīz grew up in a small town of about 20,000 people, but presently lives in Cairo. His paternal grandfather was a cloth merchant. His father pursued the same trade, doing some agricultural work as well. Professor ʿAzīz has three sisters, all of whom are housewives. He has no brothers. He laughs when I ask him how many wives he has, saying: "Only one, and one is enough!" He has three sons, all of whom specialize in fairly competitive non-religious professions. One is an agricultural engineer and the other two are pharmacists.*
>
> *The professor received his primary and secondary schooling in the Azhar institutes. Upon graduation, he had to choose between joining al-Azhar University or the Dār al-ʿUlūm. He picked the latter, being convinced that the government was funneling all the failed students into al-Azhar. After four years he received an undergraduate degree in Arabic and Islamic studies with high distinction. The professor then continued directly on to graduate study. Owing to his precociousness he was one of the few students to receive funding. He completed his master's degree in six years, spending an additional four finishing his PhD. As soon as he was done he joined the Dār al-ʿUlūm 's teaching faculty. He has remained there ever since.*
>
> *The professor describes the Dār al-ʿUlūm as an institution of "moderate and enlightened thinking" (al-fikr al-wasaṭī al-mutanawwir), which aims to bring together "authentic tradition" (al-aṣāla) and "modernity" (al-muʿāṣara). In his view it is more advanced than al-Azhar. Al-Azhar remains to some degree "stagnant" (jāmid), because it has not "benefited from modern knowledge" to the same extent as its counterpart. When I ask him what changes he expects to see at the Dār al-ʿUlūm in the wake of the revolution, he replies: "Relatively few. The Dār al-ʿUlūm is a pioneering institution. It is already ahead of its time."*

The Dār al-ʿUlūm is located on Cairo University's campus among its various other faculties. It occupies a single large nondescript building. Cairo University itself sits behind a wall manned with large numbers of police. Prior to the revolution, the wide boulevard leading up to the main entrance gate was usually lined with large numbers of police-transport trucks, projecting an ostentatious display of state power to all who approached.

Although initially an all-male institution, in the early 1950s the Dār al-ʿUlūm opened its doors to women as well.[40] While classes at the Dār al-ʿUlūm are coeducational, the sexes sit apart—men on one side of the classroom and women on the other.

Compared to the Faculty of Sharīʿa, classroom style is more standardized and overtly designed for large numbers of students. The typical lecture hall is long and rectangular. At the front end there is a raised platform. Atop the platform is a desk behind which the professor sits. The area in front of the platform is occupied by a series of long benches placed one after the other. Built into the ground, the back of each bench is designed to serve as a long extended desk for the bench immediately behind it.

Overall, the atmosphere is not significantly different from the Faculty of Sharīʿa, although the Dār al-ʿUlūm seems marginally better provided for in terms of cleanliness, upkeep, and use of computer technology. There exists a sizable prayer room. However, rather than occupying a central location, it is located in the basement. Moreover, even by the Dār al-ʿUlūm's own modest standards, its condition and upkeep have not been a financial priority. As is the case at al-Azhar, there is no audible call to prayer, nor are classes scheduled such as to allow the performance of the daily prayers in congregation. In one lecture I attended, the call to prayer from a distant mosque wafted in through the window. When the teacher saw students getting anxious about not being in the mosque, he began to warn them about "extremism" (*al-taṭarruf*). He explained: "The extremist is someone who fails to appreciate priorities. He is the kind of person who puts great stress on leaving class or leaving tests to go to the mosque when he hears the call to prayer. But this same person doesn't care when he sees cheating in the lecture hall, even though it produces greater harm for society as a whole."

In the opening years of the twentieth century, students at both the Dār al-ʿUlūm and al-Azhar dressed similarly, wearing turbans and robes to class, all being addressed by the honorific "*shaykh*."[41] By the 1930s, Dār al-ʿUlum students had abandoned such garb, and the same process had started at al-Azhar.[42] Currently, Western attire predominates at the Dār al-ʿUlūm just as it does at al-Azhar, the patterns of dress being roughly similar to those described previously for the Faculty of Sharīʿa.

The large majority of the classes I attended at the Dār al-ʿUlūm were master's-level graduate courses in the various Islamic disciplines.[43] (As is the case at

[40] Aroian 1983:2. [41] Reid 1990:50–51. [42] Riḍā 2007:18–19.

[43] I also attended graduate classes at the level of the *diblūm*, and sat in a few times in undergraduate courses.

al-Azhar, there are no classes for the doctorate). The number of students present in these classes ranged from around 30 to 70. On the other hand, teachers complained that massive numbers of enrollees were habitually absent. In one lecture, a professor expressed his anger that 40 percent of the class was missing (although it is not clear to me how widespread or accurate such a figure is).

In the classes I attended, between two-thirds and four-fifths of the students present were male. A little over half had beards. The women all veiled their heads. In this respect they were like the bulk of Cairo University's female population, where perhaps three-quarters (or more) also veil. Nevertheless, female religious students did not wear the tight clothing common on Cairo University's campus. Furthermore, around a third of the women I saw in graduate classes veiled their faces. Perhaps less than 5 percent of Cairo University's broader female student population observes this practice.

Although there is at least one female professor at the Dār al-ʿUlūm, all of the professors I saw were men, aged in their 40s to 70s. They wore suits and ties. Roughly half had beards (almost always short). The remainder were completely clean-shaven or had moustaches.

## V. REORDERING SPACE AND TIME

As they exist today, al-Azhar and the Dār al-ʿUlūm reflect the new educational models used by the government to restructure traditional religious learning beginning in the latter half of the nineteenth century. As we have seen, in late premodern Egypt, religious learning was embedded in a continuous and informal melding of lives. The reforms inaugurated a very different educational philosophy. Learning was now to be regimented by stringent spatial and temporal boundaries meant to separate it off from mundane everyday affairs and from personal interactions between teachers and students.

At the heart of the new system are periodic classes. Formally planned out by the university administration, the classes take place at particular times in particular classroom locations. Pedagogy is markedly impersonal. Teachers and students will only see each other during short class lessons. Moreover, even though a student will participate in many classes over the years, his teachers will constantly change every semester. Unlike in the traditional study-circle, students do not spend multiple years on one text with one teacher. On average, the new classes are much larger than those customary in traditional study-circles, thus inhibiting the formation of personal bonds between students and teachers. Moreover, students are aware that their success does not require building such bonds, or even coming to class in the first place (at least where attendance is not recorded). Many Azhar students I interviewed confessed that they only showed up on campus to take required tests, borrowing any needed course notes from classmates.

We are now in a position to examine the issue of educational space in more depth. Divisions of space both reflect and instill particular conceptual systems. Such is particularly pronounced in European educational models. These models put a premium on "order" because of its connection to efficiency. Inefficiency is spawned by disorder. Disorder occurs when activities are needlessly jumbled together, making them difficult to monitor and regulate with precision. Creating order necessitates placing each conceptually distinct activity in a different place. Medical care belongs in a hospital, eating belongs in a restaurant, prayer belongs in a mosque, and learning belongs in a school. Space is structured so as to prevent the intermingling of different activities.

From the perspective of the Western-style university, learning has nothing to do with informally sharing in mundane everyday activities. Hence, proper order requires that learning be separated off from such activities. This belief is manifested in the rigid division of space and time. To ensure learning is not mixed with mundane behaviors like eating and sleeping, it is required that lessons only be delivered in classrooms and that these classrooms include neither kitchen equipment nor beds. All available space is taken up by desks and chairs. Moreover, in terms of scheduling, separate times are designated for eating and sleeping as opposed to education. Temporal overlap between these disparate activities is not allowed. Contrast this general arrangement with traditional Islamic learning where lessons may take place anywhere and at any time, allowing them to be mixed with all varieties of everyday activity. Lessons given in teachers' homes easily lend themselves to such mixing. Even lessons given in the mosque occur in the midst of wide-open multipurpose space which can be (and frequently is) used for praying, sleeping, eating, and the like.

An important point to take away from the preceding remarks is that forms of institutional organization are not epistemically neutral. Different ways of ordering educational time and space embody different assumptions concerning what knowledge is and how it is transmitted. Hence, it is deeply mistaken to suppose, as is common, that the institutional changes discussed earlier merely affected "the organization of studies [at al-Azhar] rather than their spirit or substance."[44] To be sure, more recent studies have adopted subtler views. Still, a full appreciation of modernization's impact has been prevented by a failure to grasp the distinctive epistemic character of traditional Islamic education.[45] Succeeding chapters will supply additional corroboration for this assertion.

[44] Crecelius 1972:204. Also see Crecelius 1972:201; Costet-Tardieu 2005:96.

[45] To be clear, I recognize that both traditional Islamic pedagogies and modern Western pedagogies admit of variation. Yet, generally speaking, the latter evince a measure of formality that is not conducive to habitus-transmission through personal relationships.

## VI. TEACHERS AS ETHICAL EXEMPLARS

Present-day students at al-Azhar and the Dār al-ʿUlūm differ in how they appraise their teachers with regards to ethics and personal behavior. Such appraisals are shaped by students' religious identities. Wasaṭi students are inclined toward more charitable appraisals of their teachers. On the other hand, Traditionalists and Salafis often criticize their teachers. According to these criticisms, many (but not all) teachers exhibit personal behavior unworthy of religious scholars. A related criticism is that many teachers have left off Islamic behavioral norms in favor of Western behavioral norms. It is widely believed that teachers adopt Western norms because the Egyptian government pressures them to do so.

One advanced graduate student of foreign origins expressed disappointment about the behavior of professors, stating: "In the past, every teacher set himself forth as a representation (*tamthīl*) of the Prophet. He embodied his manners (*adab*). Right now there is none of that. The dean of the Faculty of Sharīʿa publicly smokes cigarettes and uses inappropriate language. How can such people perform the role of *shaykh*? We need an exemplar (*qudwa*) who can instill good dispositions (*akhlāq*). I look so hard for a *shaykh* to imitate in Egypt, but it is so rare."

One Salafi student expressed amused astonishment that I made any linkage between al-Azhar professors and ethical upbringing. Widening his eyes he exclaimed: "Are you even serious? Are we supposed to take ethics from these professors? From these professors?! We only come here for the degree. If you want ethics you must take them from elsewhere."

Interviewing one Traditionalist scholar who had repeatedly emphasized the importance of ethics in education, I asked him what he thought of the Azhar system. Despite being enrolled in the graduate program, he said that he considered his studies a waste of time. His response prompted me to ask why he was spending so many years to get a degree which he viewed so negatively. He responded:

> scholars living in the world today must operate by the conceptions of knowledge which the West has forced upon their people. Currently in Muslim countries, Egypt and elsewhere, those who run the government have internalized Western ideas, and therefore associate knowledge with possession of a university degree. These same governments have forcefully appropriated control of mosques and other religious endowments. Moreover, it is prohibited to establish new mosques or religious schools without an official permit. The officials empowered to issue permits come from a Western system, and hence cannot imagine acquiring knowledge except through the university. Even if a religious scholar has recognition from major Islamic authorities and many *ijāzas*, so long as he lacks a university degree he is considered ignorant. He will not be given a job in a government controlled mosque or even permitted to establish his own school. He will not be eligible to receive state funding for an Islamic center or to teach at a university. Such opportunities are only available for degree-holders.

The *shaykh* proceeded to explain that owing to the introduction of mass Western-style education, the population at large had also internalized European conceptions of knowledge. Consequently, they do not consider anyone without a degree knowledgeable or worthy of respect. Hence, even if an Islamic scholar considers degrees worthless, he is still compelled to acquire them, for without them he will lack the social recognition needed to do his job. The *shaykh* observed: "Religious scholars are forced to waste their entire youth at the universities, just to get master's and doctoral degrees which they cannot even complete until they are in their thirties or forties. And this is for a system they do not believe in and which produces negligible benefit. When they are forced to do this, they are diverted from helping their communities and propagating the religion (*daʿwa*)." Upon concluding his remarks, the *shaykh* told me that if I could get him into an Islamic studies PhD program in America he would gladly leave al-Azhar. Despite believing that such a program had nothing to offer him in terms of knowledge, he was convinced that a Western degree would be ideal for impressing government authorities and lay Muslims.

Many professors at al-Azhar and the Dār al-ʿUlūm attract student resentment not merely for apparently abandoning practice of the Sunna themselves, but for taking an active role in forcing students to do likewise. In one large undergraduate class at al-Azhar the lecture was interrupted when a high administrative figure (also a professor) came in for a surprise inspection of student dress. A bald clean-shaven man in his 60s, he wore a suit and tie. Leaving aside the students wearing Western attire, he expelled two individuals with beards and *jallābiyya*-robes. I was later told that the inspection was part of a new policy intended to counter the spread of "extremist" practices associated with Salafi religiosity. On another occasion I was sitting in the office of a professor at the Dār al-ʿUlūm. Comparatively young, clean-shaven, and always wearing a suit and tie, he was regarded as a rising star in the Sharīʿa department. During one of our discussions a foreign student from sub-Saharan Africa dropped in to ask a question. The fact that he was dressed in a white *jallābiyya*-robe provoked a negative reaction from the professor, who told him not to wear such clothing to the university. He explained:

> You need to understand that the *Sunna* of the Prophet does not consist in wearing traditional Arab clothing. Rather, the Prophet only wore such clothing because it was common in the society which he lived. He thereby established a principle that we should always dress in a manner which is consistent with the locally dominant custom. Hence, if you really wish to follow the Prophet's teachings you must wear the kind of attire common in Egypt [i.e., Western clothing].

Generally speaking, at al-Azhar it is tacitly understood that having a long-beard raises suspicions of "extremist" tendencies. This reduces one's chances of rising through the official Azhar hierarchy, particularly to the top levels. Students with high aspirations, or who are simply fearful of being denied state employment, are urged to show their "moderate" outlook by eschewing non-Western garb and maintaining a clean-shaven appearance.

In the eyes of many scholars, state encouragement of Western behavioral patterns is part of a foreign-inspired program to produce scholars willing to reinterpret the sacred texts in a manner more conducive to Western liberal norms. Drawing attention to British imperial control over the Egyptian government in the early twentieth century, the recently deceased Azhari Traditionalist al-Būṭī (d.2013) stresses that the reform of al-Azhar was effected in service of an imperialist agenda, asserting that such cannot be denied by any "educated person in the Arab world[46] with the slightest consciousness of the facts of modern history." Al-Būṭī explains that Lord Cromer wanted to promote the modernizing development of Egypt along Western lines. However, the Islamic religion was a source of resistance to these efforts. Hence, Cromer sought to weaken Islam's hold over Egypt by undermining the traditional system of Islamic scholarship and education. To this end, Cromer proceeded to single out religious scholars "who believed in European society in terms of much of its practices and values," encouraging them to generate new interpretations of the sacred texts. To increase their influence, under Cromer's direction "sensitive religious posts were handed over to these men, such as the position of Mufti, the position of *Shaykh al-Azhar*, and the administration of al-Azhar."[47] This enabled them to reform both al-Azhar and Islam in a manner conducive to imperial interests and the cultural Westernization of Egypt. Al-Būṭī thereby suggests that key reformist figures like ʿAbduh and al-Marāghī can be seen as agents of foreign anti-Muslim political influence.

As noted previously, among contemporary religious scholars, memories of ʿAbduh are selective and highly politicized. Many Wasaṭī scholars would reject al-Būṭī's assessment of ʿAbduh as well as his broader perspective on the reform of al-Azhar. Wasaṭī scholars are inclined to remember ʿAbduh as a hero who sought to empower Muslims by giving them access to modern liberal ideas. Moreover, they remember him as an anti-imperialist nationalist. This view receives support from his participation in the ʿUrābī revolt, and his role in publishing the anti-imperialist journal *al-ʿUrwa al-Wuthqā*. For many Wasaṭī scholars, the reform of al-Azhar has functioned to strengthen Egyptian Muslims, putting them in a better position to defend their religion and their homeland in the modern world.

Although controversial, al-Būṭī's perspective is common among non-Wasaṭī religious scholars.[48] It provides one way of reading government educational policy since the late nineteenth century. Al-Būṭī's perspective can be related to traditional learning styles, which involve learning through observation and practice using the pedagogy of companionship. Up into the first half of the twentieth century, Azhari scholars were notorious for opposing many of the government's efforts to modernize Egyptian society, arguing that they were contrary to Islam. Their opposition was grounded in a knowledge of Sharīʿa rules which had (in theory) been received from the Prophet through an unbroken *sanad*. Scholars transmitted this knowledge of Sharīʿa rules to new generations

46 Or more literally: "in this Arab world of ours."

47 Al-Būṭī 2009:112–113.

48 See, e.g., al-Ḥawālī n.d.:574–579, 593.

using the pedagogy of companionship. Hence, students acquired knowledge by observing and imitating their teachers. For instance, they observed that their teachers wore beards and turbans, and thereby inferred that Sharīʿa rules mandate (or at least encourage) wearing beards and turbans. If a student left off the practice of wearing a beard or turban, he would be disciplined by his teacher. It is essential to remember that, at this time, texts (e.g., Qurʾan, Hadith reports) were not the only sources of evidence from which students inferred knowledge of Sharīʿa rules. Rather, the observed actions of living teachers were a significant additional source of evidence. Therefore, a student's knowledge of Sharīʿa rules incorporated what he had seen from his teachers.

This traditional learning style operated to perpetuate a very conservative understanding of Sharīʿa rules. Western-inspired educational reform undermined this traditional learning style, and thereby undermined conservative understandings of Sharīʿa. This development has two aspects which merit attention. First, Western educational techniques do not sanction the idea of learning (e.g., learning Sharīʿa rules) though observation and practice. This implies that the actions of the teacher are no longer a source of evidence on Sharīʿa rules. Hence, the actions of a conservative teacher can no longer be used to perpetuate a conservative understanding of Sharīʿa rules. Second, even where reformed Islamic educational institutions retained some measure of learning through observation and practice, this form of learning no longer functioned to perpetuate a conservative understanding of Sharīʿa rules. This is because educational reform went hand in hand with the systematic removal of conservative teachers (e.g., teachers with beards and turbans). They were replaced by teachers more open to Western liberal norms (e.g), clean-shaven teachers in suits). Consequently, learning through observation and practice now functioned to perpetrate a liberal Western understanding of Sharīʿa rules. For instance, students observe that their teachers are clean-shaven and wear suits. Students thereby infer that Sharīʿa rules encourage being clean-shaven and wearing suits. If students leave off the practice of being clean-shaven and wearing suits (or at least Western attire), they (often) incur discipline at the hands of their teachers (and/or the national security apparatus).

To be clear, in my view, the modern reform of Islamic education cannot be reduced to an imperialist scheme geared toward the dissemination of Western liberal norms. Nevertheless, al-Būṭī is justified in arguing that Western liberal political projects introduced during the colonial period have played, and continue to play, an important role in guiding Islamic educational reform.

# 9

# Transforming the Act of Reading

In the modern period, traditional religious learning has been restructured in accordance with educational models that are crucially dependent upon a particular set of reading practices, which in turn require a particular type of reading materials. To appreciate the nature of these reading materials, we must first turn our attention to print technology.

## I. PREMODERN MUSLIM ATTITUDES TOWARDS PRINT

The mid-1400s witnessed the genesis of print technology in Europe. By the end of the fifteenth century Arabic copies of the Qurʾan were already being printed in Italy. By the sixteenth century, Christians had begun printing Arabic texts in Syria. Yet, it was not until the nineteenth century that print established itself among Muslims, and even then such would only occur under the pressure of European colonialism.[1] In the Ottoman Empire, printing in Turkish was banned into the 1700s. When authorization was finally issued in 1727 it did not cover religious texts. Permission to print the Qurʾan only came in 1874. Messick quotes an early European observer as explaining that Turks adopted these attitudes "because they think that the Scriptures, that is, their sacred books—would no longer be *scriptures* if they were *printed*" (emphasis in original).[2]

The first printing press was brought to Egypt by Napoleon during the French invasion of 1798. In the wake of Napoleon's departure, Muḥammad ʿAlī began operating a printing press to serve governmental needs. The overwhelming majority of the works printed concerned subjects like medicine, military matters, and the natural sciences. Less than 15 percent of the press's output was devoted to Islamic topics. It was only in the latter half of the nineteenth century that significant numbers of religious works began to be printed.[3]

Muslim resistance to print has struck many as puzzling. How is this to be explained? Mitchell highlights the importance of commentary received through a *sanad*.[4] If a text was taken through a *sanad*, there would be a teacher present to clarify its contents and prevent errors. A printed book came with no

[1] Robinson 1993:232–233. [2] Messick 1993:115–116.
[3] Skovgaard-Petersen 1997:51; Mitchell 1991:134. [4] Mitchell 1991:150–154.

The Anthropology of Islamic Law. Aria Nakissa.

such guarantee. Mitchell's insight is valuable, but also incomplete. When Muslim authors speak of the obligation to take from the mouths of *shaykhs*, they do not merely emphasize the need of commentary. They also emphasize the need for learning through observation and practice using the pedagogy of companionship.

Print threatened to drive a wedge between the study of texts and companionship. In the premodern period, books were both rare and expensive. Religious works were generally either owned by individual scholars or by educational institutions under their direct control. In these conditions, *shaykhs* could manage student reading, and compel students to undertake long-term companionship as a condition of accessing texts. *Shaykhs* exercised their power on the assumption that texts could not be properly understood without the knowledge provided through companionship.

The mass production of printed texts changed all of this. An individual no longer had to wait for a scholar to loan him a text or to dictate its contents. Printed books were readily available to all at a slight cost. Therefore, access to religious texts was no longer conditional upon submitting to long-term companionship. In the eyes of Traditionalist Muslim scholars, these developments were a sure stimulus for the proliferation of error and heresy.

Walter Ong and Jack Goody have stressed that print is not merely a more "efficient" means of communicating ideas. On the contrary, print restructures human cognitive processes.[5] Elizabeth Eisenstein has traced the enormous impact that the invention of print had on understandings of language in early modern Europe. One major consequence of these developments was a new perspective on religious texts, which played a central role in the genesis of the Protestant Reformation. Eisenstein identifies a number of distinctive print-linked Protestant beliefs. These include: (1) a belief that scripture is to be understood literally[6] and hence can be grasped by any literate individual,[7] and (2) a belief that all religious knowledge is exclusively textual in form—non-textual transmission of knowledge is thereby ruled out.[8]

As might be expected, the spread of print in Muslim societies during the nineteenth century led to radically altered understandings of language and texts. Print undermined the ancient assumption that acquiring religious knowledge requires learning though observation and practice. Instead, print fostered the belief that religious knowledge can be adequately learned through the study of texts. Print also fostered the related belief that texts can be and should be intelligible simply through their wording. These beliefs went hand in hand with a new set of practices centered on private reading. Let us take a closer look at how these developments have impacted the place of texts in religious learning.

[5] See Goody 1977; Eisenstein 1979; Ong 1982.
[6] Eisenstein 1979:364–367.
[7] Eisenstein 1979:343–344
[8] See Eisenstein 1979:319–320, 326.

## II. TEXT-BASED STUDY VERSUS TOPIC-BASED STUDY

Present-day Egyptian religious universities utilize two main methods of teaching: "text-based study" (*al-dirāsa al-naṣṣiyya*) and "topic-based study" (*al-dirāsa al-mawḍūʿiyya*). Text-based study directly descends from traditional Islamic pedagogy. A teacher reads through a text word-by-word while adding commentary. Nevertheless, there are also a number of differences. All the texts commented upon are printed. Students no longer make their own copies, even though they often inscribe the teacher's remarks in their printed editions. A second difference is that text-based study is practiced in classrooms rather than study-circles. The teacher sits behind a desk at the front of the classroom, reading the text aloud while students follow. Sometimes the teacher asks a student to do the reading, limiting himself to commentary. In the classes I attended, teachers using text-based study worked through around 15–30 pages per semester. Although it was common for multiple semesters to be devoted to the same text, only a small fraction of the total work was ever covered. While students did not precisely memorize the text, they were expected to know it in great depth and detail, at times verging on memorization. They were also responsible for full mastery of the teacher's commentary.

Topic-based study reflects the influence of modern Western pedagogy. In topic-based study, word-by-word reading of texts is assigned to students as homework. During class, the teacher offers remarks on the general topics found in the assigned text rather than going through the text itself word-by-word.

In practice, topic-based study frequently incorporates features associated with text-based study. For instance, while some professors using topic-based study refer to the class text very sparingly, others stick to it closely, holding the book before them while they teach. They cover topics in the exact order given by the text. While they do not read through the text word-by-word in its entirety, they do so with respect to subject headings and important passages (e.g., formal definitions of concepts, Hadith reports cited as proofs for arguments, etc.). Other segments of the text are paraphrased or skipped over. While proceeding through the text, the teacher adds as much lecture or commentary as he sees fit.

Whereas the books used in text-based study are almost always hundreds of years old, those used in topic-based study date from the twentieth century. They are, by Western standards, very short in length—typically between 150 and 300 pages. In the classes I attended, students were usually only responsible for one of these small books. Reflecting traditional educational tendencies, stress is put on thorough mastery of a limited amount of material rather than on reading broadly.

At al-Azhar, both text-based and topic-based methods are used at the graduate and undergraduate levels. I was told that in some courses they are utilized side by side, but I myself only saw teachers using one or the other. There seems to be a greater preference for text-based study in the more advanced classes, especially those at the graduate level. At the Dār al-ʿUlūm, I never witnessed or heard of text-based study being utilized. All lessons relied on topic-based study. Such does not mean that Dār al-ʿUlūm students never read ancient works. However, when they do so, it is for the purpose of writing research papers, theses, and dissertations. Ancient works are not studied with other students in a classroom setting.

## III. WRITING CLEARLY

At Egypt's religious universities, there has been a strong shift away from *matns*. In text-based study, I never saw independent attention given to a *matn*. Rather, teachers used written first-order commentaries in which *matns* were embedded. The *matn* was only addressed in the context of the larger work. Such contrasts with traditional study-circles, where *matns* are often taught independently.

The shift away from *matns* is even more pronounced in topic-based study. As noted earlier, topic-based study uses texts composed in the modern period. These are not structured in the form of *matns* or written commentaries on *matns*. The *matn* format is avoided for a number of reasons. First, given a declining emphasis on memorization, modern texts no longer need to be designed to be retained by heart. Second, modern texts put a premium on clarity.

Modern texts of the type used in topic-based study began to emerge in Egypt in the first quarter of the twentieth century, prompted by calls for the reform of religious instruction.[9] Muhammad al-Dusūqī, a present-day Sharīʿa professor at the Dar al-ʿUlūm, describes this process. Al-Dusūqī observes that traditional works were often "dominated by [extreme] concision, obscurity, and disputation over words."[10] The first authors of new-style works sought to change this by using "clear expression and improved organization"[11] "with the aim of making matters easy"[12] for readers to comprehend. The contemporary Syrian Azhari Wahba al-Zuḥaylī, has taken a leading role in the ongoing effort to craft such texts. He writes of how the present generation is "waiting for us to initiate a revolution in the different works of both law and legal theory, akin to what they see in the modern works dealing with the different fields of knowledge, which are distinguished by their simple style and good organization . . . "[13]

The general attitude behind the push for new-style works is well illustrated in a conversation that I describe in my fieldnotes.

> *Around 70 years of age, Professor Zubayr teaches Sharīʿa at the Dar al-ʿUlūm. He has a short gray beard and wears a suit. Meeting in his office for an interview, I asked him for his opinions on traditional pedagogy. "Older methods are not suitable for the present age. We live in an era of technology where knowledge is constantly advancing. In the past century human beings have discovered more than what their predecessors accumulated throughout the totality of human history. Modern conditions require that new information be transmitted in a speedy*

[9] See Al-Dusūqī 2009:155–167; Eccel 1984:273–275.
[10] Al-Dusūqī 2009:158–159.
[11] Al-Dusūqī 2009:159.
[12] "*Bi-qaṣd al-taysīr wa-l-tashīl.*" Al-Dusūqī 2009:155–167.
[13] Al-Zuḥaylī 2006, 1:22. Also see Khallāf 2003:8.

*fashion. Traditional pedagogy is too slow. If you go word-by-word through texts, only a few pages can be covered over the course of a semester.*

*I am not saying that students should not read older works from the Islamic heritage. They should do that, but it must be done independently. It is their own responsibility. Teachers do not have the time to read out these texts to students in class. Sharīʿa knowledge can be transmitted without the need for* sanads*. The methods of the present-day university provide a viable substitute, and one which is in better accordance with modern needs."*

*Eventually our conversation turned to the matter of akhlāq* (i.e., *good dispositions) and their connection to knowledge. Professor Zubayr remarked: "There is indeed an important relationship between akhlāq and knowledge. This is because the scholar has a single personality which incorporates both. On the other hand, intelligence always plays an independent role in the creation of knowledge, and operates separately from akhlāq.*

*These days there are some opportunities for students to take the akhlāq of their professors. For instance, they can come and visit during office hours. Nevertheless, on the whole, the size of the modern university and the present need to graduate students as fast as possible have led to a relative lack of emphasis on akhlāq. Older methods were superior in this respect."*

*Yet, despite these issues, Shaykh Zubayr was emphatic about the necessity of further reforms to religious education. "We need to use modern books rather than matns and traditional texts. These texts contain too many ancient and unfamiliar words, and are hard for students to understand. The modern era is an information age with computers. Knowledge must be accessible quickly and easily. We must use books that reflect this fact, and can be understood without difficulty."*

Newer texts strive for maximum clarity by eliminating several features characteristic of older compositions. Whereas the works used in traditional learning are often many centuries old, new-style texts make a point of replacing ancient Arabic vocabulary and stylistic conventions with words and forms of expression familiar to modern speakers. A second way of boosting clarity is by reducing the number of unexplained technical terms. Older works include many such terms for the sake of keeping texts as short (and hence as memorizable) as possible. They were to be explained in the course of *shaykhly* commentary. Newer texts either eliminate technical terms altogether or explicate their meaning.

A third way of boosting clarity is by dispensing with the compressed structure characteristic of the *matn*. Al-Ẓawāhirī observes that "most of the difficulty in [studying] law is only due to authors' forms of expression and their putting many meanings in short sentences."[14] Rather than giving students an elliptical string of key words to be elucidated by *shaykhly* commentary, newer texts proffer a fully articulated discourse.

A fourth way of boosting clarity is by eliminating poetic/artistic elements of style, such as versification and assonance. In older texts (especially *matns*) these devices help facilitate memorization. They also familiarize students with the

[14] Al-Ẓawāhirī 1904:126. Also see al-Dusūqī 2009:159.

style of the Arabic language, thereby enhancing their ability to grasp its subtleties and to speak eloquently.

Charles Hirschkind notes that nineteenth century Europeans found the aesthetics of Arabic expression acutely distasteful. For them, proper writing was to eschew embellishment and simply strive to clearly convey meaning. The fact that Muslim writing exhibited stylistic features unrelated to lucid expression was viewed as a sign of intellectual superficiality.[15]

Early religious reformers placed extraordinary importance on moving away from the "ornate" literary style characteristic of premodern writing. ʿAbduh is a good example. In an autobiographical sketch, ʿAbduh describes his life as centering around "preaching two tremendously important points."[16] The first is "liberating thought from the fetter of *taqlīd*" and the second is "reforming the style of the Arabic language used in composition." Explaining what he finds problematic about existing writing practices, ʿAbduh draws attention to the use of archaic words whose meanings are not understood.[17] He also criticizes use of an ornate literary style (*sajʿ*) overly preoccupied with rhyme (*al-fawāṣil*) and assonance (*al-jinās*), which produces writing that is "difficult to comprehend." ʿAbduh singles out graduates of al-Azhar as particularly guilty of these literary practices.[18]

ʿAbduh believes that proper writing consists in "ordinary" prose composed using contemporary words and expressions. He thereby embraces the specific style characteristic of the new European-inspired newspapers, journals, and government educational materials that had begun to emerge in nineteenth century Egypt. Timothy Mitchell attacks the presupposition that the non-literary style of these works is somehow the natural default mode of written expression, from which traditional writing deviates. He argues that the new style reflects idiosyncratic Western ideas about the nature of language; namely, that "normal" writing is perfectly clear and transparent, offering up its meaning to all readers unproblematically.[19]

ʿAbduh's views on writing are linked to his views on legal interpretation. Developing a theme touched on by his teacher al-Afghānī, ʿAbduh asserts that scripture is so clear that it can be understood by all Muslims, even those lacking a traditional religious education.[20] ʿAbduh proclaims: "It is for every Muslim to understand God [directly] from the Book of God [i.e., the Qurʾan] and to understand His Messenger [directly] from the words of His Messenger [as described in Hadith reports] without the mediation (*tawsīṭ*) of anyone from the earliest generations (*Salaf*) or the later ones." According to ʿAbduh, every Muslim is entitled to draw his or her own conclusions about what these texts mean. Anyone who alleges that these conclusions are mistaken is obliged to present clear proof for his claim.[21]

[15] Hirschkind 2006:15.
[16] "*Al-daʿwa ilā amrayn ʿazīmayn.*"
[17] "*Al-kalimāt raththa khabīth ghayr mafhūm.*"
[18] Riḍā 2006, (al-Qism al-Awwal)1:11.
[19] See Chapter 5 in Mitchell 1991.
[20] See Chapter 4 in Gesink 2010.
[21] ʿAbduh 2006, 3:307.

The basic legal issue raised by ʿAbduh can be explained as follows: The Qurʾan and Hadith reports are evidence of Sharīʿa rules. Can any Muslim understand Sharīʿa rules simply by reading the Qur'an and Hadith reports? For ʿAbduh, the default answer to this question is yes. ʿAbduh's answer is based upon an idiosyncratic modern Western understanding of language and texts. Such an understanding holds that normal texts are clear, and can convey their meaning to all readers. By extension, texts like the Qurʾan and Hadith reports are clear, and can convey their meaning to all readers. Where the Qurʾan and Hadith reports address Sharīʿa rules, they convey knowledge of Sharia rules to all readers. Such a stance conflicts with premodern Muslim views, which hold that the Qurʾan and Hadith reports are open to many different interpretations, and hence do not suffice (by themselves) to convey knowledge of Sharīʿa rules. These premodern views justify deference (through *taqlīd*) to past scholars. Hence, because the Qurʾan and Hadith reports are open to many different interpretations, to interpret them correctly one must rely on the opinions of more knowledgeable scholars from the past, like the four Imams who founded the legal schools. However, ʿAbduh dismisses such support for *taqlīd* as intellectual "stagnation" (*jumūd*)[22] and "fanaticism" (*taʿaṣṣub*).

ʿAbduh's views on language are shared by his student Riḍā, who constantly emphasizes the lucid and uncomplicated character of scripture. Riḍā asserts that scriptural texts are so simple that they were perfectly understood by the earliest Muslims despite their lack of literacy and intellectual sophistication.[23] According to Riḍā, after the first generations, Muslims were exposed to corrupting foreign cultural influences which caused them to believe that scripture was difficult to understand. As a result, Muslims came to suppose that their religion was a matter of "roughness, complicatedness and difficulty" rather than "simplicity and ease."[24]

Riḍā believes this problem has been exacerbated by the form of legal works, stating that "understanding the [texts of] Qurʾan and Sunna [directly] is easier than understanding the books of the jurists." In fact, he asserts that attempting to grasp these legal works is more than "one-hundred times" as difficult, owing to their poor style and large number of technical terms.[25]

Riḍā knows that his opinion is a controversial one, and quotes an objection from an imaginary interlocutor from al-Azhar. The interlocutor emphasizes the extreme difficulty of grasping texts, citing his own experience: "one of us remains at al-Azhar mosque twenty years and is not able to properly understand [texts] except if he takes [this understanding] from *shaykhs* who themselves have taken it from those before them."

Riḍā responds: "this is an anomalous societal disease[26] which it is necessary to treat. And when we have properly carried out the correct treatment it will vanish, and there will appear in its place the human progress (*taraqqī al-insān*)

[22] E.g., ʿAbduh 2006, 3:338–357. [23] Riḍā 2007:7–9. [24] Riḍā 2007:7–9.
[25] Riḍā 2008:55. [26] "*Maraḍ ijtimāʿī ʿāriḍ.*"

which is the custom of God. This will happen among the children of our era, akin to what is witnessed among other nations that have progressed [i.e., Europe]. . . ."

ʿAbduh and Riḍā used the new medium of print to publicize their views. The option of disseminating these views through oral transmission in traditional study circles was not particularly attractive to them. Among other things, neither possessed a *sanad* that was satisfactory to the Traditionalist circles within al-Azhar. ʿAbduh was known to have taken the controversial figure of al-Afghānī as his *shaykh*.[27] ʿAbduh's attempts to teach were met with harassment from other scholars, and for a period he was driven to move his previously public lessons into his home.[28] Riḍā's reputation as a student of ʿAbduh was likewise a liability in Traditionalist circles. Rather than trying to reform al-Azhar from the inside, both ʿAbduh and Riḍā took advantage of the new opportunities opened up by print technology. Most appealing to them were mass-circulation newspapers and journals.

Indira Falk Gesink describes the 1870s as the "boom years of Arabic journalism" and observes that al-Afghānī's various students acquired a dominant role in the Egyptian press.[29] In 1880 ʿAbduh took up work as editor of the official state newspaper "*al-Waqāʾiʿ al-Miṣriyya*" (Egyptian Happenings). By 1884 he had moved to France where he teamed with al-Afghānī to produce the reformist journal "*al-ʿUrwa al-Wuthqā*" (The Firmest Bond). The Syrian Riḍā became acquainted with ʿAbduh's ideas by reading *al-ʿUrwa al-Wuthqā*, joining him in Egypt after he returned from Europe. In 1898 Riḍā established the famous monthly journal "*al-Manār*" (The Lighthouse), for which he served as editor until his death in 1935.

It is highly significant that al-Afghānī, ʿAbduh, and Riḍā all wrote for mass circulation journals and newspapers aimed at laymen rather than producing traditional scholarly works aimed at *shaykhs*. By doing so, all three acted on their belief that the common man was capable of understanding discourses on scripture. They also thereby embraced the technology and reading practices responsible (in large part) for overthrowing the linguistic perspective upon which premodern doctrine was built.

As noted earlier, a key moment in al-Azhar's history was the appointment of ʿAbduh's student al-Marāghī to the post of Shaykh al-Azhar (1928–1929 and 1935–1945). Al-Marāghī broadly shared ʿAbduh's views on language and *taqlīd*, promoting them in the face of continued Traditionalist opposition. Hence, al-Marāghī asserts that it is possible to understand various kinds of religious texts without receiving them from *shaykhs* through an uninterrupted *sanad*.[30] He also insists that contemporary Azhari scholars are capable of independently understanding scripture and making *ijtihād*, such that they are not obliged to defer to their predecessors through *taqlīd*.[31] Countering the notion that *ijtihād* has difficult prerequisites, al-Marāghī goes so far as to suggest that *ijtihād* does not necessitate reading the Qurʾan in the original Arabic. Rather, it is possible to

[27] See Kedourie 1997:12. [28] See Gesink 2010:95. [29] Gesink 2010:77.
[30] Al-Marāghī 1959:28–30; Costet-Tardieu 2005:208–209.
[31] See al-Marāghī 1959:18–19; Costet-Tardieu 2005:189–236.

perform *ijtihād* using a translation of the Qur'an.[32] Although past Azhari scholars had repudiated ʿAbduh's views on language and *taqlīd*, al-Marāghī helped transform them into official Azhari doctrine.

## IV. LEARNING WITH CLEAR TEXTS

Written in "plain" uncompressed prose, and emptied of both technical terms and archaic expressions, modern religious texts enable the new reading practices associated with topic-based study. Clear texts help instill the notion that linguistic meaning is transparent. No longer in need of the word-by-word commentary supplied by a *shaykh*, students can be asked to do virtually all of their reading at home. No longer limited by the pace of a teacher's line-by-line commentary, students are able to proceed through texts at a much faster rate.

The fact that students read more while demanding less time from teachers is generally touted as an enormous advance in educational "efficiency." Yet, from the perspective of traditional Islamic learning, this increased "efficiency" comes at a great cost. Texts no longer serve as nodes for companionship relations which enable learning through observation and practice. Without these forms of learning, it is no longer possible to adequately transmit knowledge of Sharīʿa rules. Moreover, without these forms of learning, the ethical dimension of Islamic education is undermined.

[32] Costet-Tardieu 2005:239–241.

# 10

## Salafism and Wasaṭism

The attacks on traditional Islamic doctrine spearheaded by ʿAbduh and Riḍā ultimately brought into being two currents of reformism: Salafism and Wasaṭism. Salafism and Wasaṭism are defined by a particular stance on *ijtihād* and *taqlīd*. This stance can be understood with reference to hermeneutic theory. Earlier, I noted that *ijtihād* is a hermeneutic process whereby individuals infer knowledge of Sharīʿa rules from relevant sources of evidence. For premodern Muslims, these sources of evidence include: (1) God's statements in the Qurʾan, (2) the Prophet's actions as described in Hadith reports, (3) the reported actions of past scholars, and (4) the observed actions of present-day scholars. Salafism and Wasaṭism embrace a different notion of *ijtihād*. To put things in simplistic terms, they reduce the relevant sources of evidence used in *ijtihād*. Hence, for Salafism and Wasaṭism, the relevant sources of evidence are only: (1) God's statements in the Qurʾan, and (2) the Prophet's actions as described in Hadith reports.

Because Salafism and Wasaṭism do not recognize the reported actions of past scholars as a relevant source of evidence, both currents hold that it is legitimate to disregard the views of past scholars. In particular, it is legitimate to disregard the views of the four Imams and their legal schools. Because Salafism and Wasaṭism do not recognize the observed actions of present-day scholars as a source of evidence, they hold that it is legitimate to dispense with the pedagogy of companionship. More generally, Salafism and Wasaṭism hold that Sharīʿa rules can be adequately learned through the study of texts (i.e., the Qur'an and Hadith reports) without any need for learning through observation and practice.

Thus, Salafism and Wasaṭism envision a situation where individuals, who have never engaged in companionship, undertake *ijtihād* by inferring Sharīʿa rules from the Qurʾan and the Hadith reports. These individuals thereby come to their own independent opinions on Sharīʿa rules. Such individuals do not defer (through *taqlīd*) to the opinions of others, such as the four Imams and their legal schools.

Once again, all of this is a bit of an oversimplification. Thus, I would argue that, in practice, *proponents of Wasaṭism and Salafism do tacitly accord some measure of evidentiary value to the reported actions of past scholars and to the observed actions of present-day scholars*. Nevertheless, they accord much less value to these things than premodern scholars (and contemporary Traditionalists).

As we will see, the primary difference between Salafism and Wasaṭism concerns the interpretive methods they employ to understand the Qurʾan and Hadith reports. Salafism emphasizes a literalistic approach. Meanwhile, Wasaṭism repudiates a literalistic approach, promoting widespread and radical use of *istiṣlāḥ* and *istiḥsān*. In this chapter, I take a closer look at both currents, beginning with Salafism.

## I. SALAFISM

"Salafism" takes its name from its insistence on following the "*Salaf*" or earliest Muslim generations. Still, what distinguishes "Salafis" from other Muslims is less their reverence for the *Salaf* than their beliefs about the *Salaf*'s methods of textual interpretation. Salafis believe that the earliest generations were staunch literalists.[1] For Salafis, the *Salaf* viewed legal interpretation as a simple matter, holding that the meaning of the sacred texts is transparently expressed in their literal wording. Owing to Salafi emphasis on literal meaning, their detractors refer to them by the label "Neo-literalists" (*al-Ẓāhiriyya al-Judud*).[2]

Although Salafism consciously embraces a "literalist" approach, it is actually a complex form of literalism. Thus, Salafis do not endorse a systematic literalism (i.e., akin to the extinct Ẓāhirī school). Rather they accept the interpretive method of *qiyās* (i.e., "analogy") as a valid means of extending Sharīʿa rules. However, they generally reject the methods of *istiṣlāḥ* and *istiḥsān*. Recall that *istiṣlāḥ* involves abandoning (and possibly reforming) a rule in light of new circumstances. Meanwhile, *istiḥsān* involves making a limited exception to a rule in light of new/specific circumstances.

Understanding Salafism in Egypt requires taking into account historical linkages with Saudi Arabia. Saudi Arabia currently operates as the global center of Salafism (*al-daʿwa al-salafiyya*). Whereas Salafism is often ferociously persecuted in other parts of the Arab world, in Saudi Arabia it is the official doctrine of the state.

The modern Saudi state has a unique relationship to the Ḥanbalī school. In 1744 Ibn Saʿūd, a tribal chieftain from north central Arabia, formed an alliance with the Ḥanbalī religious reformer Muhammad bin ʿAbd al-Wahhāb (d. 1792). Ibn Saʿūd adopted Ibn ʿAbd al-Wahhāb's doctrine as the creed of his kingdom, which gradually expanded across the peninsula to produce the national entity now known as "Saudi Arabia."

Ibn ʿAbd al-Wahhāb's reformism incorporated a number of different elements. The first relates to Sufism. Contrary to what is commonly believed, Ibn ʿAbd al-Wahhāb did not question the legitimacy of Sufism itself. Indeed, he explicitly states: "We do not reject the Sufi path and the purification of the inner

[1] See al-Khujandī 2001:58.

[2] See, e.g., al-Qaraḍāwī 1999:230; al-Qaraḍāwī 2006:61.

self from the vices of sin attached to the heart and the limbs[3] so long as the person involved straightly adheres to Sharīʿa legislation...."[4] On the other hand, Ibn ʿAbd al-Wahhāb was very hostile to particular elements of medieval Sufi doctrine which seemed to lack a clear scriptural basis. He also opposed syncretic features of local Sufi practice which appeared to condone polytheism and magic.

A second element of Ibn ʿAbd al-Wahhāb's reformism was legal, reflecting his training in the Ḥanbalī school. By far the smallest of the four legal schools, Ḥanbalīs are also the most strongly inclined to interpretive literalism. While Ḥanbalīs do not hold that school doctrine should automatically be revised wher ever it conflicts with the letter of the Qurʾan and Hadith reports, a reformist faction comes close to embracing such a stance. This faction is led by Ibn Taymiyya (d.728/1328) and his student Ibn al-Qayyim (d.751/1350).[5] Ibn ʿAbd al-Wahhāb's juristic approach was influenced by both figures, although his reformism was more mild.

Ibn ʿAbd al-Wahhāb holds that *taqlīd* is inappropriate where school doctrine directly conflicts with the Qurʾan and Hadith reports. However, the mere appearance of conflict is not enough to justify revision of school doctrine unless two additional conditions are met. First, the textual proof must be clear and unequivocal. Second, the revised opinion must be endorsed by one of the other legal schools. The legal reform envisioned by Ibn ʿAbd al-Wahhāb is fairly modest, consisting in piecemeal amendments of Ḥanbalī doctrine. In common with his contemporaries, he asserts that all four schools are generally valid and that every Muslim is obliged to follow a school. He asserts that he himself remains bound in *taqlīd* to the figure of Ibn Ḥanbal.[6]

In the early twentieth century, modern reformist currents began to reshape Saudi Arabia's Wahhābī-inflected Ḥanbalism. The most important of these currents emanated from Egypt.[7] ʿAbduh himself expressed qualified admiration for Wahhābīsm, even referring to Ibn ʿAbd al-Wahhab as "the great reformer" (*al-muṣliḥ al-ʿaẓīm*).[8] ʿAbduh's belief in scientific progress made him sympathetic to Wahhābī efforts directed at rooting out magic and polytheism. Moreover, compared to the Traditionalists of al-Azhar, Wahhābī scholars were more willing to endorse departures from *taqlīd*. On the other hand, ʿAbduh had little admiration for Wahhābism's literalist tendencies. At any rate, it was Riḍā rather than ʿAbduh through which modern reformist thought entered Saudi Arabia.

3 "*La nunkir al-ṭarīqah al-ṣūfiyya wa-tanzīh al-bāṭin min radhāʾil al-maʿāṣī al-mutaʿalliqa bi-l-qalb wa-l-jawāriḥ.*"

4 See Sulayman bin Saḥmān 1342h.:54. Ibn ʿAbd al-Wahhāb's tendency to harshly criticize certain elements of Sufism while still acknowledging its validity is similar to that of other Ḥanbalīs such as Ibn Taymiyya and Ibn al-Jawzī.

5 See Ibn Taymiyya 2004, 20:247–252; Ibn al-Qayyim 2004, 2:j.4 470–479. Also see Riḍā 2008:114–115.

6 Sulaymān bin Saḥmān 1342h:44–45. For more on an Ibn ʿAbd al-Wahhāb see Dallal 1993.

7 See Riḍā 2009.

8 Wahba 2001: 7. Also see A. Amīn, n.d.:23. I was made aware of the existence of this information through the writings of Salafi authority Muḥammad Ismāʿīl al-Muqaddam.

Like ʿAbduh, Riḍā never embraced Wahhābī-style literalism.[9] Nevertheless, he was significantly more ambivalent toward European civilization than ʿAbduh, and less open to liberal-minded juristic opinions. After ʿAbduh's death in 1905, Riḍā came to develop an increasing admiration for Wahhābism, which became a prominent theme in his writings.[10] One strong point of continuity that remained between ʿAbduh and Riḍā was a categorical rejection of *taqlīd*.[11] For Riḍā, even the mild *taqlīd* of the Wahhābīs was misguided.

Riḍā's writings played a crucial role in transforming Wahhābi-inflected Ḥanbalism into Salafism. The chief figure mediating this transformation was Muḥammad Nāṣir al-Dīn al-Albānī (d.1999). Al-Albānī was born in Albania in 1914, and his father was a Ḥanafī religious scholar. While al-Albānī was still a child, his father relocated the family to Damascus. Al-Albānī received basic training in the Ḥanafī school at his father's hands. However, modernizing changes had begun to make themselves felt in Syrian life. Print technology made books and journals plentiful, and public libraries were being opened up. The bibliophilic al-Albānī took full advantage of these changes. Through enormous amounts of independent reading he became a self-taught expert in the field of Hadith reports. Unlike his predecessors, he spent little time learning from living authorities and consequently possessed few *ijāzas*.[12] During this period al-Albānī began reading Riḍā's attacks on *taqlīd* in *al-Manār*, and was influenced by the rise of similar currents within Syria.[13] In the 1950s al-Albānī began teaching an informal study-circle. Facing political persecution due to his increasing fame, around 1960 al-Albānī left Syria to accept a teaching post in Saudi Arabia.

It is with al-Albānī that the doctrine known as "Salafism" fully emerges. Al-Albānī is notable for rejecting the four legal schools outright. He criticizes those with more traditional viewpoints for "preferring their school to the Qurʾan and Sunna [i.e., Hadith reports] in cases where they differ [from each other], and making [the school] a criterion whereby to judge [how to apply the sacred texts]"[14] Al-Albānī denigrates "those who know the sayings and legal derivations of the Imams."[15] True knowledge is limited to the Qurʾan and Hadith reports. It is "not in the opinions of men."[16]

Al-Albānī's views differ significantly from the premodern reformers discussed previously. Ibn Taymiyya,[17] Ibn al-Qayyim, and Ibn ʿAbd al-Wahhāb believe in the necessity of modifying school doctrine in specific places where it conflicts with the sacred texts. Nevertheless, on issues which cannot be decided by unambiguous textual evidence, school authority is preserved and *taqlīd* remains (generally) operative. Hence, all three jurists identify as Ḥanbalīs, binding themselves to the framework of a particular legal school.

9 See Riḍā 2007b:157–162. 10 See Riḍā 2009. 11 See Riḍā 2008.

12 See Lacroix 2009:63. 13 See Lacroix 2009:63-64; Brown 2007:321–322.

14 "'*Yajʿalūnahu miʿyāran ʿalayhimā.*'" Al-Albānī 2005:86. For statements of general methodology see al-Albānī 2005; al-Albānī 2004:39–65.

15 Al-Albānī 2005:77. 16 Al-Albānī 2005:76.

17 For a general discussion of Ibn Taymiyya's relationship to the Ḥanbalī school, and how this relates to its unique structure, see Abū Zahra 2008:282–285.

Al-Albānī repudiates *taqlīd* categorically. He grants the ancient schools no authority whatsoever, refusing to affiliate himself with any one of them. For al-Albānī, every qualified jurist should derive rulings himself. Where clear texts exist, he applies them literally. Where scripture is more ambiguous, he interprets it to the best of his ability. Being absolutely free from *taqlīd*, it is not important whether his opinions accord with those of any existing school. Working on this premise, al-Albānī does not shy away from issuing unprecedented legal rulings at odds with those transmitted from past jurists.[18] Although al-Albānī is similar to Riḍā in his rejection of *taqlīd*, he differentiates himself from Riḍā by his thoroughgoing literalism.

Al-Albānī's views led him to criticize Ibn ʿAbd al-Wahhāb's acceptance of *taqlīd*. This move provoked hostility among Saudi Arabia's leading Islamic authorities. By 1963, he had been forced to relocate to Jordan. However, al-Albānī also had allies. Reform-oriented Ḥanbalīs like ʿAbd al-ʿAzīz bin Bāz (d.1999) and Muhammad bin Sālih al-ʿUthaymīn (d.2001) supported al-Albānī's ideas within the kingdom. By the last decades of the twentieth century, Ibn Bāz, Ibn ʿUthaymīn, and al-Albānī had firmly established themselves as the most influential figures in an increasingly globalizing Salafi movement. While al-Albānī himself remained outside of Saudi Arabia, Ibn Bāz became the kingdom's grand Mufti. Ibn Bāz's support ensured that state patronage would be used to promote al-Albānī's ideas both at home and abroad.

Saudi Arabian influence helped contribute to the emergence of Egyptian Salafism in the 1970s.[19] Salafism in Egypt is notable for its lack of association with specific institutions, academic or otherwise. Although there are some organizational hubs, it has spread largely through the mass production of books, pamphlets, cassettes, and DVDs. Salafis also operate some of the best organized and most informationally rich Islamic websites, containing links to thousands of free books and audio files. Nevertheless, satellite television has probably been the movement's greatest source of strength. Since 2006, several enormously successful religious channels have been launched, becoming among the most popular in Egypt of any kind.[20] These developments coincided with the increasing visibility of Salafi-type habits and forms of dress. More men began wearing long beards and more women began wearing face-veils, causing the government great alarm. The channels were banned in October 2010, three months before the 2011 Egyptian revolution broke out.

Most indigenous Egyptian Salafi authorities have never engaged in formal studies at al-Azhar or the Dār al-ʿUlūm. Moreover, unlike Traditionalists, their learning is not primarily based on study-circles or relationships with *shaykhs*. Following al-Albānī, their preference is for being self-taught through extensive

[18] For instance al-Albānī holds that "*al-dhahab muḥallaq*" is banned for women. He also holds that there is no *zakah* on "ʿurūḍ al-tijāra." See http://www.alalbany.net/fatawa_results.php?search=%DA%D1%E6%D6%20%C7%E1%CA%CC%C7%D1%C9 12/20/11. (accessed on Dec. 20, 2011). These controversial opinions have received much criticism for their lack of precedent. See, e.g., al-Qaraḍāwī 1999:230–231.

[19] For a recent study of Egyptian Salafism see Gauvain 2013.

[20] The two most important have been *al-Raḥmah* and *al-Nās*.

reading. The Salafi leadership is drawn from the most academically talented products of the non-religious educational system. A good example is provided by Alexandria, the foremost stronghold of Salafism within Egypt. The Alexandrian community is led by four scholars originally trained as medical doctors.[21] In Egypt, medicine is the most competitive specialization, attracting the brightest students. Other famous Salafi figures outside of Alexandria also come from comparatively competitive non-religious university specializations.[22] Partly owing to their elite academic status, Salafi authorities look down on formally trained scholars. Remember that the Egyptian educational system funnels the less talented students into religious studies. Salafis are also hostile to the Westernized intelligentsia and its discourse of "reason," "modernity," and "progress." For Salafis, these are analytically empty terms used in service of Occidental political agendas.

Many of those who constitute Egypt's indigenous Salafi leadership spent the 1970s and 1980s under the influence of the famous Azhari preacher ʿAbd al-Ḥamīd Kishk (d.1996).[23] Kishk distinguished himself from the Azhar establishment by his stalwart refusal to compromise on traditional Islamic prohibitions, rejecting the idea that changed social circumstances rendered them inapplicable. Twice imprisoned, and severely tortured, Kishk was notorious for fearlessly denouncing the government's subservience to the West and the fact that the Azhar establishment had been reduced to a tool of the state.

Although Kishk attracted many future Salafi leaders, he himself was critical of the doctrine's growing influence. In one 1981 sermon he states:

> ... The new fashion among pubescent thinkers is to acquire knowledge without professor or sheikh: they go directly to books but they understand nothing! ... These days, a great seventy-year-old Muslim preacher is liable to be interpellated by a pubescent boy who has read three words or a few pages of Ibn Taiymiyya or Ibn 'Abd al-Wahhab and can pose as guardian of the faith! What a farce O Azhar sheikh, and all you who slumber and who have left Islam out to pasture with anyone who happens by![24]

Over the coming years, the budding Salafi movement gradually disassociated itself from Kishk. Turning away from Egypt and al-Azhar, it realigned itself with Saudi Arabia's religious establishment. At present, the most authoritative Salafi scholars are the recently deceased triad of al-Albānī, Ibn Bāz, and Ibn ʿUthaymīn.

One Salafi scholar I spent a great deal of time with was named Nāṣir. I recorded a profile for him in my fieldnotes.

> *Nāṣir is 25 years old and Salafi in orientation. Tall with a broad build, he has a medium-sized beard. He wears a turban and jallābiyya-robe everywhere he goes. Nāṣir is honest, humble,*

[21] Their names are Muḥammad Ismāʿīl al-Muqaddam, Aḥmad Farīd, Saʿīd ʿAbd al-ʿAẓīm, and Yāsir Burhāmī.
[22] E.g., Muḥammad Ḥassān and Abū Isḥāq al-Ḥuwaynī.
[23] E.g., Abū Isḥāq al-Huwaynī and Muḥammad Ḥassān.
[24] Quoted in Kepel 1985[1984]:185.

*and sincere. Deeply principled, he has an exacting temperament which does not permit compromise where religion is concerned.*

*Nāṣir comes from a fairly well-to-do religious family. His paternal grandfather was a graduate of al-Azhar's Faculty of Uṣūl al-Dīn, thereafter working as an Arabic teacher in the national school system. Nāṣir's now-deceased father was a pediatrician with a prestigious medical degree from Cairo University. His mother graduated with a degree in business. However, she then subsequently enrolled in al-Azhar's Faculty of General (Religious) Studies, taking a second undergraduate degree in religion. Presently, she is a homemaker. Nāṣir's only sister is 29. Having previously earned a degree in the competitive field of pharmacy, she now spends her time studying at a religious institute.*

*As a child, Nāṣir attended St. George's Academy, a very elite European-style private school. Upon graduation he enrolled in ʿAyn Shams University, majoring in English literature. Two years into the program, he began to become more interested in studying Islam. One of his neighborhood friends introduced him to a Salafi* shaykh *with a study-circle meeting continuously throughout the week. The* shaykh *himself had a long beard, dressing in a turban and robe. In his 30s, he had first studied at al-Azhar and then pursued further education in Saudi Arabia. He was now a top Egyptian representative of one of the Kingdom's leading authorities. This had enabled him to accumulate a sizable following of students. In addition to teaching, the* shaykh *was also enrolled as an MA student in Sharīʿa at al-Azhar.*

*The* shaykh's *study-circle convened in a single medium-sized room on the bottom-floor of an apartment building. While lacking any furniture, the walls were lined with bookshelves filled with religious works. When Nāṣir was first introduced to the* shaykh, *he had about 30 regular students, though the number has since nearly tripled. Many students rented accommodations nearby. The* shaykh *took no money for his lessons. Indeed, he would often help students financially. In return he only demanded that students heed his moral authority and refrain from sin. To ensure compliance he periodically visited them in their homes and collected information about their personal behavior from classmates. The* shaykh's *students wore traditional robes and head coverings to class rather than Western clothes. According to the* shaykh, *those meeting to receive sacred knowledge should not dress like non-Muslims.*

*Nāṣir began attending the* shaykh's *study-circles two to three times a week, leaving his studies at ʿAyn Shams University. This continued on for nine months. These days, Nāṣir still visits the* shaykh, *but with less frequency. He is presently enrolled at the Dār al-ʿUlūm, taking Arabic courses in an open studies program. In the future he hopes to work teaching the language to non-Arab Muslims. For the time being, he sustains himself by printing and selling small quantities of religious books. He also has some property he inherited from his father.*

Salafi approaches to textual interpretation resemble those characteristic of Protestantism. Just as Protestantism emerged after the rise of print in Europe, Salafism emerged after the introduction of print to the Middle East in the nineteenth century. Nevertheless, Salafism should not be reduced to a product of print, for other factors have played a significant role in its emergence. Chief among these has been the spread of Western forms of schooling and the concomitant decline of traditional Islamic learning.

Salafis believe that the language of scriptural texts is clear and transparent. Textual interpretation is seen as a matter simple enough to be grasped by the dedicated layman, for meaning is given by wording. While Salafi scholars believe that learning from a *shaykh* is helpful, it is generally not regarded as essential. Knowledge can be acquired by independent reading. Speaking on the topic of learning, Ibn ʿUthaymīn states:

> it is necessary for the student of knowledge to seek the help of God—the Mighty and Majestic—then the people of knowledge, and to seek the help of what they have written in their books, because restricting oneself to mere reading requires a long time in contrast to the [situation of] he who sits with a scholar who explains and clarifies for him and illuminates for him the way. I do not say that he cannot attain knowledge except by taking it [directly] from the *shaykhs*.[25] Perhaps a person can attain [it] by reading, but probably, unless he devotes himself completely [to it] night and day and is granted understanding by God, he may err much. For this [reason] it is said: "whoever has a book as his guide, he errs more often than he is correct." But this [maxim] is, in truth, not to be taken [as valid] categorically.[26]

Such openness to book learning is actually opposed by a number of Saudi authorities.[27] Nevertheless, they are in a difficult position. Being caught between a premodern Ḥanbalī tradition and Salafi reforms, they must balance their hostility to book learning against widespread respect for the primarily self-taught al-Albānī. This conundrum is well illustrated in opinions expressed by the leading Saudi authority Rabī' bin Hādī al-Madkhalī. Addressing the matter of self-taught Salafis, al-Madkhalī states: "I am worried for many of these deluded individuals . . . They justify [themselves] by [invoking the example of] *Shaykh* al-Albānī—meaning that he took from books!—O my brother, *Shaykh* al-Albānī had *shaykhs*. Furthermore, he was unique (*fadhdh*), and he cannot be compared to these other people." Al-Madkhalī proceeds to admonish students of religious knowledge to be more humble and not act as if they possess the same exceptional scholastic abilities which allowed al-Albānī to teach himself.[28] At any rate, al-Madkhalī's views have had little efficacy in blunting Egyptian Salafi inclinations to autodidacticism.

Salafis believe that all individuals should strive to follow the scriptural texts without the mediation of scholars. It is recognized that laypersons, unlike scholars, typically lack the ability to research legal matters with complete independence. Accordingly, they are encouraged to ask scholars to assist them in understanding matters. The scholar supplies the correct legal opinion, but he does not ask the layman to defer to him through *taqlīd*. Rather, along with the opinion, he presents scriptural texts (*dalīl*) which prove the opinion. Grasping these proof texts, the layman can then follow them himself. The act of following

[25] "*Bi al-talaqqī min al-mashāyikh.*" [26] Ibn ʿUthaymīn 2002:62–63.

[27] Some of these views have been collected in al-Ghurbānī 1999. Nevertheless, al-Ghurabānī's presentation of source material is sometimes misleading.

[28] Quoted in al-Ghurabānī 1999:66–67.

proof texts provided by a scholar is known as "*ittbā*." Salafis hold that "*ittbāʿ*" is fundamentally different from *taqlīd*.[29]

Salafi discourse often implies that the Prophet himself worked out a full-fledged legal school (*madhhab*). Generally speaking, the teachings of this school are given by the literal wording of the sacred texts. For Salafis, it is not only illogical but blasphemous to follow one of the four legal schools rather than that of the Prophet. Al-Khujandī, the author of one well-known Salafi text, criticizes the followers of the four legal schools. He states: "Know that the only true legal school (*al-madhhab al-ḥaqq*) which it is obligatory to follow is that of our master Muḥammad the Messenger of God—peace be upon him—and that he is the greatest Imam who it is obligatory to follow . . ."[30] Al-Khujandī stresses that the classical legal schools only came into existence after the Prophet died, and thus are to be regarded as heretical innovations.[31]

For al-Khujandī, the original Islam was a simple matter guided by "holding to a literal reading of the Qurʾan and Sunna."[32] It was only later on that this was replaced with adherence to legal schools. Corrupt later jurists "obliged the people to defer through *taqlīd* to one of the four Imams and their known legal schools, and after the [the people] were bound [to a specific legal school] they barred [the people] from accepting and applying the opinion of anyone else. [It was] as if they made [the Imam of the legal school] into a prophet to be obeyed."[33] Indeed, elsewhere al-Khujandī strongly intimates that those who defer through *taqlīd* to a legal school are guilty of polytheism. This is because to leave aside the word of God for the word of men is to treat the latter as if they were divine.[34] Al-Khujandī exhorts his readers to leave *taqlīd* and embrace a proper understanding of Islam: "O Muslim, return to your religion, which consists in applying the Qurʾan and Sunna literally (*Yā ayyuhā al-Muslim irjiʿ ilā dīnika, wa huwa al-ʿamal bi-ẓāhir al-Qurʾān wa-l-Sunna*) . . ."[35]

Owing to their approach, Salafis "theologize" textual interpretation in a unique manner. As we have seen, premodern scholars strongly condemn the idea of acquiring religious knowledge by independent reading. However, the influence of Western notions about language forces a revision. For Salafis, it becomes a theological necessity to take one's knowledge directly from texts. Because the text itself is so clear as to be self-interpreting, scholarly mediation is rendered unnecessary. Scholarly opinion becomes something essentially distinct from and opposable to textual meaning. Favoring the opinion of a scholar over the self-evident literal meaning of a text then becomes tantamount to treating him as a prophet, or even divinizing him as a god.

Western language ideology also motivates Salafis to categorically repudiate Sufism. Such a repudiation is distinctly modern in character. As noted previously,

[29] See al-Albānī 2005:71–93. For a traditionalist criticism of this view see al-Būṭī 2009.

[30] Al-Khujandī 2001:69. [31] Al-Khujandi 2001:63.

[32] "*Wa kull wāḥid mimman yuḥfaẓ ʿanhu al-ʿilm wa-l-dīn min aʾimmat al-salaf qad tamassaka bi-ẓāhir al-Kitāb wa-l-Sunna.*" Al-Khujandī 2001:56.

[33] Al-Khujandī 2001:60. [34] Al-Khujandi 2001:72. [35] Al-Khujandī 2001:65.

it cannot be traced to Ibn ʿAbd al-Wahhāb. Remember that Sufism focuses on the acquisition of dispositions, emphasizing the need to take them from a *shaykh*. For Salafis, Islam is simply a matter of texts. Habitus acquisition from living exemplars has no essential place. As a result, claims that one must pass one's life reverently clinging to a *shaykh* and serving him appear bizarre and theologically suspect. If there is no rationally intelligible ethical or intellectual benefit from spending time with *shaykhs*, then it seems to follow that those who engage in such behavior have ulterior motives, like worshipping *shaykhs* as gods. Consequently, Salafis habitually portray Sufism as similar to polytheism.

On one occasion, I asked a Salafi scholar for his thoughts on the practice of offering oneself as a servant to a *shaykh* in order to acquire knowledge. He responded:

> This is a form of extremism (*ghuluww*). Scholars themselves are not where knowledge is located. They are only a means to knowledge which is ultimately found in books. The job of scholars is to point you to books and to help you understand what is in books— like the Qurʾan and Hadith reports. The contents of these books provide a standard by which to judge scholars—to determine which of them is right and which of them is wrong.
>
> Some people, especially Sufis, exaggerate the importance of men, whether it be scholars or even the Prophet—peace be upon him—and his family. Hence, they refer to these figures using terms like "my master" (*sayyidī*) and "our lord" (*mawlānā*). And they kiss their hands. But all these things are heretical innovations (*bidʿa*) used to raise various figures above their actual status as mere human beings.
>
> Sufis are also always exaggerating the importance of the *sanad*. Maybe it had a purpose in the past. But it has been rendered irrelevant by changes in technology. Now if we want to make sure that the contents of a book are authentic, we just need to get our hands on a trustworthy printed copy. Taking from a *shaykh* is unnecessary.
>
> I myself have never engaged in companionship with a *shaykh*, although I did attend the lessons of a particular *shaykh* regularly for four or five years. Then I stopped going. I had already taken what he had to offer in terms of knowledge. I also eventually noticed that some of what he was teaching was incorrect.

In the preceding pages, I have tried to assess some of the ways in which Salafi perspectives relate to those found in premodern times. The fact that there are differences between the two has been highlighted in many studies.[36] Still, all too often, the identification of differences has been harnessed in service of ideologically driven attempts to impugn and discredit the Salafi movement. In order to prevent my findings from being distorted I would like to be clear on a few points.

First, I would like to dissociate my conclusions from inter-Muslim religious polemics. These polemics summarily dismiss all Salafi perspectives as the simple

[36] See, e.g., Meijer 2009.

by-product of modern alienation from the Islamic heritage. Such polemics are often put forth by contemporary Traditionalists who wish to defend a particular set of controversial juristic doctrines and Sufi practices which persisted into the late premodern period. Salafis criticize these doctrines and practices. However, it should be stressed that many of these criticisms are traceable to premodern figures like Ibn Taymiyya, Ibn al-Qayyim, and Ibn ʿAbd al-Wahhāb. Indeed, some of these criticisms actually echo views of very early figures like Imam al-Shāfiʿī.[37] Obviously, Salafi criticisms that originate with premodern jurists cannot be regarded as a mere by-product of modern alienation.

Second, any evaluation of Salafi views must give due consideration to political context. Many Egyptians I interviewed stated that they wished it were possible for them to rely on the opinions of scholars. However, this was difficult because the government had subjugated religious institutions to the interests of the state. In these circumstances, it was necessary for laypersons to formulate an independent understanding of the sacred texts in order to avoid manipulation. In other words, the Egyptian state's aggressive attempts to control religious education have inadvertently played a role in fostering support for Salafi-type lay interpretation.

## II. WASAṬISM

Wasaṭism, like Salafism, rejects *taqlīd* and holds that contemporary scholars should interpret scripture for themselves rather than deferring to the ancient legal schools. However, the Wasaṭi rejection of *taqlīd* leads to a juristic approach rather different than the conscious literalism prized by Salafism.

Certain elements of Wasaṭism can be traced back to the period between 1830 and 1880. It was during this period that Muslim religious scholars and intellectuals first began considering how liberal ideas might be reconciled with the Islamic tradition. Generally speaking, such figures came from Middle Eastern and South Asian Muslim populations facing the expansion of the British and French empires. Important figures from this period include Rifāʿa al-Ṭahṭāwī (1801–1873), ʿAbd al-Qādir al-Jazāʾirī (1808–1883), Sayyid Aḥmad Khān (1817–1898), Khayr al-Dīn al-Tūnisī (1822–1890), Jamāl al-Dīn al-Afghānī (1839–1897), Namık Kemal (1840–1888), Chirāgh ʿAlī (1844–1895), and Amīr ʿAlī (1849–1928). Nevertheless, Wasaṭism as a distinctive juristic approach began to crystallize in the writings of ʿAbduh (1849–1905) and his student Riḍā (1865–1935). Compared with most earlier figures, ʿAbduh and Riḍā did a better job of situating their ideas in relation to premodern legal doctrines. Moreover, both figures were able to draw on the unique authority of al-Azhar to help disseminate their views.[38]

[37] E.g., particular criticisms of *taqlīd*. See El Shamsy 2013.

[38] Riḍā was able to draw on al-Azhar's authority by collaborating with Azhari figures like ʿAbduh and al-Marāghī.

In earlier chapters we looked at ʿAbduh and Riḍā's rejection of *taqlīd*. Here, I will focus on other elements of their legal thought.

Aside from his rejection of *taqlīd*, the most important feature of ʿAbduh's reformist vision is his stance on *maṣlaḥa*. As noted earlier, premodern jurists hold that God desires to secure specific benefits (*maṣlaḥa*) for human beings, and He laid down Sharīʿa rules as a means to this end. This implies that Sharīʿa rules may need to be abandoned and reformed due to new circumstances. After all, a rule which suffices to secure a benefit under one set of circumstances (e.g., seventh century Arabia) may not suffice to secure this benefit under a different set of circumstances. This general line of thinking legitimates the premodern interpretive methodologies of *istiṣlāḥ* and *istiḥsān*. Such methodologies can be used to justify substantial departures from the literal meaning of scripture. However, premodern jurists used these methodologies cautiously and sparingly, preferring to remain close to the literal meaning of scripture. By contrast, ʿAbduh suggests the need for more radical departures from the literal meaning of scripture.[39] In his view, this is necessary to secure the benefits desired by God in the radically new circumstances of modernity. ʿAbduh's ideas receive further elaboration at the hands of Riḍā.

In developing ʿAbduh's ideas, Riḍā draws on premodern legal doctrine. Recall that premodern jurists divide Sharīʿa rules into two general categories: *ʿibādāt* rules and *muʿāmalāt* rules. *ʿIbādāt* rules pertain to ritual worship (e.g., prayer, fasting, pilgrimage). These rules exist to secure otherworldly benefits (e.g., eternal salvation). On the other hand, *muʿāmalāt* rules regulate human social life (e.g., criminal law, commercial law). Such rules exist to secure worldly benefits (e.g., protection of life, protection of property). While the distinction between *ʿibādāt* rules and *muʿāmalāt* rules is medieval in origin, Riḍā gives it unprecedented importance and puts it to novel uses.

For Riḍā, *ʿibādāt* rules are immutable in nature, and texts dealing with them should be interpreted in a straightforward literal fashion. Notably, in Riḍā's view, the category of *ʿibādāt* rules encompasses not only rules related to ritual worship but also most rules related to family affairs (i.e., marriage, divorce, custody, and inheritance).[40] Family law is assimilated to ritual law because in neither case is it seen as appropriate to probe the precise reasons undergirding legislation.[41]

Riḍā views *muʿāmalāt* rules as more complex than *ʿibādāt* rules. This is because the former must be responsive to changing historical circumstances. For Riḍā, all things being equal, a text addressing *muʿāmalāt* rules should be applied literally. However, Riḍā emphasizes that such a text *may* need to be reinterpreted where it does not secure benefits (desired by God) under prevailing circumstances.[42]

[39] See, e.g., ʿAbduh 2006, 2:88–92; ʿAbduh 2006, 3:257–376.

[40] See Riḍā 1922:543.

[41] E.g., asking why there are five daily prayers rather than seven is like asking why men may marry 4 women rather than 10.

[42] See Riḍā 2007:157-173. Also see Kerr 1966:187–208; Hallaq 1997:214–220; Lombardi 2006:83–92; Zaman 2012:111–123.

In other words, the rule found in the text may been to be abandoned and/or reformed.

Recall, for instance, that God has laid down a Qur'anic a rule requiring that Muslims obtain horses for war. This is because God desires that Muslims have the benefit of military strength. Riḍā holds that this rule must be reformed in order to fit present-day circumstances. Today the rule requires that Muslims prepare for war by obtaining modern military technologies (e.g., tanks, aircraft, missiles) rather than horses.[43] Consider a second more controversial example: Interest-based financial transactions are forbidden by the Qur'anic text. Whereas in the past these transactions often functioned to exploit the poor, it can be argued that they are generally beneficial in the context of the modern world economy. Hence, in the modern economy, interest-based financial transactions facilitate the investment needed for a nation's economic growth, thereby raising the standard of living and alleviating poverty and sickness. We may posit that God desires that poverty and sickness be alleviated. And, if this is the case, it can be argued that, in modern circumstances, He would allow such interest-based transactions.[44] These are the types of issues being contemplated by Riḍā.

Riḍā's position suggests that where *muʿāmalāt* rules are concerned, it is necessary to make more extensive use of methods like *istiṣlāḥ* and *istiḥsān*. However, he does not specify how extensively they should be used. This leaves his position vague and ambiguous. Consequently, Riḍā's approach is capable of accommodating very different legal visions. At one extreme, highly liberal proponents of Riḍā's thought can invoke it to justify the systematic abandonment and reformation of *muʿāmalāt* rules. For these scholars, virtually all traditional *muʿāmalāt* rules do not fit present-day circumstances. Such scholars typically posit that rules modeled on contemporary liberal Western norms do fit present-day circumstances. This leads to a situation where traditional *ʿibādāt* rules are retained, but virtually all *muʿāmalāt* rules are replaced by rules modeled on contemporary liberal Western norms. At the other extreme, highly conservative proponents of Riḍā's thought can invoke it to justify retaining the bulk of traditional *muʿāmalāt* rules. For such scholars, most of these rules do fit present-day circumstances, even if they acknowledge that some traditional *muʿāmalāt* rules must be replaced. Between these extremes exist a range of intermediate positions.

## III. THE ONGOING DEVELOPMENT OF WASAṬISM

Although Wasaṭism continues to evolve historically, its conceptual core derives from Riḍā's elaboration of ʿAbduh's ideas. While Wasaṭi-type thought can be found in all Muslim countries, it has a particularly strong association with Egypt.

[43] Riḍā 1368h, 10:68–71.

[44] Relevant here is al-ʿAshmāwī 1996:114–121.

By the middle of the twentieth century, Wasaṭism had displaced Traditionalism as the leading doctrine at both al-Azhar and the Dār al-ʿUlūm.

Wasaṭism today is best represented by the Egyptian Azhari Yūsuf al-Qaraḍāwī, arguably the most famous Islamic scholar in the world. Al-Qaraḍāwī explains Wasaṭism as a middle ground between two opposite extremes. On the one hand, there is the "approach of restrictiveness and severity"[45] which treats Sharīʿa rules as inflexible and does not pay sufficient attention to human needs. Al-Qaraḍāwī places Salafism and Traditionalism in this category.[46] At the other end of the spectrum is the "approach of excessive accommodation."[47] Al-Qaraḍāwī associates this latter approach with kowtowing to foreign cultural and political power.[48] It is characteristic of those who embrace more radically "liberal" or "modernist" opinions. Al-Qaraḍāwī describes such individuals as "Westernizers" (*al-madrasa al-taghrībiyya*) who use the pretext of Islam's flexibility to legitimate practices which do not accord with its spirit.[49] Al-Qaraḍāwī explains that Wasaṭism aims to strike a balance between the opposite poles of excessive restriction and excessive accommodation. "The Wasaṭi school proceeds according to the middle way . . . it does not follow extremists in their extremism nor does it follow the lax in their laxity . . . it refuses both fanaticism and dissoluteness, believing in balance and moderation."[50]

As indicated earlier, Riḍā's thought is fundamentally ambiguous and highly vague. Put differently, it does not offer precise guidance in terms of methodology. Accordingly, a fundamental feature of Wasaṭism, and one constantly highlighted by its opponents, is its lack of concrete principles (*ḍawābiṭ*).[51] Consider al-Qaraḍāwī's juristic vision. An abstract commitment to "moderation" provides little determinate guidance in juridical matters. Which principles define what counts as "excessive restriction" or "excessive accommodation"? Which factors are relevant in striking the right balance between them? Wasaṭis are comfortable leaving these questions relatively open, allowing individual jurists to work out their own solutions. Ritual and family law aside, every trained scholar is equally entitled to formulate his/her own opinion.

Professors at al-Azhar and the Dār al-ʿUlūm often cite a Hadith report in which the Prophet states: "If the judge makes *ijtihād* and is correct he receives two rewards. If he makes *ijtihād* and is incorrect he [still] receives one reward."[52] This is seen as implying that a jurist need not fear being punished for a wrong answer. Professors also make continuous recourse to the medieval maxim: "every interpreter is correct in his juristic opinion" (*kull mujtahid muṣīb*). Although in the premodern period both the preceding Hadith report and the preceding maxim were understood differently,[53] today they are interpreted as licensing interpretive subjectivism.

[45] "*Ittijāh al-Taḍyīq wa-l-Tashdīd.*"
[46] Qaraḍāwī, *al-Ijtihād* 229–231.
[47] "*Ittijāh al-Ghuluww fi al-Tawassuʿ.*"
[48] Al-Qaraḍāwī 1999:231–233.
[49] Al-Qaraḍāwī 2006:137. Also see al-Qaraḍāwī 1999:232–233; al-Qaraḍāwī 2008a:192–193.
[50] Al-Qaraḍāwī 2006:137.
[51] See al-Būṭī 2005. Also see Chapter 17 in Hallaq 2009.
[52] Cited in al-ʿUmari 1986:148–149.
[53] Among other things they only were seen to apply (in their full form) to the ancient and extinct class of the *mujtahid muṭlaq*, rather than to latter-day jurists.

The nebulousness of Wasaṭism allows it to serve as an umbrella for widely divergent viewpoints. For instance, these days much attention is given to questions such as whether it is permissible for men and women to shake hands with one another, whether it is permissible for Muslims to engage in credit transactions which produce interest,[54] whether it is permissible for Muslims to inherit from non-Muslims,[55] and whether it is permissible for Muslim women to leave off veiling for the sake of pursuing educational opportunities otherwise unavailable.[56] Hewing closely to the literal meaning of scripture, the most conservative Wasaṭis ban all of the above. By contrast, the most liberal Wasaṭis rule that all are allowed. Other Wasaṭis adopt intermediate positions, banning some items while permitting others.

It is worth noting that Wasaṭi scholars do not merely argue for the need to reinterpret sacred texts in response to changed historical circumstances. Some also claim that past generations misunderstood scripture even as it applied to their own times. Put differently, Wasaṭi scholars are given to asserting that scripture has been misconstrued throughout history. For instance, various Wasaṭi scholars have argued that contrary to premodern views, scripture does not endorse punishing apostasy or offensive jihad,[57] that polygamy is only allowed in exceptional circumstances,[58] that it is permitted to take interest on loans,[59] and that it is permissible for Muslims to establish secular states which do not impose Islamic law.[60] Wasaṭis who advocate these unprecedented opinions recognize that they are contradicting the ancient jurists. However, Wasaṭis reject *taqlīd* and do not believe they must defer to their predecessors.

Such opinions strike Traditionalist scholars as shocking. Thus, the eminent Traditionalist Muḥammad Zāhid al-Kawtharī (d. 1951) attacks perspectives of this type, asking whether it is really possible for someone to believe that:

> all the legal interpreters of Islam, up until this day, have been in error, and that he, at the end of time, is correcting them with the truth that has lain hidden from the Muslim nation since the dawn of the sun of Islam until today. [If so] this [claim] is reckless and arbitrary to the utmost extreme.[61]

Top-level state-appointed religious authorities generally subscribe to very liberal forms of Wasaṭism.[62] Two good contemporary examples are the late Shaykh al-Azhar Muḥammad Sayyid Ṭanṭāwī (d.2010) as well as ʿAlī Jumʿa. Jumʿa is a particularly influential figure both inside and outside of Egypt. He received his doctorate in legal theory from al-Azhar, thereafter being appointed to a professorship. From 2003 to 2013 he served as state Mufti. Erudite and witty, with a flair

[54] See, e.g., Chapter 10 in Skovgaard-Petersen 1997.

[55] See, e.g., al-Qaraḍāwī 2006:277–283.

[56] See, e.g., Zeghal 2007:122–128.

[57] See, e.g., al-Ṣaʿīdī 2012[1955]; Zebiri 1993:68.

[58] See ʿAbduh 2006, 2:88–92; Riḍā 1367h, 4:357–358. Also see Zebiri 1993:65–67.

[59] See, e.g., al-ʿAshmāwī 1996:114–121. Also see Zebiri 1993:74–77.

[60] See, e.g., ʿAbd al-Rāziq 1972.

[61] Al-Kawtharī 1993:166.

[62] E.g., the late *Shaykh al-Azhar* Muḥammad Sayyid Ṭanṭāwī as well as the recent State Mufti ʿAlī Jumʿa.

for the controversial, Jumʿa is an ubiquitous media presence. His favorite topics include the ignorant extremism of Salafis and the dangers posed by Islamist political movements. Although Jumʿa reviles Salafism, he has a very strong admiration for particular elements of Traditionalism.

Jumʿa's juristic opinions are very liberal. Indeed, he has gone so far as to argue that Egypt's European-style legal system, properly understood, can be seen as more or less in complete "conformance with the Sharīʿa" ("*muṭābiq li-l-Sharīʿa*").[63] Notably, similar opinions can be found at al-Azhar's Faculty of Sharīʿa, where some professors are accustomed to asserting that "eighty to ninety percent" of Egyptian law is already consistent with the Sharīʿa. Jumʿa acknowledges that the national legal system allows interest-based financial transactions and does not implement any of the Qurʾanic criminal penalties. Nevertheless, Jumʿa believes that the suspension of such legislation can be justified based on Islam's flexibility and responsiveness to modern circumstances. At any rate, he asserts that issues of this type are open to variant interpretations, and that all opinions should be respected. He associates less pluralistic perspectives with "terrorist" thought.[64]

Contrary to what I initially expected, conservative Wasaṭis I interacted with generally had a great deal of respect for liberal Wasaṭi religious authorities. Hence, it would seem that Wasaṭism's absence of well-defined juristic principles promotes a large measure of tolerance and pluralism among scholars. The absence of clear standards makes it difficult to definitively establish that any religious authority is mistaken. It is even harder to prove that the alleged mistake arose from wickedness and corruption rather than simple confusion stemming from a lack of guidelines. Practically speaking, as long as a scholar has sufficiently strong educational credentials, he is given an extraordinary amount of leeway in formulating opinions.

Although conservative Wasiṭis rarely exhibit enmity toward their more liberal counterparts, they are highly critical of the state for which the latter serve as spokesmen. Conservative Wasiṭis are often affiliated with the Islamist Muslim Brotherhood, the Mubārak regime's chief political opposition. Prominent examples include Muḥammad al-Ghazālī (d.1996) as well as al-Qaraḍāwī himself.

Not all scholars endorse Wasaṭism's tolerance of different legal opinions. Salafis and Traditionalists habitually complain that Wasaṭism's characteristic modes of argumentation can be used to justify anything and are open to manipulation by foreign powers. Thus, even though al-Qaraḍāwī sees himself as opposed to "Westernizers," his detractors place him firmly in this camp. They highlight his perceived penchant for interpreting away traditional prohibitions to allow the adoption of Western practices. The Salafi Muqbil bin Hādī al-Wādiʿī (d.2001), a prominent student of al-Albānī, notoriously describes him as a "howling dog"[65]

[63] He also says the legal system "*lā yukhālif al-sharīʿa illā ʿalā sabīl al-ijtihād*"—that is that all apparent divergences from the Sharīʿa can claim to be legitimate products of *ijtihād*.

[64] This is recorded in a videotaped lecture I purchased outside of the Sulṭān Ḥasan mosque. It is entitled "al-Tajriba al-Miṣriyya."

[65] Al-Wādiʿī 2005:5–6, 8.

who "it is necessary to keep under legal guardianship until examined by a psychologist, it being feared that the enemies of Islam have brain-washed him and he has become delusional."[66] Salafis often joke that al-Qaraḍāwī's best-selling legal work "The Permitted and Prohibited in Islam"[67] is more appropriately titled "The Permitted and the Permitted in Islam." Al-Qaraḍāwī's supporters respond that a book of Salafi opinions would merit the title: "The Prohibited and the Prohibited in Islam."

Wasaṭi approaches have provoked the hostility of Traditionalists as well as Salafis. Thus, in a famous treatise published in the 1960s, the Syrian Azhari al-Būṭī expresses concern over how the loose legal reasoning characteristic of Wasaṭism has been manipulated to legitimate laws of liberal and communist origin which are repugnant to Islam.[68]

In comparing Traditionalism, Salafism, and Wasaṭism one cannot avoid touching on long-standing debates over theory and practice in the history of Islamic law. Earlier Western scholarship posited that, in reality, Sharīʿa rules were only implemented to a very limited extent in premodern Muslim societies.[69] However, later studies suggest a more complex view. According to this view, the extent to which Sharīʿa rules were implemented in a given community depended upon the nature of its social and political institutions, and a number of other factors (e.g., the length of time the community had been Muslim, the circumstances under which it had become Muslim). In many societies, Sharīʿa rules were implemented to a significant extent, even if they were not implemented fully.[70] Premodern Muslim scholars persistently promoted the implementation of Sharīʿa rules to the best of their ability, and over time their efforts often bore fruit. As indicated earlier, scholars were willing to abandon and reform some Sharīʿa rules in light of changes in circumstances, thereby facilitating the implementation of these rules. Nevertheless, scholars resisted radical reform of Sharīʿa rules. In many cases they also resigned themselves to the fact that their societies would inevitably ignore many Sharīʿa rules. Put differently, premodern scholars learned to live with an (often sizable) gap between Sharīʿa doctrine in theory and the implementation of this doctrine in practice. In modern Egypt, an attitude of this type is common among Traditionalists and Salafis. By contrast, Wasaṭis seek to close the gap between Sharīʿa doctrine and practice through sweeping and sometimes radical reform of Sharīʿa rules.

In modern Egypt, Traditionalism and Salafism offer a personal path to salvation for principled individual Muslims. Such individuals can commit themselves to the demanding requirements of these approaches. Nevertheless, given the nature of modern Egyptian society, Traditionalists and Salafis have had difficulty establishing organizations that comply with their teachings. Moreover, with regard to actual government legislation, Traditionalist and Salafi viewpoints are habitually ignored as impractical and unrealistic. I do not mean to suggest that

[66] Al-Wādiʿī 2005:24. [67] See al-Qaraḍāwī 2007. [68] See al-Būṭī 2005:26–28.

[69] This view is represented by Christiaan Snouck Hurgronje and Joseph Schacht.

[70] See Udovitch 1970; Peters 2005; Hallaq 2009.

it is pointless for Traditionalists and Salafis to try and realize their visions of a proper Islamic society. I would simply note that their success has hitherto been limited in important ways. The projects of Traditionalists and Salafis have run up against hegemonic modern social and political institutions based on norms of liberalism, secularism, and capitalism. Given its greater flexibility, Wasaṭism has had more success in accommodating itself to such institutions. Wasaṭis have been able to establish organizations consistent with their teachings and have even had a voice in shaping certain government policies and laws. Judging from the elections which took place in the wake of the 2011 Egyptian revolution, one might posit the following. If an Islamist party were ever to come to power in the country it would almost certainly be a Wasaṭi party.[71] To the extent that Traditionalists and Salafis[72] seek to enter politics, they will be under enormous pressure to compromise on their principles. Such compromise would involve embracing a more flexible approach to law—one akin to that found among conservative Wasaṭis.

[71] E.g., Muslim Brotherhood, Ḥizb al-Wasaṭ.

[72] E.g., Ḥizb al-Nūr.

# Conclusion: Rethinking the Islamic Legal Tradition

Cultural, legal, and religious traditions typically contain rules. In this book, I have tried to elucidate how knowledge of such rules is transmitted over time. In particular, I have focused on knowledge of Sharīʿa rules, giving attention to Islamic legal doctrine and religious education. In analyzing these issues, I have drawn on two analytic frameworks; namely, hermeneutic theory and practice theory. Where appropriate, I have also incorporated insights from planning theory.

Hermeneutic theory and practice theory are both concerned with the relationship between action and mind (i.e., mental attributes). However, they analyze this relationship in different ways. Hermeneutic theory emphasizes that actions reveal mental attributes. Meanwhile practice theory emphasizes that repeated actions (i.e., practice) instill mental attributes.

The rise of practice theory in recent decades has coincided with the increasing marginalization of hermeneutic theory within many fields of social research, including anthropology. In this book, I have argued against the current trend toward marginalizing hermeneutic theory in favor of practice theory. This is because cultural, legal, and religious traditions (like Islam) have important dimensions that can only be addressed through hermeneutic theory. Proponents of practice theory tend to overlook these dimensions. In particular, proponents of practice theory overlook the hermeneutic process whereby members of a tradition (e.g., Muslims scholars) engage with that tradition. This process involves synthesizing a coherent overall picture of a mind from its effects/signs. Many proponents of practice theory have also come to promote a perspective on rules and rule-learning which is unsatisfactory. Thus, practice theory fails to recognize that, in many traditions, knowledge of rules is knowledge of a mind (i.e., beliefs, desires, intentions). Practice theory tends to reduce rules to the literal meaning of verbal statements (even though rules are often better conceptualized as intentions). Practice theory does not appreciate that (oftentimes) rules (like intentions) are partially instrumentally rational and partially arbitrary/non-rational. Practice theory also does not provide an adequate account of how new circumstances can prompt the abandonment and reformation of rules. In pointing out these problems, I have not denied the great value of practice theory. Rather, I have argued that practice theory, *taken alone*, does not suffice

The Anthropology of Islamic Law. Aria Nakissa.

as a framework for analyzing cultural, legal, and religious traditions—especially traditions which contain rules (like Islam). For this reason, it is necessary to draw on both hermeneutic theory and practice theory in analyzing traditions.

I have offered some ideas about how hermeneutic theory and practice theory can be brought together to facilitate the analysis of cultural, legal, and religious traditions (particularly those which contain rules). My basic argument is that in many traditions, knowledge of rules is knowledge of a mind/mental attributes (i.e., intentions, beliefs, and desires). Mental attributes cause chains of effects, and these effects are signs of the mental attributes which have caused them. It is possible to synthesize a coherent overall picture of a mind from its effects/signs (i.e., from the effects/signs caused by mental attributes). This mode of analysis is an intuitive one. Hence, we engage in this mode of analysis when we synthesize a coherent overall picture of a general's mind from the obedient actions of his soldiers (as these actions are effects/signs caused by the general's mental attributes). Likewise, we engage in this mode of analysis when we synthesize a coherent overall picture of a king's mind (e.g., God's mind) from the obedient actions of his subjects (e.g., the Prophet and Muslim scholars). This mode of analysis is often tied to particular methods of learning (i.e., learning through texts, learning through observation, learning through practice). These methods enable a student to synthesize a coherent overall picture of a mind.

I have used the preceding ideas to offer a historical and ethnographic analysis of Islamic legal doctrine and Islamic learning, focusing on higher religious education in modern Egypt. Hence, I have argued that knowledge of Sharīʿa rules is knowledge of God's mind. Or, to be more specific, knowledge of Sharīʿa rules is knowledge of God's will/intentions, and the desires and beliefs on which they are based. Knowledge of this kind is inferred from signs/effects of God's mental attributes. These signs/effects include: (1) God's statements in the Qurʾan, (2) the reported obedient actions of the Prophet Muḥammad (Sunna), (3) the reported obedient actions of religious scholars from the past, and (4) the observed obedient actions of present-day religious scholars. These signs/effects play a central role in Islamic education, where they are embedded in different methods of learning, including learning through texts, learning through observation, and learning through practice.

I have sought to explain how the preceding insights from hermeneutic theory and practice theory can be used to analyze the full range of concepts found in Islamic legal doctrine (e.g., Sharīʿa, Qurʾan, Sunna, *ijmāʿ*, *qiyās*, *istiṣlāḥ*, *istiḥsān*, *maṣlaḥa*, *Maqāṣid al-Sharīʿa*, *taqlīd*, *ijtihād*, *madhhab*). I have likewise sought to explain how the preceding insights from hermeneutic theory and practice theory can be used to analyze the full range of concepts associated with religious learning and (with some exceptions) Sufism (e.g., *akhlāq*, *malaka*, *ṣifa*, *qalb*, *fanāʾ*, *shaykh*, *tarbiya*, *ṣuḥba*, *mushāhada*, *iqtidāʾ*, *mushāfaha*, *sanad*, *ijāza*). In this way, I have tried to provide the reader with a detailed, comprehensive, and theoretically informed treatment of Islamic legal doctrine and religious learning.

In writing this book, I have sought to build upon, and bridge, anthropological and Islamicist approaches to Islamic law. In doing so, I have tried to put forth a more adequate understanding of what Sharīʿa rules are. Drawing on practice theory, recent anthropological scholarship is generally content to affirm that Sharīʿa rules are rules. But I have argued that Sharīʿa rules are not merely rules. Rather, Sharīʿa rules should be conceptualized as intentions. Islamicist scholarship does often recognize that Sharīʿa rules are (God's) intentions (or "will"). On the other hand, Islamicist analysis does not engage with the complex nature of intentions. It is necessary to go beyond such analysis, and recognize that intentions (and hence Sharīʿa rules) are based upon beliefs and desires, are partially instrumentally rational and partially non-rational, and may be abandoned/reformed in response to new circumstances. Accordingly, Sharīʿa rules can be conceptualized as a coherent, and complexly structured, system of intentions, beliefs, and desires—one which has some capacity to evolve in response to changing circumstances. This system embodies the semi-autonomous inner logic of Sharīʿa rules. Throughout history, this system has shaped the ways in which Muslims have thought about and applied Sharīʿa rules. Admittedly, there have always been different understandings of this system, and these different understandings have always been influenced by factors like power and political interest. Yet, it would be a mistake to disregard the system for these reasons, or to reduce the analysis of Sharīʿa rules to the analysis of power and political interests. In my view, anthropologists and Islamicists must pay attention to this system when investigating how Muslim scholars and laypersons think about and apply Sharīʿa rules. Anthropologists and Islamicists must also pay attention to how Muslim scholars and laypersons transmit knowledge of this system through actions, statements, and material structures/artifacts, both within the context of Islamic learning and in other less formal contexts.

I end by again turning back to the issue of generalization. I have argued that various currents within the (Sunni) Islamic tradition exhibit a type of coherence. This is due to the fact that these currents take (either explicitly or implicitly) the Qurʾan, the Prophet Muḥammad, and past religious scholars as fundamental sources of religious knowledge. Such is most evident in premodern Islam as well as contemporary Traditionalism. But it also holds with respect to Wasaṭism and Salafism (for in practice, most Wasaṭis and Salafis treat past scholars as fundamental sources of religious knowledge).

The fact that the (Sunni) Islamic tradition recognizes the Qurʾan, the Prophet Muḥammad, and past religious scholars as fundamental sources of religious knowledge does not preclude substantial variation in forms of Islamic religiosity. Nevertheless, it engenders certain widely shared transhistorical and transregional patterns in Islamic education and legal thought. In describing these patterns, I have made a number of general claims about the Islamic tradition. I fully recognize that such an approach will invite criticism from scholars who are methodologically committed to the view that broad generalizations are inherently problematic, and that the sole aim of proper Islamicist scholarship is to precisely delineate local and historically specific manifestations of

Islam. However, I have suggested that scholarship on Islam should pay attention both to broad patterns as well as local and historically specific manifestations of Islam. The present work has attempted to do exactly this. In other words, it has attempted to discern broad patterns within the Islamic tradition, while also examining a local and historically specific manifestation of Islam in modern Egyptian religious education.

# *Bibliography*

Abaza, Mona 2002 Debates on Islam and Knowledge in Malaysia and Egypt: Shifting Worlds. London: RoutledgeCurzon.

Abduh, Muḥammad 2006 Al-Aʿmāl al-Kāmila li-l-Imām al-Shaykh Muḥammad ʿAbduh. Edited by Muḥammad ʿImara. 5 Vols. Cairo: Dār al-Shurūq.

Abd al-Rāziq, ʿAlī 1972 Al-Islām wa Uṣūl al-Ḥukm li-ʿAlī ʿAbd al-Rāziq: Dirāsa wa Wathāʾiq bi-Qalam Muḥammad ʿImāra. Beirut: al-Muʾassasa al-ʿArabiyya li-Dirāsāt wa al-Nashr.

Abū Dāwud 1998 Kitāb al-Sunan. Edited by Muḥammad ʿAwwāma. 5 Vols. Beirut: Muʾassasa al-Rayyān.

Abū Ghudda, ʿAbd al-Fattāh 1992 Al-Isnād min al-Dīn wa-Safḥa Mushriqa min Tarīkh Samāʿ al-Ḥadīth ʿinda al-Muḥaddithīn. Beirut: Dār al-Qalam.

Abū Ghudda, ʿAbd al-Fattāh 2008 Lamaḥāt min Tarīkh al-Sunna wa ʿUlūm al-Ḥadīth. Beirut: Dār al-Bashāʾir al-Islāmiyya.

Abu-Lughod, Lila 2005 Dramas of Nationhood: The Politics of Television in Egypt. Chicago: University of Chicago Press.

Abū Zahra, Muḥammad 2002 Mālik: Ḥayātuhu wa-ʿAṣruhu – Ārāʾuhu wa-Fiqhuhu. Cairo: Dār al-Fikr al-ʿArabī.

Abū Zahra, Muḥammad 2008 Ibn Taymiyya: Ḥayātuhu wa-ʿAṣruhu – Ārāʾuhu wa-Fiqhuhu. Cairo: Dār al-Fikr al-ʿArabī.

Abū Zahra, Muḥammad 2009 Tārīkh al-Madhāhib al-Islāmiyya. Cairo: Dār al-Fikr al-ʿArabī.

ʿAfīfī, Ṭalʿat Muḥammad 2005 Al-Taʿlīm bayna al-Naẓrat al-Islāmiyya wa-l-Naẓrat al-Gharbiyya. Cairo: Maktaba al-Īmān.

Agar, Michael 1980 Hermeneutics in Anthropology. Ethos 8(3): 253–272.

Agrama, Hussein Ali 2012 Questioning Secularism: Islam, Sovereignty, and the Rule of Law in Modern Egypt. Chicago: University of Chicago Press.

Ahmed, Shahab 2016 What Is Islam?: The Importance of Being Islamic. Princeton, NJ: Princeton University Press.

Ahmed, Shahab and Nenad Filipovic 2004 The Sultan's Syllabus: A Curriculum for the Ottoman Imperial Medreses Prescribed in a Fermān of Qānūnī I Süleymān, Dated 973 (1565). Studia Islamica, No. 98/99: 183–218.

al-Ājurī, Abū Bakr bin al-Ḥusayn bin 'Abdullah 1985 Akhlāq al-'Ulamā'. Beirut: Dar al-Kutub al-ʿIlmiyya.

al-Albānī, Muḥammad Nāṣir al-Dīn 2004 Ṣifa Ṣalāh al-Nabī. al-Riyāḍ: Maktaba al-Maʿārif.

al-Albānī, Muḥammad Nāṣir al-Dīn 2005 Al-Ḥadīth: Ḥujja fī al-Aqāʾid wa-l-Aḥkām. Riyadh: Maktaba al-Maʿārif.

Ali, Kamran Asdar 2002 Planning the Family in Egypt: New Bodies, New Selves. Austin: University of Texas Press.

Algar, Hamid 1976 The Naqshbandī Order: A Preliminary Survey of Its History and Significance. Studia Islamica 44: 123–152.

Amīn, Aḥmad N.d. Zuʿamāʾ al-Iṣlāḥ fī al-ʿAsr al-Ḥadīth. Beirut: Dār al-Kitāb al-ʿArabı.

Anjum, Ovamir 2012 Politics, Law, and Community in Islamic Thought. New York: Cambridge University Press.

The Anthropology of Islamic Law. Aria Nakissa.

Ansari, Ishaq Zafar 2004 Islamic Juristic Terminology before al-Shafi'i: A Semantic Analysis with Special Reference to Kufa. In The Formation of Islamic Law, edited by Wael Hallaq, 211–256. Vermont: Ashgate.

al-Anṣārī, ʿAbd al-ʿAlī Muḥammad bin Niẓām al-Dīn 2002 Fawātiḥ al-Raḥamūt bi-Sharḥ Musallam al-Thubūt. 2 Vols. Beirut: Dār al-Kutub al-ʿIlmiyya.

Anscombe, G.E.M. 2000[1957] Intention. Cambridge, MA: Harvard University Press.

Arjomand, Said Amir 1984 The Shadow of God and the Hidden Imam. Chicago: University of Chicago Press.

Aroian, Lois A. 1983 The Nationalization of Arabic and Islamic Education in Egypt: Dar Al-Ulum and Al-Azhar. The Cairo Papers in Social Science, Vol. 6, Monograph 4. Cairo: The American University in Cairo.

Asad, Talal 1986 The Idea of an Anthropology of Islam. Occasional Papers Series. Washington DC: Center for Contemporary Arab Studies, at Georgetown University.

Asad, Talal 1993 Genealogies of Religion. Baltimore: Johns Hopkins University Press.

Asad, Talal 2003 Formations of the Secular: Christianity, Islam, Modernity. Stanford, CA: Stanford University Press.

al-ʿAshmāwī, Muḥammad Saʿīd 1996 Uṣūl al-Sharīʿa. Cairo: Maktaba Madbūlī al-Ṣaghīr.

Audi, Robert 2006 Practical Reasoning and Ethical Decision. New York: Routledge.

Austin, J.L. 1962 How to Do Things with Words. New York: Oxford University Press.

al-Azharī, Ṣāliḥ ʿAbd al-Samīʿ al-Ābī 2006 Jawāhir al-Iklīl. 2 Vols. Beirut: al-Maktaba al-ʿAṣriyya.

Al-Azhar University N.d. Jāmiʿa al-Azhar: 2007–2008 (Official Manual).

Al-Azmeh, Aziz 1993 Islams and Modernities. New York: Verso.

Azmi, Mohammad Mustafa 1968 Studies in Early Ḥadīth Literature. Beirut: Al-Maktab Al-Islami.

al-Badakhshī, Muḥammad bin al-Ḥasan N.d. Sharḥ al-Badakhshī wa maʿahu Sharḥ al-Isnawī. 3 Vols. Beirut: Dār al-Kutub al-ʿIlmiyya.

Bamyeh, Mohammed 1999 The Social Origins of Islam: Mind, Economy, Discourse. Minneapolis: University of Minnesota Press.

al-Bājūrī, Ibrāhīm bin Muḥammad 2001 al-Mawāhib al-Laduniyya ʿalā al-Shamāʾil al-Muḥammadiyya, edited by Muḥammad ʿAwwāma. Dār al-Yusr.

Baring, Evelyn 1916 Modern Egypt. 2 Vols. New York: Macmillan.

al-Barzanjī, ʿAbd al-Laṭīf 1996 Al-Taʿāruḍ wa-l-Tarjīḥ bayna al-Adilla al-Sharʿiyya. Beirut: Dār al-Kutub al-ʿIlmiyya.

Bashir, Shahzad 2011 Sufi Bodies: Religion and Society in Medieval Islam. New York: Columbia University Press.

Beiser, Frederick 2011 The German Historicist Tradition. New York: Oxford University Press.

Berkey, Jonathan 1992 The Transmission of Knowledge in Medieval Cairo: A Social History of Islamic Education. Princeton, NJ: Princeton University Press.

Betti, Emilio 1990 Hermeneutics as the General Methodology of the Geisteswissenschaften. In The Hermeneutical Tradition: From Ast to Ricouer, edited by Gayle Ormiston and Alan Schrift, 159–197. Albany: State University of New York Press.

Betti, Emilio 2017 General Theory of Interpretation, Book 7. Translated by Giorgio Pinton. CreateSpace.

Biltājī, Muḥammad 2006 Manhaj ʿUmar bin al-Khaṭṭāb fī al-Tashrīʿ. Cairo: Dār al-Salām.

Bloor, David 2006[1997] Wittgenstein, Rules and Institutions. New York: Routledge.

Boas, Franz 1887 The Study of Geography. Science 9 (210): 137–141.
Bohannan, Paul 1968 Justice and Judgment among the Tiv. New York: Oxford University Press.
Bourdieu, Pierre 1977 Outline of a Theory of Practice. Translated by Richard Nice. New York: Cambridge University Press.
Bourdieu, Pierre 1984 Distinction: A Social Critique of the Judgment of Taste. Translated by Richard Nice. Cambridge, MA: Harvard University Press.
Bourdieu, Pierre 1987 The Force of Law: Toward a Sociology of the Juridical Field. Translated by Richard Terdiman. Hastings Law Journal 38:805–853.
Bourdieu, Pierre 1990 The Logic of Practice. Translated by Richard Nice. Stanford, CA: Stanford University Press.
Bourdieu, Pierre 1998 Practical Reason: On the Theory of Action. Stanford, CA: Stanford University Press.
Bouveresse, Jacques 1999 Rules, Dispositions, and the Habitus. In Bourdieu: A Critical Reader, edited by Richard Shusterman, 45–63. Oxford: Blackwell.
Bowen, John 2003 Islam, Law, and Equality in Indonesia: An Anthropology of Public Reasoning. New York: Cambridge University Press.
Bowen, John 2007 Why the French Don't Like Headscarves: Islam, the State, and Public Space. Princeton, NJ: Princeton University Press.
Bowen, John. 2010 Can Islam Be French?: Pluralism and Pragmatism in a Secularist State. Princeton, NJ: Princeton University Press.
Bowen, John 2012 A New Anthropology of Islam. Cambridge: Cambridge University Press.
Bowen, John 2016 On British Islam: Religion, Law, and Everyday Practice in Sharīʿa Councils. Princeton, NJ: Princeton University Press.
Bratman, Michael 1987 Intention, Plans, and Practical Reason. Cambridge, MA: Harvard University Press.
Bratman, Michael 1999 Faces of Intention. New York: Cambridge University Press.
Bratman, Michael 2007 Structures of Agency. New York: Oxford University Press.
Bratman, Michael 2014 Shared Agency: A Planning Theory of Acting Together. New York: Oxford University Press.
Bravmann, M. M. 1972 The Spiritual Background of Early Islam: Studies in Ancient Arab Concepts. Leiden: Brill.
Brenneis, Donald 1994 Discourse and Discipline at the National Research Council: A Bureaucratic Bildungsroman. Cultural Anthropology 9(1): 23–36.
Brown, Jonathan 2007 The Canonization of al-Bukhari and Muslim: The Formation of the Sunni Ḥadīth Canon. Boston: Brill.
Brown, Jonathan 2009 Ḥadīth: Muhammad's Legacy in the Medieval and Modern World. Oxford: Oneworld.
Brunner, Rainer 2009 Education, Politics, and the Struggle for Intellectual Leadership: al-Azhar between 1927 and 1945. In Guardians of the Faith in Modern Times, edited by Meir Hatina, 109–140. Leiden: Brill.
Buckley, Thomas 1996 The Little History of Pitiful Events. In Volksgeist as Method and Ethic: Essays on Boasian Ethnography and the German Anthropological Tradition, edited by George Stocking, 257–297. Madison: University of Wisconsin Press.
al-Bukhārī, Muḥammad bin Ismāʿīl 2002 Ṣaḥīḥ al-Bukhārī. Damascus: Dār Ibn Kathīr.
Bunzl, Matti 1996 Franz Boas and the Humboldtian Tradition. In Volksgeist as Method and Ethic: Essays on Boasian Ethnography and the German Anthropological Tradition, edited by George Stocking, 17–78. Madison: University of Wisconsin Press.

Burak, Guy 2013 Dynasty, Law, and the Imperial Provincial Madrasa: The Case of al-Madrasa al-ʿUthmaniyya in Ottoman Jerusalem. International Journal of Middle East Studies 45: 111–125.

Burak, Guy 2015 The Second Formation of Islamic Law: The Hanafi School in the Early Modern Ottoman Empire. New York: Cambridge University Press.

al-Būṭī, Muḥammad Saʿīd Ramaḍān 2005 Ḍawābiṭ al-Maṣlaḥah fī al-Sharīʿah al-Islāmiyyah. Damascus: Dār al-Fikr.

al-Būṭī, Muḥammad Saʿīd Ramaḍān 2009 al-Lāmadhabiyya: Akhṭar Bid'a tuhaddid al-Sharīʿa al-Islāmiyya. Damascus: Dār al-Farābī.

al-Būṭī, Muḥammad Saʿīd Ramaḍān and Ṭayyib Tīzīnī 1999 Al-Islām wa-l-ʿAsr: Taḥadiyyāt wa-Āfāq. Damascus: Dār al-Fikr.

Calder, Norman 1993 Studies in Early Muslim Jurisprudence. New York: Oxford University Press.

Calder, Norman 1996 Al-Nawawī's Typology of Muftīs and Its Significance for a General Theory of Islamic Law. Islamic Law and Society 3(2): 137–164.

Calder, Norman 2006 Interpretation and Jurisprudence in Medieval Islam, edited by Jawid Mojaddedi and Andrew Rippin. Burlington, VT: Ashgate.

Calhoun, Craig 1993 Habitus, Field, and Capital: The Question of Historical Specificity. In Bourdieu: Critical Perspectives, edited by Craig Calhoun, Edward LiPuma, and Moishe Postone, 61–88. Chicago: University of Chicago Press.

Chamberlain, Michael 1994 Knowledge and Social Practice in Medieval Damascus, 1190–1350. New York: Cambridge University Press.

Chibnik, Michael 2011 Anthropology, Economics, and Choice. Austin: University of Texas Press.

Clarke, Morgan 2012 The Judge as Tragic Hero: Judicial Ethics in Lebanon's Shari'a Courts. American Ethnologist 39(1): 106–121.

Clifford, James 1988 The Predicament of Culture. Cambridge, MA: Harvard University Press.

Clifford, James and George Marcus, eds. 1986 Writing Culture. Berkeley: University of California Press.

Collingwood, R. G. 1993 The Idea of History. Oxford: Clarendon Press.

Comaroff, John and Simon Roberts 1981 Rules and Processes: The Cultural Logic of Dispute in an African Context. Chicago: University of Chicago.

Conley, John and William O'Barr. 1993 Legal Anthropology Comes Home: A Brief History of the Ethnographic Study of Law. Loyola of Los Angeles Law Review 27: 41–64.

Cook, Bradley James 2000 Egypt's National Education Debate. Comparative Education 36(4): 477–490.

Cook, Michael 1997 The Opponents of the Writing of Tradition in Early Islam. Arabica 44 (Fasc.4): 437–530.

Cornell, Vincent 1983 The Logic of Analogy and the Role of the Sufi Shaykh in Post-Marinid Morocco. International Journal of Middle East Studies 15(1): 67–93.

Costet-Tardieu, Francine 2005 Un réformiste à l'université al-Azhar: Oeuvre et pensée de Mustafâ al-Marâghî (1881–1945) Cairo: CEDEJ.

Crapanzano, Vincent 1980 Tuhami: Portrait of a Moroccan. Chicago: University of Chicago Press.

Crecelius, Daniel 1972 Nonideological Responses of the Egyptian Ulama to Modernization. In Scholars, Saints, and Sufis: Muslim Religious Institutions in the Middle East since 1500, edited by Nikki Keddie, 167–210. Berkeley: University of California Press.

Crone, Patricia 1987 Roman, Provincial and Islamic Law: The Origin of the Islamic Patronate. New York: Cambridge University Press.

Crone, Patricia 1999 Weber, Islamic Law, and Rise of Capitalism. In Max Weber and Islam, edited by Toby Huff and Wolfgang Schluchter, 247–272. New Brunswick, NJ: Transaction.

al-Dabbāgh, ʿAbd al-Raḥmān bin Muḥammad N.d. Mashāriq Anwār al-Qulūb. Beirut: Dār Ṣādir.

al-Dabbūsī, Abū Zayd 2001 Taqwīm al-Adilla. Beirut: Dār al-Kutub al-ʿIlmiyya.

Dallal, Ahmad 1993 The Origins and Objectives of Islamic Revivalist Thought, 1750–1850. Journal of the American Oriental Society 113(3): 341–359.

Daniel, Valentine 1984 Fluid Signs: Being a Person the Tamil Way. Berkeley: University of California Press.

Dār al-ʿUlūm N.d. Dalīl: 2010–2011 (Official Manual).

N.d. Dalīl Rasāʾil al-Mājistīr wa al-Duktūrāh allatī nūqishat fī kulliyya Dār al-ʿUlūm mundhu ʿāmm 1950 wa ḥattā nihāya 2000. Iʿdād: Mahā Aḥmad ʿAlām, Fāṭima ʿAbbās ʿAbd al-Raḥmān, and Sulaymān Ibrāhīm al-Bilkīmī. Ishrāf: Kamāl al-Sayyid Khafājī.

Davidson, Donald 2001[1980] Essays on Actions and Events. 2nd ed. New York: Oxford University Press.

Davidson, Donald 2001[1984] Inquiries into Truth and Interpretation. New York: Oxford University Press.

Dennett, Daniel 1987 The Intentional Stance. Cambridge, MA: The MIT Press.

al-Dihlawī, Shāh Walī Allah 1398h ʿIqd al-Jīd fī Aḥkām al-Ijtihād wa-l-Taqlīd. Cairo: al-Maṭbaʿa al-Salafiyya.

al-Dijwī, Yūsuf 1981 Maqālāt wa Fatāwā al-Shaykh Yūsuf al-Dijwī. 2 Vols. Cairo: al-Hayʾa al-ʿĀmma li-Shuʾūn al-Matābiʿ al-Amīriyya.

Dilthey, Wilhelm 1972[1900] The Rise of Hermeneutics. Translated by Frederic Jameson. New Literary History 3(2): 229–244.

Dilthey, Wilhelm 1988[1883] Introduction to the Human Sciences. Translated by Ramon Betanzos. Detroit, MI: Wayne State University Press.

Dilthey, Wilhelm 2002[1910] The Formation of the Historical World in the Human Sciences: Wilhelm Dilthey, Selected Works, Vol. 3., edited by Rudolph Makkreel and Frithjof Rodi. Princeton, NJ: Princeton University Press.

Dodge, Bayard 1961 Al-Azhar: A Millenium of Muslim Learning. Washington, DC: The Middle East Institute.

Douglas, Mary 2002[1962] Purity and Danger. New York: Routledge.

Douglas, Mary 2003[1970] Natural Symbols. New York: Routledge.

Droysen, Johann Gustav 1893 Outline of the Principles of History. Translated by E. Benjamin Andrews. Boston: The Athaneum Press.

Dupret, Baudouin 2007 What Is Islamic Law: A Praxiological Answer and an Egyptian Case Study. Theory, Culture & Society 24(2): 79–100.

Duranti, Alessandro 2015 The Anthropology of Intentions: Language in a World of Others. New York: Cambridge University Press.

al-Dusūqī, Muḥammad 2009 Madkhal li-ʿIlm al-Uṣūl. Sisila al-Kutub al-Irshādiyya. Cairo: Rābiṭa al-Jāmiʿa al-Islāmiyya.

Dutton, Yasin 1999 The Origins of Islamic Law. New York: Curzon.

Dwyer, Kevin 1982 Moroccan Dialogues. Baltimore: Johns Hopkins University Press.

Eccel, A. Chris 1984 Egypt, Islam, and Social Change: Al-Azhar in Conflict and Accomodation. Berlin: Klaus Schwarz Verlag.

Eickelman, Dale 1978 The Art of Memory: Islamic Education and Its Social Reproduction. Comparative Studies in Society and History 20(4): 485–516.
Eickelman, Dale 1985 Knowledge and Power in Morocco: The Education of Twentieth-Century Notable. Princeton, NJ: Princeton University Press.
Eisenstein, Elizabeth L. 1979 The Printing Press as an Agent of Change: Communications and Cultural Transformation in Early-Modern Europe. 2 Vols. New York: Cambridge University Press.
Ekins, Richard 2012 The Nature of Legislative Intent. New York: Oxford University Press.
El Shamsy, Ahmad 2008 Rethinking *Taqlīd* in the Early Shafi'i School. Journal of the American Oriental Society, 128(1): 1–24.
El Shamsy, Ahmad 2013 The Canonization of Islamic Law: A Social and Intellectual History. New York: Cambridge University Press.
El-Zein, Abdul Hamid 1977 Beyond Ideology and Theology: The Search for the Anthropology of Islam. Annual Review of Anthropology 6: 227–252.
Emon, Anver 2010 Islamic Natural Law Theories. New York: Oxford University Press.
Ephrat, Daphna 2000 A Learned Society in a Period of Transition: The Sunni "Ulama" of Eleventh-Century Baghdad. Albany: State University of New York Press.
Ephrat, Daphna 2008 Spiritual Wayfarers, Leaders in Piety: Sufis and the Dissemination of Islam in Medieval Palestine. Cambridge, MA: Harvard Center for Middle Eastern Studies.
Erlanger, Howard, Bryant Garth, Jane Larson, Elizabeth Mertz, Victoria Nourse, and David Wilkins 2005 Is It Time for a New Legal Realism? Wisconsin Law Review 2005(2): 335–363.
Erie, Matthew 2016 China and Islam: The Prophet, the Party, and the Law. Cambridge: Cambridge University Press.
al-Fādānī, Abū Fayḍ Muḥammad Yāsīn bin ʿĪsā 2008 Asānīd wa-Ijāzāt wa-Musalsalāt al-Fādānī. Beirut: Dār al-Bashāʾir al-Islāmiyya.
Fadel, Mohammad 1996 The Social Logic of *Taqlīd* and the Rise of the Mukhtaṣar. Islamic Law and Society 3)2(: 193–233.
Fakhry, Majid 1994 Ethical Theories in Islam. 2nd ed. New York: Brill.
Farquhar, Michael 2017 Circuits of Faith: Migration, Education, and the Wahhabi Mission. Stanford, CA: Stanford University Press.
Faubion, James 2011 An Anthropology of Ethics. New York: Cambridge University Press.
al-Fāwī, ʿAbd al-Fattāḥ 2004 Fī al-Akhlāq. Cairo: Dār al-Hānī.
Fischer, Michael M. J. 1980 Iran: From Religious Dispute to Revolution. Madison: The University of Wisconsin Press.
Fischer, Michael M. J. and Mehdi Abedi 1990 Debating Muslims: Cultural Dialogues in Postmodernity and Tradition. Madison: University of Wisconsin Press.
Foucault, Michel 1972 The Archaeology of Knowledge and The Discourse on Language. Translated by A. M. Sheridan Smith. New York: Pantheon.
Foucault, Michel 1990[1978] The History of Sexuality: An Introduction. Translated by Robert Hurley. New York: Vintage Books.
Foucault, Michel 1990[1985] The Use of Pleasure. Translated by Robert Hurley. New York: Vintage Books.
Foucault, Michel 1995[1977] Discipline and Punish: The Birth of the Prison. Translated by Alan Sheridan. New York: Vintage Books.
Foucault, Michel 1998[1969] What Is an Author? In Aesthetics, Method, and Epistemology. Translated by Robert Hurley et al. New York: The New Press.
Gadamer, Hans-Georg [1960]2006 Truth and Method. New York: Continuum.

Gauvain, Richard 2013 Salafi Ritual Purity: In the Presence of God. New York: Routledge.

Geertz, Clifford 1960 Religion of Java. Glencoe, IL: The Free Press.

Geertz, Clifford 1968 Islam Observed. New Haven, CT: Yale University Press.

Geertz, Clifford 1973 The Interpretation of Cultures: Selected Essays. New York: Basic Books.

Geertz, Clifford 1980 Negara. Princeton, NJ: Princeton University Press.

Geertz, Clifford 1983 Local Lnowledge: Further Essays in Interpretive Anthropology. New York: Basic Books.

Gerber, Haim 1994 State, Society, and Law in Islam: Ottoman Society in Comparative Perspective. Albany: State University of New York Press.

Gesink, Indira Falk 2010 Islamic Reform and Conservatism: Al-Azhar and the Evolution of Modern Sunni Islam. New York: I. B. Tauris.

al-Ghāwajī, Wahbī 2004 Kalima ʿIlmiyya Hādiya fī al-Bidʿa wa Aḥkāmihā. Damascus: Dār al-Bashāʾir.

al-Ghazālī, Abū Ḥāmid 1964 Mīzān al-ʿAmal. Cairo: Dār al-Maʿārif bi-Misr.

al-Ghazālī, Abū Ḥāmid 1971 Shifāʾ al-Ghalīl. Baghdad: Maṭbaʿa al-Irshād.

al-Ghazālī, Abū Ḥāmid 1999 Al-Maqṣad al-Asnā fī Sharḥ Asmāʾ Allah al-Ḥusnā. Damascus: Maṭbaʿa al-Ṣabāḥ.

al-Ghazālī, Abū Ḥāmid 2000 Al-Mustaṣfā fī ʿIlm al-Uṣūl. Beirut: Dār al-Kutub al-ʿIlmiyya.

al-Ghazālī, Abū Ḥāmid 2003 Maqāṣid al-Falāsifa. Beirut: Dār al-Kutub al-ʿIlmiyya.

al-Ghazālī, Abū Ḥāmid 2004a Iḥyāʾ ʿUlūm al-Dīn. Cairo: Dār al-Ḥadīth.

al-Ghazālī, Abū Ḥāmid 2004b al-Iqtiṣād fi al-Iʿtiqād. Beirut: Dār al-Kutub al-ʿIlmiyya.

al-Ghazālī, Abū Ḥāmid 2005 Iḥyāʾ ʿUlūm al-Dīn. Beirut: Dār Ibn Ḥazm.

al-Ghazālī, Muḥammad 1987 Khuluq al-Muslim. Cairo: Dār al-Rayyān.

al-Ghurbānī, Abū ʿAbdullah Khālid bin Muḥammad 1999 Al-Saḥafiyyūn. Cairo: Dār al-Kitāb wa-l-Sunna.

Giddens, Anthony 1968 "Power" in the Recent Writings of Talcott Parsons. Sociology 2(3): 257–272.

Giddens, Anthony 1979 Central Problems in Social Theory: Action, Structure and Contradiction in Social Analysis. Berkeley: University of California Press.

Giddens, Anthony 1984 The Constitution of Society: Outline of the Theory of Structuration. Cambridge: Polity Press.

Gilsenan, Michael 1982 Recognizing Islam. London: Croom Helm.

Gleave, Robert 2012 Islam and Literalism: Literal Meaning and Interpreation in Islamic Legal Theory. Edinburgh: Edinburgh University Press.

Gluckman, Max 1967 The Judicial Process among the Barotse of Northern Rhodesia. Manchester: Manchester University Press.

Goody, Jack 1977 The Domestication of the Savage Mind. New York: Cambridge.

Graham, William 1983 Islam in the Mirror of Ritual. In Islam's Understanding of Itself, edited by Richard G. Hovannisian and Speros Vryonis Jr., 53–71. Malibu: Undena.

Graham, William 1993 Traditionalism in Islam: An Essay in Interpretation. The Journal of Interdisciplinary History 23(3): 495–522.

Green, Nile 2010 The Uses of Books in a Late Mughal Takiyya: Persianate Knowledge between Person and Paper. Modern Asian Studies 44(2): 241–265.

Grice, H.P. 1957 Meaning. The Philosophical Review 66(3): 377–388.

Grice, H.P. 1969 Utterer's Meaning and Intention. The Philosophical Review 78(2): 147–177.

Grice, H.P. 1971 Intention and Uncertainty. New York: Oxford University Press.

Grice, H.P. 1989 Retrospective Epilogue. In Studies in the Way of Words. Cambridge, MA: Harvard University Press: 339–385.

Griffel, Frank 2009 Al-Ghazālī's Philosophical Theology. New York: Oxford University Press.
Habermas, Jurgen 1971 Knowledge and Human Interests. Translated by Jeremy Shapiro. Boston: Beacon Press.
Habermas, Jurgen 1984 The Theory of Communicative Action: Reason and the Rationalization of Society. Translated by Thomas McCarthy. Boston: Beacon Press.
Habermas, Jurgen 1987 The Theory of Communicative Action: Lifeworld and System: A Critique of Functionalist Reason. Translated by Thomas McCarthy. Boston: Beacon Press.
Habermas, Jurgen 1996 Between Facts and Norms: Contributions to a Discourse Theory of Law and Democracy. Translated by William Rehg. Cambridge, MA: MIT Press.
Hacker, P. M. S. 1993[1990] Wittgenstein: Meaning and Mind. Part I: Essays. Oxford: Blackwell.
Hadot, Pierre 1995[1987] Philosophy as a Way of Life. Malden, MA: Blackwell.
al-Ḥafnāwī, Muḥammad 2007 Al-Taʿāruḍ wa-l-Tarjīḥ ʿinda al-Uṣūliyyīn wa atharuhumā fī al-Fiqh al-Islāmī. al-Manṣūra: Dār al-Wafāʾ.
Hallaq, Wael 1984 Was the Gate of Ijtihād Closed? International Journal of Middle Eastern Studies 16(1): 3–41.
Hallaq, Wael 1986 On the Origins of the Controversy about the Existence of Mujtahids and the Gate of Ijtihād. Studia Islamica 63: 129–141.
Hallaq, Wael 1992 Uṣūl al-Fiqh: Beyond Tradition. Journal of Islamic Studies 3(2): 172–202.
Hallaq, Wael 1997 A History of Islamic Legal Theories. New York: Cambridge University Press.
Hallaq, Wael 2001 Authority, Continuity, and Change in Islamic Law. New York: Cambridge University Press.
Hallaq, Wael.2002 The Quest for Origins or Doctrine? Islamic Legal Studies as Colonialist Discourse. UCLA Journal of Islamic and Near Eastern Law 2(1): 1–31.
Hallaq, Wael. 2005 The Origins and Evolution of Islamic Law. New York: Cambridge University Press.
Hallaq, Wael 2009 Sharī'a: Theory, Practice, Transformation. New York: Cambridge University Press.
Hallaq, Wael 2013 The Impossible State. New York: Columbia University Press.
Hallaq, Wael B., ed. 2004 The Formation of Islamic Law. Burlington, VT: Ashgate.
Hamdy, Sherine 2009 Islam, Fatalism, and Medical Intervention: Lessons from Egypt on the Cultivation of Forebearance (*sabr*) and Reliance on God (*tawakkul*). Anthropological Quarterly 82: 173–196.
Hanks, William 2005 Bourdieu and the Practices of Language. Annual Review of Anthropology 34: 67–83.
Ḥasb Allah, 'Alī 1997 Uṣūl al-Tashrī' al-Islāmī. Cairo: Dār al-Fikr al-'Arabī.
al-Ḥawālī, Safar N.d. Al-ʿIlmāniyya: Nashʾatuhā wa Taṭawwuruhā wa Āthāruhā fī al-Ḥayāh al-Islāmiyya al-Muʿāsira. Markaz al-Baḥth al-ʿIlmī wa Iḥyā' al-Turāth al-Islāmī.
Heck, Paul 2002a The Epistemological Problem of Writing in Islamic Civilization: al-Ḫaṭīb al-Baġdādī's (d.463/1071) 'Taqyīd al-'ilm'. Studia Islamica 94:85–114.
Heck, Paul 2002b The Construction of Knowledge in Islamic Civilization: Qudama b. Ja'far and his Kitab al-Kharaj wa sina'at al-kitaba. Boston: Brill.
Heil, John and Alfred Mele, eds. 1993 Mental Causation. New York: Oxford University Press.
Hefner, Robert 1985 Hindu Javanese: Tengger Tradition and Islam. Princeton, NJ: Princeton University Press.

Herrera, Linda 2006 Islamization and Education: Between Politics, Profit, and Pluralism. In Cultures of Arab Schooling: Critical Ethnographies from Egypt, edited by Linda Herrera and Carlos Alberto Torres, 25–52. Albany: State University of New York.

Heyworth-Dunne, J. 1968[1939] An Introduction to the History of Education in Modern Egypt. London: Frank Class and Co. Ltd.

Ḥilmī, Muṣṭafā 2005 Ibn Taymiyya wa-l-Taṣawwuf. Cairo: Dār Ibn al-Jawzī.

Hirsch, Susan 1998 Pronouncing and Persevering: Gender and the Discourses of Disputing in an African Islamic Court. Chicago: University of Chicago Press.

Hirschkind, Charles 2006 The Ethical Soundscape: Cassette Sermons and Islamic Counterpublics. New York: Columbia University Press.

Hoffman, Valerie 1995 Sufism, Mystics, and Saints in Modern Egypt. Columbia: University of South Carolina Press.

Hoffman, Valerie 1999 Annihilation in the Messenger of God: The Development of a Sufi Practice. International Journal of Middle East Studies 31(3): 351–369.

Holton, Richard 2009 Willing, Wanting, Waiting. New York: Oxford University Press.

Horkheimer, Max 2004[1947] Eclipse of Reason. New York: Continuum.

Hourani, Albert 2007[1983] Arabic Thought in the Liberal Age (1798–1939). New York: Cambridge University Press.

Hourani, George 1985 Reason and Tradition in Islamic Ethics. New York: Cambridge University Press.

Huff, Toby 1984 Max Weber and the Methodology of the Social Sciences. New Brunswick, NJ: Transaction Books.

Huff, Toby and Wolfgang Schluchter 1999 Max Weber and Islam. New Brunswick, NJ: Transaction.

Hull, Matthew 2012 Government of Paper: The Materiality of Bureaucracy of in Urban Pakistan. Berkeley: University of California Press.

Hymes, Dell 1977 Foundations in Sociolinguistics: An Ethnographic Approach. London: Tavistock.

Ibn ʿAbd al-Barr, Abū ʿUmar 2006 Jāmiʿ Bayān al-ʿIlm wa Faḍlihi. Beirut: Dār Ibn Ḥazm.

Ibn ʿAbd al-Salām, ʿIzz al-Dīn 1999 Qawāʾid al-Aḥkām fī Maṣāliḥ al-Anām. Beirut: Dār al-Kutub al-ʿIlmiyya.

Ibn ʿAbd al-Salām, ʿIzz al-Dīn 2004 Maqāṣid al-Ṣalāh. ʿAbd al-Fattāḥ Ḥusayn Muḥammad Hamām, Dirāsa wa Taḥqīq. Cairo: Maktaba Awlād al-Shaykh li-Turāth.

Ibn ʿĀbidīn 2000 Radd al-Muḥtār. Beirut: Dār al-Fikr.

Ibn ʿĀbidīn 1325h Majmūʿa Rasāʾil Ibn ʿĀbidīn. 2 Vols. Damascus: Sharika al-Ṣahāfiyya al-ʿUthmāniyya.

Ibn Amīr al-Ḥājj 1999 Al-Taqrīr wa-l-Taḥbīr. 3 Vols. Beirut: Dār al-Kutub al-ʿIlmiyya.

Ibn ʿĀshūr, Muḥammad al-Ṭāhir 2001 Maqāṣid al-Sharīʿa al-Islāmiyya. ʿAmmān: Dār al-Nafāʾis.

Ibn ʿĀshūr, Muḥammad al-Ṭāhir 2006 Ibn Ashur: Treatise on Maqasid al Sharīʿah. Translated and Annotated by Mohamed El-Tahir El-Mesawi. Washington, DC: The International Institute of Islamic Thought.

Ibn Ḥajar al-ʿAsqalānī 2004 Fatḥ al-Bārī. Cairo: Dār al-Ḥadīth.

Ibn Ḥajar al-ʿAsqalānī 2008 Bulūgh al-Marām. Beirut: Dār Ibn Ḥazm.

Ibn al-Ḥājj, Muḥammad bin Muḥammad 2008 al-Madkhal. 2 Vols. Beirut: al-Maktaba al-ʿAsriyya.

Ibn Jamāʿa, Badr al-Dīn Muḥammad 2009 Tadhkira al-Sāmiʿ wa-l-Mutakallim. Beirut: Dār al-Bashāʾir.

Ibn Kathīr, ʻImād al-Dīn 2005 Tafsīr al-Qurʾan al-ʿAẓīm. 10 Vols. Cairo: Dār al-Ḥadīth, 2005.
Ibn Khaldūn, ʿAbd al-Raḥmān bin Muḥammad 1967[1958] The Muqaddimah: An Introduction to History. Translated by Franz Rosenthal. 3 Vols. Princeton, NJ: Princeton University Press.
Ibn Khaldūn, ʿAbd al-Raḥmān bin Muḥammad 2010 Muqaddima Ibn Khaldūn. Cairo: Nahḍa Miṣr
Ibn Manẓūr, Muḥammad bin Mukarram 2003 Lisān al-ʿArab. 9 Vols. Cairo: Dār al-Ḥadīth.
Ibn Miskawayh, Abū ʿAlī Aḥmad bin Muḥammad 2006 Tahdhīb al-Akhlāq. Beirut: Dār Ṣādir.
Ibn Nujaym, Zayn al-Dīn bin Ibrāhīm bin Muḥammad 1999 Al-Ashbāh wa-l-Naẓāʾir ʿalā Madhhab Abī Ḥanīfa al-Nuʾmān. Beirut: Dār al-Kutub al-ʿIlmiyya.
Ibn Qayyim al-Jawziyya 1423h. Iʿlām al-Muwaqqiʿīn ʿan Rabb al-ʿĀlamīn. al-Dammām: Dār Ibn al-Jawzī.
Ibn Qayyim al-Jawziyya 2004 Iʿlām al-Muwaqqiʿīn. 2 Vols. Cairo: Dār al-Ḥadīth.
Ibn Qayyim al-Jawziyya 2005 Madārij al-Sālikīn. Cairo: Dār al-Ḥadīth.
Ibn Qayyim al-Jawziyya 2007 Al-Ṭibb al-Nabawī. Damascus: Maktaba Dār al-Bayān.
Ibn Qudāma, Muwaffaq al-Dīn 1994 Rawḍa al-Nāẓir wa-Janna al-Munāẓir. Beirut: Dār al-Kutub al-ʿIlmiyya.
Ibn Rajab 2004 Jāmiʿ al-ʻUlūm wa-l-Ḥikam fī Sharḥ Khamsīn Ḥadīthan min Jawāmiʿ al-Kalim. Cairo: Dār al-Salām.
Ibn Sabʿīn 2007 Anwār al-Nabi: Asrāruhā wa-Anwāʿuhā. Cairo: Dār al-Āfāq al-ʿArabiyya.
Ibn al-Ṣalāḥ, Abū ʿAmr ʻUthman 1989 Muqaddima Ibn al-Ṣalāḥ. Cairo: Dār al-Maʿārif.
Ibn al-Ṣalāḥ, Abū ʿAmr ʻUthman 2009 Adab al-Fatwā. Cairo: Maktaba al-Khānajī bi-l-Qāhira.
Ibn Taymiyya, Taqī al-Dīn 2004 Majmūʿ Fatāwā Shaykh al-Islām Ibn Taymiyya, edited by ʿAbd al-Rahmān bin Muḥammad bin Qāsim. 37 Vols. Al-Madīna al-Munawwara: Mujammaʿ al-Mālik Fahd.
Ibn Taymiyya, Taqī al-Dīn 1982 Al-Furqān bayna Awliyāʿ al-Raḥmān wa Awliyāʾ al-Shayṭān. al-Riyāḍ: Maktaba al-Maʿārif.
Ibn Taymiyya, Taqī al-Dīn 2008 al-Musawwada fī Uṣūl al-Fiqh li-Āl Taymiyya. Beirut: Dār Ibn Ḥazm.
al-Ījī, ʿAḍud al-Dīn 2000 Sharḥ al-ʿAḍud ʿalā Mukhtaṣar al-Muntahā al-Uṣūlī. Beirut: Dār al-Kutub al-ʿIlmiyya.
al-Ījī, ʿAḍud al-Dīn 2004 Sharḥ Mukhtaṣar al-Muntahā al-Uṣūlī. 3 Vols. Beirut: Dār al-Kutub al-ʿIlmiyya.
Ibrahim, Ahmed Fekry 2016a Rethinking the *Taqlīd* Hegemony: An Institutional, Longue-Durée Approach. Journal of the American Oriental Society 136(4):801–816.
Ibrahim, Ahmed Fekry 2016b Rethinking the *Taqlīd-Ijtihād* Dichotomy: A Conceptual-Historical Approach. Journal of the American Oriental Society 136(2): 285–303.
ʿIlīsh, Muḥammad 1958 Fatḥ al-ʿAlī al-Mālik fī al-Fatwā ʿalā Madhhab al-Imām Mālik. Cairo: Maṭbaʿa Muṣṭafā al-Bābī al-Ḥalabī wa-Awlādihi.
ʿĪsā, ʿAbd al-Qādir 1993 Haqāʾiq ʿan al-Taṣawwuf. Ḥalab: Dār al-ʿIrfān.
al-Iṣfahānī, al-Rāghib 2007 Kitāb al-Dharīʿa ilā Makārim al-Sharīʿa. Cairo: Dār al-Salām.
Al-Jabartī, ʿAbd al-Raḥmān N.d. ʿAjāʾib al-Āthār fī al-Tarājim wa-l-Akhbār. 3 Vols. Beirut: Dār al-Jīl.
Jackson, Michael, ed. 1996 Things as They Are: New Direction in Phenomenological Anthropology. Bloomington: Indiana University Press.
Jackson, Sherman 1996 *Taqlīd*, Legal Scaffolding and the Scope of Legal Injunctions in Post-formative Theory *Muṭlaq* and *ʿĀmm* in the Jurisprudence of *Shihāb al-Dīn al-Qarāfī*. Islamic Law and Society 3(2): 165–192.

Jackson, Sherman 2004 Discipline and Duty in a Medieval Muslim Elementary School: Ibn Ḥajar al-Haythamī's *Taqrīr al-Maqāl*. In Law and Education in Medieval Islam, edited by Joseph Lowry, Devin Stewart, and Shawkat Toorawa, 18–32._Warminster: E. J. W. Gibb Memorial Trust.

Jarrār, Ḥusnī Adham 1997 Al-Qudwa al-Ṣāliḥa: Akhlāq Qurʾāniyya wa Namādhij Rabbāniyya. ʿAmman: Dār al-Ḍiyāʾ.

al-Jaṣṣāṣ, Abū Bakr 2000 Uṣūl al-Jaṣṣāṣ. 2 Vols. Beirut: Dār al-Kutub al-ʿIlmiyya.

Johansen, Baber 1988 The Islamic Law on Land Tax and Rent. London: Croom Helm.

Johansen, Baber 1998 Contingency in a Sacred Law: Legal and Ethical Norms in the Muslim Fiqh. Boston: Brill.

Johansen, Julian 1996 Sufism and Islamic Reform in Egypt: The Battle for Islamic Tradition. New York: Oxford University Press.

Johnston, David 2007 Maqāṣid al-Sharīʿa: Epistemology and Hermeneutics of Muslim Theologies of Human Rights. Die Welt des Islams 47(2): 149–187.

Jumʿa, ʿAlī 2004 Qawl Ṣaḥābī ʿinda al-Uṣūliyyīn. Cairo: Dār al-Risāla.

Joseph, Marc 2014 Donald Davidson. New York: Routledge.

al-Jurjānī, al-Sayyid al-Sharīf 2004 Muʿjam al-Taʿrīfāt Cairo: Dār al-Faḍīla

al-Juwaynī, Imām al-Ḥaramayn 2002 al-Burhān. 2 Vols. Beirut: Dar Iḥyāʿ al-Turāth al-ʿArabī.

Kahn, Paul 1999 The Cultural Study of Law. Chicago: University of Chicago.

Kamali, Mohammed 2013 Principles of Islamic Jurisprudence. 3rd ed. Cambridge: Islamic Texts Society.

Karzūn, Anis Aḥmad 2008 Ādāb Ṭālib al-ʿIlm. Beirut: Dār Ibn Ḥazm.

Katz, Marion 2013 Prayer in Islamic Thought and Practice. New York: Cambridge University Press.

al-Kawtharī, Muḥammad Zāhid 1993 Maqālāt al-Kawtharī. Beirut: Dār al-Ahnāf.

al-Kawtharī, Muḥammad Zāhid 2004 Al-Fiqh wa-Uṣūl al-Fiqh min Aʿmāl al-Imām Muḥammad Zāhid al-Kawtharī. Beirut: Dār al-Kutub al-ʿIlmiyya.

Kedourie, Elie 1997 Afghānī and ʿAbduh: An Essay on Religious Unbelief and Political Activism in Modern Islam. London: Frank Cass & Co.

Kepel, Gilles 1985[1984] Muslim Extremism in Egypt: The Prophet and Pharaoh. Translated by Jon Rothschild. Berkeley: University of California Press.

Kerr, Malcolm H. 1966 Islamic Reform: The Political and Legal Theories of Muhammad Abduh and Rashid Riḍā. Berkeley: University of California Press.

al-Khādimī, Abū Saʿīd 1314h Barīqa Maḥmūdiyya fī Sharḥ al-Ṭariqa al-Muḥammadiyya. Istanbul: Maṭbaʿa Sharika Siḥāfiyya ʿUthmāniyya.

Khafājī, Muḥammad Abd al-Mun'im 1987 Al-Azhar fī Alf ʿĀmm. 3 Vols. Beirut: ʿĀlam al-Kutub.

Khallāf, ʿAbd al-Wahhāb 2003 ʿIlm Uṣūl al-Fiqh. Cairo: Dār al-Ḥadīth.

al-Khujandī, Muḥammad Sulṭān al-Maʿṣūmī 2001 Hal al-Muslim Mulzam bi-Ittibāʿ Madhhab Muʿayyan min al-Madhāhib al-Arbaʿa. Cairo: Dar Ibn ʿAffān.

al-Kinānī, Ashraf 2005 Al-Adilla al-Istithnāʾiyya ʿinda al-Uṣūliyyīn. ʿAmman: Dār al-Nafāʾis.

Kohn, Eduardo 2013 How Forests Think. Berkeley: University of California.

Krawietz, Birgit 2002 Cut and Paste in Legal Rules: Designing Islamic Norms with *Talfiq*. Die Welt des Islams, New Series, 42(1): 3–40.

Kroeber, Alfred and Talcott Parsons 1958 The Concepts of Culture and of the Social System. American Sociological Review 23(5): 582–583.

Kulick, Don and Christopher Stroud 1990 Christianity, Cargo and Ideas of Self: Patterns of Literacy in a Papua New Guinean Village. Man, New Series, 25(2): 286–304.

Kugle, Scott 2007 Sufis and Saints' Bodies: Mysticism, Corporeality, and Sacred Power in Islam. Chapel Hill: University of North Carolina Press.

Lacroix, Stephane 2009 Between Revolution and Apoliticism: Nasir al-Din al-Albani and His Impact on the Shaping of Contemporary Salafism. In Global Salafism: Islam's New Religious Movement, edited by Roel Meijer, 58–80. New York: Columbia.

Laffan, Michael 2011 The Makings of Indonesian Islam: Orientalism and the Narration of a Sufi Past. Princeton, NJ: Princeton University Press.

Laidlaw, James 2002 For an Anthropology of Ethics and Freedom. Journal of the Royal Anthropological Institute 8(2): 311–332.

Lambek, Michael 1991 Tryin' to Make It Real but Compared to What?" Culture 11 (1–2): 43–51.

Lambek, Michael 1993 Knowledge and Practice in Mayotte: Local Discourses of Islam, Sorcery, and Spirit Possession. Toronto: University of Toronto Press.

Lambek, Michael 2015 The hermeneutics of Ethical Encounters: Between Traditions and Practice. Hau: Journal of Ethnographic Theory 5(2): 227–250.

Lambek, Michael, ed. 2010 Ordinary Ethics: Anthropology, Language, and Action. New York: Fordham University Press.

Lane, Edward 2005[1836] Manners and Customs of the Modern Egyptians. New York: Cosimo Classics.

Lane, Edward 1968 An Arabic-English Lexicon. Beirut: Librairie du Liban.

Lapidus, Ira 1984 Knowledge, Virtue, and Action: The Classical Muslim Conception of Adab and the Nature of Religious Fulfillment in Islam. In Moral Conduct and Authority: The Place of Adab in South Asian Islam, edited by Barbara Metcalf, 38–61. Berkeley: University of California.

Latour, Bruno and Steve Woolgar 1986 Laboratory Life: The Construction of Scientific Facts. Princeton, NJ: Princeton University Press.

Lemke, Wolf-Dieter 1980 Maḥmūd Šaltut (1893–1963) und die Reform der Azhar. Frankfurt: P. D. Lang.

LePore, Ernest 1986 Truth and Interpretation: Perspectives on the Philosophy of Donald Davidson. Oxford: Basil Blackwell.

Levinson, Stephen 1983 Pragmatics. New York: Cambridge University Press.

Llewellyn, Karl and E. Adamson Hoebel 1941 The Cheyenne Way. Norman: University of Oklahoma Press.

Lombardi, Clark 2006 State Law as Islamic Law in Modern Egypt. Boston: Brill, 2006.

Lowry, Joseph 2007 Early Islamic Legal Theory: The Risālā of Muḥammad ibn Idrīs al-Shāfiʿī. Boston: Brill.

Lukacs, Georg 1971[1923] History and Class Consciousness. Translated by Rodney Livingstone. Cambridge: MIT Press.

MacIntyre, Alasdair 1990 Three Rival Versions of Moral Inquiry. Notre Dame, IN: University of Notre Dame Press.

MacIntyre, Alasdair 2008[1981] After Virtue: A Study in Moral Theory. Notre Dame, IN: University of Notre Dame Press.

Madkūr, ʿAbd al-Ḥamīd 2010 Al-Manhaj al-ʿIrfānī al-Dhawqī ʿinda Sūfiyya al-Islām. In al-Manhajiyya al-Islāmiyya. Vol 1. Cairo: Dār al-Salām.

Mahmood, Saba 2005 Politics of Piety: The Islamic Revival and the Feminist Subject. Princeton, NJ: Princeton University Press.

Makdisi, George 1981 The Rise of Colleges: Institutions of Learning in Islam and the West. Edinburgh: Edinburgh University Press.

Makdisi, George 1991 Religion, Law and Learning in Classical Islam. London: Variorum.

Malinowski, Bronislaw 1984[1922] Argonauts of the Western Pacific. Long Grove, IL: Waveland Press.

al-Mansī, Muḥammad 2005 Ḍawābiṭ Istiftā᾽ al-Qalb fī al-Sharīʿa al-Islāmiyyya. Cairo: Dār al-Hānī.

al-Marāghī, Muṣṭafā 1959 Al-Ijtihād fī al-Islām. Cairo: Al-Maktab al-Fannī li-l-Nashr.

al-Mārdīnī 2004 Al-Raḥabiyya fī ʿIlm al-Farā᾽iḍ bi-Sharḥ Sibt al-Mārdīni wa-Ḥāshiya al-Allāma al-Baqrī. Damascus: Dār al-Qalam.

Mauss, Marcel 1992[1934] Techniques of the Body. In Incorporations, edited by Jonathan Crary and Sanford Kwinter, 455–477. New York: Zone.

Mauss, Marcel 2000[1950] The Gift. New York: W. W. Norton.

Mayyāra, Muḥammad bin. Aḥmad 2007 Al-Durar al-Thamīn wa-l-Mawrid al-Muʿīn. Beirut: al-Maktaba al-ʿAṣriyya.

Meijer, Roel, ed. 2009 Global Salafism: Islam's New Religious Movement. New York: Columbia.

Melchert, Christopher 1997 The Formation of Sunni Schools of Law, 9th–10th Centuries C.E. New York: Brill.

Melchert, Christopher 2004 The Etiquette of Learning in the Early Islamic Study Circle. In Joseph Lowry, ed. Law and Education in Medieval Islam. Warminster, England: E. J. W. Gibb Memorial Trust.

Merry, Sally Engle 1990 Getting Justice and Getting Even: Legal Consciousness among Working-Class Americans. Chicago: University of Chicago Press.

Merry, Sally Engle 2003 Human Rights Law and the Demonization of Culture (And Anthropology along the Way). Political and Legal Anthropology Review 26(1): 55–76.

Merry, Sally Engle 2006 Human Rights and Gender Violence: Translating International Law into Local Justice. Chicago: University of Chicago Press.

Mertz, Elizabeth 2007 The Language of Law School: Learning to "Think Like a Lawyer." New York, Oxford University Press.

Messick, Brinkley 1993 The Calligraphic State: Textual Domination and History in a Muslim Society. Berkeley: University of California Press.

Mir-Hosseini, Ziba 1999 Islam and Gender. Princeton, NJ: Princeton University Press.

Mitchell, Timothy 1991[1988] Colonising Egypt. Berkeley: University of California Press.

Mitchell, Peter 1997 Introduction to Theory of Mind: Children, Autism and Apes. New York: Oxford University Press.

Mittermaier, Amira 2011 Dreams That Matter: Egyptian Landscapes of the Imagination. Berkeley: University of California Press.

McGinn, Colin 1984 Wittgenstein on Meaning. New York: Basil Blackwell.

Moore, Sally Falk 1986 Social Facts and Fabrications: "Customary" Law on Kilimanjaro, 1880–1980. New York: Cambridge University Press.

Moore, Sally Falk 2000[1978] Law as Process: An Anthropological Approach. New Introduction by Martin Chanock. Oxford: James Currey.

Motzki, Harald 2002 The Origins of Islamic Jurisprudence: Meccan Fiqh before the Classical Schools. Translated by Marion H. Katz. Boston: Brill.

Muslim, Abū al-Ḥusayn 1426h Saḥīḥ Muslim. Riyadh: Dār Ṭība.

Nakissa, Aria 2014a An Ethical Solution to the Problem of Legal Indeterminacy: Sharīʿa Scholarship at Egypt's al-Azhar. Journal of the Royal Anthropological Institute 20(1):93–112.

Nakissa, Aria 2014b An Epistemic Shift in Islamic Law: Educational Reform at al-Azhar and the Dār al-ʿUlūm. Islamic Law and Society 21: 209–251.

Naṣr, ʿAbdullah Salāma 2009 Al-Azhar al-Sharīf fī Ḍawʾ Sīra Aʿlāmihi al-Ajillāʾ. Cairo: Maktaba al-Īmān.

al-Nawawī, Yaḥyā bin Sharaf 1929 Saḥīḥ Muslim bi-Sharḥ al-Nawawī. Cairo: al-Maṭbaʿat al-Miṣriyya bi-l-Azhar.

al-Nawawī, Yaḥyā bin Sharaf 1987 Adab al-ʿĀlim wa-l-Mutaʿallim: Muqaddimat al-Majmūʿ. Tanta: Maktaba al-Ṣahāba.

al-Nawawī, Yaḥyā bin Sharaf 2002 Al-Maqasid: Nawawi's Manual of Islam. 2nd ed. Translation and Notes by Nuh Ha Mim Keller. Beltsville, MD: Amana.

N.d. Kitāb al-Majmūʿ: Sharḥ al-Muhadhdhab li-l-Shīrāzī. Jidda: Maktaba al-Irshād.

Nussbaum, Martha 1986 The Fragility of Goodness: Luck and Ethics in Greek Tragedy and Philosophy. New York: Cambridge University Press.

Ong, Walter 2002[1982] Orality and Literacy. London: Methuen.

Opwis, Felicitas 2010 Maṣlaḥa and the Purpose of the Law: Islamic Discourse on Legal Change from the 4th/10th to 8th/14th Century. Boston: Brill.

Ortner, Sherry 1984 Theory in Anthropology since the Sixties. Comparative Studies in Society and History 26(1): 126–166.

Ortner, Sherry 1999 Introduction. In The Fate of "Culture": Geertz and Beyond, edited by Sherry Ortner, 1–13. Berkeley: University of California Press.

Ortner, Sherry 2006 Anthropology and Social Theory: Culture, Power, and the Acting Subject. Durham, NC: Duke University Press.

Osanloo, Arzoo 2009 The Politics of Women's Rights in Iran. Princeton, NJ: Princeton University Press.

Parsons, Talcott 1949[1937] The Structure of Social Action. Glencoe, IL: The Free Press.

Parsons, Talcott 1964[1951] The Social System. New York: The Free Press of Glencoe.

Parsons, Talcott and Edward Shils, eds. 1951 Towards a General Theory of Action. Cambridge, MA: Harvard University Press.

Peletz, Michael 2002 Islamic Modern: Religious Courts and Cultural Politics in Malaysia. Princeton, NJ: Princeton University Press.

Peters, Rudolph 1980 Idjtihad and Taqlīd in 18th and 19th Century Islam. Die Welt des Islams, New Series 20(3/4): 131–145.

Peters, Rudolph 2005 Crime and Punishment in Islamic Law. New York: Cambridge University Press.

Peters, Rudolph Poscher, Ralf 2015 Hermeneutics, Jurisprudence and Law. In The Routledge Companion to Hermeneutics, edited by Jeff Malpas and Hans Helmuth Gander, 451–465. New York: Routledge, 2015.

Pospisil, Leopold 1974 Anthropology of Law: A Comparative Theory. New Haven, CT: HRAF Press.

Powers, David 1989 Orientalism, Colonialism, and Legal History: The Attack on Muslim Family Endowments in Algeria and India. Comparative Studies in Society and History 31(3): 535–571.

Powers, David 2002 Law, Society and Culture in the Maghrib, 1300–1500. New York: Cambridge University Press.

al-Qābisī 1986 Al-Risāla al-Mufaṣṣila li-Aḥwāl al-Mutaᶜallimīn wa-Aḥkām al-Muᶜallimīn wa-l-Mutaᶜallimīn, edited by Aḥmad Khālid. Tunis: al-Sharika al-Tūnisiyya li-l-Tawzīᶜ.
al-Qāḍī Abū Yaᶜlā 2002 Al-ᶜUdda fī Uṣūl al-Fiqh. 2 Vols. Beirut: Dār al-Kutub al-ᶜIlmiyya.
al-Qaraḍāwī, Yūsuf 1999 Al-Ijtihād fī al-Sharīᶜa al-Islāmiyya. Kuwait: Dār al-Qalam.
al-Qaraḍāwī, Yūsuf 2006 Dirāsa fī Fiqh Maqāṣid al-Sharīᶜa. Cairo: Dār al-Shurūq.
al-Qaraḍāwī, Yūsuf 2007 Al-Ḥalāl wa-l-Ḥarām fī al-Islām. Cairo: Maktaba Wahba.
al-Qaraḍāwī, Yūsuf 2008a Al-Ṣaḥwa al-Islāmiyya min al-Murāhaqa ilā al-Rushd. Cairo: Dār al-Shurūq.
al-Qaraḍāwī, Yūsuf 2008b Kalimāt fī al-Wasaṭiyya al-Islāmiyya wa-Maᶜālimihā. Cairo: Dār al-Shurūq.
al-Qarāfī, Shihāb al-Dīn 2005 Tanqīḥ al-Fuṣūl. Cairo: al-Maktaba al-Azhariyya li-l-Turāth.
al-Qurtubī, Abū ᶜAbdullah Muḥammaad bin Aḥmad 2010 Al-Jāmiᶜ li-Aḥkām al-Qurʾān. Cairo; Dār al-Ḥadīth.
al-Qushayrī, Abū al-Qāsim 2001 Al-Risāla al-Qushayriyya. Beirut: Dār al-Kutub al-ᶜIlmiyya.
Rabinow, Paul 1977 Reflections on Fieldwork in Morocco. Berkeley: University of California Press.
Rabinow, Paul and William Sullivan 1987 Interpretive Social Science: A Second Look. Berkeley: University of California Press.
Ramberg, Bjorn 2015 Davidson and Rorty: Triangulation and Anti-foundationalism. In The Routledge Companion to Hermeneutics, edited by Jeff Malpas and Hans Helmuth Gander, 216–235. New York: Routledge.
al-Raysūnī, Aḥmad 2006 Imām Al-Shāṭibī's Theory of the Higher Objectives and Intents of Islamic Law. Translated by Nancy Roberts. Washington, DC: The International Institute of Islamic Thought.
al-Raysūnī, Aḥmad 2013 Fiqh al-Thawra: Murājaᶜāt fī al-Fiqh al-Siyāsī al-Islāmī. Cairo: Dār al-Kalima.
al-Rāzī, Fakhr al-Dīn N.d. Al-Maḥṣūl fī ᶜIlm Uṣūl al-Fiqh. Dirāsa wa-Taḥqīq li-Ṭaha Jābir al-ᶜAlwānī. Beirut: Muʾassasa al-Risālah.
al-Rāzī, Fakhr al-Dīn 1981 Tafsīr al-Fakhr al-Rāzī. Beirut: Dār al-Fikr.
Reid, Donald Malcolm 1990 Cairo University and the Making of Modern Egypt. New York: Cambridge University Press.
Reimann, Mathias 1990 Nineteenth Century German Legal Science. Boston College Law Review 31(4): 837–897.
Ricoeur, Paul 1971 The Model of the Text: Meaningful Action Considered as a Text. Social Research 38(3): 529–562.
Ricoeur, Paul 1981 Hermeneutics and the Human Sciences. New York: Cambridge University Press.
Riḍā, Rashīd 1922 Madaniyyat al-Qawānīn. Al-Manār 23: 539–548.
Riḍā, Rashīd 2006 Tārīkh al-Ustādh al-Imām al-Shaykh Muḥammad ᶜAbduh. Cairo: Dār al-Faḍīla.
Riḍā, Rashīd 2007a Yusr al-Islām wa-Uṣūl al-Tashrīᶜ al-ᶜĀmm. Minneapolis, MN: Dar Almanar.
Riḍā, Rashīd 2007b al-Manār wa al-Azhar. Minneapolis, MN: Dar Almanar.
Riḍā, Rashīd 2008 Muḥāwarāt al-Muslih wa-l-Muqallid wa al-Waḥda al-Islāmiyya. Minneapolis, MN: Dar Almanar.
Riḍā, Rashīd 2009 al-Wahhābiyyūn wa-l-Ḥijāz. Minneapolis, MN: Dar Almanar.
Riḍā, Rashīd 1367h Tafsīr al-Manār. 3rd.ed. Vol. 4 Cairo: Dār al-Manār.
Riḍā, Rashīd 1368h Tafsīr al-Manār. 2nd.ed. Vol. 10 Cairo: Dār al-Manār.

Riles, Annelise 2001 The Network Inside Out. Ann Arbor: University of Michigan Press.
Rippin, Andrew 2006 Muslims: Their Religious Beliefs and Practices. New York: Routledge.
Robinson, Francis 1993 Technology and Religious Change: Islam and the Impact of Print. Modern Asian Studies 27(1): 229–251.
Robson, J. 1978 Isnad. In Encyclopedia of Islam. New Edition, edited by E. van Donzel, B. Lewis, Ch. Pellat. Vol. 4. Leiden: Brill.
Rodinson, Maxime 1973 Islam and Capitalism. Translated by Brian Pearce. New York: Pantheon Books.
Rosaldo, Michelle 1982 The Things We Do with Words: Ilongot Speech Acts and Speech Act Theory in Philosophy. Language in Society 11(2): 203–237.
Roseberry, William 1982 Balinese Cockfights and the Seduction of Anthropology. Social Research 49(4): 1013–1028.
Rosen, Lawrence 1989 The Anthropology of Justice: Law as Culture in Islamic Society. New York: Cambridge University Press.
Rosen, Lawrence, ed. 1995 Other Intentions. Santa Fe, NM: School of American Research Press.
Rosenthal, Franz 2007 Knowledge Triumphant: The Concept of Knowledge in Medieval Islam. With an Introduction by Dimitri Gutas. Boston: Brill.
Ross, David, trans. 2009 The Nicomachean Ethics. Revised with an Introduction and Notes by Lesley Brown. New York: Oxford University Press.
Ryle, Gilbert 2002[1949] The Concept of Mind. Introduction by Daniel C. Dennett. Chicago: The University of Chicago Press.
Sadeghi, Behnam 2013 The Logic of Law Making in Islam. New York: Cambridge University Press.
Sahlins, Marshall 1976 Culture and Practical Reason. Chicago: University of Chicago Press.
Sahlins, Marshall 1981 Historical Metaphors and Mythical Realities: Structure in the Early History of the Sandwich Islands Kingdom. Ann Arbor: University of Michigan Press.
Said, Edward 1994[1978] Orientalism. New York: Vintage Books.
al-Ṣaʿīdi, ʿAbd al-Mutaʿāl 2012[1955] Al-Ḥurriya al-Dīniyya fī al-Islām. Cairo: Dār al-Kitāb al-Miṣrī.
Salvatore, Armando 1997 Islam and the Political Discourse of Modernity. Reading, UK: Garnet.
Salvatore, Armando and Dale Eickelman 2004 Public Islam and the Common Good. Boston: Brill.
al-Samʿānī, Manṣūr bin Muḥammad 1419h Qawātiʿ al-Adilla fī Uṣūl al-Fiqh. 5 Vols. Al-Riyāḍ: Saudi Arabia: Maktaba al-Tawba.
Sarat, Austin and Jonathan Simon 2003 Cultural Analysis, Cultural Studies, and the Law. Durham, NC: Duke University Press.
al-Sarrāj Abū Naṣr 1960 al-Lumaʿ. Cairo: Dār al-Kutub al-Ḥadītha.
Savigny, Frederick Charles von 1831 The Vocation of Our Age. Translated by Abraham Hayward. London: Littlewood.
al-Sayyid, Mahmūd 2000 Daʿwa Anṣār al-Sunna wa Sanawāt min al-ʿAtāʾ. Cairo: Maktaba al-Ḥurriya.
al-Sayyid, Usāma 2010 Al-Iḥyāʾ al-Kabīr li-Maʿālim al-Manhaj al-Azharī al-Munīr. Dubai: Kalām li-l-Buḥūth wa-l-I'lām.
Sayyid-Marsot, Afaf Lutfi 1972 The Ulama of Cairo in the Eighteenth and Nineteenth Centuries. In Scholars, Saints, and Sufis: Muslim Religious Institutions in the Middle East since 1500, edited by Nikki Keddie, 149–166. Berkeley: University of California Press.

Schacht, Joseph 1965 An Introduction to Islamic Law. New York: Oxford University Press.
Schacht, Joseph 1967[1950] The Origins of Muhammadan Jurisprudence. New York: Oxford University Press.
Schimmel, Annemarie 1975 Mystical Dimensions of Islam. Chapel Hill: University of North Carolina Press.
Schleiermacher, Friedrich [1838]1998 Hermeneutics and Criticism and Other Writings, edited by Andrew Bowie. New York: Cambridge University Press.
Schluchter, Wolfgang 1999 Hindrances to Modernity: Max Weber on Islam. In Max Weber and Islam, edited by Toby Huff and Wolfgang Schluchter, 53–138. New Brunswick, NJ: Transaction.
Schneider, David 1968 American Kinship: A Cultural Account. Chicago: University of Chicago Press.
Schneider, Mark 1987 Culture-as-Text in the Work of Clifford Geertz. Theory and Society 16(6): 809–839.
Schoeler, Gregor 2006 The Oral and the Written in Early Islam, edited by James E. Montgomery. Translated by Uwe Vagelphol. New York: Routledge.
Schutz, Alfred 1962 Collected Papers Vol. 1: The Problem of Social Reality, edited by Maurice Natanson. Boston: Martinus Nijhoff.
Schutz, Alfred 1967[1932] The Phenomenology of the Social World. Translated by George Walsh and Frederick Lehnert. Evanston, IL: Northwestern University Press.
Schutz, Alfred 1970 On Phenomenology and Social Relations, edited by Helmut Wagner. Chicago: University of Chicago Press.
Schutz, Alfred and Thomas Luckmann 1973 The Structures of the Life-World, Vol. 1. Translated by Richard Zaner and H. Tristram Engelhardt. Evanston, IL: Northwestern University Press.
Searle, John 1969 Speech Acts. Cambridge: Cambridge University Press.
Searle, John 1978 Literal Meaning. Erkenntnis 13: 207–224.
Searle, John 1983 Intentionality. Cambridge: Cambridge University Press.
Sedgwick, Mark 2009 Muhammad Abduh: A Biography. Cairo: The American University in Cairo Press.
Sewell, William 2005 Logics of History: Social Theory and Social Transformation. Chicago: University of Chicago Press.
Shalabī, Aḥmad 1999 Al-Tarbiya wa-l-Taʿlīm fi al-Fikr al-Islāmī. Cairo: Maktaba al-Nahḍa al-Miṣriyya.
Shalabī, Muḥammad Muṣṭafā 1947 Taʿlīl al-Aḥkām. Cairo: Maṭbaʿa al-Azhar.
Shankman, Paul 1984 The Thick and the Thin: On the Interpretive Theoretical Program of Clifford Geertz. Current Anthropology 25(3): 261–280.
al-Shāfiʿī, Muhammad bin Idris N.d. Al-Risala, edited by Aḥmad Shākir. Beirut: Dār al-Kutub al-ʿIlmiyya.
Shapiro, Scott 2002 Law, Plans, and Practical Reason. Legal Theory 8(4): 387–441.
Shapiro, Scott 2008 How Rules Affect Practical Reasoning. In Reasons and Intentions, edited by Bruno Verbeek, 133–152. Burlington, VT: Ashgate.
Shapiro, Scott 2011 Legality. Cambridge, MA: Harvard University Press.
al-Shāṭibī, Abū Isḥāq 2004 al-Muwāfaqāt fī Uṣūl al-Sharīʿa. Beirut: Dār al-Kutub al-ʿIlmiyya.
al-Shawkānī, Muḥammad bin ʿAlī 1994 Irshād al-Fuḥūl. Beirut: Dār al-Kutub al-ʿIlmiyya.
Sherif, Mohamed Ahmed 1975 Ghazali's Theory of Virtue. Albany: State University of New York Press.

al-Shinnāwī, ʿAbd al-ʿAzīz Muḥammad 1984 al-Azhar Jāmiʿan wa-Jāmiʿatan. 2 Vols. Cairo: Maktaba al-Anjlū al-Miṣriyya.

al-Shinqīṭī, Aḥmad bin Muḥammad 2008 Madārij al-Ṣuʿūd ilā Marāqī al-Suʿūd. Riyāḍ: Maktaba al-Rushd.

al-Siddīqī, Muḥammad bin ʿAllān N.d. Kitāb al-Futūḥāt al-Rabbāniyya ʿalā al-Adhkār al-Nūrāniyya. Beirut: Dār Iḥyāʾ al-Turāth al-ʿArabī.

Silverstein, Brian 2011 Islam and Modernity in Turkey. New York: Palgrave Macmillan.

Silverstein, Michael 1972 Linguistic Theory: Syntax, Semantics, Pragmatics. Annual Review of Anthropology 1: 349–382.

Silverstein, Michael 1976 Shifters, Linguistic Categories, and Cultural Description. In Meaning in Anthropology, edited by Keith Basso, 11–55. Albuquerque: University of New Mexico.

Silverstein, Michael 1979 Language Structure and Linguistic Ideology. In The Elements: A Parasession on Linguistic Units and Levels, edited by W. Hanks, 193–247. Chicago: Chicago Linguistic Society.

Skovgaard-Petersen, Jakob 1997 Defining Islam for the Egyptian State: Muftis and Fatwas of the Dār al-Iftā. New York: Brill.

Sperber, Dan and Deirdre Wilson 2002 Pragmatics, Modularity, and Mind-Reading. Mind and Language 17(1&2): 3–23.

Starrett, Gregory 1995 The Hexis of Interpretation: Islam and the Body in the Egyptian Popular School. American Ethnologist 22(4):953–969.

Starrett, Gregory 1998 Putting Islam to Work: Education, Politics, and Religious Transformation in Egypt. Berkeley: University of California Press.

Stewart, Devin 2004 The Doctorate of Law in Mamluk Syria and Egypt. In Law and Education in Medieval Islam, edited by Joseph Lowry, Devin Steward, and Shawkat Toorawa. _Warminster: E.J.W. Gibb Memorial Trust.

Stiles, Erin 2009 An Islamic Court in Context: An Ethnographic Study of Judicial Reasoning. New York: Palgrave Macmillan.

Strathern, Marilyn 2006 Bullet-Proofing: A Tale from the United Kingdom. In Documents: Artifacts of Modern Knowledge, edited by Annelise Riles. Ann Arbor: University of Michigan Press.

Stauth, Georg 1987 Civilizing the Soul: German Orientalists. Issue 90 of Working paper, Universität Bielefeld Forschungsschwerpunkt Entwicklungssoziologie.

Stocking, George 1974 Introduction. In A Franz Boas Reader, edited by George Stocking. Chicago: University of Chicago Press.

al-Sulamī, ʿAbd al-Raḥman 1986 Ṭabaqāt al-Ṣūfiyya. Cairo: Maṭbaʿa al-Madanī

Sulayman bin Saḥmān 1342h Al-Hadiyya al-Saniyya wa-l-Tuḥfa al-Wahhābiyya al-Najdiyya. Cairo: Maṭbaʿa al-Manār.

al-Suyūṭī, Jalāl al-Dīn 1983a Al-Radd ʿalā man Akhlada ilā al-Arḍ wa jahila anna al-Ijtihād fi Kull ʿAsr Farḍ. Beirut: Dār al-Kutub al-ʿIlmiyya.

al-Suyūṭī, Jalāl al-Dīn 1983b al-Ashbāh wa-l-Naẓāʾir. Beirut: Dār al-Kutub al-ʿIlmiyya.

al-Ṭabarī, Abū Jaʿfar Muḥammad bin Jarīr 2010 Tafsīr al-Ṭabarī. 12 Vols. Cairo: Dār al-Ḥadīth.

al-Taftāzānī, Saʿd al-Dīn N.d. Al-Talwīḥ ʿalā al-Tawḍīḥ. 2 Vols. Beirut: Dār al-Kutub al-ʿIlmiyya.

Ṭanṭāwī, Muḥammad Sayyid 2004 al-ʿAqīda wa-l-Akhlāq. Cairo: Dār al-Saʿāda.

N.d. Al-Wasīṭ fī al-Fiqh al-Muyassar ʿalā al-Madhāhib al-Arbaʿa: al-Juzʾ al-Awwal li-l-Ṣaff al-Awwal al-Thānawī, Qism al-ʿIbādāt 2009–2010. Cairo: Dār al-Saʿāda.

N.d. Al-Wasīṭ fī al-Fiqh al-Muyassar ʿalā al-Madhāhib al-Arbaʿah: al-Juzʾ al-Thānī li-l-Ṣaff al-Thānī, Qism: al-Muʿāmalāt - al-Qaḍāʾ- al-Jihād - al-Ḥudūd 2011–2012. Cairo: Dār al-Saʿāda.

Taylor, Charles 1971 Interpretation and the Sciences of Man. The Review of Metaphysics 25(1): 3–51.

Taylor, Charles 1999 "To Follow a Rule . . . " In Bourdieu: A Critical Reader, edited by Richard Shusterman, 29–44. Oxford: Blackwell.

al-Tirmidhī, Muḥammad bin ʿĪsā 2008 Shamāʾil al-Nabī. Tunis: Dār al-Gharb al-Islāmī.

Tönnies, Ferdinand 2001[1887] Community and Civil Society. Translated by Jose Harris and Margaret Hollis. New York: Cambridge University Press.

Treiger, Alexander 2012 Inspired Knowledge in Islamic Thought: Al-Ghazālī's Theory of Mystical Cognition and Its Avicennian Foundation. New York: Routledge.

al-Ṭūfī, Najm al-Dīn 2009 Sharḥ li-l-ʿArbaʿīn al-Nawawiyya. Cairo: Dār al-Baṣāʾir.

Turner, Bryan 1974 Weber and Islam. New York: Routledge.

Turner, Victor 1967 The Forest of Symbols: Aspects of Ndembu Ritual. Ithaca, NY: Cornell University Press.

al-ʿUmarī, Nādiya 1986 Al-Ijtihād fī al-Islām. Beiruṭ: Muʾassasa al-Risāla.

al-ʿUthaymīn, Muḥammad bin Ṣāliḥ 2002 Kitāb al-ʿIlm. Riyadh: Dār al-Thurayyā.

al-ʿUthaymīn, Muḥammad bin Ṣāliḥ 2003 Sharḥ al-ʿAqīda al-Wāsiṭiyya. Cairo: Dār al-ʿAqīda.

Udovitch, Abraham 1970 Theory and Practice of Islamic Law: Some Evidence from the Geniza. Studia Islamica 32: 289–303

Vargas, Manuel and Gideon Yaffe, eds. 2014 Rational and Social Agency: The Philosophy of Michael Bratman. New York: Oxford University Press.

Vishanoff, David 2011 The Formation of Islamic Hermeneutics. New Haven, CT: American Oriental Society.

von Benda-Beckmann, Franz 2009 Riding or Killing the Centaur? Reflections on the Identities of Legal Anthropology. In Law and Anthropology, edited by Michael Freeman and David Napier, 13–46. New York: Oxford University Press.

Waardenburg, Jacques 2007 Muslims as Actors: Islamic Meanings and Muslim interpretations in the Perspective of the Study of Religions. Berlin: Walter de Gruyter.

al-Wādiʿī, Muqbil bin Hādī 2005 Radd ʿalā al-Qaraḍāwī. Ṣanʿāʾ: Dār al-Āthār.

Wahbah, Ḥāfiẓ 2001 Khamsūn ʿĀmm fī Jazīra al-ʿArab. Cairo: Dār al-Āfāq al-ʿArabiyya.

Ware, Rudolph 2014 The Walking Qurʾan: Islamic Education, Embodied Knowledge, and History in West Africa. Chapel Hill: University of North Carolina Press.

Weber, Max 1946[1915] The Social Psychology of the World's Religions. In From Max Weber: Essays in Sociology, edited by H.H. Gerth and C. Wright Mills. New York: Oxford University Press.

Weber, Max 1975 Roscher and Knies: The Logical Problems of Historical Economics. Translated by Guy Oakes. New York: The Free Press.

Weber, Max 1978[1922] Economy and Society: an Outline of Interpretive Sociology, edited by Guenther Roth and Claus Wittich. 2 Vols. Berkeley: University of California Press.

Weber, Max 2000[1930] The Protestant Ethic and the Spirit of Capitalism. Translated by Talcott Parsons. New York: Routledge.

Weiss, Bernard 1978 Interpretation in Islamic Law: The Theory of *Ijtihād.* The American Journal of Comparative Law 26(2): 199–212.

Weiss, Bernard 1998 The Spirit of Islamic Law. Athens: University of Georgia Press.

Wittgenstein, Ludwig 1965[1958] The Blue and Brown Books. New York: Harper & Row.

Wittgenstein, Ludwig 1972[1969] On Certainty. Translated by Denis Paul and G.E.M. Anscombe. NY: Harper & Row.

Wittgenstein, Ludwig 1999[1922] Tractatus Logico-Philosophicus. Translated by C.K. Ogden. With an Introduction by Bertrand Russell. NY: Dover.

Wittgenstein, Ludwig 2001[1953] Philosophical Investigations. Translated by G. E. M. Anscombe. Oxford: Blackwell.

Woolard, Kathryn and Bambi Schieffelin 1994 Language Ideology. Annual Review of Anthropology 23: 55–82.

Yunis Ali, Mohamed 2000 Medieval Islamic Pragmatics: Sunni Legal Theorists' Models of Textual Communication. New York: Routledge.

Zaman, Muhammad Qasim 2002 The Ulama in Contemporary Islam. Princeton, NJ: Princeton University Press.

Zaman, Muhammad Qasim 2012 Modern Islamic Thought in a Radical Age. New York: Cambridge University Press.

al-Zarkashī, Badr al-Dīn 2007 al-Baḥr al-Muḥīṭ. 4 Vols. Beirut: Dār al-Kutub al-ʿIlmiyya.

al-Zarnūjī, Burhān al-Islām 2004 Taʿlīm al-Mutaʿallim Ṭarīq al-Taʿallum. Khartoum: al-Dār al-Sūdāniyya li-l-Kutub.

al-Ẓawāhirī, Muḥammad al-Aḥmadī 1904 Al-ʿIlm wa-l-ʿUlamāʾ wa-Niẓām al-Taʿlīm. Al-Maṭbaʿa al-ʿUmūmiyya bi-Ṭanṭā.

Zebiri, Kate 1993 Mahmūd Shaltūt and Islamic Modernism. New York: Oxford University Press.

Zeghal, Malika 1996 Gardiens de l'Islam: les oulemas d'Al Azhar dans l'Egypte comtemporaine. Paris: Presses de Sciences Po.

Zeghal, Malika 1999 Religion and Politics in Egypt: The Ulema of al-Azhar, Radical Islam, and the State (1952–94). International Journal of Middle East Studies 31(3): 371–399.

Zeghal, Malika 2007 The "Recentering" of Religious Knowledge and Discourse: The Case of al-Azhar in Twentieth-Century Egypt. In Schooling Islam: The Culture and Politics of Modern Muslim Education, edited by Robert Hefner and Muhammad Qasim Zaman, 107–130. Princeton, NJ: Princeton University Press.

Zigon, Jarrett 2008 Morality: An Anthropological Perspective. New York: Berg.

Zubaida, Sami 1990 Exhibitions of Power. Economy and Society 19(3): 359–375.

Zubaida, Sami 2003 Law and Power in the Islamic World. New York: I. B. Tauris.

al-Zuḥaylī, Wahba 2006 Uṣūl al-Fiqh al-Islamī. 2 Vols. Damascus: Dār al-Fikr.

Zysow, Aron 2013[1984] The Economy of Certainty: An Introduction to the Typology of Islamic Legal Theory. Atlanta, GA: Lockwood Press.

# Index




The Anthropology of Islamic Law. Aria Nakissa.